Early Christian Fathers

General Editors

John Baillie (1886–1960) served as President of the World Council of Churches, a member of the British Council of Churches, Moderator of the General Assembly of the Church of Scotland, and Dean of the Faculty of Divinity at the University of Edinburgh.

John T. McNeill (1885–1975) was Professor of the History of European Christianity at the University of Chicago and then Auburn Professor of Church History at Union Theological Seminary in New York.

Henry P. Van Dusen (1897–1975) was an early and influential member of the World Council of Churches and served at Union Theological Seminary in New York as Roosevelt Professor of Systematic Theology and later as President.

THE LIBRARY OF CHRISTIAN CLASSICS

Early Christian Fathers

Edited and translated by
CYRIL C. RICHARDSON, ThD, DD

In collaboration with
EUGENE R. FAIRWEATHER, ThD
EDWARD R. HARDY, PhD
and
MASSEY H. SHEPHERD, JR., PhD

Westminster John Knox Press
LOUISVILLE • LONDON

© 1953 The Westminster Press

Paperback reissued 2006 by Westminster John Knox Press, Louisville, Kentucky.

Cover design by designpointinc.com

Published by Westminster John Knox Press
Louisville, Kentucky

This book is printed on acid-free paper that meets the American National Standards Institute Z39.48 standard. ⊛

PRINTED IN THE UNITED STATES OF AMERICA

Library of Congress Cataloging-in-Publication Data is on file at the Library of Congress, Washington, D.C.

ISBN-13: 978-0-664-22747-0
ISBN-10: 0-664-22747-3

GENERAL EDITORS' PREFACE

The Christian Church possesses in its literature an abundant and incomparable treasure. But it is an inheritance that must be reclaimed by each generation. THE LIBRARY OF CHRISTIAN CLASSICS is designed to present in the English language, and in twenty-six volumes of convenient size, a selection of the most indispensable Christian treatises written prior to the end of the sixteenth century.

The practice of giving circulation to writings selected for superior worth or special interest was adopted at the beginning of Christian history. The canonical Scriptures were themselves a selection from a much wider literature. In the Patristic era there began to appear a class of works of compilation (often designed for ready reference in controversy) of the opinions of well-reputed predecessors, and in the Middle Ages many such works were produced. These medieval anthologies actually preserve some noteworthy materials from works otherwise lost.

In modern times, with the increasing inability even of those trained in universities and theological colleges to read Latin and Greek texts with ease and familiarity, the translation of selected portions of earlier Christian literature into modern languages has become more necessary than ever; while the wide range of distinguished books written in vernaculars such as English makes selection there also needful. The efforts that have been made to meet this need are too numerous to be noted here, but none of these collections serves the purpose of the reader who desires a library of representative treatises spanning the Christian centuries as a whole. Most of them embrace only the age of the Church Fathers, and some of them have long been out of print. A fresh translation of a work already translated may shed much new light upon its meaning. This is true even of Bible translations despite the work of many experts through the centuries. In some instances old translations have been adopted in this series, but wherever necessary or desirable, new ones have been made. Notes have been supplied where these were needed to explain the author's meaning. The introductions provided for the several treatises and extracts will, we believe, furnish welcome guidance.

JOHN BAILLIE
JOHN T. McNEILL
HENRY P. VAN DUSEN

CONTENTS

PREFACE

In this volume we have attempted to give new translations of some of the basic Christian writings of the first two centuries. Our aim has been to render the originals in clear, idiomatic English, and to facilitate the reading of these classics by revising the standard paragraphs and by relegating the chapter and verse numbers to the margins.

In view of the fact that most of the material in our book has been rendered into English so frequently as well as so recently, the translations offered cannot but reflect some knowledge of those already published. While our work has been done without conscious borrowing, the same turn oᴸ phrases is likely to occur to more than one translator, and acquaintance with previous renderings cannot be, and should not be, eradicated from the memory.

We have sought to provide adequate introductory material, and to add such notes as are necessary for understanding the text. The lists of books are purposely more extensive than in some other series, and are planned to aid the student who wishes to study these particular documents more thoroughly.

The division of work among the contributors is indicated by the Table of Contents. I should like to thank the general editors for their assistance in the preparation of the manuscript and for their many helpful suggestions; the three contributors for their splendid co-operation; and Dr. Bard Thompson for his help with the notes for Athenagoras.

CYRIL C. RICHARDSON.

Union Theological Seminary.

Introduction to Early Christian
Literature and Its Setting

THE LITERATURE

The most striking facts about early Christian literature are its rich variety and its almost exclusively Gentile authorship. Outside the New Testament writings little belongs to the first century, the only considerable document being Clement's Letter to the Church of Rome. But the second century saw an increasing literary activity among Christians, which swelled to a flood toward its end.

To choose the works of the first two centuries that can be called "classics" is a difficult, even an arbitrary, task. It is the purpose of this volume to select a number of the most notable treatises, having in mind their representative character as well as their intrinsic worth. Thus an early sermon has been included despite its somewhat banal nature, while more weighty works such as the Apologies of Tatian and Theophilus have been excluded. Justin and Athenagoras must suffice to indicate that class of literature. It has not, however, been possible to include every type of early Christian writing. There is no apocalypse, no apocryphal gospel, no Christian poetry. Yet the selection made will give a good indication of the temper of second century Christianity and the quality of its literature.

The earliest Christian writings after the New Testament are customarily known under the title "Apostolic Fathers." It is to a French scholar of the seventeenth century, Jean Cotelier, that we owe this grouping. In 1672 he published two volumes entitled *SS. Patrum qui temporibus apostolicis floruerunt . . . opera edita et inedita, vera et suppositicia.* This collection included the letter ascribed to Barnabas, the Shepherd of Hermas, two letters of Clement (of which only one is genuine), seven of Ignatius, and one of Polycarp, along with the account of the latter's martyrdom. All but Barnabas and Hermas will be found in this volume. Later on, the anonymous brief addressed to Diognetus and the fragments of Papias and Quadratus were added to the collection by Andreas Gallandi in his *Bibliotheca veterum Patrum*, 1765. Finally, with the discovery of the Didache by Byrennios in 1873, this tractate too came to find a place in editions of the Apostolic Fathers.

These writings do not form a unity either in date or in type. The earliest is Clement's Letter, about A.D. 96. The latest are the sermon mistakenly known as his Second Letter, and the brief addressed to Diognetus. Both these were written somewhat before the middle of the second century. Other Christian literature not included in the Apostolic Fathers also comes from this period, as, for instance, the Apology of Aristides (about A.D. 130) and the Odes of Solomon (before A.D. 150). Yet, on the whole, the collection can be said to comprehend most of the significant Christian literature between the New Testament period and that of the great Apologists.

In type, the letter predominates. Even the account of Polycarp's martyrdom is a letter, from the church of Smyrna to that of Philomelium. The Letter of Barnabas is a theological tract, which attempts to grapple with the problem of the significance of the Old Testament for Christianity. It is a good example of the use of the epistolary form for a literary convention. Another instance is the piece addressed to Diognetus. While it bears the title of a letter, it is really a brief for Christianity. The earliest Christian sermon, as we have observed, is misleadingly called "Clement's Second Letter." Actually, however, it is a homily, and only by accident did it get dubbed an epistle.

Of the other works in this group, the Shepherd of Hermas is an apocalpyse, dealing with repentance after baptism; the Didache is a Church manual; while the fragments of Papias and Quadratus are from theological treatises. The former wrote five books entitled Explanations of the Lord's Sayings. They were apparently a running commentary on Jesus' utterances, interspersed with a good deal of oral tradition. Quadratus' work was an apology addressed to the emperor Hadrian.

What marks these writings, taken as a whole, is their literary simplicity, their earnest religious conviction, and their independence of Hellenistic philosophy and rhetoric. They are closer to the New Testament in their artlessness, and while they may lack something of its spiritual depth, they reveal an intense concern for its basic message. They come from a time when the Church was warring on two fronts—against pagan attack and internal schism. Hence their peculiar concern is for order. The unity of the Church around its leaders and the preservation of the faith from perversion are their dominant themes. In consequence the religious spontaneity of the New Testament writings gives place to a more moral and ecclesiastical note.

The next important group of Christian writings in the second century is that of the Apologists. The earliest is perhaps the brief addressed to Diognetus. There follow the Apologies of Aristides, Justin, Tatian, Athenagoras, Theophilus, and, by the end of the century, of Clement of Alexandria and Tertullian. They are notable contributions to Christian literature. In Athenagoras, Clement, and Tertullian emerge writers of no small literary merit, who can vie with the best rhetoricians of the day. Their purpose is to defend the faith by making contact with the prevalent philosophies and by showing the superiority of Christianity. By means of the Logos doctrine which appears in John's Gospel and is clearly formulated in Justin, they relate the revelation in Christ to a current way of thinking. But their leading theme is monotheism; and their sharpest attacks fall on the weaknesses of the ancient mythology. They do not primarily emphasize the place of Jesus Christ in the faith. They are addressing Gentiles who are not inheritors of the Old Testament monotheism. Hence the unity of God is their first concern. Particularly is this true of Athenagoras' Plea.

A third group of early Christian writings is the apocryphal literature.[1] Of this a great deal has come down to us. Much of it, however, is later than the second century, and much of it is heretical in nature, being tinged with a Docetic point of view. In general this literature is Christian romance. There are tales of Jesus and the apostles which are told to satisfy the curiosity awakened by the paucity of incident in many of the New Testament accounts, and to meet the yearning for the miraculous. Popular folklore is blended with Gospel material, and legend upon legend is created in the style of a novelist with a pious imagination.

Then there is Christian poetry. Little of this has survived, the most significant work being the Odes of Solomon.[2] This

---

[1] See the collection made by M. R. James, *The Apocryphal New Testament.* Oxford, 1924.

[2] J. R. Harris and A. Mingana, *The Odes of Solomon,* 2 vols. Manchester, 1916–1920.

is the first Christian hymnbook that we possess. It was almost certainly written in Greek sometime before A.D. 150, though it has come down to us only in Syriac, and in a partial Coptic version. The Odes are hymns of praise, displaying a mystical spirit akin to that of John and Ignatius, and free from speculative thought.

Another group of early Christian writings is composed of the stories of martyrdoms. The simple but stirring tale of Polycarp's suffering forms the theme of the Letter of the Church of Smyrna to that of Philomelium. Other important accounts concern the persecutions in Lyons and Vienne; the martyrdoms of Perpetua and Felicitas in Carthage; of Carpus, Papylus, and Agathonice in Pergamon; and of Apollonius in Rome.[3] There have also been preserved some official court proceedings of the trials and executions of Christians. Notable are those of Justin, and of the martyrs of Scili in North Africa.

Finally, there are the Christian forms of Gnostic and anti-Gnostic literature. Most of the former has perished, though excerpts in the writings of Church Fathers enable us to reconstruct the systems of the great Gnostic teachers such as Valentinus, with some accuracy.[4] A number of the early Fathers wrote against Gnosticism—Justin, Rhodo, Melito, Theophilus, Modestus, and others—but their works have not survived. The five books of Irenaeus, Refutation and Overthrow of the Pretended but False Gnosis (usually referred to as Against Heresies), are the first full-length treatise we have giving the Catholic reply to various Gnostic systems. It is, indeed, more than this, for it includes a careful exposition of the faith; and it is unfortunate that its text has been preserved only in a Latin translation. The significance of Irenaeus cannot be over-estimated. While he is neither a penetrating nor a systematic thinker, he sums up the main lines of the Catholic development of the second century; and from him there flow the two differing streams of Western and Eastern Christianity.

Such are the types of Christian writing in the first two centuries. Almost all of it was penned by Gentiles. Practically no Jewish Christian literature has survived. It is possible that

[3] A selection has been translated and published by E. C. E. Owen, *Some Authentic Acts of the Early Martyrs*. 1927.

[4] A notable document, for instance, is the letter of Ptolemy to Flora, preserved in Epiphanius' *Panarion*. See the new edition by G. Quispel, Éditions du Cerf, Paris, 1950 (in Sources chrétiennes). An English translation is given by R. M. Grant in his *Second Century Christianity*, pp. 30–37. S.P.C.K., London, 1946.

Clement of Rome and Hermas were Hellenistic Jews; and it is to our loss that the Memoirs of Hegesippus, a Hellenistic Jew of the Orient, have perished. These Memoirs comprised five books and constituted a polemic against Gnosticism. They contained also some historical details of the early Palestinian Church, of which Eusebius has preserved some fragments in his *Ecclesiastical History*. At the end of the second century one of the main sources underlying the pseudo-Clementine literature [5] was written; and this gives us some knowledge of Jewish Christianity. But it is remarkable with what rapidity the Christian faith, born in the obscure environment of Galilee, should have become a Gentile religion, enlisting the efforts of Gentile writers of distinction, while Jewish Christianity should have dwindled in importance. Judaizers were, to be sure, a force to be reckoned with in the days of Ignatius, and from time to time we hear of them in the writings of later Church Fathers such as Epiphanius. But they have left no significant body of literature. Separated from their countrymen by their religious convictions, and from the Holy City by the destruction under Titus, Jewish Christians eked out a precarious and isolated existence, until, having splintered into various groups, they were almost extinct by the fifth century, though a number of their ideas survived in Islam. It was the Greek, rather than the Jew, who became the inheritor of the Christian message—a fact which should give pause to those who unduly exaggerate the importance of Hebrew above Greek thinking.

THE SETTING

The introductions to the various documents in our volume will provide the reader with the requisite information to appreciate their setting and importance. It may, however, be appropriate here to characterize briefly the main lines of the Christian development in the second century.

The expansion of Christianity in this period was rapid and far-flung. It penetrated Mesopotamia to Edessa and Arbela and reached as far west as the interior of Spain, and perhaps the southern coast of Britain. Christians were to be found on the Rhone in Gaul, and even on the Rhine. The Dalmatian coast was beginning to be missionized. The Church was taking root in North Africa, Cyrenaica, and interior Egypt, as well

---

[5] I.e., *The Sermons of Peter*. See the recent study by H. J. Schoeps, *Theologie und Geschichte des Judenchristentums*. J. C. B. Mohr, Tübingen, 1949.

as consolidating and enlarging its gains in Syria, Greece, Asia Minor, and Italy. The spread of the new faith naturally followed the great trade routes and was centered in the cities. Only gradually did it win the rural areas, where ancient traditions were more stubbornly defended.

Primary among the marks of the period is the rise of the Catholic consciousness. By this phrase is meant the emergence of a distinctly ecclesiastical point of view, evident in the ordering of Church life. The kerygma, or "preaching," of the New Testament becomes the *regula fidei* of the early Fathers. Didactic and ethical interests come to the fore. The faith is more carefully prescribed and the Church more exactly organized. The leading concern is to conserve the apostolic witness, and, while showing its relevance to pagan modes of thought, to guard against the extremes of Gnostic speculation and prophetic enthusiasm.

Under the single bishop who, with his council of presbyters, rules the congregation, there is built up a closely knit organization which will be able to withstand the concerted persecutions of the third century. The bishop is the successor of the apostles, representing the localizing of the prophetic, teaching, and liturgical functions of the original apostolate. He becomes the center of the Church's life, the living witness and guardian of its faith. Exactly how it came about that a single bishop should succeed to powers earlier vested in local bodies of presbyters, is not altogether clear; though much may be explained by the occasional settling of an apostle, prophet, or teacher of the original missionary ministry, in some locality. What, however, is clear is that the development was orderly, and that it was very widespread by the time of Ignatius. The obvious convenience of having a single administrative head, the economic necessity whereby a congregation could afford to maintain only one full-time official, the dominance of certain leading personalities, together with the suitability of having a single celebrant for worship—all these factors doubtless played a role in the rise of the monepiscopate. It is, indeed, already foreshadowed in the Pastoral Epistles, where Timothy and Titus are viewed as Paul's delegates, entrusted with the supervision of the presbyteries in Ephesus and Crete. The final step is taken in the communities reflected in Ignatius' correspondence. There the bishop is the bishop of a local congregation, and the term, originally synonymous with "presbyter," now characterizes this distinctive office.

The bishop is the living center of the Christian tradition. He is a prophetic as well as a sacramental person; and nothing more clearly reveals the second century attitude toward the episcopate than the description the Smyrnaeans give of their martyred bishop, Polycarp: he was "an apostolic and prophetic teacher" (Mart. Poly. 16:2).

With the rise of the episcopate there emerges the importance of the great sees of Christendom, claiming apostolic foundation. The significance of the episcopate in Irenaeus, for instance, does not lie in a sacramental chain of ordinations, but in a chain of authorized teachers, which reaches back to the apostles. Of first importance among such sees is Rome, the center of Western Christianity, whose place of eminence is due both to its being the imperial city and to its being the city of Peter and Paul. It is, too, Christendom in miniature, for there Christians from all lands eventually turn up. In consequence, Rome is the ideal center from which to set one's compass of orthodoxy.

The tradition of the faith, however, was incorporated in more than living personalities. It was enshrined in a book, and expressed in brief, formal statements suitable for baptismal confessions. The second century saw the rise of the New Testament canon and the formation of the earliest creeds. Both were partly determined by the pressure of heresy and the consequent necessity for the Church to make its message clear. But heresy was only one factor in the development. The internal needs of the Church were such that the tradition should be preserved in accepted writings and in authentic confessions.

The New Testament canon has its origin in the high regard with which Christians from the first viewed the logia of the Lord and the writings of apostles. Until A.D. 150, however, the only Bible of Christians was the Septuagint, the Greek Old Testament. This the Church had inherited from Judaism, and at first it sufficed. The Christian message entailed the explication of the Old Testament in the light of the acts and words of the Messiah. What was foreshadowed in the sacred books of the Law and the Prophets had now come to pass in the Christ. Hence Christian preaching was founded on the Old Testament and on the living tradition of Jesus, passed from mouth to mouth. This feeling for personal witness was very strong in the Early Church. Papias, for instance, records his disdain for books and his preference for "the living and abiding voice." The tradition was not something dead, but a vital reality to be discovered from living persons. Yet the corruptions to which oral tradition was subject soon necessitated the writing of Christian books; and as the living witnesses to Christ and the apostles passed away, these books took on a new significance. They came to be read in worship, and by A.D. 150 they had gained the authority that had once belonged exclusively to the Old Testament.

The actual formation of the canon, however, was both determined and hastened by the Gnostic rejection of the Old Testament. The sharp dualism of the Gnostics, who viewed the Jewish and Christian revelations as antithetical, found its clearest expression in Marcion, who flourished in the middle of the second century. He contrasted the good God revealed in Jesus Christ with the Old Testament God of retaliation and vengeance, whom he viewed as responsible for the evil in creation. In consequence, he did away with the Old Testament as the sacred book of Christians, and in its place he supplied a canon called "The Gospel and the Apostle." The "Gospel" was a form of our present Luke; the "Apostle" was a corpus of ten letters of Paul. Both the Gospel and Paul he expurgated of Old Testament references, to suit his theology. The Catholic canon was doubtless framed with Marcion's in view, though it was not until the fourth century that there was final unanimity on which books should be included. Three of the works in our present volume (I Clement, II Clement, and the Didache) were at one time part of the New Testament in some areas of the Church.

The creed developed as a baptismal formula. The most important is the Roman symbol which underwent various revisions until the seventh century, and came finally to be known as "The Apostles' Creed." Its primitive form is reflected in Irenaeus, and at the end of the second century Hippolytus[6] gives us the first text of the three statements to which the baptized yielded assent on their immersion.

The process whereby the faith became ordered in the episcopate, preserved in the canon, and defined in a creed, has its counterpart in the development of the liturgy. Throughout the second century prayer was still extemporaneous, though set forms and phrases had been taken over from the Jewish synagogue, and Christian prayers were gradually becoming stereotyped. We have an instance of a traditional intercessory prayer in I Clement (chs. 59 to 61), and some reflections of the Eucha-

[6] Apostolic Tradition, ch. 21. For the early dating of this work, see my article in the *Anglican Theological Review*, January, 1948, pp. 38–44.

ristic prayer will be observed in Polycarp's Martyrdom (ch. 14). The primitive prayers of the Didache survived in Alexandria, and, indeed, turn up two centuries later in Egyptian liturgies. But it was the structure, rather than the exact wording of the liturgy, that was early established. The way in which the Church should continue the action of Jesus at the Last Supper was a matter of grave importance. It was an action that was the center of the Church's life, for by this mystery the Christian believed he was incorporated into the very humanity of Christ (Justin, Apol. I, ch. 66).

By the turn of the first century the Eucharist was no longer a supper meal. The ceremony of the bread and wine had been attached to a service of lections and prayer, derived from the synagogue. The first description we have is in Justin's Apology (I, chs. 65; 67). The service takes place about dawn in a private house, and its order is as follows: lections, sermon, intercessory prayers, kiss of peace, offering of the bread and wine, consecration prayer, Communion. By the end of the century we have a text of the consecration prayer in Hippolytus, though that learned Roman is careful to indicate that he is giving a pattern, not insisting on the exact words to be followed.[7]

The change from a supper meal to a dawn service arose from several factors. For one thing, slaves, who formed a significant part of a Christian congregation, were not free to attend an evening meal. Then again, imperial edicts had forbidden unlicensed clubs to hold such suppers. Moreover, to Gentiles, who dated their days from midnight, a supper on Saturday evening would have seemed an odd way of celebrating the day of the resurrection. Jews dated their days from sundown, and so the primitive Christian communities (envisaged in the liturgical section of the Didache) naturally celebrated the day of the resurrection with a Saturday supper. For Gentiles, however, this cannot but have seemed inappropriate.

Practically all the documents in our volume refer to the persecution of Christians, and of this a brief word may be said. It is a disputed point whether Christians in this early period were persecuted because of an official, imperial rescript forbidding their existence, or whether the action taken against them rested only on the general police powers of Roman magistrates. In any case there was persecution; but it was neither so incessant nor so widespread as is often imagined. There were spasmodic outbreaks of a savage nature, as Nero's

[7] Apostolic Tradition, chs. 4; 10:4.

action, or the condemnations of Ignatius and Polycarp, or the sad tale of the martyrs in Lyons and Vienne. But the State made no concerted attempt to stamp out Christianity until the days of Decius in the middle of the third century. Yet by their attacks on the Roman gods and by their refusal to sacrifice to the imperial genius, the Christians were always liable both to popular vengeance and to criminal prosecution.

Internally, the life of the Church in the second century was disturbed by two important movements—Gnosticism and Montanism. The former was an attempt to modernize the faith by accommodating it to the syncretic spirit of the age. During our period the type of Christianity that flourished in two widely separated centers, Edessa and Alexandria, was avowedly Gnostic; and not, indeed, until the turn of the second century did there emerge significant Catholic minorities in those areas.

Gnosticism [8] is older than Christianity. It represents the fusion of Oriental and Greek ideas into various elaborate systems whose aim is to acquire "gnosis" or knowledge of the divine. Ancient mythological material is blended with philosophic and religious ideas. Sometimes the dominating interest is the philosophic one—the problem of the one and the many. At other times the religious element is primary, and salvation is sought from the insecurity and evil of the natural world. Popular magical notions and astrology also enter in; and the vast movement of Gnosis had manifold forms throughout the Hellenistic world. Gnosis is knowledge based on revelation, but it is not intellectual knowledge. It is saving knowledge, enabling the soul to escape from the flux and change of life and to find the assurance of immortality. By the true gnosis the soul is freed from the evil prison house of the body into which it has fallen, and empowered to ascend to its original home in the spiritual world.

In the Christian forms of Gnosis there are instances where the Christian element is clearly a superficial addition to a system already complete. But in other cases, as in those of the great Alexandrine teachers, Basilides and Valentinus, the Christian factor is fundamental. Yet all Gnostic systems depend upon a principle that is at variance with Christianity—the dualism of matter and spirit. That the body was basically evil, and in no sense the creation of a good God, was a central tenet. It

---

[8] For a clear and cogent survey of Gnosticism, with some reference to the recent discoveries in Egypt, see G. Quispel, *Gnosis als Weltreligion.* Origo Verlag, Zurich, 1951.

led Gnostics to dispute the underlying message of the Old Testament, and to contrast the creator-God with the God revealed in Jesus Christ. In consequence, as we have already seen, the Old Testament was rejected, and new Christian books were substituted in its place. It is interesting that not only the first New Testament canon comes from Gnostic sources, but Gnostics were the first to give New Testament passages the authority once enjoyed by the Old Testament (Basilides), to write a New Testament commentary (Heracleon), and to make a Gospel harmony (Tatian). This peculiar interest in a *New* Testament stems from the rejection of the Old.

Other serious consequences followed from the Gnostic disparagement of the body. The doctrine of the incarnation was denied. Jesus only "appeared": he did not genuinely take on human flesh. Hence these Gnostics came to be known as "Docetics" (from *dokeō*, appear); and it is against this aspect of their teaching that Ignatius' letters are primarily aimed.

In the ethical sphere the Gnostics either espoused a strict asceticism or else indulged in antinomianism. In the one case they argued that the soul should cut itself as loose as possible from the material world; in the other case they contended that, because creation was outside the sphere of the good God, the soul's relation to it was a matter of indifference. Both these attitudes were challenged by the anti-Gnostic writers, such as Irenaeus; while it 'is against the second that the earliest Christian sermon (II Clement) is directed.

At the opposite pole to Gnosticism stands the Montanist movement of the latter half of the second century. In essence this was an earnest attempt to recover the prophetic note in primitive Christianity, and to challenge both the intellectualistic tendencies in Gnosticism and the ecclesiastical trend of the second century Church. It was a revival of the religion of the Spirit—an ecstatic outburst, eagerly expectant of the end of the world and rigorous in its ascetic demands. It opposed the developing laxity in Christian morals, which went hand in hand with the Church's claim to forgive sins after baptism, and the antinomianism to which some forms of Gnosticism had led. Born in Phrygia in Asia Minor, it passed eventually to North Africa, where it won for its cause the vehement Tertullian, in whose writings it takes on a severely puritanical note. But its most characteristic feature was its revival of prophecy and its emphasis on the Spirit. Wrapped in ecstatic visions, Montanus and his prophetesses declared new revelations, foretelling the coming of the New Jerusalem, forbidding second marriages and second repentance, and insisting on rigorous fasts and other ascetic practices.

The Catholic opposition to Montanism rested on the conviction that the Christian revelation was complete. Nothing new in principle could be added to the apostolic deposit of the faith. The Church, too, was cautious about ecstasies in which the prophet lost the use of his reason and identified himself with God. "I am come neither as an angel, nor as an ambassador, but as God the Father," said Montanus. Against such extravagant claims, the Church insisted on the sufficiency of the apostolic tradition.

The ascetic tendencies in Gnosticism and Montanism affected the ethical life of the Catholic Church. While the extremes of both positions were renounced, an increasing veneration of celibacy and virginity is to be observed. In both Justin and Athenagoras this is apparent; and it reaches its full expression in the development of monasticism in the fourth century.

To conclude: The dominant interest of the second century Church was the ordering of its life and teaching. To preserve the apostolic witness against Gnostic perversions and Montanist extravagancies, the episcopate, the canon, and the creed were developed. To interpret it to the Gentile mind, its affinities with the best in pagan religious thought were utilized. To maintain it against persecution, the martyr was willing to suffer. Finally, to ensure the perpetuity of the faith, the Church built up a closely knit organization which was as uncompromising toward heresy and schism as it was toward the demands of the State.

BASIC WORKS ON EARLY CHRISTIAN LITERATURE AND HISTORY

In addition to the books mentioned in the introductions to the various documents, the following more comprehensive works may be consulted. In the list below and elsewhere in this volume the names of publishers are given only for books published since 1928.

MANUALS OF EARLY CHRISTIAN LITERATURE

Altaner, B., *Patrologie*, 2d ed. J. C. Herder, Freiburg, 1950.

Bardenhewer, O., *Geschichte der altkirchlichen Literatur*, 5 vols. J. C. Herder, Freiburg, 1913–1932.

Goodspeed, E. J., *A History of Early Christian Literature*. University of Chicago Press, Chicago, 1942.

Harnack, A., *Geschichte der altchristlichen Literatur bis Eusebius*, 5 vols. Leipzig, 1893–1904.

Labriolle, P. de, *Histoire de la littérature latine chrétienne*. Paris, 1924.

Monceaux, P., *Histoire de la littérature latine chrétienne*. Paris, 1924.

Puech, A., *Histoire de la littérature grecque chrétienne jusqu'à la fin du IVe siècle*, 3 vols. Société d'édition "Les Belles Lettres," Paris, 1928–1930.

Quasten, J., *Patrology*, Vol. I (the best manual in English). Spectrum Publishers, Utrecht, 1950.

Raemers, S. A., *A Handbook of Patrology* (based on J. Tixeront, *Mélanges de patrologie*). J. C. Herder, St. Louis, 1934.

Stählin, O., *Die altchristliche griechische Literatur* (in W. von Christ, *Geschichte der griechischen Literatur*, 2.2), 6th ed. Munich, 1924.

HISTORIES OF THE EARLY CHURCH

Duchesne, L., *Early History of the Christian Church*, 3 vols. London, 1909–1924.

Elliott-Binns, L. E., *The Beginnings of Western Christendom*. Lutterworth Press, London, 1948.

Eusebius, *Ecclesiastical History*. Greek text by Schwartz, E., in Die griechischen christlichen Schriftsteller der ersten drei Jahrhunderte. Leipzig, 1903. English translations with copious notes by McGiffert, A. C., in Select Library of Nicene and Post-Nicene Fathers, Series 1, Vol. I, New York, 1890; and by Lawlor, H. J., and Oulton, J. E. L., London, 1928.

Harnack, A., *The Expansion of Christianity*, English translation by J. Moffatt, 2 vols. New York, 1904–1905.

Kidd, B. J., *A History of the Church to A.D. 461*, 3 vols. (standard work, carefully documented). Oxford, 1922.

Latourette, K. S., *The First Five Centuries* (Vol. 1 of A History of the Expansion of Christianity). Harper & Brothers, New York, 1937.

Lebreton, J., and Zeiller, J., *The History of the Primitive Church*, 2 vols., English translation by E. C. Messenger. The Macmillan Company, New York, 1949.

Lietzmann, H., *The Beginnings of the Christian Church*, English translation by B. L. Woolf. Charles Scribner's Sons, New York, 1937.
The Founding of the Church Universal, English translation by B. L. Woolf. Charles Scribner's Sons, New York, 1938.

Moffatt, J., *The First Five Centuries* (brief sketch with rich bibliography, including novels with early Christian background). University of London Press: Hodder, London, 1938.

HISTORIES OF EARLY CHRISTIAN DOCTRINE AND PRACTICE

Bauer, W., *Rechtgläubigkeit und Ketzerei im ältesten Christentum* (fundamental study of relation of orthodoxy to heresy, somewhat radical). J. C. B. Mohr, Tübingen, 1934.

Bethune-Baker, J. F., *Introduction to the Early History of Christian Doctrine* (standard work), 5th ed. Cambridge University Press, London, 1933.

Cadoux, C. J., *The Early Church and the World* (clearly organized and well-documented work on early Christian ethics). Edinburgh, 1925.

Dix, G., *The Shape of the Liturgy* (standard work on liturgy, deals largely with early period). The Dacre Press, London, 1944.

Harnack, A., *A History of Dogma*, English translation by N. Buchanan, 7 vols. London, 1894 ff.

Lebreton, J., *Histoire de la dogme de la Trinité*, 2 vols. Paris, 1927–1928. English translation of Vol. I by A. Thorold. Burns, London, 1939.

McGiffert, A. C., *A History of Christian Thought*, 2 vols. Charles Scribner's Sons, New York, 1931.

Seeberg, R., *Textbook of the History of Doctrines*, English translation by C. E. Hay. Philadelphia, 1905.

Srawley, J. H., *The Early History of the Liturgy*. Cambridge University Press, Cambridge, 1947.

The New Testament in the Apostolic Fathers. Oxford, 1905.

Tixeront, J., *History of Dogmas*, English translation by H. L. B., 3 vols. St. Louis, 1923 ff.

Source Books

Ayer, J. C., *A Source Book for Ancient Church History*. Charles Scribner's Sons, New York, 1933.

Grant, R. M., *Second Century Christianity* (a small volume of some important fragments). S.P.C.K., London, 1946.

James, M. R., *The Apocryphal New Testament*. Oxford, 1924.

Collections of Early Christian Writings

Migne, J. P., *Patrologia cursus completus*: Series Graeca, Paris, 1857–1866; Series Latina, Paris, 1844–1855.

Berlin Corpus: *Die griechischen christlichen Schriftsteller der ersten drei Jahrhunderte*. Berlin, 1897 ff.

Vienna Corpus: *Corpus scriptorum ecclesiasticorum latinorum*. Vienna, 1866 ff.

Corpus scriptorum christianorum orientalium. Paris, 1903 ff. There are four series, Syriac, Coptic, Arabic, and Ethiopic.

Patrologia Orientalis, ed. Graffin, R., and Nau, F. Paris, 1907 ff.

Patrologia Syriaca, ed. Graffin, R. Paris, 1894–1926.

Collections of Early Christian Writings in Translation

The Ante-Nicene Fathers (reprint of the Edinburgh edition by A. Roberts and J. Donaldson, revised by A. C. Coxe). Buffalo, 1884–1886.

Translations of Christian Literature, ed. W. J. Sparrow-Simpson and W. K. Lowther Clarke. Four series: Greek Texts, Latin Texts, Liturgical Texts, and Oriental Texts. London, 1917 ff.
Ancient Christian Writers, ed. J. Quasten and J. C. Plumpe. Newman Press, Westminster, Maryland, 1946 ff.
The Fathers of the Church, ed. L. Schopp. Cima Publishing Company, New York, 1947 ff.
Bibliothek der Kirchenväter, ed. O. Bardenhewer, Th. Schermann, and C. Weyman, Jos. Kösel, Kempten, 1911–1930; Second Series, 1932–1939.
Sources chrétiennes, ed. H. de Lubac and J. Daniélou. Éditions du Cerf, Paris, 1941 ff.

DICTIONARIES

The Catholic Encyclopedia. New York, 1907–1914.
Dictionnaire d'archéologie chrétienne et de liturgie. Paris, 1907 ff.
Dictionnaire de la théologie catholique. Paris, 1903 ff.
Dictionary of the Apostolic Church. Edinburgh, 1915–1918.
Dictionary of Christian Biography. London, 1877–1888.
Realencyclopädie für protestantische Theologie und Kirche, 3d ed. Leipzig, 1896–1913.
Reallexikon für Antike und Christentum. Hiersemann Verlag, Leipzig, 1941 ff.

ATLASES

Heussi, K., and Mulert, H., *Atlas zur Kirchengeschichte.* Tübingen, 1919.
Shepherd, W. R., *Historical Atlas.* 7th ed. Henry Holt & Company, Inc., New York, 1929.
Wright, G. E., and Filson, F. V., *The Westminster Historical Atlas to the Bible.* The Westminster Press, Philadelphia, 1945.

BIBLIOGRAPHY

Richardson, E. C., *Bibliographical Synopsis* in The Ante-Nicene Library, Vol. 10. New York, 1899.
See also the relevant sections in the manuals listed, especially Altaner and Quasten.

INDEXES

Goodspeed, E. J., *Index Patristicus* (Greek index of the Apostolic Fathers). Leipzig, 1907.
Goodspeed, E. J., *Index Apologeticus* (Greek index of the Greek Apologists). Leipzig, 1912.

LETTERS IN CRISES

The Letter of the Church of Rome
to the Church of Corinth,
Commonly Called Clement's First Letter

INTRODUCTION

OUTSIDE THE NEW TESTAMENT WRITINGS, THE earliest Christian document we possess is an anonymous letter of the church of Rome to the church of Corinth. It was written about A.D. 96, and was so highly esteemed in Christian antiquity that for a while it was even reckoned as part of the canon in Egypt and Syria.[1] Very ancient tradition ascribes the letter to a certain Clement who, according to the early episcopal lists, was the third bishop of Rome. The style of the document is simple and clear, though it is marked by some rhetorical devices, notably a fondness for synonyms. The importance of the letter lies in the picture it gives us of early Roman Christianity. Here we see a version of the gospel which, while reflecting Paulinism, is more strongly influenced by Hellenistic Judaism, and which, in several ways, foreshadows the leading emphases of later Roman Catholicism.

DATE

Some references in the letter itself indicate that it stems from the period of the second generation of Christians. The Neronian persecution of A.D. 64 is already past (chs. 5; 6): the Corinthians are viewed as an "ancient church" (ch. 47:6), and there are in Rome those who from youth to old age have lived irreproachable Christian lives (ch. 63:3). Yet Peter and Paul can be described as heroes belonging to "our own generation" (ch. 5:1); and while the apostles have passed away, there still

---

[1] Clement of Alexandria cites it as Scripture, and it is found in Syriac and Coptic codices of the N.T. as well as being appended to the Codex Alexandrinus.

survive some whom they appointed as presbyters (ch. 44). Certain calamities have again befallen the church (chs. 1:1; 7:1). These are distinguished from the Neronian persecution (ch. 7:1), and are generally taken to refer to Domitian's capricious attacks on Christians. While we are not well informed about these, there is sufficient evidence to credit them.[2] A further indication that the letter belongs to the first century is the lack of a knowledge of the canonical Gospels. All in all, there can be little doubt that A.D. 96 or 97 (the end of Domitian's reign or the beginning of Nerva's) is the correct date.

THE OCCASION OF THE LETTER

The occasion of the letter was a schism in the Corinthian church. The same factious spirit that Paul had encountered there had once again provoked serious dissension. It appears that some young men had been the ringleaders of a revolt which had succeeded in deposing the ruling presbyters (chs. 3:3; 44:6). Exactly what lay behind this action is not altogether clear. It may be that these youths, restless under the rule of clergy considerably older than themselves and who held office for life, sought to introduce a more flexible system into the ministry. Following the custom of the cults, they may have wished for annual elections and for a constant change of officers. It is probable, however, that an even deeper issue was involved. There are hints in the letter that the rebels claimed to have particular spiritual gifts which (in their judgment) were not receiving adequate recognition. They were ascetics observing continence (ch. 38:2). They boasted of "gnosis"—secret knowledge of the faith, that is, revealed only to the elite (ch. 48:5). Perhaps, too, they spoke with tongues, though the references are equally open to the interpretation that they were persuasive and powerful speakers (chs. 21:5; 57:2). These slight indications might lead us to suppose that the strife was between charismatics and the regular ministry. In the course of the Church's history those with special spiritual gifts have not seldom felt slighted if they received insufficient recognition or failed to be elected to office. This is the reverse of the situation reflected in the Didache, where the visiting prophet is held in high esteem and it is the claims of the local ministry that have to be pressed (chs. 11:3 ff.; 13; 15:1, 2).

[2] The relevant passages will be found in J. B. Lightfoot, *The Apostolic Fathers*, Part 1, Vol. I, pp. 104 ff.

News of the dissension seems to have reached Rome through hearsay (ch. 47:7). It is possible that some traveling Romans had not been accorded the usual welcome, as visitors, by the rebellious faction, and on returning home had spread the report. This would account for the emphasis on hospitality (chs. 1:2; 11; 12). In any case there is no evidence that Corinth applied to Rome for a judgment in the matter. Rome's intervention is to be explained from other factors.

It was nothing extraordinary for leaders of one church to send a letter of advice and warning to another congregation. The apostolic prerogative exercised by Paul had set a wide precedent which was followed by the author of the seven letters in the Revelation, by Ignatius, by Polycarp, by Dionysius of Corinth,[3] by Serapion,[4] and by many others. Each Christian community seems to have felt a sufficient sense of responsibility for the others so that its leaders could admonish them with solicitude. In some instances, of course, the authors claimed a special right to speak. The seer of the Revelation and the martyr Ignatius are examples. But the point to bear in mind is that the local churches did not conceive of themselves as isolated and autonomous units. They were part of the wider Church, and were not unconcerned with what happened in other congregations. This is most forcibly brought home to us by the style of our document. For it is not written in the name of an individual, but of a congregation. It is very far from a papal decree, though it was doubtless written by one of the leaders of the Roman church. It makes no claim to superior authority, but, basing itself on the authority of Scripture, it tries to persuade an errant congregation to return to the right way.

Furthermore, that Rome should intervene in the internal affairs of the Corinthian church is partly to be explained by the close relations between the two cities. Refounded as a Roman colony in the middle of the first century, Corinth had built up a peculiarly intimate connection in trade and culture with the mother city. Indeed, excavations have made clear how exactly Corinth tried to mimic Rome—in its sculpture, architecture, organization, and even its names. Neither the church at Rome nor that at Corinth was, it is true, Latin in race or language. The predominant element in both congregations was doubtless converted Hellenistic Jews. Yet these affinities between the two cities help to explain even the

[3] Eusebius, *Hist. eccl.*, IV, ch. 23.
[4] *Ibid.*, V, ch. 19; VI, 12:3-6.

Christian connections. Corinth, moreover, by being a natural halt on the route between Rome and the East would be in constant touch with the imperial capital.

Yet it cannot be denied that these two explanations do not fully account for the tone of the letter. Rome very definitely regards it as her duty to intervene (ch. 63) and sends envoys to see that matters are put right (ch. 65). Something of her unique place as the church of the imperial city, and the church of Peter and Paul (ch. 5), must surely have been in the writer's mind. Among the Roman clergy (as we learn from Hermas, Vis., II, ch. 4) there seems to have been one who acted as a sort of "foreign secretary" for the church, sending abroad various advices and exhortations as well as gifts of charity.[5] This implies more than a casual relation with other churches; and while this should not be pressed to vindicate much later papal claims, it does indicate that the Roman community took most seriously its responsibility as a sister church for the welfare of other congregations. Here, in germ, is that exercise of authority which was to become the papal primacy.

THE AUTHOR

While the letter was written in the name of the church of Rome and its subscription did not originally mention Clement, there can be little doubt that he was the author. The Greek manuscripts attribute it to him, and, as early as A.D. 170, Dionysius of Corinth ascribes it to him. He speaks of it as the letter "which was previously written to us through Clement," and he mentions the fact it was still read publicly in the Corinthian church on Sundays (Eusebius, *Hist. eccl.* IV. 23:11).

Precisely who Clement was is not altogether clear. The earliest episcopal lists, those of Irenaeus and Hegesippus, make him the third bishop of Rome. This tradition, however, implies that the monepiscopate was very early established in that city, and doubtless reads back a later situation into the more primitive period. Certainly the terms "bishop" and "presbyter" were not yet clearly distinguished in Clement's time, for he uses them as synonyms or at any rate to refer to the same class of persons, the church rulers (cf. chs. 42:4; 44:4, 5; 47:6; 57:1). Exactly what the situation was in those early years we do not know. The only hint we derive is from the Roman prophet

---

[5] The far-flung charity of the Roman church is noted by Ignatius, Rom. 1:2. Cf. Dionysius of Corinth *apud* Eusebius, *Hist. eccl.* IV. 23:10.

Hermas, who in the course of his visions relates rather epigrammatically that he is bidden to write "two little books and [to] send one to Clement and one to Grapte. Clement must then send it to the cities abroad, for that is his duty, and Grapte shall exhort the widows and orphans" (Hermas, Vis. II. 4:3). The date of this vision is the late first century, and it doubtless refers to our Clement, among whose duties was that of acting as a kind of foreign secretary for the church. That he had some of the functions later vested in the episcopate may well be true; but that he was exactly a "bishop" in the later sense is open to doubt. It must suffice to call him a leading—perhaps *the* leading—presbyter-bishop of the Roman church.

More than that we do not know of Clement. The attempts to identify him with the Clement mentioned in Paul's Philippians (ch. 4:3),[6] or with the family of the consul Titus Flavius Clemens, are only conjectures. The name is a very frequent one in this period, especially in military circles. Yet it must be conceded that the hypothesis that has been elaborated by J. B. Lightfoot, that Clement was a freedman of the Flavian family, is attractive and not entirely lacking in substance. The consul Titus Flavius Clemens was a cousin of Domitian, and according to Dion Cassius he was executed by the emperor on the charge of atheism. This may possibly mean that he was a Christian, since the accusation of atheism was frequently brought against the new faith. Furthermore, his wife Domitilla was exiled; and it appears that one of the oldest Roman catacombs, the *Coemeterium Domitillae*, was situated on an estate belonging to her. Slight as these indications are, they do lend support to the theory that the consul and his wife were Christians. By virtue of his position he certainly could never have been a church official; but it is not altogether unlikely that someone connected with his household and bearing his name was the author of our letter.

CLEMENT'S CHRISTIANITY

The most striking feature of Clement's letter is its blending of Old Testament and Christian themes with Hellenistic ideas and expressions. Its author is saturated in the Old Testament, citing the Septuagint with frequency and finding in the heroes of Israel the patterns of Christian conduct. He is familiar with Pauline writings, especially with I Corinthians, which he uses

6 Origen, Com. in John 6:36 and Eusebius, *Hist. eccl.*, III, ch. 15.

as a model for his own letter, imitating its hymn on love (chs. 49; 50) and enlarging on its teachings regarding the resurrection (ch. 24) and schism (ch. 47). But these Jewish and Christian elements often take on a Stoic dress (e.g., chs. 20; 21); and while sometimes Clement speaks in the very tones of Paul, as for instance on justification by faith (ch. 32:4), his leading convictions are somewhat different.

There is a strain of moralism in his religion, which links him on the one hand with Hellenistic Judaism and on the other with Stoicism. Where, for Paul, Abraham was the hero whose faith alone made him right with God, for Clement, he is the pattern of obedience, of hospitality, of humility, and of righteousness (chs. 10:1, 7; 17:2; 31:2). Again, while our author is aware of the grave issue raised by the doctrine of justification by faith, viz., that men might continue to sin that grace should abound, the answer he gives to this dilemma is very different from Paul's. Where the latter in Rom., ch. 6, emphasizes the mystical dying of the Christian to sin, Clement stresses the moral imitation by the Christian of the Creator's good works (ch. 33). Once again, in defending the doctrine of the resurrection, Clement, like Paul, can base his case on a natural theology (ch. 24; cf. I Cor. 15:36), and is well aware that Christ is the first fruits of those that slept (ch. 24:1; cf. I Cor. 15:20). Yet his crowning argument is not the victory won by Christ over sin and the law, but the incredible tale of the phoenix (ch. 25)! Finally, where Paul reaches to the very heart of the issue of schism by asking the incisive question, "Is Christ divided?" Clement expatiates on the orderliness of nature (ch. 20) and the consequences of envy and rivalry (chs. 4 to 6).

These instances must suffice to indicate the extent to which Clement has moved away from the Pauline gospel into an atmosphere more concerned with the moral life, and in particular with the virtues of humility and order. Where ethical injunctions are secondary to Paul's letters, they are primary in Clement. We observe, too, a tendency, very evident in chs. 20; 24 to 25, to emphasize natural theology. All these are marks of that later Romanism to which Clement's Letter points.

It is, however, in the treatment of church order that Clement most clearly foreshadows later Catholicism. The deposition of the local Corinthian rulers leads him to set forth a hierarchical view of the ministry and to stress the need of submission to the duly elected clergy. It is claimed (chs. 42 to 44) that the apostles appointed their first converts as presbyter-bishops and provided for a future ministry should these eventually die. It is not entirely clear how the new clergy were to be installed, save that the congregation was to elect them. It is possible that they were to be ordained by the remaining presbyter-bishops, though it is more likely that Clement intends something different, viz., that they were to be ordained by a special class of ministers who succeeded to the apostolic prerogatives (see note on ch. 44). Here we have in essence the doctrine of apostolic succession. Emphasis, moreover, is laid upon the liturgical functions of these presbyter-bishops who stand in the apostolic line. It is they who lead worship and have the right to "offer the gifts" (ch. 44:4), just as the duly appointed priests of the Old Testament performed the various sacrifices (chs. 42 to 44). The sacrificial understanding of the Lord's Supper here comes to the fore and is clearly connected with the theme of apostolic succession.

It has been already observed that Clement still uses the terms "presbyter" and "bishop" for the same class of persons, the church rulers, and we are not therefore to suppose that the monepiscopate has been fully established. The local church seems to be governed by a board of presbyter-bishops, though one of its number may have had special powers and privileges. What, however, is important to note is that the main lines of the later development are so plainly prefigured.

Conclusion

To summarize: Clement's Letter reflects the movement away from the Pauline faith to a type of Christianity in which ethical interests and concern for law and order predominate. This does not, however, exclude both acquaintance with, and some grasp of, the Pauline gospel. The cleavage is not so sharp as is sometimes made out. Nor do the Stoic expressions to be found in Clement or his interest in, and familiarity with, the pagan world (note chs. 37 and 55:1), indicate that he has capitulated to an alien culture. Rather must we say that Roman Christianity is giving evidence of its background in Hellenistic Judaism, and adapting itself to the imperial capital.

MANUSCRIPTS AND BOOKS

Despite the fact that Clement's Letter was widely read in Christian antiquity, and at one time formed part of the New

Testament canon in Egypt and Syria, its text was unknown in
the West through the Middle Ages. Not until 1628, when the
fifth century Codex Alexandrinus· reached England, was it
recovered. This Codex of the Bible was the gift of Cyril Lucar,
the Patriarch of Constantinople, to Charles I. At the end of the
New Testament two epistles of Clement are appended. The
first is our document; the second is not an epistle at all but a
second century homily, wrongly attributed to Clement.
Patrick Young (Junius) edited the first edition of Clement's
Letter from this Codex in 1633. This text, unfortunately
defective in one page (chs. 57:7 to 63:4 being wanting), was
the only one known until the discovery of the eleventh century
Jerusalem Codex by Philotheos Byrennios, which he published
in 1875. An autotype of the latter manuscript is given by J. B.
Lightfoot in his *Apostolic Fathers*, Part 1, Vol. I, pp. 425-474.

There are four other witnesses to the text. There is a Syriac
version, extant in one twelfth century manuscript, now in
Cambridge. It was published by R. H. Kennett (from Professor
Bensley's work) in 1899. There is a Latin version, edited by
Dom G. Morin in *Anecdota Maredsolana*, Vol. II, 1894. The
manuscript belongs to the eleventh century, but the translation
is very ancient, going back to the second or third century.
There are finally two Coptic versions independent of each other
and in the Akhmimic dialect. The better preserved of the two
is a Berlin papyrus of the fourth century, edited by C. Schmidt
in Texte und Untersuchungen, XXXII. 1, 1908. Chapters
34:6 to 42:2 are lacking. The other and more fragmentary one
is from a Strassburg manuscript of the fifth century, edited by
F. Rösch in 1910, *Bruchstücke des I Klemensbriefes*. It breaks off
at ch. 26:2.

The best modern edition of the Greek text, and the one used
for this translation, is that by Karl Bihlmeyer in his revision
of F. X. Funk's *Die apostolischen Väter*, Part 1, Tübingen, 1924.
The editions of J. B. Lightfoot, *The Apostolic Fathers*, Part 1,
"S. Clement of Rome," revised edition, London, 1890, and
of Kirsopp Lake, *The Apostolic Fathers* (Loeb Classics), London,
1912, should also be consulted. The text by H. Hemmer in
Hemmer and Lejay, *Les Pères apostoliques*, Part 2, Paris, 1909,.
is based on Funk, *Patres apostolici* of 1901.

There are a number of important modern translations. As
well as the renderings by Lightfoot and Lake in the works just
mentioned, there are two excellent idiomatic ones: by J. A.
Kleist, *The Epistles of St. Clement of Rome and St. Ignatius of*

Antioch, Newman Press, Westminster, Maryland, 1946, in the series Ancient Christian Writers; and by F. X. Glimm, *The Apostolic Fathers,* Cima Publishing Company, New York, 1947, in the series The Fathers of the Church. In the style of the Revised Version of the Bible is W. K. Lowther Clarke, *The First Epistle of Clement to the Corinthians,* S.P.C.K., London, 1937. The most recent translation is by Edgar Goodspeed in his *The Apostolic Fathers: An American Translation,* Harper & Brothers, New York, 1950.

In German there are renderings by Adolf Harnack, *Das Schreiben der römischen Kirche an die korinthische aus der Zeit Domitians,* J. C. Hinrichs, Leipzig, 1929; by Rudolf Knopf, *Die Lehre der Zwölf Apostel: Die zwei Klemensbriefe,* Tübingen, 1920, in Handbuch zum N. T.; by F. Zeller, *Die apostolischen Väter,* Munich, 1918, in the 2d series of the Bibliothek der Kirchenväter; and by Knopf and Krüger in E. Hennecke, *Neutestamentliche Apokryphen,* 2d ed., Tübingen, 1924.

In French there is the translation by H. Hemmer in the edition already mentioned.

In Italian there is a rendering by G. Bosio, *I Padri apostolici,* Part 1, Società editrice internazionale, Turin, 1940, Vol. VII of the series Corona Patrum Salesiana.

All these editions have introductions and notes. The most illuminating are those by Lightfoot, Kleist, Lowther Clarke, Harnack, and Hemmer. Knopf is especially good on the lexicographical side and on parallel literature. For clarity, incisiveness, and penetration, Harnack's work, despite its brevity, is unsurpassed. Written some half a century after he first published an edition of Clement, it represents the fruit of a lifetime of patristic scholarship. Many of his points are reproduced in English dress by Lowther Clarke.

Studies in Clement are numerous. The most significant are these: W. Wrede, *Untersuchungen zum ersten Klemensbrief* (a basic early work), Göttingen, 1891; W. Scherer, *Der erste Klemensbrief an die Korinther nach seiner Bedeutung für die Glaubenslehre der katholischen Kirche untersucht,* Regensburg, 1902; Th. Schermann, *Griechische Zauberpapyri und das Gemeinde- und Dankgebet im ersten Klemensbrief,* in Texte und Untersuchungen, XXXIV. 2b (useful material, but not incisively treated), Leipzig, 1909; F. Gerke, *Die Stellung des ersten Klemensbriefes innerhalb der Entwicklung der altchristlichen Gemeindeverfassung und des Kirchenrechts,* in Texte und Untersuchungen, XLVII. 1, J. C. Hinrichs (an elaborate attack on Sohm's theory about Church law),

Leipzig, 1931; L. Sanders, *L'Hellénisme de Saint Clément de Rome et le Paulinisme* (especially good on the parallels with Stoic thought and literary forms, but underestimates Clement's break with Pauline theology), Louvain, 1943.
There are also a number of important articles: F. S. Marsh, "Clement of Rome" in *Dictionary of the Apostolic Church* (the best summary of significant issues), 2d ed., 1926; L. Lemme, "Das Judenchristentum der Urkirche und der Brief des Klemens Romanus," in *Neues Jahrbuch für deutsche Theologie*, I, pp. 325–480, 1892; V. Schweizer, "Glaube und Werke bei Klemens Romanus," in *Theologische Quartalschrift*, 85, pp. 417–437; 547–575, 1903; W. Praetorius, "Die Bedeutung der beiden Klemensbriefe für die älteste Geschichte der kirchlichen Praxis," in *Zeitschrift für die Kirchengeschichte*, 33, pp. 347–363, 1912; 501–528; E. Dubowy, "Klemens von Rom über der Reise Pauli nach Spanien," in *Biblische Studien*, XIX. 3, Freiburg, 1914; A. Plummer, "Danaïds and Dirces," in *The Expository Times*, 26, pp. 560–562, 1915; T. Merill, "On Clement of Rome," in *American Journal of Theology*, 22, pp. 426–442, 1918; G. Bardy, "Expressions stoïciennes dans le I*ᵉ* Clementis," in *Recherches de science religieuse*, 12, pp. 78–85, 1922; R. van Cauwelaert, "L'Intervention de l'Église de Rome à Corinth vers l'an 96," in *Revue d'histoire ecclésiastique*, 31, pp. 267–306, 1935; J. Zeiller, "À propos de l'intervention de l'Église de Rome à Corinth," *ibid.*, pp. 762–764; R. van Cauwelaert, "Réponse aux remarques de M. J. Zeiller," *ibid.*, pp. 765–766; O. Cullmann, "Les Causes de la mort de Pierre et de Paul d'après le témoignage de Clément Romain," in *Revue d'histoire et de philosophie religieuses*, 10, pp. 294–300, 1930; S. Lösch, "Der Brief des Klemens Romanus. Die Probleme und ihrer Beurteilung in der Gegenwart," in *Studi dedicati alla memoria de Paolo Ubaldi*, pp. 177–188, Milan, 1937; P. Meinhold, "Geschehen und Deutung im ersten Klemensbrief," in *Zeitschrift für die Kirchengeschichte*, 58, pp. 82–129, 1939; R. L. P. Milburn, "The Persecution of Domitian," in *Church Quarterly Review*, 139, pp. 154–164 (disputes the traditional view), 1945; J. Klevinghaus, *Die theologische Stellung der apostolischen Väter zur alttestamentlichen Offenbarung*, pp. 45–77, C. Bertelsmann, Gütersloh, 1948; W. C. Van Unnik, "Is I Clement 20 Purely Stoic?" in *Vigiliae Christianae*, 4, pp. 181–189, 1950.

The Letter of the Church of Rome
to the Church of Corinth,
Commonly Called Clement's First Letter

THE TEXT

The church of God, living in exile[7] in Rome, to the church of God, exiled in Corinth—to you who are called and sanctified by God's will through our Lord Jesus Christ. Abundant grace and peace be yours from God Almighty through Jesus Christ.

Due, dear friends, to the sudden and successive misfortunes 1 and accidents we have encountered,[8] we have, we admit, been rather long in turning our attention to your quarrels. We refer to the abominable and unholy schism, so alien and foreign to those whom God has chosen, which a few impetuous and headstrong fellows have fanned to such a pitch of insanity that your good name, once so famous and dear to us all, has fallen into the gravest ill repute. Has anyone, indeed, stayed 2 with you without attesting the excellence and firmness of your faith? without admiring your sensible and considerate Christian piety? without broadcasting your spirit of unbounded hospitality?[9] without praising your perfect and trustworthy knowledge? For you always acted without partiality and walked in 3 God's laws. You obeyed your rulers and gave your elders the proper respect. You disciplined the minds of your young people in moderation and dignity. You instructed your women to do everything with a blameless and pure conscience, and to give

---

[7] The Greek word implies a colony of aliens without full civic rights. Christians are strangers and pilgrims on earth, their true fatherland being heaven. Cf. I Peter 2:11; Phil. 3:20; Heb. 11:9.

[8] The reference is to persecution under Domitian—the same persecution reflected in John's Apocalypse.

[9] Hospitality is emphasized several times in the letter. It is a virtue appropriate to churches on the great trade route of the Empire, Corinth being a natural halt between Rome and the East.

their husbands the affection they should. You taught them, too, to abide by the rule of obedience and to run their homes with dignity and thorough discretion.

2 You were all humble and without any pretensions, obeying orders rather than issuing them, more gladly giving than receiving.[10] Content with Christ's rations and mindful of them, you stored his words carefully up in your hearts and held his sufferings before your eyes.

2 In consequence, you were all granted a profound and rich peace and an insatiable longing to do good, while the Holy 3 Spirit was abundantly poured out on you all. You were full of holy counsels, and, with zeal for the good and devout confidence, you stretched out your hands[11] to almighty God, beseeching him to have mercy should you involuntarily have 4 fallen into any sin. Day and night you labored for the whole brotherhood, that by your pity and sympathy the sum of his 5 elect might be saved. You were sincere and guileless and bore 6 no grudges. All sedition and schism were an abomination to you. You wept for the faults of your neighbors, while you reck-7 oned their shortcomings as your own. You never regretted all 8 the good you did, being "ready for any good deed."[12] Possessed of an excellent and devout character, you did everything in His fear. The commands and decrees of the Lord were engraven 3 on the tablets of your heart.[13] You were granted great popularity and growing numbers, so that the word of Scripture was fulfilled: "My beloved ate and drank and filled out and grew fat and started to kick."[14]

2 From this there arose rivalry and envy, strife and sedition, 3 persecution and anarchy, war and captivity. And so "the dishonored" rose up "against those who were held in honor,"[15] those of no reputation against the notable, the stupid against 4 the wise, "the young against their elders."[16] For this reason righteousness and peace are far from you, since each has abandoned the fear of God and grown purblind in his faith, and ceased to walk by the rules of his precepts or to behave in a way worthy of Christ. Rather does each follow the lusts

---

10 Cf. Acts 20:35.
11 Indicative of the ancient posture of prayer, standing upright with the hands outstretched.
12 Titus 3:1.
13 Cf. Prov. 7:3.
14 Deut. 32:15.
15 Isa. 3:5.
16 Isa. 59:14.

of his evil heart, by reviving that wicked and unholy rivalry,[17] by which, indeed, "death came into the world."[18]

For Scripture runs thus: "And it happened after some days 4 that Cain brought God a sacrifice from the fruits of the earth, while Abel made his offering from the first-born of the sheep and of their fat. And God looked with favor on Abel and on 2 his gifts; but he did not heed Cain and his sacrifices. And Cain 3 was greatly upset and his face fell. And God said to Cain, 4 'Why are you so upset, and why has your face fallen? If you have made a correct offering but not divided it correctly, have you not sinned?[19] Keep quiet. Your brother will turn to you 5 and you shall rule over him.'[20] And Cain said to his brother 6 Abel, 'Let us go into the field.' And it happened that while they were in the field Cain attacked his brother Abel and killed him."[21]

You see, brothers, rivalry and envy are responsible for 7 fratricide. Because of rivalry our forefather Jacob fled from the 8 presence of his brother Esau. It was rivalry that caused Joseph 9 to be murderously persecuted and reduced to slavery. Rivalry 10 forced Moses to flee from the presence of Pharaoh, the king of Egypt, when he heard his fellow clansman say: "Who made you a ruler or judge over us? Do you want to slay me as you did the Egyptian yesterday?"[22] By reason of rivalry Aaron and 11 Miriam were excluded from the camp. Rivalry cast Dathan 12 and Abiram alive into Hades because they revolted against Moses, God's servant. Because of rivalry David not only 13 incurred the envy of foreigners but was even persecuted by Saul, the king of Israel.

But, passing from examples in antiquity, let us come to the 5 heroes[23] nearest our own times. Let us take the noble examples of our own generation. By reason of rivalry and envy 2 the greatest and most righteous pillars[24] [of the Church]

---

[17] A key word in this letter opposing schism. "Rivalry" is used in a very broad sense and in Clement's mind is a primary source of evil. With many examples he traces the persecution of the righteous to the jealous hatred which goodness inspires.

[18] Wis. 2:24.

[19] The sentence is obscure, but seems to imply that Cain's gift was rejected, not because it was sheep instead of fruits, but because he kept back for himself the best parts.

[20] The meaning here is obscure.   [21] Gen. 4:3–8.   [22] Ex. 2:14.

[23] Literally "athletes," "combatants," "champions," the metaphor being taken from the Greek games. Cf. Heb. 12:1.

[24] Cf. Gal. 2:9.

3 were persecuted, and battled to the death. Let us set before
4 our eyes the noble apostles: Peter,[25] who by reason of wicked
jealousy, not only once or twice but frequently endured suffering and thus, bearing his witness,[26] went to the glorious place
5 which he merited. By reason of rivalry and contention[27] Paul
6 showed how to win the prize for patient endurance. Seven
times he was in chains; he was exiled, stoned, became a
herald [of the gospel] in East and West, and won the noble
7 renown which his faith merited. To the whole world he taught
righteousness, and reaching the limits of the West[28] he bore
his witness before rulers. And so, released from this world, he
was taken up into the holy place and became the greatest
example of patient endurance.

6   To these men who lived such holy lives there was joined a
great multitude of the elect who by reason of rivalry were the
victims of many outrages and tortures and who became out-
2 standing examples among us. By reason of rivalry women were
persecuted in the roles of Danaïds and Dircae.[29] Victims of
dreadful and blasphemous outrages, they ran with sureness the
course of faith to the finish, and despite their physical weakness
3 won a notable prize. It was rivalry that estranged wives from
their husbands and annulled the saying of our father Adam,
4 "This is now bone of my bone and flesh of my flesh."[30] Rivalry
and contention have overthrown great cities and uprooted
mighty nations.

7   We are writing in this vein, dear friends, not only to admonish you but also to remind ourselves. For we are in the same
2 arena and involved in the same struggle. Hence we should

25 The sequence Peter and Paul is interesting in a Roman document,
though it also occurs in Ignatius (Rom. 4:3). This passage is good proof
of Peter's martyrdom in Rome, as well as of Paul's, under Nero.

26 The word "bear witness," *martureō*, in Christian usage often, but not
necessarily, implies martyrdom (cf. Acts 22:20).

27 This has been interpreted to refer to a quarrel between the Petrine
and Pauline parties in Rome, similar to the one in Antioch (Gal. 2:11 ff.).
The suggestion is not necessary, but such a quarrel might have been a
factor in the Neronian outbreak.

28 The source of Clement's information is unknown. The reference is sometimes taken to imply that Paul was released from his first imprisonment
in Rome and carried out his intention to visit Spain (Rom. 15:24).

29 A reference to spectacles in the arena where criminals were forced to
play mythological roles. Dirce was tied to the horns of a bull and dragged
to death. The daughters of Danaüs were married off by being offered
as prizes in a foot race. It is likely that Christian girls were thus raped
before being martyred.

30 Gen. 2:23.

give up empty and futile concerns, and turn to the glorious and holy rule of our tradition.[31] Let us note what is good, what 3 is pleasing and acceptable to Him who made us. Let us fix 4 our eyes on the blood of Christ and let us realize how precious it is to his Father, since it was poured out for our salvation and brought the grace of repentance to the whole world. Let 5 us go through all the generations and observe that from one generation to another the Master "has afforded an opportunity of repentance"[32] to those who are willing to turn to him. Noah preached repentance and those who heeded him 6 were saved. Jonah preached destruction to the Ninevites; and 7 when they had repented of their sins, they propitiated God with their prayers and gained salvation despite the fact they were not God's people.

The ministers of God's grace spoke about repentance through 8 the Holy Spirit, and the Master of the universe himself spoke 2 of repentance with an oath: "For as I live, says the Lord, I do not desire the death of the sinner, but his repentance." He added, too, this generous consideration: "Repent, O house 3 of Israel, of your iniquity. Say to the sons of my people, Should your sins reach from earth to heaven, and be redder than scarlet and blacker than sackcloth, and should you turn to me with your whole heart and say 'Father!' I will heed you as though you were a holy people."[33] And in another place this 4 is what he says: "Wash and become clean: rid your souls of wickedness before my eyes. Cease from your wickedness, learn to behave well, devote yourselves to justice, rescue the wronged, uphold the rights of the orphan and grant the widow justice. And come, let us reason together, says the Lord; and if your sins are like purple, I will make them white as snow, and if they are like scarlet, I will make them white as wool. And if you are willing and heed me, you shall eat the good things of the earth. But if you are unwilling and do not heed me, the sword shall devour you. For it is the mouth of the Lord that has spoken thus."[34] Since, therefore, he wanted all those he 5 loved to have an opportunity to repent, he confirmed this by his almighty will.

31 A characteristically Roman phrase, but not yet in a technical or legalistic sense. "Tradition," furthermore, means something *living* handed *over*, not something *dead* handed *down*.
32 Wis. 12:10.
33 Ezek. 33:11–27. The citation differs from the canonical version and may be due to Clement's free rendering or more likely to a variant text he was following.   34 Isa. 1:16–20.

9   So, then, let us fall in with his magnificent and glorious intention, and let us prostrate ourselves before him as suppliants of his mercy and kindness. Let us turn to his compassion and give up useless ventures and strife, and rivalry that leads to
2 death. Let us fasten our eyes on those who have served his
3 magnificent glory to perfection. Let us take Enoch, for instance, who, because he proved upright by his obedience, was trans-
4 lated and never died. Noah proved faithful in his ministry and preached a new birth to the world. Through him, therefore, the Master saved those living creatures that entered peacefully
10 into the ark. Abraham, who was called "The Friend," proved
2 faithful in obeying God's words. It was obedience which led him to quit his country, his kindred, and his father's house, so that, by leaving a paltry country, a mean kindred, and an
3 insignificant house, he might inherit God's promises. For he told him: "Depart from your country and from your kindred and from the house of your father, and go to a land which I will show you. And I will make you great among the nations and I will bless you and I will make your name great and you will be blessed. And I will bless those who bless you and curse those who curse you, and all the tribes of the earth will be
4 blessed through you."35 And again, when he separated from Lot, God told him: "Lift up your eyes and from where you now are look to the North, the South, the East, and the West, for all the land that you see I will give you and your seed forever.
5 And I will make your seed like the dust of the earth. If anybody can count the dust of the earth, then your seed will be
6 counted."36 And again he says: "God led Abraham out and told him: Look up to heaven and count the stars, if you can. That is how numerous your seed will be! And Abraham believed God and this was put down to his credit as an upright
7 deed."37 Because of his faith and hospitality a son was granted to him in his old age, and he obediently offered him as a sacri-
11 fice to God on one of the hills which he indicated. Because of his hospitality and religious devotion, Lot was saved from Sodom, when the whole countryside was condemned to fire and brimstone. In that way the Master made it clear that he does not forsake those who put their hope on him, but delivers to punishment and torment those who turn away from him.
2 Of this latter, to be sure, his wife became an example. After quitting the city with him, she changed her mind and fell out

35 Gen. 12:1–3.   36 Gen. 13:14–16.
37 Gen. 15:5, 6.

with him, with the result that she became a pillar of salt that exists to this day. In this way it was made evident to all that the double-minded and those who question God's power are condemned and become a warning to all generations.

Because of her faith and hospitality Rahab the harlot was 12 saved. For when the spies were sent to Jericho by Joshua the 2 son of Nun, the king of the land got to know that they had come to spy on his country. Consequently he sent out men to capture them, intending to arrest them and put them to death. The hospitable Rahab, however, took them in and hid them 3 in a room upstairs under stalks of flax. When the king's men 4 learned of it, they said to her: "The men who are spying on our country went into your house. Bring them out, for this is the king's command." But she at once answered, "The men you seek came into my house, but they immediately departed and are on their way," and she pointed in the opposite direction. And she said to the men: "I am absolutely certain that 5 the Lord God is handing this country over to you; for fear and terror of you have fallen on all its people. When, therefore, you come to take it, rescue me and my father's house." And they 6 said to her: "It shall be exactly as you say. When you learn of our approach, you shall gather together all your family under your roof and they shall be saved. But whoever is found outside the house will perish." And in addition they gave her a sign 7 that she should hang a piece of scarlet from her house. By this they made it clear that it was by the blood of the Lord that redemption was going to come to all who believe in God and hope on him. You see, dear friends, that not only faith but proph- 8 ecy as well is exemplified in this woman.

Let us then, brothers, be humble and be rid of all pretensions 13 and arrogance and silliness and anger. Let us act as Scripture bids us, for the Holy Spirit says: "Let not the wise man boast of his wisdom or the strong man of his might or the rich man of his wealth. But let him that boasts boast of the Lord; and so he will seek Him out and act justly and uprightly."[38] Especially let us recall the words of the Lord Jesus, which he uttered to teach considerateness and patience. For this is what 2 he said: "Show mercy, that you may be shown mercy. Forgive, that you may be forgiven. As you behave to others, so they will behave to you. As you give, so will you get. As you judge, so you will be judged. As you show kindness, so will you receive kindness. The measure you give will be the measure you

[38] Cf. Jer. 9:23, 24; I Sam. 2:10; I Cor. 1:31; II Cor. 10:17.

3 get."³⁹ Let us firmly hold on to this commandment and these injunctions so that in our conduct we may obey his holy words
4 and be humble. For Holy Scripture says, "On whom shall I look except on him who is humble and gentle and who trembles at my words?"⁴⁰

14   It is right, then, and holy, brothers, that we should obey God rather than follow those arrogant and disorderly fellows
2 who take the lead in stirring up loathsome rivalry. For we shall incur no ordinary harm, but rather great danger, if we recklessly give ourselves over to the designs of men who launch out into strife and sedition to alienate us from what is right.
3 Let us be kind to one another in line with the compassion and
4 tenderness of him who created us. For it is written: "The kind shall inhabit the land, and the innocent shall be left upon it. But those who transgress shall be destroyed from off it."⁴¹
5 And again he says: "I saw an ungodly man exalted and elevated like the cedars of Lebanon. But I passed by and, look, he had vanished! And I searched for his place and could not find it. Maintain innocence and have an eye for uprightness, for a man of peace will have descendants."⁴²

15   Let us, then, attach ourselves to those who are religiously devoted to peace, and not to those who wish for it hypo-
2 critically. For somewhere it is said, "This people honors me
3 with its lips, but its heart is far removed from me."⁴³ And again, "They blessed with their mouth, but they cursed with their
4 heart."⁴⁴ And again it says: "They loved him with their mouth, but they lied to him with their tongue. Their heart was not straightforward with him, and they were not faithful to his
5 covenant. Therefore let the deceitful lips that speak evil against the righteous be struck dumb."⁴⁵ And again: "May the Lord destroy all deceitful lips and the tongue that boasts unduly and those who say, 'We will boast of our tongues; our lips are our
6 own; who is Lord over us?' Because of the wretchedness of the poor and the groans of the needy I will now arise, says the Lord. I will place him in safety: I will act boldly in his cause."⁴⁶

16   It is to the humble that Christ belongs, not to those who exalt
2 themselves above his flock. The scepter of God's majesty, the

---

³⁹ Cf. Matt. 5:7; 6:14, 15; 7:1, 2, 12; Luke 6:31, 36–38. It is probable that both here and in ch. 46:8 Clement is drawing on an extracanonical collection of Jesus' sayings.
⁴⁰ Isa. 66:2.
⁴² Ps. 37:35–37.
⁴⁴ Ps. 78:36, 37; 62:4.
⁴⁶ Ps. 12:3–5.
⁴¹ Prov. 2:21, 22; Ps. 37:9, 38.
⁴³ Isa. 29:13; Mark 7:6.
⁴⁵ Ps. 31:18.

Lord Jesus Christ, did not come with the pomp of pride or arrogance, though he could have done so. But he came in humility just as the Holy Spirit said of him. For Scripture 3 reads: "Lord, who has believed what we heard? And to whom has the arm of the Lord been revealed? Before him we announced that he was like a child, like a root in thirsty ground. He has no comeliness or glory. We saw him, and he had neither comeliness nor beauty. But his appearance was ignominious, deficient when compared to man's stature. He was a man marred by stripes and toil, and experienced in enduring weakness. Because his face was turned away, he was dishonored and disregarded. He it is who bears our sins and suffers pain 4 for us. And we regarded him as subject to toil and stripes and affliction. But it was for our sins that he was wounded and for 5 our transgressions that he suffered. To bring us peace he was punished: by his stripes we were healed. Like sheep we have 6 all gone astray: each one went astray in his own way. And 7 the Lord delivered him up for our sins; and he does not open his mouth because he is abused. Like a sheep he is led off to be slaughtered; and just as a lamb before its shearers is dumb, so he does not open his mouth. In his humiliation his condemnation ended. Who shall tell about his posterity? For his life was 8 taken away from the earth. Because of the transgressions of 9 my people he came to his death. And I will give the wicked as 10 an offering for his burial and the rich for his death. For he did no iniquity and no deceit was found in his mouth. And the Lord's will is to cleanse him of his stripes. If you make an offer- 11 ing for sin, your soul will see a long-lived posterity. And the 12 Lord's will is to do away with the toil of his soul, to show him light and to form him with understanding, to justify an upright man who serves many well. And he himself will bear their sins. For this reason he shall have many heirs and he shall share 13 the spoils of the strong, because his life was delivered up to death and he was reckoned among transgressors. And he it was who 14 bore the sins of many and was delivered up because of their sins."[47]

And again he himself says: "I am a worm and not a man, a 15 disgrace to mankind and despised by the people. All those who 16 saw me mocked me, they made mouths at me and shook their heads, saying: 'He hoped on the Lord. Let him rescue him, let him save him, since he is pleased with him!' "[48]

You see, dear friends, the kind of example we have been 17

[47] Isa. 53:1–12.　　　　[48] Ps. 22:6–8.

given. And so, if the Lord humbled himself in this way, what should we do who through him have come under the yoke of
17 his grace? Let us be imitators even of those who wandered around "in the skins of goats and sheep,"[49] and preached the coming of the Christ. We refer to the prophets Elijah and Elisha—yes, and Ezekiel, too—and to the heroes of old as
2 well. Abraham was widely renowned and called the Friend of God. When he gazed on God's glory, he declared in his humil-
3 ity, "I am only dust and ashes."[50] This is what is written about Job: "Job was an upright and innocent man, sincere, devout,
4 and one who avoided all evil."[51] But he was his own accuser when he said, "There is none who is free from stain, not even
5 if his life lasts but a single day."[52] Moses was called "faithful in all God's house"[53] and God used him to bring His judgment on Egypt with scourges and torments. Yet even he, despite the great glory he was given, did not boast; but when he was granted an oracle from the bush, said: "Who am I that you
6 send me? I have a feeble voice and a slow tongue."[54] And again he says, "I am but steam from a pot."[55]
18   And what shall we say of the famous David? God said of him, "I have discovered a man after my own heart, David the son of Jesse: I have anointed him with eternal mercy."[56]
2 But he too says to God: "Have mercy upon me, O God, according to your great mercy; and according to the wealth
3 of your compassion wipe out my transgression. Wash me thoroughly from my iniquity and cleanse me from my sin, for I acknowledge my transgression and my sin is ever before me.
4 Against you only have I sinned; and I have done evil in your sight. The result is that you are right when you speak and are
5 acquitted when you are judged. For, see, I was conceived in
6 iniquity, and in sin did my mother bear me. For, see, you have loved the truth: you have revealed to me the mysteries and
7 secrets of your wisdom. You shall sprinkle me with hyssop and I shall be cleansed. You shall wash me and I shall be whiter
8 than snow. You will make me hear joy and gladness: the bones
9 which have been humbled shall rejoice. Turn your face from
10 my sins and wipe away all my iniquities. Create in me a pure
11 heart, O God, and renew a right spirit in my very core. Cast me not away from your presence, and do not take your Holy
12 Spirit away from me. Give me back the gladness of your salva-

49 Heb. 11:37.   50 Gen. 18:27.   51 Job 1:1.
52 Job 14:4, 5.   53 Num. 12:7; Heb. 3:2.   54 Ex. 3:11; 4:10.
55 The source is unknown.   56 Ps. 89:20; Acts 13:22.

tion, and strengthen me with your guiding spirit. I will teach 13
your ways to the wicked, and the godless shall turn back to you.
Save me from bloodguiltiness, O God, the God of my salvation. 14
My tongue will rejoice in your righteousness. You will open 15
my mouth, O Lord, and my lips will proclaim your praise.
For if you had wanted sacrifice, I would have given it. You will 16
not find pleasure in burnt offerings. The sacrifice for God is a 17
broken spirit: a broken and a humbled heart, O God, you will
not despise."[57]

The humility and obedient submissiveness of so many and 19
so famous heroes have improved not only us but our fathers
before us, and all who have received His oracles in fear and
sincerity. Since, then, we have benefited by many great and 2
glorious deeds, let us run on to the goal of peace, which was
handed down to us from the beginning. Let us fix our eyes on
the Father and Creator of the universe and cling to his magnificent and excellent gifts of peace and kindness to us. Let us see 3
him in our minds and look with the eyes of our souls on his
patient purpose. Let us consider how free he is from anger toward his whole creation.

The heavens move at his direction and peacefully obey 20
him. Day and night observe the course he has appointed them, 2
without getting in each other's way. The sun and the moon 3
and the choirs of stars roll on harmoniously in their appointed
courses at his command, and with never a deviation. By 4
his will and without dissension or altering anything he has
decreed the earth becomes fruitful at the proper seasons and
brings forth abundant food for men and beasts and every living
thing upon it. The unsearchable, abysmal depths and the in- 5
describable regions[58] of the underworld are subject to the same
decrees. The basin of the boundless sea is by his arrangement 6
constructed to hold the heaped up waters, so that the sea does
not flow beyond the barriers surrounding it, but does just as
he bids it. For he said, "Thus far you shall come, and your 7
waves shall break within you."[59] The ocean which men cannot 8
pass, and the worlds beyond it, are governed by the same
decrees of the Master. The seasons, spring, summer, autumn, 9
and winter, peacefully give way to each other. The winds 10
from their different points perform their service at the proper
time and without hindrance. Perennial springs, created for
enjoyment and health, never fail to offer their life-giving
breasts to men. The tiniest creatures come together in harmony

[57] Ps. 51:1–17.   [58] Emending *krimata* to *klimata*.   [59] Job 38:11.

11 and peace. All these things the great Creator and Master of the universe ordained to exist in peace and harmony. Thus, he showered his benefits on them all, but most abundantly on us who have taken refuge in his compassion through our Lord

12 Jesus Christ, to whom be glory and majesty forever and ever. Amen.[60]

21 Take care, dear friends, that his many blessings do not turn out to be our condemnation, which will be the case if we fail to live worthily of him, to act in concert, and to do what is

2 good and pleasing to him. For he says somewhere, "The Spirit of the Lord is a lamp which searches the hidden depths of the

3 heart."[61] Let us realize how near he is, and that none of our

4 thoughts or of the ideas we have escapes his notice. It is right, therefore, that we should not be deserters, disobeying his will.

5 Rather than offend God, let us offend foolish and stupid men who exalt themselves and boast with their pretensions to fine

6 speech. Let us reverence the Lord Jesus Christ whose blood was given for us. Let us respect those who rule over us. Let us honor our elders. Let us rear the young in the fear of God. Let

7 us direct our women to what is good. Let them show a purity of character we can admire. Let them reveal a genuine sense of modesty. By their reticence let them show that their tongues are considerate. Let them not play favorites in showing affection, but in holiness let them love all equally, who fear God.

8 Let our children have a Christian training. Let them learn the value God sets on humility, what power pure love has with him, how good and excellent it is to fear him, and how this means salvation to everybody who lives in his fear with holiness

9 and a pure conscience. For he is the searcher of thoughts and of desires. It is his breath which is in us; and when he wants to, he will take it away.

22 Now Christian faith confirms all this. For this is how Christ addresses us through his Holy Spirit: "Come, my children,

2 listen to me. I will teach you the fear of the Lord. What man is

3 there that desires life, and loves to see good days? Keep your

4 tongue from evil and your lips from uttering deceit. Refrain

5, 6 from evil and do good. Seek peace and follow after it. The eyes of the Lord are over the upright and his ears are open to their

---

[60] This chapter bears some relation to the Christian thanksgiving for creation, which opened the consecration prayer of the primitive Eucharist. There is an affinity of ideas, and even some verbal parallels, with later liturgies. But the spirit of the chapter is Clement's.

[61] Prov. 20:27.

petitions. But the face of the Lord is turned against those who
do evil, to eradicate their memory from the earth. The upright 7
man cried out and the Lord heeded him and delivered him
out of all his troubles. Manifold are the plagues of the sinner, 8
but his mercy will enfold those who hope on the Lord."[62]

The all-merciful and beneficent Father has compassion on 23
those who fear him, and with kindness and love he grants his
favors to those who approach him with a sincere heart. For 2
this reason we must not be double-minded, and our souls must
not harbor wrong notions about his excellent and glorious gifts.
Let that verse of Scripture be remote from us, which says: 3
"Wretched are the double-minded, those who doubt in their
soul and say, 'We have heard these things even in our fathers'
times, and, see, we have grown old and none of them has
happened to us.' You fools! Compare yourselves to a tree. 4
Take a vine: first it sheds its leaves, then comes a bud, then a
leaf, then a flower, and after this a sour grape, and finally a
ripe bunch."[63] You note that the fruit of the tree reaches its
maturity in a short time. So, to be sure, swiftly and suddenly 5
his purpose will be accomplished, just as Scripture, too, testifies:
"Quickly he will come and not delay, and the Lord will come
suddenly into his temple, even the Holy One whom you
expect."[64]

Let us consider, dear friends, how the Master continually 24
points out to us that there will be a future resurrection. Of this
he made the Lord Jesus Christ the first fruits by raising him
from the dead. Let us take note, dear friends, of the resurrection 2
at the natural seasons. Day and night demonstrate resurrection. 3
Night passes and day comes. Day departs and night returns.
Take the crops as examples. How and in what way is the seeding 4
done? The sower goes out and casts each of his seeds in the 5
ground.[65] When they fall on the ground they are dry and bare,
and they decay. But then the marvelous providence of the
Master resurrects them from their decay, and from a single seed
many grow and bear fruit.

Let us note the remarkable token which comes from the 25
East, from the neighborhood, that is, of Arabia. There is a bird 2
which is called a phoenix. It is the only one of its kind and lives

---

[62] Ps. 34:11–17; 32:10.
[63] The source of this citation is unknown. It may possibly come from the
lost apocalypse of Eldad and Modat. Cf. Hermas, Vis. II. 3:4.
[64] Mal. 3:1.
[65] Cf. Matt. 13:3, etc.

five hundred years. When the time for its departure and death draws near, it makes a burial nest for itself from frankincense, myrrh, and other spices; and when the time is up, it gets into
3 it and dies. From its decaying flesh a worm is produced, which is nourished by the secretions of the dead creature and grows wings. When it is full-fledged, it takes up the burial nest containing the bones of its predecessor, and manages to carry them all the way from Arabia to the Egyptian city called Heliopolis.
4 And in broad daylight, so that everyone can see, it lights at the altar of the sun and puts them down there, and so starts
5 home again. The priests then look up their dated records and discover it has come after a lapse of five hundred years.[66]
26 Shall we, then, imagine that it is something great and surprising if the Creator of the universe raises up those who have served him in holiness and in the assurance born of a good faith, when he uses a mere bird to illustrate the greatness of his promise?
2 For he says somewhere: "And you shall raise me up and I shall give you thanks"[67]; and, "I lay down and slept: I rose up
3 because you are with me."[68] And again Job says, "And you will make this flesh of mine, which has endured all this, to rise up."[69]
27   With this hope, then, let us attach ourselves to him who is
2 faithful to his promises and just in his judgments. He who bids us to refrain from lying is all the less likely to lie himself.
3 For nothing is impossible to God save lying.[70] Let us, then, rekindle our faith in him, and bear in mind that nothing is
4 beyond his reach. By his majestic word he established the uni-
5 verse, and by his word he can bring it to an end. "Who shall say to him, What have you done? Or who shall resist his mighty strength?"[71] He will do everything when he wants to and as he wants to. And not one of the things he has decreed will fail.
6 Everything is open to his sight and nothing escapes his will.
7 For "the heavens declare God's glory and the sky proclaims the work of his hands. Day pours forth words to day; and night imparts knowledge to night. And there are neither words nor speech, and their voices are not heard."[72]
28   Since, then, he sees and hears everything, we should fear

---

[66] The story of the phoenix was famous in antiquity. It is in Hesiod, Herodotus, Ovid, Pliny the Elder, etc. Tacitus is more critical toward the legend than Clement (*Ann.* 6:28).
[67] Source unknown. Cf. Ps. 28:7.   [68] Ps. 3:5.
[69] Job 19:26.   [70] Cf. Heb. 6:18.   [71] Wis. 12:12.
[72] Ps. 19:1–3.

him and rid ourselves of wicked desires that issue in base deeds. By so doing we shall be sheltered by his mercy from the judgments to come. For where can any of us flee to escape his mighty 2 hand? What world is there to receive anyone who deserts him? For Scripture says somewhere: "Where shall I go and where 3 shall I hide from your presence? If I go up to heaven, you are there. If I go off to the ends of the earth, there is your right hand. If I make my bed in the depths, there is your spirit." [73] Where, then, can anyone go or where can he flee to escape 4 from him who embraces everything?

We must, then, approach him with our souls holy, lifting 29 up pure and undefiled hands to him, loving our kind and compassionate Father, who has made us his chosen portion. For thus it is written: "When the Most High divided the 2 nations, when he dispersed the sons of Adam, he fixed the boundaries of the nations to suit the number of God's angels. [74] The Lord's portion became his people, Jacob: Israel was the lot that fell to him." [75] And in another place it says: "Behold, 3 the Lord takes for himself a people from among the nations, just as a man takes the first fruits of his threshing floor; and the Holy of Holies shall come forth from that nation." [76]

Since, then, we are a holy portion, we should do everything 30 that makes for holiness. We should flee from slandering, vile and impure embraces, drunkenness, rioting, filthy lusts, detestable adultery, and disgusting arrogance. "For God," says 2 Scripture, "resists the arrogant, but gives grace to the humble." [77] We should attach ourselves to those to whom 3 God's grace has been given. We should clothe ourselves with concord, being humble, self-controlled, far removed from all gossiping and slandering, and justified by our deeds, not by words. For it says: "He who talks a lot will hear much in reply. 4 Or does the prattler imagine he is right? Blessed is the one his 5 mother bore to be short-lived. Do not indulge in talking overmuch." [78] We should leave God to praise us and not praise 6 ourselves. For God detests self-praisers. Let others applaud our 7 good deeds, as it was with our righteous forefathers. Presump- 8 tion, audacity, and recklessness are traits of those accursed by

[73] Ps. 139:7, 8.
[74] The idea is that each nation has its guardian angel.
[75] Deut. 32:8, 9.
[76] A conflation of a number of O.T. phrases: Deut. 4:34; 14:2; Num. 18:27; II Chron. 31:14; Ezek. 48:12.
[77] Prov. 3:34; James 4:6; I Peter 5:5.
[78] Job 11:2, 3. The text is corrupt in the LXX, which Clement cites.

God. But considerateness, humility, and modesty are the traits of those whom God has blessed.

31 Let us, then, cling to his blessing and note what leads to it. 2 Let us unfold the tale of the ancient past. Why was our father Abraham blessed? Was it not because he acted in righteous- 3 ness and truth, prompted by faith? Isaac, fully realizing what 4 was going to happen, gladly let himself be led to sacrifice. In humility Jacob quit his homeland because of his brother. He went to Laban and became his slave, and to him there were **32** given the twelve scepters of the tribes of Israel. And if anyone will candidly look into each example, he will realize the magnificence of the gifts God gives.

2 For from Jacob there came all the priests and the Levites who serve at God's altar. From him comes the Lord Jesus so far as his human nature goes. From him there come the kings and rulers and governors of Judah. Nor is the glory of the other tribes derived from him insignificant. For God promised that 3 "your seed shall be as the stars of heaven." [79] So all of them received honor and greatness, not through themselves or their own deeds or the right things they did, but through his will. 4 And we, therefore, who by his will have been called in Jesus Christ, are not justified of ourselves or by our wisdom or insight or religious devotion or the holy deeds we have done from the heart, but by that faith by which almighty God has justified all men from the very beginning. To him be glory forever and ever. Amen.

33 What, then, brothers, ought we to do? [80] Should we grow slack in doing good and give up love? May the Lord never permit this to happen at any rate to us! Rather should we be energetic in doing "every good deed" [81] with earnestness and 2 eagerness. For the Creator and Master of the universe himself 3 rejoices in his works. Thus by his almighty power he established the heavens and by his inscrutable wisdom he arranged them. He separated the land from the water surrounding it and fixed it upon the sure foundation of his own will. By his decree he brought into existence the living creatures which roam on it; and after creating the sea and the creatures which inhabit it, 4 he fixed its boundaries by his power. Above all, with his holy and pure hands he formed man, his outstanding and greatest 5 achievement, stamped with his own image. For this is what God said: "Let us make man in our own image and likeness.

[79] Gen. 15:5; 22:17; 26:4.   [80] Cf. Rom. 6:1.
[81] Titus 3:1.

And God made man: male and female he created."[82] And 6
so, when he had finished all this, he praised it and blessed it
and said, "Increase and multiply."[83] We should observe that 7
all the righteous have been adorned with good deeds and the
very Lord adorns himself with good deeds and rejoices. Since, 8
then, we have this example, we should unhesitatingly give ourselves to his will, and put all our effort into acting uprightly.

The good laborer accepts the bread he has earned with his 34
head held high; the lazy and negligent workman cannot look
his employer in the face. We must, then, be eager to do good; 2
for everything comes from Him. For he warns us: "See, the 3
Lord is coming. He is bringing his reward with him, to pay each
one according to his work."[84] He bids us, therefore, to believe 4
on him with all our heart, and not to be slack or negligent in
"every good deed."[85] He should be the basis of our boasting 5
and assurance. We should be subject to his will. We should
note how the whole throng of his angels stand ready to serve
his will. For Scripture says: "Ten thousand times ten thousand 6
stood by him, and thousands of thousands ministered to him
and cried out: Holy, holy, holy is the Lord of Hosts: all creation
is full of his glory."[86] We too, then, should gather together 7
for worship in concord and mutual trust, and earnestly beseech
him as it were with one mouth, that we may share in his great
and glorious promises. For he says, "Eye has not seen and ear 8
has not heard and man's heart has not conceived what he has
prepared for those who patiently wait for him."[87]

How blessed and amazing are God's gifts, dear friends! 35
Life with immortality, splendor with righteousness, truth with 2
confidence, faith with assurance, self-control with holiness!
And all these things are within our comprehension. What, 3
then, is being prepared for those who wait for him? The Creator
and Father of eternity, the all-holy, himself knows how great
and wonderful it is. We, then, should make every effort to be 4
found in the number of those who are patiently looking for
him, so that we may share in the gifts he has promised. And 5
how shall this be, dear friends? If our mind is faithfully fixed
on God; if we seek out what pleases and delights him; if we
do what is in accord with his pure will, and follow in the way

---

[82] Gen. 1:26, 27.   [83] Gen. 1:28.
[84] A conflation from: Isa. 40:10; 62:11; Prov. 24:12; Rev. 22:12.
[85] Titus 3:1.   [86] Dan. 7:10; Isa. 6:3.
[87] I Cor. 2:9; Isa. 64:4. This does not imply that Clement viewed I Corin-
    thians as canonical. He merely cites an O.T. text via a rendering in Paul.

of truth. If we rid ourselves of all wickedness, evil, avarice, contentiousness, malice, fraud, gossip, slander, hatred of God,
6 arrogance, pretension, conceit, and inhospitality.[88] God hates those who act in this way; "and not only those who do these
7 things but those who applaud them."[89] For Scripture says: "But God told the sinner: Why do you speak of my statutes
8 and have my covenant on your lips? You hated discipline and turned your back on my words. If you saw a thief you went along with him, and you threw in your lot with adulterers. Your mouth overflowed with iniquity, and your tongue wove deceit. You sat there slandering your brother and putting a
9 stumbling block in the way of your mother's son. This you did, and I kept silent. You suspected, you wicked man, that I
10 would be like you. I will reproach you and show you your very
11 self. Ponder, then, these things, you who forget God, lest he seize
12 you like a lion and there be no one to save you. A sacrifice of praise will glorify me, and that is the way by which I will show him God's salvation."[90]
36   This is the way, dear friends, in which we found our salvation, Jesus Christ, the high priest of our offerings, the protector and
2 helper of our weakness. Through him we fix our gaze on the heights of heaven. In him we see mirrored God's pure and transcendent face. Through him the eyes of our hearts have been opened. Through him our foolish and darkened understanding springs up to the light. Through him the Master has willed that we should taste immortal knowledge. For, "since he reflects God's splendor, he is as superior to the angels as his
3 title is more distinguished than theirs."[91] For thus it is written: "He who makes his angels winds, and his ministers flames of
4 fire."[92] But of his son this is what the Master said: "You are my son: today I have begotten you. Ask me and I will give you the nations for you to inherit, and the ends of the earth for you to
5 keep."[93] And again he says to him: "Sit at my right hand until
6 I make your enemies your footstool."[94] Who are meant by "enemies"? Those who are wicked and resist his will.
37   Really in earnest, then, brothers, we must march under his
2 irreproachable orders. Let us note with what discipline, readiness, and obedience those who serve under our generals carry
3 out orders. Not everybody is a general, colonel, captain, sergeant, and so on. But "each in his own rank"[95] carries out the

---

[88] Cf. Rom. 1:29–32.   [89] *Ibid.*   [90] Ps. 50:16–23.
[91] Heb. 1:3, 4.   [92] Heb. 1:7; Ps. 104:4.   [93] Heb. 1:5; Ps. 2:7, 8.
[94] Heb. 1:13; Ps. 110:1.   [95] I Cor. 15:23.

orders of the emperor and of the generals. The great cannot 4
exist without the small; neither can the small exist without the
great. All are linked together; and this has an advantage. Take 5
our body, for instance. The head cannot get along without
the feet. Nor, similarly, can the feet get along without the head.
"The tiniest parts of our body are essential to it," [96] and are
valuable to the total body. Yes, they all act in concord, and
are united in a single obedience to preserve the whole body.

Following this out, we must preserve our Christian body too 38
in its entirety. Each must be subject to his neighbor, according
to his special gifts. The strong must take care of the weak; the 2
weak must look up to the strong. The rich must provide for the
poor; the poor must thank God for giving him someone to
meet his needs. The wise man must show his wisdom not in
words but in good deeds. The humble must not brag about his
humility; but should give others occasion to mention it. He
who is continent must not put on airs. He must recognize that
his self-control is a gift from another. We must take to heart, 3
brothers, from what stuff we were created, what kind of
creatures we were when we entered the world, from what a
dark grave he who fashioned and created us brought us into
his world. And we must realize the preparations he so generously made before we were born. Since, then, we owe all this to 4
him, we ought to give him unbounded thanks. To him be glory
forever and ever. Amen.

Thoughtless, silly, senseless, and ignorant folk mock and jeer 39
at us, in an effort, so they imagine, to exalt themselves. But 2
what can a mere mortal do? What power has a creature of
earth? For it is written: "There was no shape before my eyes, 3
but I heard a breath and a voice. What! Can a mortal be pure 4
before the Lord? Or can a man be blameless for his actions, if
he does not believe in His servants and finds something wrong
with His angels? Not even heaven is pure in His sight: let 5
alone those who live in houses of clay—of the very same clay
of which we ourselves are made. He smites them like a moth;
and they do not last from dawn to dusk. They perish, for they
cannot help themselves. He breathes on them, and they die 6
for lack of wisdom. Call out and see if anyone will heed you, 7
or if you will see any of the holy angels. For wrath destroys a
stupid man, and rivalry is the death of one in error. I have seen 8
the foolish taking root, but suddenly their home is swept away.
May their sons be far from safety! May they be mocked at the 9

96 I Cor. 12:21, 22.

doors of lesser men, and there will be none to deliver them. For what has been prepared by them, the righteous will eat; and they shall not be delivered from troubles."⁹⁷

40 Now that this is clear to us and we have peered into the depths of the divine knowledge, we are bound to do in an orderly fashion all that the Master has bidden us to do at the 2 proper times he set. He ordered sacrifices and services to be performed; and required this to be done, not in a careless and 3 disorderly way, but at the times and seasons he fixed. Where he wants them performed, and by whom, he himself fixed by his supreme will, so that everything should be done in a holy way and with his approval, and should be acceptable to his 4 will. Those, therefore, who make their offerings at the time set, win his approval and blessing. For they follow the Master's 5 orders and do no wrong. The high priest is given his particular duties: the priests are assigned their special place, while on the Levites particular tasks are imposed. The layman is bound by the layman's code.

41 "Each of us," brothers, "in his own rank"⁹⁸ must win God's approval and have a clear conscience. We must not transgress the rules laid down for our ministry, but must perform it 2 reverently. Not everywhere, brothers, are the different sacrifices—the daily ones, the freewill offerings, and those for sins and trespasses—offered, but only in Jerusalem. And even there sacrifices are not made at any point, but only in front of the sanctuary, at the altar, after the high priest and the ministers 3 mentioned have inspected the offering for blemishes. Those, therefore, who act in any way at variance with his will, suffer 4 the penalty of death. You see, brothers, the more knowledge we are given, the greater risks we run.

42 The apostles received the gospel for us from the Lord Jesus 2 Christ; Jesus, the Christ, was sent from God. Thus Christ is from God and the apostles from Christ. In both instances the 3 orderly procedure depends on God's will. And so the apostles, after receiving their orders and being fully convinced by the resurrection of our Lord Jesus Christ and assured by God's word, went out in the confidence of the Holy Spirit to preach 4 the good news that God's Kingdom was about to come. They preached in country and city, and appointed their first converts, after testing them by the Spirit, to be the bishops and deacons 5 of future believers. Nor was this any novelty, for Scripture had mentioned bishops and deacons long before. For this is what

⁹⁷ Job 4:16–18; 15:15; chs. 4:19 to 5:5.   ⁹⁸ I Cor. 15:23.

Scripture says somewhere: "I will appoint their bishops in righteousness and their deacons in faith."[99]

And is it any wonder that those Christians whom God had **43** entrusted with such a duty should have appointed the officers mentioned? For the blessed Moses too, "who was a faithful servant in all God's house,"[1] recorded in the sacred books all the orders given to him, and the rest of the prophets followed in his train by testifying with him to his legislation. Now, when **2** rivalry for the priesthood arose and the tribes started quarreling as to which of them should be honored with this glorious privilege, Moses bid the twelve tribal chiefs bring him rods, on each of which was written the name of one of the tribes. These he took and bound, sealing them with the rings of the tribal leaders; and he put them in the tent of testimony on God's table. Then he shut the tent and put seals on the keys just **3** as he had on the rods. And he told them: "Brothers, the tribe **4** whose rod puts forth buds is the one God has chosen for the priesthood and for his ministry." Early the next morning he **5** called all Israel together, six hundred thousand strong, and showed the seals to the tribal chiefs and opened the tent of testimony and brought out the rods. And it was discovered that Aaron's rod had not only budded, but was actually bearing fruit. What do you think, dear friends? Did not Moses know in **6** advance that this was going to happen? Why certainly. But he acted the way he did in order to forestall anarchy in Israel, and so that the name of the true and only God might be glorified. To Him be the glory forever and ever. Amen.

Now our apostles, thanks to our Lord Jesus Christ, knew **44** that there was going to be strife over the title of bishop. It was **2** for this reason and because they had been given an accurate knowledge of the future, that they appointed the officers we have mentioned. Furthermore, they later added a codicil to the effect that, should these die, other approved men should succeed to their ministry.[2] In the light of this, we view it as a **3**

99 Isa. 60:17.   1 Num. 12:7; Heb. 3:5.

2 In this sentence and the one following there are a number of ambiguities in the Greek, which have given rise to three possible interpretations. (a) The apostles provided that, if they themselves should die, other approved men should succeed to the apostolic prerogatives. These men would take over the right to appoint the local presbyteries, and are the ones referred to by the phrase, "Others of the proper standing." (b) The apostles provided that should their first converts (i.e., the first local presbyters) die, others should succeed them. This succession would be in the hands of the apostles and, later on, of "others of the proper standing,"

breach of justice to remove from their ministry those who were appointed either by them [i.e., the apostles] or later on and with the whole church's consent, by others of the proper standing, and who, long enjoying everybody's approval, have ministered to Christ's flock faultlessly, humbly, quietly, and

4 unassumingly. For we shall be guilty of no slight sin if we eject from the episcopate men who have offered the sacrifices with

5 innocence and holiness. Happy, indeed, are those presbyters who have already passed on, and who ended a life of fruitfulness with their task complete. For they need not fear that anyone

6 will remove them from their secure positions. But you, we observe, have removed a number of people, despite their good conduct, from a ministry they have fulfilled with honor and

45 integrity. Your contention and rivalry, brothers, thus touches matters that bear on our salvation.

2 You have studied Holy Scripture, which contains the truth

3 and is inspired by the Holy Spirit. You realize that there is nothing wrong or misleading written in it. You will not find that upright people have ever been disowned by holy men.

4 The righteous, to be sure, have been persecuted, but by wicked men. They have been imprisoned, but by the godless. They have been stoned by transgressors, slain by men prompted

5 by abominable and wicked rivalry. Yet in such sufferings they

6 bore up nobly. What shall we say, brothers? Was Daniel cast

7 into a den of lions by those who revered God? Or was Ananias, Azarias, or Mishael shut up in the fiery furnace by men devoted to the magnificent and glorious worship of the Most High? Not for a moment! Who, then, was it that did such things? Detestable men, thoroughly and completely wicked, whose factiousness drove them to such a pitch of fury that they tormented those who resolutely served God in holiness and innocence. They failed to realize that the Most High is the champion and defender of those who worship his excellent

i.e., men like Timothy and Titus with apostolic rank. (c) The apostles provided that should their first converts (i.e., the first local presbyters) die, others should succeed them. This succession, begun by the apostles, would be continued by self-perpetuating presbyteries. In this view, the phrase, "Others of the proper standing," would refer to the same class of persons as does the phrase, "The officers we have mentioned," in the preceding sentence, i.e., to presbyters. The reader will observe that, while the titles "presbyter" and "bishop" appear to be synonymous in Clement, the first two interpretations favor the "episcopal" view of the early ministry, while the third favors the "presbyterian."

name with a pure conscience. To him be the glory forever and
ever. Amen. But those who held out with confidence inherited 8
glory and honor. They were exalted, and God inscribed them
on his memory forever and ever. Amen.

Brothers, *we* must follow such examples. For it is written: 46, 2
"Follow the saints, because those who follow them will become
saints."³ Again, it says in another place: "In the company 3
of the innocent, you will be innocent; in the company of the
elect, you will be elect; and in a crooked man's company you
will go wrong."⁴ Let us, then, follow the innocent and the 4
upright. They, it is, who are God's elect. Why is it that you 5
harbor strife, bad temper, dissension, schism, and quarreling?
Do we not have one God, one Christ, one Spirit of grace which 6
was poured out on us? And is there not one calling in Christ?
Why do we rend and tear asunder Christ's members and raise 7
a revolt against our own body? Why do we reach such a pitch
of insanity that we are oblivious of the fact we are members
of each other? Recall the words of our Lord Jesus. For he said: 8
"Woe to that man! It were better for him not to have been born
than to be the occasion of one of my chosen ones stumbling. It
were better for him to have a millstone around his neck and to
be drowned in the sea, than to pervert one of my chosen."⁵ Your 9
schism has led many astray; it has made many despair; it has
made many doubt; and it has distressed us all. Yet it goes on!

Pick up the letter of the blessed apostle Paul. What was the 47, 2
primary thing he wrote to you, "when he started preaching
the gospel?"⁶ To be sure, under the Spirit's guidance, he wrote 3
to you about himself and Cephas and Apollos, because even
then you had formed cliques. Factiousness, however, at that 4
time was a less serious sin, since you were partisans of notable
apostles and of a man they endorsed. But think now who they 5
are who have led you astray and degraded your honorable
and celebrated love of the brethren. It is disgraceful, exceed- 6
ingly disgraceful, and unworthy of your Christian upbringing,
to have it reported that because of one or two individuals the
solid and ancient Corinthian Church is in revolt against its
presbyters. This report, moreover, has reached not only us, 7
but those who dissent from us as well.⁷ The result is that the
Lord's name is being blasphemed because of your stupidity,
and you are exposing yourselves to danger.

³ Source unknown.   ⁴ Ps. 18:26, 27.
⁵ Matt. 26:24; Luke 17:1, 2, and parallels.
⁶ Phil. 4:15.   ⁷ I.e., Jews and pagans.

48 We must, then, put a speedy end to this. We must prostrate ourselves before the Master, and beseech him with tears to have mercy on us and be reconciled to us and bring us back to

2 our honorable and holy practice of brotherly love. For it is this which is the gate of righteousness, which opens the way to life, as it is written: "Open the gates of righteousness for me,

3 so that I may enter by them and praise the Lord. This is the

4 Lord's gate: the righteous shall enter by it." [8] While there are many gates open, the gate of righteousness is the Christian gate. Blessed are all those who enter by it and direct their way "in holiness and righteousness," [9] by doing everything without disorder.

5 Let a man be faithful, let him be capable of uttering "knowledge," [10] let him be wise in judging arguments, let him be

6 pure in conduct. But the greater he appears to be, the more humble he ought to be, and the more ready to seek the common

49 good in preference to his own. Whoever has Christian love must

2 keep Christ's commandments. Who can describe the bond of

3 God's love? Who is capable of expressing its great beauty?

4, 5 The heights to which love leads are beyond description. Love unites us to God. "Love hides a multitude of sins." [11] Love puts up with everything and is always patient. There is nothing vulgar about love, nothing arrogant. Love knows nothing of schism or revolt. Love does everything in harmony. By love all God's elect were made perfect. Without love nothing can

6 please God. By love the Master accepted us. Because of the love he had for us, and in accordance with God's will, Jesus Christ our Lord gave his blood for us, his flesh for our flesh, and his life for ours.

50 You see, brothers, how great and amazing love is, and how

2 its perfection is beyond description. Who is able to possess it save those to whom God has given the privilege? Let us, then, beg and implore him mercifully to grant us love without human

3 bias and to make us irreproachable. All the generations from Adam to our day have passed away, but those who, by the grace of God, have been made perfect in love have a place among the saints, who will appear when Christ's Kingdom

4 comes. For it is written: "Go into your closets for a very little while, until my wrath and anger pass, and I will remember a

5 good day and I will raise you up from your graves." [12] Happy

---

[8] Ps. 118:19, 20.   [9] Luke 1:75.
[10] *Gnosis* in its technical sense of mystical knowledge.
[11] Prov. 10:12; I Peter 4:8.   [12] Isa. 26:20; Ezek. 37:12.

are we, dear friends, if we keep God's commandments in the harmony of love, so that by love our sins may be forgiven us. For it is written: "Happy are those whose iniquities are for- 6 given and whose sins are covered. Happy is the man whose sin the Lord will not reckon, and on whose lips there is no deceit."[13] This is the blessing which was given to those whom 7 God chose through Jesus Christ our Lord. To him be the glory forever and ever. Amen.

Let us, then, ask pardon for our failings and for whatever 51 we have done through the prompting of the adversary. And those who are the ringleaders of the revolt and dissension ought to reflect upon the common nature of our hope. Those, cer- 2 tainly, who live in fear and love would rather suffer outrages themselves than have their neighbors do so. They prefer to endure condemnation themselves rather than bring in reproach our tradition of noble and righteous harmony. It is better for 3 a man to confess his sins than to harden his heart in the way those rebels against God's servant Moses hardened theirs. The verdict against them was made very plain. For "they went 4 down to Hades alive,"[14] and "death will be their shepherd."[15] Pharaoh and his host and all the princes of Egypt and "the 5 chariots and their riders"[16] were engulfed in the Red Sea and perished, for no other reason than that they hardened their foolish hearts after Moses, God's servant, had done signs and wonders in Egypt.

The Master, brothers, has no need of anything. He wants 52 nothing of anybody save that he should praise him. For his 2 favorite, David, says: "I will praise the Lord; and this will please him more than a young calf with horns and hoofs. Let the poor observe this and rejoice."[17] And again he says: "Offer to God 3 the sacrifice of praise, and pay your vows to the Most High. Call on me in the day of your affliction and I will rescue you, and you will glorify me. For the sacrifice God wants is a broken 4 spirit."[18]

You know the Holy Scriptures, dear friends—you know 53 them well— and you have studied God's oracles. It is to remind you of them that we write the way we do. When Moses ascended 2 the mountain and spent forty days and forty nights in fasting and humiliation, God said to him: "Get quickly down from here, for your people, whom you led out of the land of Egypt, have broken the law. They have quickly turned from the way

13 Ps. 32:1, 2; Rom. 4:7–9. 14 Num. 16:33. 15 Ps. 49:14.
16 Ex. 14:23. 17 Ps. 69:30–32. 18 Ps. 50:14, 15; 51:17.

you bid them take. They have cast idols for themselves."[19]
3 And the Lord told him: "I have spoken to you once, yes, twice, saying, I have looked at this people and, see, it is obstinate. Let me exterminate them, and I will wipe out their name from under heaven, and I will make you into a great and wonderful
4 nation, much larger than this one."[20] And Moses answered: "No, no, Lord. Pardon my people's sin, or else eliminate me too from the roll of the living."[21]
5   O great love! O unsurpassed perfection! The servant speaks openly to his Lord. He begs pardon for his people or requests
54 that he too will be wiped out along with them. Well, then, who of your number is noble, large-hearted, and full of love?
2 Let him say: "If it is my fault that revolt, strife, and schism have arisen, I will leave, I will go away wherever you wish, and do what the congregation orders. Only let Christ's flock live in
3 peace with their appointed presbyters." The man who does this will win for himself great glory in Christ, and will be welcome everywhere. "For the earth and its fullness belong to
4 the Lord."[22] This has been the conduct and will always be the conduct of those who have no regrets that they belong to the city of God. .
55   Let us take some heathen examples:[23] In times of plague many kings and rulers, prompted by oracles, have given themselves up to death in order to rescue their subjects by their own blood.[24] Many have quit their own cities to put an end to
2 sedition.[25] We know many of our own number who have had themselves imprisoned in order to ransom others. Many have sold themselves into slavery and given the price to feed others.
3 Many women, empowered by God's grace, have performed
4 deeds worthy of men. The blessed Judith, when her city was under siege, begged of the elders to be permitted to leave it for
5 the enemy's camp. So she exposed herself to danger and for love of her country and of her besieged people, she departed. And the Lord delivered Holofernes into the hands of a woman.
6 To no less danger did Esther, that woman of perfect faith, expose herself in order to rescue the twelve tribes of Israel when they were on the point of being destroyed. For by her fasting and humiliation she implored the all-seeing Master,

---

[19] Deut. 9:12 (Ex. 32:7, 8).   [20] Deut. 9:13, 14 (Ex. 32:9, 10).
[21] Ex. 32:31, 32.   [22] Ps. 24:1.
[23] The influence of pagan culture on Clement is evident here, as in his references to the phoenix (ch. 25) and to the Roman army (ch. 37).
[24] Cf. Cicero, *Tusc.* 1:116.   [25] E.g., Solon, Lycurgus, Scipio Africanus.

the eternal God; and he beheld the humility of her soul and rescued her people for whose sake she had faced danger.

So we too must intercede for any who have fallen into sin, 56 that considerateness and humility may be granted to them and that they may submit, not to us, but to God's will. For in that way they will prove fruitful and perfect when God and the saints remember them with mercy. We must accept correction, 2 dear friends. No one should resent it. Warnings we give each other are good and thoroughly beneficial. For they bind us to God's will. This is what the Holy Word says about it: "The 3 Lord has disciplined me severely and has not given me up to death. For the Lord disciplines the one he loves, and punishes 4 every son he accepts." [26] For, it says, "the upright man will 5 discipline me with mercy and reprove me. But let not the oil of sinners anoint my head." [27] And again it says: "Happy is 6 the man the Lord reproves. Do not refuse the Almighty's warning. For he inflicts pain, and then makes all well again. He smites, but his hands heal. Six times will he rescue you from 7, 8 trouble; and on the seventh evil will not touch you. In famine 9 he will rescue you from death; in war he will deliver you from the edge of the sword. From the scourge of the tongue he 10 will hide you, and you will not be afraid of evils when they come. You will ridicule the wicked and lawless, and not be afraid 11 of wild beasts; for wild beasts will leave you in peace. Then 12, 13 you will discover that your house will be peaceful, and the tent in which you dwell will be safe. You will find, too, that your 14 seed will be numerous, and your children like the grass of the fields. You will come to your tomb like ripe wheat harvested 15 at the appropriate season, or like a heap on the threshing floor gathered together at the right time." [28]

You see, dear friends, how well protected they are whom 16 the Master disciplines. Yes, he is like a good Father, and disciplines us so that the outcome of his holy discipline may mean mercy for us. And that is why you who are responsible 57 for the revolt must submit to the presbyters. You must humble your hearts and be disciplined so that you repent. You must 2 learn obedience, and be done with your proud boasting and curb your arrogant tongues. For it is better for you to have an insignificant yet creditable place in Christ's flock than to appear eminent and be excluded from Christ's hope. For this is what 3 the excellent Wisdom says: "See, I will declare to you the utterance of my Spirit: I will teach you my word. Since I called 4

[26] Ps. 118:18; Prov. 3:12 (Heb. 12:6).   [27] Ps. 141:5.   [28] Job 5:17–26.

and you did not listen, since I poured out words and you did not heed, but disregarded my plans and disobeyed my reproofs, therefore I will laugh at your destruction. And I will rejoice when ruin befalls you and when confusion suddenly overtakes you, and catastrophe descends like a hurricane, or when perse-
5 cution and siege come upon you. Yes, it will be like this: when you call upon me, I will not heed you. The wicked shall look for me and shall not find me. For they detested wisdom, and did not choose the fear of the Lord. They had no desire to heed
6 my counsels, and mocked at my reproofs. For this reason they shall eat the fruit of their ways and fill themselves with impiety.
7 Because they wronged babes, they will be slain; and by being searched out the impious shall be destroyed. But he that listens to me will dwell in confident hope and live quietly, free from the fear of any misfortune."[29]

58   So, then, let us obey his most holy and glorious name and escape the threats which Wisdom has predicted against the disobedient. In that way we shall live in peace, having our
2 confidence in his most holy and majestic name. Accept our advice, and you will never regret it. For as God lives, and as the Lord Jesus Christ lives and the Holy Spirit (on whom the elect believe and hope), the man who with humility and eager considerateness and with no regrets does what God has decreed and ordered will be enlisted and enrolled in the ranks of those who are saved through Jesus Christ. Through him be the glory to God forever and ever. Amen.

59   If, on the other hand, there be some who fail to obey what God has told them through us, they must realize that they will
2 enmesh themselves in sin and in no insignificant danger. We, for our part, will not be responsible for such a sin. But we will beg with earnest prayer and supplication that the Creator of the universe will keep intact the precise number of his elect in the whole world, through his beloved Child[30] Jesus Christ. It was through him that he called us "from darkness to light,"[31]
3 from ignorance to the recognition of his glorious name,[32] to hope on Your name, which is the origin of all creation. You have opened "the eyes of our hearts"[33] so that we realize you

29 Prov. 1:23–33.
30 Cf. Acts 4:27. The epithet is derived from the Servant passages of Isaiah and occurs in early liturgical language.   31 Acts 26:18.
32 It is possible that there is a lacuna here; but it may be that the awkwardness of construction is due to the fact that Clement is citing a familiar form of prayer, into which his train of thought has led him.
33 Eph. 1:18.

alone are "highest among the highest, and ever remain holy among the holy."[34] "You humble the pride of the arrogant, overrule the plans of the nations, raise up the humble and humble the haughty. You make rich and make poor; you slay and bring to life; you alone are the guardian of spirits and the God of all flesh."[35] You see into the depths:[36] you look upon men's deeds; you aid those in danger and "save those in despair."[37] You are the creator of every spirit and watch over them. You multiply the nations on the earth, and from out of them all you have chosen those who love you through Jesus Christ, your beloved Son. Through him you have trained us, made us saints, and honored us.

We ask you, Master, be our "helper and defender."[38] 4 Rescue those of our number in distress; raise up the fallen; assist the needy; heal the sick; turn back those of your people who stray; feed the hungry; release our captives; revive the weak; encourage those who lose heart. "Let all the nations realize that you are the only God,"[39] that Jesus Christ is your Child, and "that we are your people and the sheep of your pasture."[40]

You brought into being the everlasting structure of the world 60 by what you did. You, Lord, made the earth. You who are faithful in all generations, righteous in judgment, marvelous in strength and majesty, wise in creating, prudent in making creation endure, visibly good, kind to those who trust in you, "merciful and compassionate,"[41]—forgive us our sins, wickedness, trespasses, and failings. Do not take account of every sin 2 of your slaves and slave girls, but cleanse us with the cleansing of your truth, and "guide our steps so that we walk with holy hearts and do what is good and pleasing to you"[42] and to our rulers.

Yes, Master, "turn your radiant face toward us"[43] in peace, 3 "for our good,"[44] that we may be shielded "by your powerful

[34] Isa. 57:15.
[35] A conflation of Biblical phrases. See Isa. 13:11; Ps. 32:10; Job 5:11; I Sam. 2:7 (cf. Luke 1:53); Deut. 32:39; I Sam. 2:6; II Kings 5:7; Num. 27:16.
[36] Cf. Sir. 16:18, 19.   [37] Judith 9:11.   [38] Judith 9:11; Ps. 119:114.
[39] I Kings 8:60; II Kings 19:19; Ezek. 36:23.
[40] Ps. 79:13; 95:7; 100:3.
[41] Joel 2:13; Sir. 2:11; II Chron. 30:9.
[42] Ps. 40:2; 119:133; I Kings 9:4; Deut. 12:25, 28; 13:18; 21:9.
[43] Ps. 67:1; 80:3, 7, 19; Num. 6:25, 26.
[44] Gen. 50:20; Jer. 21:10; 24:6; Amos 9:4.

hand"[45] and rescued from every sin "by your uplifted arm."[46]
4 Deliver us, too, from all who hate us without good reason. Give
us and all who live on the earth harmony and peace, just as
you did to our fathers when they reverently "called upon you
in faith and truth."[47] And grant that we may be obedient to
your almighty and glorious name, and to our rulers and
governors on earth.

61   You, Master, gave them imperial power through your
majestic and indescribable might, so that we, recognizing it
was you who gave them the glory and honor, might submit to
them, and in no way oppose your will. Grant them, Lord,
health, peace, harmony, and stability, so that they may give
no offense in administering the government you have given
2 them. For it is you, Master, the heavenly "King of eternity,"[48]
who give the sons of men glory and honor and authority over
the earth's people. Direct their plans, O Lord, in accord with
"what is good and pleasing to you,"[49] so that they may
administer the authority you have given them, with peace,
3 considerateness, and reverence, and so win your mercy. We
praise you, who alone are able to do this and still better things
for us, through the high priest and guardian of our souls, Jesus
Christ. Through him be the glory and the majesty to you now
and for all generations and forevermore. Amen.

62   We have written enough to you, brothers, about what befits
our religion and is most helpful to those who want reverently
2 and uprightly to lead a virtuous life. We have, indeed, touched
on every topic—faith, repentance, genuine love, self-control,
sobriety, and patience. We have reminded you that you must
reverently please almighty God by your uprightness, truthful-
ness, and long-suffering. You must live in harmony, bearing no
grudges, in love, peace, and true considerateness, just as our
forefathers, whom we mentioned, won approval by their
humble attitude to the Father, God the Creator, and to all
3 men. We were, moreover, all the more delighted to remind you
of these things, since we well realized we were writing to
people who were real believers and of the highest standing,
and who had made a study of the oracles of God's teaching.
63 Hence it is only right that, confronted with such examples and
so many of them, we should bow the neck and adopt the
attitude of obedience. Thus, by giving up this futile revolt, we

45 Ex. 6:1; Deut. 4:34; 5:15; Jer. 32:21; Ezek. 20:34.
46 Jer. 32:21; Ezek. 20:33, 34.   47 Ps. 145:18; I Tim. 2:7.
48 I Tim. 1:17; Tob. 13:6, 10.   49 Deut. 12:25, 28; 13:18.

may be free from all reproach and gain the true goal ahead of us. Yes, you will make us exceedingly happy if you prove 2 obedient to what we, prompted by the Holy Spirit, have written, and if, following the plea of our letter for peace and harmony, you rid yourselves of your wicked and passionate rivalry.

We are sending you, moreover, trustworthy and discreet 3 persons who from youth to old age have lived irreproachable lives among us. They will be witnesses to mediate between us. We have done this to let you know that our whole concern 4 has been, and is, to have peace speedily restored among you.

And now may the all-seeing God and Master "of spirits" 64 and Lord "of all flesh,"[50] who chose the Lord Jesus Christ and us through him "to be his own people,"[51] grant to every soul over whom His magnificent and holy name has been invoked,[52] faith, fear, peace, patience, long-suffering, self-control, purity, and sobriety. So may we win his approval through our high priest and defender, Jesus Christ. Through him be glory, majesty, might, and honor to God, now and forevermore. Amen.

Be quick to return our delegates in peace and joy, Claudius 65 Ephebus and Valerius Bito, along with Fortunatus.[53] In that way they will the sooner bring us news of that peace and harmony we have prayed for and so much desire, and we in turn will the more speedily rejoice over your healthy state.

The grace of our Lord Jesus Christ be with you and with all everywhere whom God has called through him. Through him be glory, honor, might, majesty, and eternal dominion to God, from everlasting to everlasting. Amen.

The Letter of the Romans to the Corinthians[54]

---

[50] Num. 16:22; 27:16.   [51] Deut. 14:2.

[52] A reference to the invocation of the triune name of God in baptism.

[53] Nothing is known of these men. The names of the first two suggest that they were Greek residents in Rome, who had taken Roman names from the imperial house of Claudius and of his wife Messalina, of the *Gens Valeria*. Perhaps they were freedmen of "Caesar's household" (Phil. 4:22).

[54] This form of the title, preserved in the Coptic, is doubtless the original one. The other MSS. attribute the Letter explicitly to Clement.

The Letters of Ignatius, Bishop of Antioch

INTRODUCTION

THE SIGNIFICANCE OF THESE SEVEN LETTERS LIES IN their being intimate, familiar, and popular. They do not, in the first instance, reveal a set of ideas though they are not lacking in thoughtfulness. Rather do they reveal a man. So much of early Christian literature is impersonal that it is refreshing to stumble upon letters reminiscent of the frank and personal note of Paul's correspondence.

The conditions under which Ignatius' letters were written did not make for careful reflection. They are the letters of a prisoner on his way to martyrdom. Their religious character is popular rather than deep. Their style is compressed and turbulent, reflecting the brusque and impetuous nature of their author (Trall., ch. 4), as well as the irritation of a captive subjected to brutality (Rom. 5:1). Their metaphors change with alarming abruptness, and are often more striking than apt (Eph., ch. 9). Their grammar is not free from carelessness. Yet for these very reasons they have a peculiar value. They disclose a real person, expressing himself in the moment of crisis, and so making clear the ruling passions of his life.

Our knowledge of Ignatius is confined almost entirely to these letters. The later acts of his martyrdom are pure romances, resting on no historical foundations. It is only for the few days when he journeys from Philadelphia to Troas under a military guard that we catch a glimpse of this early second century bishop.

It appears that he was bishop of Antioch in Syria,[1] and

[1] According to Origen (Hom. 6 in Luc., P.G. 13, 1814–1815) and Eusebius (*Hist. eccl.* III. 22, 36), the second bishop of Antioch. Eusebius gives Euodius as the first. In Rom. 2:2, Ignatius calls himself "the bishop

during a short but intense persecution of that city had been
condemned to fight with wild beasts in Rome. Perhaps others
had suffered the same fate, but this is not altogether clear unless
we so interpret the reference in Rom., ch. 10.[2] In any case,
chained to a squad of soldiers, he is taken by the overland route
through Cilicia and Asia Minor, and thence to Rome. Where
the way forks at Laodicea, the northern road is chosen. He
halts at Philadelphia, and then again at Smyrna, where he is
welcomed by Polycarp, the bishop of that city, and by delegates
from the neighboring churches of Ephesus, Magnesia, and
Tralles. It is from Smyrna too that he writes the first four of his
letters—three to the churches that had sent delegates and one
to the church at Rome. Pressing northward, he stops again at
Troas. From here he corresponds with the churches of Philadelphia and Smyrna, and adds a personal note to Polycarp.
We gather that he crossed by sea to Neapolis and halted once
more at Philippi, where the Christians welcomed him.[3] After
that he passes out of sight. We may, however, conjecture that
he reached Italy by way of Dyrrhacium and Brundisium.
Furthermore, we may be fairly sure that he was eventually
martyred in the Coliseum sometime during Trajan's reign
(A.D. 98–117).[4]

Ignatius' letters are dominated by three concerns. First
is his approaching martyrdom. To "imitate the Passion of my
God" (Rom. 6:3) is the exclusive theme of the letter to the
Romans, but it underlies the others as well. This, for him, is the
way to become a "real disciple," a "genuine Christian." He is
clearly impatient to "get to God"[5] by way of martyrdom; and
to brace himself for the ordeal he pictures in startling detail
what this must mean for him (Rom. 5:2, 3). We are not, therefore, surprised that the same line of thought is reflected in
other aspects of the letters. His theology, for instance, revolves
around the blood of Christ (cf. the striking and compressed

of Syria," but this doubtless means no more than "the bishop from
Syria," "the Syrian bishop." The phrase has no connection with the
much later organization of dioceses. In Ignatius' time a bishop was the
bishop of a local congregation, not of a far-flung diocese.

[2] Cf. also Polycarp, Phil. 9:1.   [3] *Ibid.*, chs. 9; 13.

[4] Cf. Irenaeus, *Adv. haer.* V. 28:4; Origen and Eusebius, *op. cit.*

[5] A very frequent phrase in Ignatius. The use of *tugchanein* and *epitugchanein*
with a genitive in just this sense is unusual, but not unique. Certainly
the phrase does not mean to "attain divinity," but to "reach God"
(see Rom. 7:2). Perhaps something of the uncertainty (cf. Trall. 13:3)
and the good fortune involved are also implied by the phrase.

thought of Eph. 1:1); and he emphasizes the reality of Christ's Passion by pointing to his own imminent death (Smyr. 4:2).

The second concern is for the unity of the Church. Against threatening schisms, Ignatius is persistent in his stress on obedience to the Church authorities. In his letters there first emerges the picture of the local congregation governed by a single bishop who is supported by a council of presbyters and assisted by deacons. In this Ignatius betrays a stage of development beyond the situation reflected in the Pastoral Epistles, the Didache, and I Clement. There the titles "bishop" and "presbyter," and perhaps the offices too, are not clearly distinguished. The local congregations are ruled by boards of officials (sometimes called bishops, sometimes presbyters), subject only to apostolic figures, such as Timothy and Titus, or to itinerant prophets. In Ignatius, on the contrary, the single bishop is the leading figure in the Church. Without his approval no services are to be held (Smyr. 8:2) or other action taken (Trall. 7:2). He seems to represent the localizing of the teaching, ruling, and prophetic functions of the original missionary ministry of apostles, prophets, and catechists. This process had, indeed, already started in the Didache (see ch. 13); but in Ignatius it is complete.

What, however, is most striking about this appearance of the monepiscopate in Ignatius is the lack of an explicit doctrine of apostolical succession. For him the authority of the Church officers is not derived from a chain of teaching chairs (as in Irenaeus) or from a succession of ordinations (as in Augustine), but from the fact that their offices are the earthly antitype of a heavenly pattern. The bishop, for instance, represents God; the presbyters, the apostles; and the deacons, Christ (Mag. 6:1). Such teaching stems from a Platonic way of looking at things, and stands in marked contrast with those views of authority that emphasize the historical connection between the episcopate and the apostles. Rather is it a mystical nexus between the earthly Church and the sphere of the divine, which is fundamental in Ignatius. It is this that makes it possible for him to urge that deference to the bishop is the same thing as deference to God (Eph. 5:3–6).

The bishop in Ignatius, moreover, is not only an administrative and liturgical officer. He is also a prophet. This is especially true in his own case. In Philad., ch. 7, he gives us an instance of his gifts in this direction, while the name Theophorus ("God-inspired"), which he assumes, is likely not a proper name but an epithet to indicate his prophetic character. One may note, similarly, how he urges Polycarp to seek for heavenly revelations (Poly. 2:2). Not inappropriately, therefore, did the Smyrnaeans remember Polycarp as "an apostolic and *prophetic* teacher" (Mart. Poly. 16:2).

The third concern in Ignatius is to unmask those heretical movements which are leading to schism. Two of these are prevalent; and while he does not go into detail, believing as he does more in order than in argument, we may gather their main features from his casual references.

In Philadelphia he came into personal contact with a Judaizing movement similar to the one attacked by Paul in his Letter to the Galatians and mentioned later in the Apocalypse (ch. 3:9). It was, to be sure, not so thoroughgoing as that faced by Paul, circumcision not being demanded of its Gentile devotees (Philad. 6:1). But the observance of the Sabbath was involved, along with belief in certain Jewish traditions and allegories (Mag., chs. 8; 9).

At the opposite pole to this error was the Docetic heresy, rife in Smyrna. Here the attempt to accommodate the gospel to Greek culture had gone to the limit of denying the reality of the Lord's body. The basic Hellenistic idea that matter was evil led inevitably to disbelief in the incarnation. God could not have a direct relation with the sensible world, since this was the province of evil. Accordingly, Christ could not have been genuinely man. He only appeared or seemed to have a body (whence "Docetism," from the Greek *dokeō*, seem), being as it were a phantom from the heavenly sphere. The way Ignatius plays on this theme is interesting. By inventing a sham Christ (a Christ who only "seems" to be), the Docetics prove themselves to be a sham, and they will end up by becoming apparitions! (Trall., ch. 10; Smyr., ch. 2).

Against such views Ignatius introduces two of the leading emphases of his theology. One is the divinity of Christ. This was compromised by the Judaizing movement, which viewed him as the last of the prophets. For Ignatius, Christ is "our God." He can even speak of the "Christ God" (Smyr. 10:1), revealing by such an expression his own Christocentric faith and also something of the liberal use of the word *theos* (god) to be found in Hellenistic circles.

The other emphasis of Ignatius' Christianity falls upon the reality of the incarnation, Passion, and resurrection of the Christ. He continually stresses the genuine and actual nature of these occurrences and the inseparable unity of flesh and spirit —even after the resurrection (Smyr., ch. 3). So much so, that such repeated phrases as "in flesh and in spirit" become expressions similar to our "body and soul," and are used as synonyms for "thoroughly" or "completely" (cf. Eph. 10:3; Mag. 13:2).

While these are two of the central themes of Ignatius' thought, recent study has drawn attention to other aspects of it. One concerns the affinities between Ignatius and the Gnostics. There are, indeed, traces of Gnostic terminology in the letters, and a number of ideas (as for instance those in Eph., chs. 19; 20) which were later elaborated in the Valentinian and other systems. But Ignatius was not a Gnostic: he was very far from it. His was not a speculative mind. Indeed, it is the simplicity and uncompromising quality of his basic convictions, so frequently expressed in compact, credal statements, which are most characteristic of him. That is not, however, to deny that Ignatius is hospitable to quite a few phrases and ideas familiar from Hellenistic religion and alien to the general stream of Biblical thought. The Eucharist is "the medicine of immortality" (Eph. 20:2); Christians are "full of God" (Mag., ch. 14); God is *Sigē* (silence, Mag. 8:2); and the divine sphere is *Plērōma* (fullness, Eph., inscr.). Again, Ignatius alludes to the myth of the New Man (Eph. 20:1), and has touches of Gnostic influence in his Church mysticism, where the earthly order reflects the heavenly pattern. Yet, for all that, the central convictions of the Christian faith are clearly—even dogmatically—affirmed, while against the basic Gnostic tenet that matter is evil he wages a constant warfare.

Closely connected with this issue are others which bear upon Ignatius' relation to the New Testament faith. How far does he deviate from the Pauline gospel? Is he influenced by John? Does he depart from John? It is not needful here to review these complex questions at length. Rather should the reader bear them in mind as he surveys the letters. One or two points, however, may be noted.

Ignatius knew several letters of Paul—perhaps the original corpus of seven. He was most familiar with I Corinthians. He probably knew Ephesians; and there may be reminiscences of others. Some parts of the Pauline gospel—above all, the sense of fellowship with the crucified and risen Christ—he understood well. Others were strange to him. He never grasped Paul's teaching on justification, on deliverance from *sarx* (flesh), or on the indwelling Spirit. Nor did he penetrate the fullness of Paul's view of faith as receptivity, the opposite of boasting. In Ignatius faith is primarily conviction. Sometimes, indeed, he uses Pauline phrases with meanings that widely differ from the original (e.g., Rom. 5:1; Eph. 8:2).

With John the question is more difficult. There are a number of possible reminiscences (Mag. 7:1; Rom. 7:2, 3; Philad. 7:1; 9:1), but none is decisive. All of them can be explained by a common religious ethos. Yet their weight is cumulative, and there is a close relation between the views of John and Ignatius on the Eucharist (cf. John 6:54 with Eph. 20:2, and Smyr. 7:1).

In general it would be true to say that the Christianity of Ignatius represents a step removed from the central New Testament faith. It lacks the freshness and depth of the Pauline and Johannine gospels, though this can easily be exaggerated. The process by which the faith became ordered and organized, thereby losing something of its original spontaneity and reliance on the Spirit, is evident in the New Testament itself, especially in the Pastoral Epistles. Ignatius carries the development a little farther, striking out on a line of Church mysticism somewhat different from the moral note of the Pastorals and I Clement. But at the same time it is impossible to miss in Ignatius the intense devotion to the person of Christ and the consciousness of fellowship with his sufferings.

"A soul seething with the divine *eros*"—such is Chrysostom's description of Ignatius in his eulogy delivered on the martyr's feast in Antioch.[6] It is an apt phrase, for more reasons than Chrysostom intended. There is a religious vehemence about these letters, even an impatience and a heat of excitement, which is more fittingly expressed by the classical *eros* than by the uniquely Christian *agapē*. Ignatius is himself aware of his lack of gentleness and calm (Trall. 4:2). He had, too, something of those sharp alternations of pride and humility, which we meet in Paul (Trall., chs. 4; 5). His letter to the Romans, moreover, expresses that exaggerated passion for martyrdom which the Church later sought to restrain. In the light of these traits it is interesting to notice how struck Ignatius was by the bishops of Ephesus and Philadelphia (Eph., ch. 6; Philad. 1:1). He saw in their modest and retiring character what was most lacking in his own. By their quietness they seemed the more effectual and, as bishops, were the better able to mirror the divine nature which their office represented (Eph., chs. 6; 15). God's

6 *In S. Martyrem Ignatium* I, P.G. 50:588.

essential character was that of silence—a silence broken only at the incarnation, and even then with reserve and modesty (Eph., ch. 19).

Yet, for all this, there is a nobility about this Oriental martyr. He can recognize his weakness, and he has grasped the central truth of the Christian gospel, incorporating it into his very life. He will suffer with Christ and so become a genuine disciple.

MANUSCRIPTS AND BOOKS

THE MANUSCRIPTS OF IGNATIUS' LETTERS

The letters of Ignatius were first collected by Polycarp, the bishop of Smyrna,[7] who sent copies of them to the church at Philippi not long after Ignatius had left that city on his way across Macedonia (Phil., ch. 13). Whether this collection contained all seven letters is not clear. Possibly Polycarp did not have access to the one to the Romans, though this was early in circulation, being quoted by Irenaeus (*Adv. haer.* V. 28:4), and known, of course, to Eusebius. It is likely that copies of all the letters were kept by Ignatius' amanuensis, the Ephesian Burrhus (see Philad. 11:2), and that Polycarp obtained them from him.

We possess no pure manuscript of the original corpus, for in the fourth century the letters were interpolated and six additional ones added (Mary of Cassobola to Ignatius; Ignatius to Mary, to the Tarsians, Philippians, Antiochenes, and to Hero, deacon of Antioch). The aim of these forgeries was to gain for a diluted form of Arianism the authority of a primitive martyr. Finally, in the Middle Ages—perhaps around the twelfth century, which saw a new development of the cult of the Virgin—a correspondence between Ignatius and Mary, as well as two letters of Ignatius to John, was fabricated in the West.

The greater part of the extant manuscripts contains the seven interpolated letters along with five or six of the spurious ones,

---

[7] It would seem that the Greek, Latin, and Armenian manuscripts which preserve the genuine text of the letters have retained Polycarp's original order: Smyrnaeans, Polycarp, Ephesians, Magnesians, Philadelphians, Trallians, and probably Romans. Philadelphians and Trallians are reversed in the Armenian. Romans was often embedded in the Martyrology (see below).

some of the Latin versions adding the medieval forgeries. The first edition of the Latin was by J. Faber Stapulensis (Lefèvre d' Étaples), Paris, 1498, and of the Greek by Valentinus Paceas, Dillingae, 1557.

With the revival of learning in the Renaissance a critical spirit toward the Ignatian corpus first arose; but it was not until the labors of Theodor Zahn and J. B. Lightfoot in the nineteenth century that the question was finally settled and the genuine form of the letters of Ignatius was fully established.

A pioneer work which attempted to separate the wheat from the chaff was that of the Genevan professor Nicholaus Vedelius in 1623. He printed the seven letters known to Eusebius by themselves, relegating the six spurious ones to a separate volume. He recognized, too, that even the seven genuine ones had been interpolated. It was, however, Archbishop James Ussher who in the seventeenth century first discovered the pure text of the letters, though in a Latin version. The controversy with the Puritans over episcopacy brought the question of the genuineness of Ignatius' correspondence into the foreground; and, in his efforts to defend this, Ussher came upon two Latin manuscripts that contained versions of the text corresponding to that known to Eusebius and other fathers. These manuscripts did, indeed, contain five of the forged letters as well; but the remarkable thing was that the text of the genuine seven had not been interpolated. Ussher published his text in 1644, and his guess that Robert Grosseteste (the learned medieval bishop of Lincoln) had been the translator has since been confirmed.

Two years later (1646) Isaac Voss in Amsterdam published the Greek text of this Latin version from an eleventh century Florentine manuscript. In this the letter to the Romans is wanting, the manuscript being defective and breaking off in the middle of the Epistle to the Tarsians. But as it was customary to separate Romans from the others and to embed it in the Acts of Ignatius' Martyrdom, it was doubtless in the original manuscript. These Acts would have come at the end, as they do in Ussher's Latin versions. Anyway, the defect was supplied by the discovery of a tenth century Greek manuscript of the Martyrology, published by T. Ruinart in 1689.

The authenticity of the text defended by Ussher and Voss was soon attacked by French Calvinists (notably by Jean Daillé in Geneva, 1666); but a full and learned reply was offered by Bishop John Pearson in his *Vindiciae Ignatianae*, 1672.

Considerably later (1845) an English canon, Dr. W. Cureton, published a Syriac version of three of the letters (Polycarp, Ephesians, and Romans). This text (based finally on three manuscripts) was considerably more brief than the Vossian; and in his learned work *Corpus Ignatianum* (1849) Cureton argued that it represented the genuine form of the letters. His theory, however, did not win acceptance. The works of Theodor Zahn (*Ignatius von Antiochien*, Gotha, 1873) and of J. B. Lightfoot (*The Apostolic Fathers*, Part 2, Vol. I, London, 1885) have convincingly shown that Cureton's text represents a rather crude abridgment of the original letters.

To summarize: the letters of Ignatius have come down to us in three forms. There is the long recension, interpolated in the fourth century. There is the short Syriac recension, which is an abridgment of the authentic letters. Finally there is the middle recension, or genuine text.

A full description of the manuscripts (including the Armenian, and the Syriac and Coptic fragments) will be found in Lightfoot, *op. cit.*, pp. 70–126; 587–598. To this must be added the fifth century Berlin papyrus fragment of *Smyrnaeans* (in Greek: see C. Schmidt and W. Schubert in *Altchristliche Texte*, Berliner Klassikertexte, Heft VI, 1910), and the Coptic fragments published by Carl Wessely in *Sitzungsberichte der kais. Akademie der Wissenschaften in Wien*, Vol. CLXXII, Part 4, 1913.

THE ACTS OF IGNATIUS' MARTYRDOM

The Acts of Ignatius' Martyrdom are current in five forms. Of these only two are independent, the so-called Antiochene and Roman Acts. The others are combinations and modifications of them.

The Antiochene Acts derive their name from the fact that their center of interest is Antioch, where Ignatius is tried by Trajan and whither his bones are brought back from Rome. These Acts date from the fifth century and rest on no historical foundation. Their textual history, however, is important, since the genuine text of Ignatius' Letter to the Romans is embedded in them. They are current in Latin, Greek, and Syriac.

Even more crudely legendary are the Roman Acts, which belong to the sixth century and record Ignatius' trial before Trajan and the Senate and his martyrdom in the amphitheater. They are extant in Greek and Coptic.

TEXTS AND STUDIES

The best Greek text, and the one used for this translation, is by Karl Bihlmeyer in his revision of F.X. Funk's *Die apostolischen Väter*, Part 1, Tübingen, 1924. More recent, but based on this, is P. Th. Camelot's *Ignace d'Antioche, Lettres*, Éditions du Cerf, Paris, 1944 (in the series Sources chrétiennes, with translation). Kirsopp Lake did the text with translation for the Loeb Classics, *The Apostolic Fathers*, London, 1912. Lightfoot's text and translation is in Part 2, Vol. II, of his *Apostolic Fathers*, revised ed., London, 1889.

The more important translations are as follows: by Lake and Lightfoot in the editions mentioned; by J. H. Srawley, *The Epistles of St. Ignatius, Bishop of Antioch*, London, 1919; by J. A. Kleist, *The Epistles of St. Clement of Rome and St. Ignatius of Antioch*, Newman Press, Westminster, Maryland, 1946, in the series Ancient Christian Writers; by Gerald G. Walsh, *The Apostolic Fathers*, Fathers of the Church Press, New York, 1946, in the series The Fathers of the Church. The last two versions bring out Ignatius' meaning in modern, idiomatic English. The Letter to the Trallians has been characteristically rendered by James Moffatt in an article in the *Harvard Theological Review*, 29, 1936, pp. 1–38, "An Approach to Ignatius." The latest English translation (exact and pointed, but not bold) is by Edgar Goodspeed in *The Apostolic Fathers: An American Translation*, Harper & Brothers, New York, 1950.

The best French translation, incisive and idiomatic, is by Auguste Lelong in Hemmer and Lejay, *Les Pères apostoliques*, Vol. III, Paris, 2d ed. 1927. In addition there are the more literal renderings of Camelot (already mentioned) and H. Delafosse in his *Les Lettres d'Ignace d'Antioche*, Paris, 1927 (where he adduces a radical theory of their late date and fictitious character).

In German there are these versions: by Walter Bauer, *Die Briefe des Ignatius von Antiochien*, in the series Handbuch zum N.T., Tübingen, 1920; by G. Krüger in Hennecke, *Neutestamentliche Apokryphen*, 2d ed., J. C. B. Mohr, Tübingen, 1924; and by F. Zeller, *Die apostolischen Väter*, in the 2d series of the Bibliothek der Kirchenväter, Munich, 1918.

In Italian there is *I Padri apostolici*, Part 2a, by G. Bosio, Vol. XIV, in the series Corona Patrum Salesiana, Turin, 1942.

All these editions have introductions and notes, the most valuable being those of Lightfoot, Srawley, Kleist, and Bauer.

In addition to the works of Zahn and Lightfoot previously mentioned, the following are the more important recent studies in Ignatius: E. von der Goltz, *Ignatius von Antiochien als Christ und Theologe* (a fundamental work) in Texte und Untersuchungen, Vol. XII, Part 3, Leipzig, 1894; M. Rackl, *Die Christologie des heiligen Ignatius von Antiochien* (rich in bibliography) in Freiburger theologische Studien, 14, 1914; H. Schlier, *Religionsgeschichtliche Untersuchungen zu den Ignatiusbriefen* (a valuable study but one that exaggerates Ignatius' dependence on Gnostic and "mystery" sources), A. Töpelmann, Giessen, 1929; H. W. Bartsch, *Gnostisches Gut und Gemeindetradition bei Ignatius von Antiochien* (which further pursues the Gnostic theme), C. Bertelsmann, Gütersloh, 1940; C. C. Richardson, *The Christianity of Ignatius of Antioch* (a survey of main concepts), Columbia University Press, New York, 1935, and "The Church in Ignatius of Antioch" in *The Journal of Religion*, 17, pp. 428–443, 1937; F. A. Schilling, *The Mysticism of Ignatius of Antioch*, Thesis, University of Pennsylvania, Philadelphia, 1932; E. Bruston, *Ignace d'Antioche, ses epîtres, sa vie, sa théologie*, Paris, 1897; H. de Genouillac, *L'Église chrétienne au temps de Saint Ignace d'Antioche*, Paris, 1907. The trinitarian question has been studied by Jules Lebreton in his article "La Théologie de la Trinité d'après Saint Ignace d'Antioche" in *Recherches de science religieuse*, 15, pp. 97–126, 393–419, 1925, and in his *Histoire du dogme de la Trinité*, Vol. II, pp. 282–331, Paris, 1928. James Moffatt has characterized Ignatius' faith in "A Study in Personal Religion" in *The Journal of Religion*, 10, pp. 169–186, 1930, an essay which is supplemented by his article in the *Harvard Theological Review*, January, 1936, already cited. The connection between Ignatius and John has been investigated by P. Dietze, "Die Briefe des Ignatius von Antiochien und das Johannesevangelium" in *Studien und Kritiken*, 78, pp. 563–603, 1905; by W. J. Burghardt in *Theological Studies*, 1, pp. 1–26, 140–156, 1940; and more recently by C. Maurer in his *Ignatius von Antiochien und das Johannesevangelium*, Zurich, 1949. This last study, along with the chapters on Ignatius in J. Klevinghaus, *Die theologische Stellung der apostolischen Väter zur alttestamentlichen Offenbarung*, C. Bertelsmann, Gütersloh, 1948, and in T. F. Torrance, *The Doctrine of Grace in the Apostolic Fathers*, Oliver, Ltd., Edinburgh, 1948, represents a modern Protestant tendency to emphasize the decline of the New Testament faith in the post-Apostolic period, without fully appreciating the connection between the New Testament and the subapostolic writers. Finally mention may be made of Th. Preiss's article "La Mystique de l'imitation du Christ et de l'unité chez Ignace d'Antioche" in *Revue d'histoire et de philosophie religieuses*, 18, pp. 197–241, 1938; of M. H. Shepherd's essay "Smyrna in the Ignatian Letters" in *The Journal of Religion*, 20, pp. 141–159, 1940; and of the note by Henry Chadwick, "The Silence of Bishops in Ignatius," in the *Harvard Theological Review*, April, 1950, pp. 169–172.

The Letter of Ignatius, Bishop of Antioch

TO THE EPHESIANS

Written from Smyrna, where Ignatius and his military guard made a halt on their way to Rome via the northern road to Troas, this is the longest of his letters. Four delegates, including the modest and retiring bishop Onesimus, had been sent by the neighboring Ephesian church to greet and encourage the martyr. One of them, the deacon Burrhus, later accompanied Ignatius as far as Troas, and perhaps acted as his amanuensis (Philad. 11:2).

Ignatius takes the occasion to thank the Ephesians for their kindness. While praising them for their unity and orthodoxy, he proceeds to warn them against schism and the prevalent Docetic heresy which was being disseminated by itinerant teachers.

THE TEXT

Heartiest greetings of pure joy in Jesus Christ from Ignatius, the "God-inspired,"[8] to the church at Ephesus in Asia.[9] Out of the fullness[10] of God the Father you have been blessed with large numbers and are predestined from eternity to enjoy forever continual and unfading glory. The source of your unity and election is genuine suffering which you undergo by

---

[8] "Theophorus," literally "God-bearer." It is probably not a proper name but an epithet indicating his prophetic gifts. He is "full of God" (cf. Mag., ch. 14). Perhaps the church at Antioch dubbed him thus.

[9] Ephesus, the scene of Paul's mission and traditionally of John's later activity, was the capital of the Roman province of Asia. It was, too, the central port of the trade route which joined the Aegean with the East. Hence the reference in ch. 12:2.

[10] The term has a Gnostic ring, *plērōma* referring in later Gnostic systems to the sphere of the divine.

the will of the Father and of Jesus Christ, our God. Hence you
deserve to be considered happy.

1　I gave a godly welcome to your church which has so endeared
itself to us by reason of your upright nature, marked as it is
by faith in Jesus Christ, our Saviour, and by love of him. You
are imitators of God; and it was God's blood that stirred you
up once more to do the sort of thing you do naturally and have
2 now done to perfection. For you were all zeal to visit me when
you heard that I was being shipped as a prisoner from Syria
for the sake of our common Name[11] and hope. I hope, indeed, by
your prayers to have the good fortune to fight with wild beasts
3 in Rome, so that by doing this I can be a real disciple. In God's
name, therefore, I received your large congregation in the
person of Onesimus,[12] your bishop in this world,[13] a man whose
love is beyond words. My prayer is that you should love him
in the spirit of Jesus Christ and all be like him. Blessed is He
who let you have such a bishop. You deserved it.

2　Now about my fellow slave[14] Burrhus, your godly deacon,
who has been richly blessed. I very much want him to stay
with me. He will thus bring honor on you and the bishop.
Crocus too, who is a credit both to God and to you, and whom
I received as a model of your love, altogether raised my spirits
(May the Father of Jesus Christ grant him a similar comfort!), as
did Onesimus, Burrhus, Euplus, and Fronto. In them I saw and
2 loved you all. May I always be glad about you, that is, if I deserve
to be! It is right, then, for you to render all glory to Jesus Christ,
seeing he has glorified you. Thus, united in your submission, and
subject to the bishop and the presbytery, you will be real saints.

3　I do not give you orders as if I were somebody important.
For even if I am a prisoner for the Name, I have not yet
reached Christian perfection. I am only beginning to be a
disciple, so I address you as my fellow students. I needed your
coaching in faith, encouragement, endurance, and patience.
2 But since love forbids me to keep silent about you, I hasten
to urge you to harmonize your actions with God's mind. For
Jesus Christ—that life from which we can't be torn—is the
Father's mind, as the bishops too, appointed the world over,
reflect the mind of Jesus Christ.

11 I.e., the name of "Christian."
12 In welcoming Onesimus, Ignatius felt that he received the whole
　Ephesian church which the bishop represented.
13 In contrast to their heavenly bishop, Christ.
14 A Pauline reminiscence. All Christians are slaves of Christ.

Hence you should act in accord with the bishop's mind, as **4** you surely do. Your presbytery, indeed, which deserves its name and is a credit to God, is as closely tied to the bishop as the strings to a harp. Wherefore your accord and harmonious love is a hymn to Jesus Christ. Yes, one and all, you should **2** form yourselves into a choir,[15] so that, in perfect harmony and taking your pitch from God, you may sing in unison and with one voice to the Father through Jesus Christ. Thus he will heed you, and by your good deeds he will recognize you are members of his Son. Therefore you need to abide in irreproachable unity if you really want to be God's members forever.

If in so short a time I could get so close to your bishop— **5** I do not mean in a natural way, but in a spiritual—how much more do I congratulate you on having such intimacy with him as the Church enjoys with Jesus Christ, and Jesus Christ with the Father. That is how unity and harmony come to prevail everywhere. Make no mistake about it. If anyone is **2** not inside the sanctuary,[16] he lacks God's bread.[17] And if the prayer of one or two has great avail, how much more that of the bishop and the total Church. He who fails to join in your **3** worship shows his arrogance by the very fact of becoming a schismatic. It is written, moreover, "God resists the proud."[18] Let us, then, heartily avoid resisting the bishop so that we may be subject to God.

The more anyone sees the bishop modestly silent, the more **6** he should revere him. For everyone the Master of the house sends on his business, we ought to receive as the One who sent him. It is clear, then, that we should regard the bishop as the Lord himself. Indeed, Onesimus spoke very highly of your **2** godly conduct, that you were all living by the truth and harboring no sectarianism. Nay, you heed nobody beyond what he has to say truthfully about Jesus Christ.[19]

Some, indeed, have a wicked and deceitful habit of flaunting **7** the Name about, while acting in a way unworthy of God. You must avoid them like wild beasts. For they are mad dogs which

---

15 The many musical metaphors in Ignatius led to the later legend that he had introduced antiphonal singing into the Church (Socrates, *Hist. eccl.*, VI, ch. 8.

16 The metaphor is taken from that area of the Temple in which faithful Jews gathered for the usual sacrifices. It is contrasted with the outer Court of the Gentiles. The point here is that the true Holy Place is the faithful congregation regularly assembled under its bishop.

17 Cf. John 6:33.   18 Prov. 3:34.

19 Adopting the reading of Lightfoot.

bite on the sly. You must be on your guard against them, for it
2 is hard to heal their bite. There is only one physician—of flesh
yet spiritual, born yet unbegotten, God incarnate, genuine life
in the midst of death, sprung from Mary as well as God,
first subject to suffering then beyond it—Jesus Christ our
Lord.[20]

8   Let no one mislead you, as, indeed, you are not misled, being
wholly God's. For when you harbor no dissension that can
harass you, then you are indeed living in God's way. A cheap
sacrifice[21] I am, but I dedicate myself to you Ephesians—a
2 church forever famous. Carnal people cannot act spiritually,[22]
or spiritual people carnally, just as faith cannot act like unbelief, or unbelief like faith. But even what you do in the flesh you
do spiritually. For you do everything under Christ's control.[23]

9   I have heard that some strangers came your way with a
wicked teaching. But you did not let them sow it among you.
You stopped up your ears to prevent admitting what they
disseminated. Like stones of God's Temple, ready for a building
of God the Father, you are being hoisted up by Jesus Christ,
as with a crane (that's the cross!), while the rope you use is the
Holy Spirit. Your faith is what lifts you up, while love is the
way you ascend to God.

2   You are all taking part in a religious procession,[24] carrying
along with you your God, shrine, Christ, and your holy objects,
and decked out from tip to toe in the commandments of Jesus
Christ. I too am enjoying it all, because I can talk with you in
a letter, and congratulate you on changing your old way of
life and setting your love on God alone.

---

20 The first of several compact credal statements in Ignatius. While they
are stamped with his originality, they doubtless draw upon primitive
formulas used in catechetical instruction and baptism.

21 The term *peripsēma* (scum, filth), which occurs several times in Ignatius,
was used of common criminals who were sacrificed in times of adversity
to avert the wrath of the gods. Ignatius uses it as an expression of humility
and devotion, to refer to his anticipated martyrdom.

22 Cf. Rom. 8:5, 8.

23 Literally "in Christ," a phrase which has a wide variety of meaning
in Ignatius and is derived from Saint Paul. In the latter, as probably
here in Ignatius, the underlying idea parallels that of demon possession
(cf. Mark 1:23, "*in* an unclean spirit"). The Christian is "possessed
by Christ," is "under his control" and "influence."

24 An abrupt change of metaphor, suggested by the building of a temple.
This time the reference is to a heathen procession—perhaps in honor of
the Ephesian Artemis. The devotees would be in festive attire and would
carry small shrines and amulets of the goddess.

"Keep on praying"[25] for others too, for there is a chance 10 of their being converted and getting to God. Let them, then, learn from you at least by your actions. Return their bad 2 temper with gentleness; their boasts with humility; their abuse with prayer. In the face of their error, be "steadfast in the faith."[26] Return their violence with mildness and do not be intent on getting your own back. By our patience let us show 3 we are their brothers, intent on imitating the Lord, seeing which of us can be the more wronged, robbed, and despised. Thus no devil's weed will be found among you; but thoroughly pure and self-controlled, you will remain body and soul united to Jesus Christ.

The last days are here. So let us abase ourselves and stand in 11 awe of God's patience, lest it turn out to be our condemnation. Either let us fear the wrath to come or let us value the grace we have: one or the other. Only let our lot be genuine life in Jesus Christ. Do not let anything catch your eye besides him, 2 for whom I carry around these chains—my spiritual pearls! Through them I want to rise from the dead by your prayers. May I ever share in these, so that I may be numbered among the Ephesian Christians who, by the might of Jesus Christ, have always been of one mind with the very apostles. I realize 12 who I am and to whom I am writing. I am a convict; you have been freed. I am in danger; you are safe. You are the route for 2 God's victims.[27] You have been initiated into the [Christian] mysteries with Paul, a real saint and martyr, who deserves to be congratulated. When I come to meet God may I follow in his footsteps, who in all his letters[28] mentions your union with Christ Jesus.

Try to gather together more frequently to celebrate God's 13 Eucharist and to praise him. For when you meet with frequency, Satan's powers are overthrown and his destructiveness is undone by the unanimity of your faith. There is nothing better 2 than peace, by which all strife in heaven and earth is done away.

You will not overlook any of this if you have a thorough 14 belief in Jesus Christ and love him. That is the beginning and end of life: faith the beginning and love the end.[29] And

---

25 I Thess. 5:17.   26 Col. 1:23.

27 Ephesus lay on the route by which criminals from the provinces would be brought to Rome to supply victims for the amphitheater.

28 An exaggeration of the fact that in several of Paul's letters he refers to Ephesus and Ephesians.   29 Cf. I Tim. 1:5.

when the two are united you have God, and everything else
2 that has to do with real goodness is dependent on them. No one
who professes faith falls into sin, nor does one who has learned
to love, hate. "The tree is known by its fruit."[30] Similarly,
those who profess to be Christ's will be recognized by their
actions. For what matters is not a momentary act of professing,
but being persistently motivated by faith.

15   It is better to keep quiet and be real, than to chatter and be
unreal. It is a good thing to teach if, that is, the teacher
practices what he preaches. There was one such Teacher,
who "spoke and it was done"[31]; and what he did in silence[32]
2 is worthy of the Father. He who has really grasped what Jesus
said can appreciate his silence. Thus he will be perfect: his
words will mean action, and his very silence will reveal his
character.

3   The Lord overlooks nothing. Even secrets are open to him.
Let us, then, do everything as if he were dwelling in us. Thus
we shall be his temples[33] and he will be within us as our God—
as he actually is. This will be clear to us just to the extent
that we love him rightly.

16   Make no mistake, my brothers: adulterers will not inherit
2 God's Kingdom.[34] If, then, those who act carnally suffer death,
how much more shall those who by wicked teaching corrupt
God's faith for which Jesus Christ was crucified. Such a vile
creature will go to the unquenchable fire along with anyone
who listens to him.

17   The reason the Lord let the ointment be poured on his
head was that he might pass on the aroma of incorruption to
the Church. Do not be anointed with the foul smell of the teaching of the prince of this world, lest he capture you and rob you
2 of the life ahead of you. Why do we not all come to our senses
by accepting God's knowledge, which is Jesus Christ? Why do we
stupidly perish, ignoring the gift which the Lord has really sent?

18   I am giving my life (not that it's worth much!)[35] for the cross,
which unbelievers find a stumbling block, but which means
to us salvation and eternal life. "Where is the wise man?
Where is the debater?"[36] Where are the boasts of those
2 supposedly intelligent? For our God, Jesus the Christ, was
conceived by Mary, in God's plan being sprung both from the

---

[30] Matt. 12:33.   [31] Ps. 33:9.
[32] I.e., unobtrusively, and with special reference to his silence at his trial.
[33] Cf. I Cor. 3:16.   [34] Cf. I Cor. 6:9, 10.
[35] See note 21.   [36] I Cor. 1:20.

seed of David[37] and from the Holy Spirit. He was born and baptized that by his Passion he might hallow water.

Now, Mary's virginity and her giving birth escaped the **19** notice of the prince of this world, as did the Lord's death— those three secrets crying to be told, but wrought in God's silence.[38] How, then, were they revealed to the ages? A star[39] **2** shone in heaven brighter than all the stars. Its light was indescribable and its novelty caused amazement. The rest of the stars, along with the sun and the moon, formed a ring around it; yet it outshone them all, and there was bewilderment whence this unique novelty had arisen. As a result all magic **3** lost its power and all witchcraft ceased. Ignorance was done away with, and the ancient kingdom [of evil] was utterly destroyed, for God was revealing himself as a man, to bring newness of eternal life.[40] What God had prepared was now beginning. Hence everything was in confusion as the destruction of death was being taken in hand.

If Jesus Christ allows me, in answer to your prayers, and it **20** is his will, I will explain to you more about [God's] plan in a second letter I intend to write. I have only touched on this plan in reference to the New Man Jesus Christ, and how it involves believing in him and loving him, and entails his Passion and resurrection. I will do this especially if the Lord shows me that **2** you are all, every one of you, meeting together under the influence of the grace that we owe to the Name,[41] in one faith and in union with Christ, who was "descended from David according to the flesh"[42] and is Son of man and Son of God. At these meetings you should heed the bishop and presbytery attentively, and break one loaf, which is the medicine of immortality, and the antidote which wards off death but yields continuous life in union with Jesus Christ.

I am giving my life for you and for those whom you, to God's **21** honor, sent to Smyrna. I am writing to you from there, giving the Lord thanks and embracing Polycarp and you too in my love. Bear me in mind, as Jesus Christ does you. Pray for the **2** church in Syria, whence I am being sent off to Rome as a prisoner. I am the least of the faithful there—yet I have been privileged to serve God's honor. Farewell in God the Father and in Jesus Christ, our common hope.

[37] Cf. Rom. 1:3.
[38] God's modesty and reserve in the incarnation were something for which Satan was unprepared.
[39] An expansion of the story in Matt. 2:2, and influenced by Gen. 37:9.
[40] Cf. Rom. 6:4.   [41] I.e., the name of "Christian."   [42] Rom. 1:3.

TO THE MAGNESIANS

Like the Ephesians, the Christians at Magnesia (a town some fifteen miles from Ephesus) sent delegates to greet Ignatius in Smyrna. Among them was their youthful bishop, Damas. In his letter to them Ignatius instructs them on not presuming on the youthfulness of their bishop, emphasizes the importance of unity and subjection to the Church officers, and warns them against Judaistic errors.

THE TEXT

Every good wish in God the Father and in Jesus Christ from Ignatius, the "God-inspired," to the church at Magnesia on the Maeander. In Christ Jesus, our Saviour, I greet your church which, by reason of its union with him, is blessed with the favor of God the Father.

1 I was delighted to hear of your well-disciplined and godly love; and hence, impelled by faith in Jesus Christ, I decided 2 to write to you. Privileged as I am to have this distinguished and godly name,[43] I sing the praises of the churches, even while I am a prisoner. I want them to confess that Jesus Christ, our perpetual Life, united flesh with spirit. I want them, too, to unite their faith with love—there is nothing better than that. Above all, I want them to confess the union of Jesus with the Father. If, with him to support us, we put up with all the spite of the prince of this world and manage to escape, we shall get to God.

2 Yes, I had the good fortune to see you, in the persons of Damas

43 I.e., Theophorus, "God-inspired." The point would seem to be that, despite his status as a convict, he makes prophetic utterances in praise of the churches.

your bishop (he's a credit to God!), and of your worthy
presbyters, Bassus and Apollonius, and of my fellow slave, the
deacon Zotion. I am delighted with him, because he submits
to the bishop as to God's grace, and to the presbytery as to the
law of Jesus Christ.

Now, it is not right to presume on the youthfulness of your 3
bishop. You ought to respect him as fully as you respect the
authority of God the Father. Your holy presbyters, I know,
have not taken unfair advantage of his apparent youthfulness,
but in their godly wisdom have deferred to him—nay, rather,
not so much to him as to the Father of Jesus Christ, who is
everybody's bishop. For the honor, then, of him who loved us, 2
we ought to obey without any dissembling, since the real issue
is not that a man misleads a bishop whom he can see, but that
he defrauds the One who is invisible. In such a case he must
reckon, not with a human being, but with God who knows his
secrets.

We have not only to be called Christians, but to be Christians. 4
It is the same thing as calling a man a bishop and then doing
everything in disregard of him. Such people seem to me to be
acting against their conscience, since they do not come to the
valid and authorized services.

Yes, everything is coming to an end, and we stand before 5
this choice—death or life—and everyone will go "to his own
place."⁴⁴ One might say similarly, there are two coinages, one
God's, the other the world's. Each bears its own stamp—
unbelievers that of this world; believers, who are spurred by
love, the stamp of God the Father through Jesus Christ. And
if we do not willingly die in union with his Passion, we do not
have his life in us.

I believed, then, that I saw your whole congregation in these 6
people I have mentioned, and I loved you all. Hence I urge you
to aim to do everything in godly agreement. Let the bishop
preside in God's place, and the presbyters take the place of the
apostolic council, and let the deacons (my special favorites)
be entrusted with the ministry of Jesus Christ who was
with the Father from eternity and appeared at the end [of the
world].

Taking, then, the same attitude as God, you should all 2
respect one another. Let no one think of his neighbor in a
carnal way; but always love one another in the spirit of Jesus
Christ. Do not let there be anything to divide you, but be in

44 Acts 1:25.

accord with the bishop and your leaders. Thus you will be an example and a lesson of incorruptibility.

7   As, then, the Lord did nothing without the Father[45] (either on his own or by the apostles) because he was at one with him, so you must not do anything without the bishop and presbyters. Do not, moreover, try to convince yourselves that anything done on your own is commendable. Only what you do together is right. Hence you must have one prayer, one petition, one mind, one hope, dominated by love and unsullied joy—that means you must have Jesus Christ. You cannot have anything better than that.

2   Run off—all of you—to one temple of God, as it were, to one altar, to one Jesus Christ, who came forth from one Father, while still remaining one with him, and returned to him.

8   Do not be led astray by wrong views or by outmoded tales[46] that count for nothing. For if we still go on observing Judaism,

2 we admit we never received grace. The divine prophets themselves lived Christ Jesus' way. That is why they were persecuted, for they were inspired by his grace to convince unbelievers that God is one, and that he has revealed himself in his Son Jesus Christ, who is his Word issuing from the silence [47] and who won the complete approval of him who sent him.

9   Those, then, who lived by ancient practices arrived at a new hope. They ceased to keep the Sabbath and lived by the Lord's Day, on which our life as well as theirs shone forth, thanks to Him and his death, though some deny this.[48] Through this mystery we got our faith, and because of it we stand our ground

2 so as to become disciples of Jesus Christ, our sole teacher. How, then, can we live without him when even the prophets, who were his disciples by the Spirit, awaited him as their teacher? He, then, whom they were rightly expecting, raised them from the dead, when he came.[49]

10   We must not, then, be impervious to his kindness. Indeed, were he to act as we do, we should at once be done for. Hence, now we are his disciples, we must learn to live like Christians— to be sure, whoever bears any other name does not belong to

2 God. Get rid, then, of the bad yeast[50]—it has grown stale and

[45] Cf. John 5:19, 30; 8:28.

[46] The reference is to apocryphal Jewish legends and allegorical interpretations of the Old Testament (cf. I Tim. 1:4).

[47] The idea is that by the incarnation God broke his silence, cf. Ignatius, Eph., ch. 19.

[48] A passing allusion to the other current heresy, Docetism.

[49] Cf. Matt. 27:52.   [50] Cf. I Cor. 5:7.

sour—and be changed into new yeast, that is, into Jesus Christ. Be salted in him, so that none of you go bad, for your smell will give you away. It is monstrous to talk Jesus Christ 3 and to live like a Jew. For Christianity did not believe in Judaism, but Judaism in Christianity. People of every tongue have come to believe in it, and so been united together in God. [51]

I do not write in this way, my dear friends, because I have 11 heard that any of you are like that. Rather do I, well aware of my humble position, want to caution you ahead, lest you fall a prey to stupid ideas, and to urge you to be thoroughly convinced of the birth, Passion, and resurrection, which occurred while Pontius Pilate was governor. Yes, all that was actually and assuredly done by Jesus Christ, our Hope. God forbid that any of you should lose it!

I want to be glad about you ever so much, if, that is, I 12 deserve to be. For though I am a prisoner, I cannot compare with one of you who are free. I realize that you are not conceited, for you have Jesus Christ within you. And more, I know you are self-conscious when I praise you, just as Scripture says, "The upright man is his own accuser." [52]

Make a real effort, then, to stand firmly by the orders of 13 the Lord and the apostles, so that "whatever you do, you may succeed" [53] in body and soul, in faith and love, in Son, Father, and Spirit, from first to last, along with your most distinguished bishop, your presbytery (that neatly plaited spiritual wreath!), and your godly deacons. Defer to the bishop and to one another 2 as Jesus Christ did to the Father in the days of his flesh, and as the apostles did to Christ, to the Father, and to the Spirit. In that way we shall achieve complete unity.

I realize you are full of God. Hence I have counseled you 14 but briefly. Remember me in your prayers, that I may get to God. Remember too the church in Syria—I do not deserve to be called a member of it. To be sure, I need your united and holy prayers and your love, so that the church in Syria may have the privilege of being refreshed by means of your church.

The Ephesians greet you from Smyrna. I am writing to you 15 from there. Like you, they came here for God's glory and have revived me considerably, as has Polycarp, the bishop of Smyrna. The other churches also send their greetings to you in honor of Jesus Christ. Farewell—be at one with God, for you possess an unbreakable spirit, which is what Jesus Christ had.

51 Cf. Isa. 66:18.   52 Prov. 18:17, LXX. The Hebrew is quite different.
53 Ps. 1:3, LXX.

TO THE TRALLIANS

The Christians at Tralles (a town some seventeen miles east of Magnesia) had sent their bishop, Polybius, to greet Ignatius in Smyrna. His letter in response is characteristic. Its leading themes are unity and obedience to the Church officials—themes provoked by the spreading danger of the Docetic heresy. It contains, too, several flashes that reveal Ignatius' character. Particularly striking is ch. 4, where he discloses his own impetuous and fervent nature which contrasts with the calm gentleness of Polybius.

THE TEXT

Full hearty greetings in apostolic style,[54] and every good wish from Ignatius, the "God-inspired," to the holy church at Tralles in Asia. You are dear to God, the Father of Jesus Christ, elect and a real credit to him, being completely at peace by reason of the Passion of Jesus Christ, who is our Hope, since we shall rise in union with him.

1 Well do I realize what a character you have—above reproach and steady under strain. It is not just affected, but it comes naturally to you, as I gathered from Polybius, your bishop. By God's will and that of Jesus Christ, he came to me in Smyrna, and so heartily congratulated me on being a prisoner for Jesus
2 Christ that in him I saw your whole congregation. I welcomed, then, your godly good will, which reached me by him, and I gave thanks that I found you, as I heard, to be following God.

2 For when you obey the bishop as if he were Jesus Christ, you are (as I see it) living not in a merely human fashion but in Jesus Christ's way, who for our sakes suffered death that you

54 I.e., in imitation of Paul's inscriptions.

might believe in his death and so escape dying yourselves. It 2 is essential, therefore, to act in no way without the bishop, just as you are doing. Rather submit even to the presbytery as to the apostles of Jesus Christ. He is our Hope,[55] and if we live in union with him now, we shall gain eternal life. Those too who 3 are deacons of Jesus Christ's "mysteries"[56] must give complete satisfaction to everyone. For they do not serve mere food and drink,[57] but minister to God's Church. They must therefore avoid leaving themselves open to criticism, as they would shun fire.

Correspondingly, everyone must show the deacons respect. 3 They represent Jesus Christ, just as the bishop has the role of the Father, and the presbyters are like God's council and an apostolic band. You cannot have a church without these. I am 2 sure that you agree with me in this.

In your bishop I received the very model of your love, and I have him with me. His very bearing is a great lesson, while his gentleness is most forceful. I imagine even the godless respect him.

While I could write about this matter more sharply, I spare 3 you out of love. Since, too, I am a convict, I have not thought it my place to give you orders like an apostle. God has granted 4 me many an inspiration, but I keep my limits, lest boasting should be my undoing. For what I need most at this point is to be on my guard and not to heed flatterers. Those who tell me . . . they are my scourge.[58] To be sure, I am ever so eager 2 to be a martyr, but I do not know if I deserve to be. Many people have no notion of my impetuous ambition. Yet it is all the more a struggle for me. What I need is gentleness by which the prince of this world is overthrown.

Am I incapable of writing to you of heavenly things?[59] 5 No, indeed; but I am afraid to harm you, seeing you are mere babes. You must forgive me, but the chances are you could not accept what I have to say and would choke yourselves. Even in my own case, it is not because I am a prisoner and can 2

---

55 Cf. I Tim. 1:1.   56 I Cor. 4:1.

57 The reference is primarily to the Eucharist. In Ignatius' time this was still a supper meal, which the deacons served. There is also an allusion to the distribution of charity for which the deacons, under the bishop, were responsible.

58 What his flatterers said to him is either suppressed by Ignatius from fear of boasting or has fallen out of the text. We might supply, "You are a true martyr."

59 Cf. I Cor. 3:1, 2.

grasp heavenly mysteries, the ranks of the angels, the array of principalities, things visible and invisible[60]—it is not because of all that that I am a genuine disciple as yet. There is plenty missing, if we are not going to be forsaken by God.

6   I urge you, therefore—not I, but Jesus Christ's love—use only Christian food. Keep off foreign fare, by which I mean
2 heresy. For those people mingle Jesus Christ with their teachings just to gain your confidence under false pretenses. It is as if they were giving a deadly poison mixed with honey and wine, with the result that the unsuspecting victim gladly accepts it and drinks down death with fatal pleasure.

7   Be on your guard, then, against such people. This you will do by not being puffed up and by keeping very close to [our][61] God, Jesus Christ, and the bishop and the apostles' precepts.
2 Inside the sanctuary a man is pure; outside he is impure. That means: whoever does anything without bishop, presbytery, and deacons does not have a clear conscience.

8   It is not because I have heard of any such thing in your case that I write thus. No, in my love for you I am warning you ahead, since I foresee the devil's wiles. Recapture, then, your gentleness, and by faith (that's the Lord's flesh) and by love (that's Jesus Christ's blood) make yourselves new creatures.
2 Let none of you hold anything against his neighbor. Do not give the heathen opportunities whereby God's people should be scoffed at through the stupidity of a few. For, "Woe to him by whose folly my name is scoffed at before any."[62]

9   Be deaf, then, to any talk that ignores Jesus Christ, of David's lineage, of Mary; who was really born, ate, and drank; was really persecuted under Pontius Pilate; was really crucified and
2 died, in the sight of heaven and earth and the underworld. He was really raised from the dead, for his Father raised him, just as his Father will raise us, who believe on him, through Christ Jesus, apart from whom we have no genuine life.

10   And if, as some atheists (I mean unbelievers) say, his suffering was a sham (it's really *they* who are a sham!), why, then, am I a prisoner? Why do I want to fight with wild beasts? In that case I shall die to no purpose. Yes, and I am maligning the Lord too!

11   Flee, then, these wicked offshoots which produce deadly fruit. If a man taste of it, he dies outright. They are none of the
2 Father's planting.[63] For had they been, they would have shown

60 Cf. Col. 1:16.   61 Text uncertain.
62 Isa. 52:5.   63 Cf. Matt. 15:13.

themselves as branches of the cross, and borne immortal fruit. It is through the cross, by his suffering, that he summons you who are his members. A head cannot be born without limbs, since God stands for unity. It is his nature.

From Smyrna I send you my greetings in which the churches 12 of God that are here with me join. They have altogether raised my spirits—yes, completely. My very chains which I carry 2 around for Jesus Christ's sake, in my desire to get to God, exhort you, "Stay united and pray for one another!"

It is right that each one of you and especially the presbyters should encourage the bishop, in honor of the Father, Jesus Christ, and the apostles.

Out of love I want you to heed me, so that my letter will not 3 tell against you. Moreover, pray for me. By God's mercy I need your love if I am going to deserve the fate I long for,[64] and not prove a "castaway."[65]

The Smyrnaeans and Ephesians send their greetings with 13 love. Remember the church of Syria in your prayers. I am not worthy to be a member of it: I am the least of their number. Farewell in Jesus Christ. Submit to the bishop as to [God's] 2 law, and to the presbytery too. All of you, love one another with an undivided heart. My life is given for you, not only now but 3 especially when I shall get to God.[66] I am still in danger. But the Father is faithful: he will answer my prayer and yours because of Jesus Christ. Under his influence may you prove to be spotless.

[64] Text and meaning uncertain.   [65] I Cor. 9:27.
[66] I.e., when I am martyred.

TO THE ROMANS

His final letter from Smyrna, Ignatius writes to the church of Rome. Unlike his other letters, this one is not concerned with questions of heresy and Church unity. Rather is it an intensely personal document. In it he reveals most clearly the spirit of the Oriental martyr; and in a double way it is a letter to prepare his martyrdom. It is, on the one hand, a plea to the Romans not to interfere with the fate in store for him; and on the other hand it is, as it were, a letter to himself to brace him for the coming ordeal. It betrays an excess of zeal which is strange to most of us, and even repugnant to some. It must, however, be read in the light of the fact that Ignatius was tormented by the brutality of his Roman guard (his "ten leopards" as he calls them, ch. 5:1), and reacted with the intemperance of a man who had already given his life away. Some will find in the letter a perverted masochism; others will discern in it all the splendor of the martyr spirit. No one, however, will miss its burning sincerity or the courageous zeal of a disciple to suffer with his Lord.

The significant place that the Roman church held in the imagination of Ignatius is clear from the flattering inscription, with its emphasis on the extensiveness of that church's charity, and from the mention of Peter and Paul (in that order!) in ch. 4:3.

THE TEXT

Greetings in Jesus Christ, the Son of the Father, from Ignatius, the "God-inspired," to the church that is in charge of affairs in Roman quarters[67] and that the Most High Father

[67] Bizarre as some of Ignatius' expressions are, this one is most perplexing, and has exercised commentators not a little. The Greek is: *prokathētai en topō chōriou Rōmaiōn.* The words *en topō* might conceivably be taken as

and Jesus Christ, his only Son, have magnificently embraced
in mercy and love. You have been granted light both by the
will of Him who willed all that is, and by virtue of your believing in Jesus Christ, our God, and of loving him. You are a
credit to God: you deserve your renown and are to be congratulated. You deserve praise and success and are privileged to be
without blemish. Yes, you rank first in love,[68] being true to
Christ's law and stamped with the Father's name.[69] To you,
then, sincerest greetings in Jesus Christ, our God, for you cleave
to his every commandment—observing not only their letter but
their spirit—being permanently filled with God's grace and
purged of every stain alien to it.

Since God has answered my prayer to see you godly people, 1
I have gone on to ask for more. I mean, it is as a prisoner for
Christ Jesus that I hope to greet you, if indeed it be [God's]
will that I should deserve to meet my end.[70] Things are off 2
to a good start. May I have the good fortune to meet my
fate without interference! What I fear is your generosity which
may prove detrimental to me. For you can easily do what you
want to, whereas it is hard for me to get to God unless you let
me alone. I do not want you to please men, but to please God,[71] 2
just as you are doing. For I shall never again have such a chance
to get to God, nor can you, if you keep quiet, get credit for a
finer deed. For if you quietly let me alone, people will see in
me God's Word. But if you are enamored of my mere body,
I shall, on the contrary, be a meaningless noise. Grant me no 2
more than to be a sacrifice for God while there is an altar at
hand. Then you can form yourselves into a choir and sing

"in dignity," and the whole clause rendered: "Which has a precedence
of dignity over the district of the Romans." Another suggestion has been
to read *Christou* for *chōriou*: "Which presides over the district of the Romans
in the place of Christ." The most usual rendering has been: "Which
presides [has the chief seat] in the district of the region of the Romans."
This is somewhat barbarous. It also presents an ambiguity: is the presi-
dence exercised over the *whole* Church or only over the district in which
the Roman church has its seat? My own rendering is modeled on the
phrase *ho topos tēs chōras*, which means "the local circumstances of the
district." If, then, the Greek text is correct and *topos* has the sense of
"local circumstances," the expression, literally rendered, would be:
"Which has the chief seat in the local circumstances of the district of the
Romans."
68 The Roman church was early renowned for its extensive acts of charity.
69 A reference to the invocation of the Father's name over the Christian
in baptism. The implication is that the Christian by sharing the Father's
name shares too the Father's generous nature.
70 I.e., martyrdom.   71 Cf. I Thess. 2:4.

praises to the Father in Jesus Christ that God gave the bishop of Syria the privilege of reaching the sun's setting when he summoned him from its rising. It is a grand thing for my life to set on the world, and for me to be on my way to God, so that I may rise in his presence.

3   You never grudged anyone. You taught others.[72] So I want you to substantiate the lessons that you bid them heed.
2 Just pray that I may have strength of soul and body so that I may not only talk [about martyrdom], but really want it. It is not that I want merely to be called a Christian, but actually to *be* one. Yes, if I prove to be one, then I can have the name. Then, too, I shall be a convincing Christian only when the
3 world sees me no more. Nothing you can see has real value. Our God Jesus Christ, indeed, has revealed himself more clearly by returning to the Father. The greatness of Christianity lies in its being hated by the world, not in its being convincing to it.

4   I am corresponding with all the churches and bidding them all realize that I am voluntarily dying for God—if, that is, you do not interfere. I plead with you, do not do me an unseasonable kindness. Let me be fodder for wild beasts—that is how I can get to God. I am God's wheat and I am being ground
2 by the teeth of wild beasts to make a pure loaf for Christ. I would rather that you fawn on the beasts so that they may be my tomb and no scrap of my body be left. Thus, when I have fallen asleep, I shall be a burden to no one. Then I shall be a real disciple of Jesus Christ when the world sees my body no more. Pray Christ for me that by these means I may become
3 God's sacrifice. I do not give you orders like Peter and Paul. They were apostles: I am a convict. They were at liberty: I am still a slave.[73] But if I suffer, I shall be emancipated by Jesus Christ; and united to him, I shall rise to freedom.

     Even now as a prisoner, I am learning to forgo my own
5 wishes. All the way from Syria to Rome I am fighting with wild beasts, by land and sea, night and day, chained as I am to ten leopards (I mean to a detachment of soldiers), who only get worse the better you treat them. But by their injustices I am becoming a better disciple, "though not for that reason am
2 I acquitted."[74] What a thrill I shall have from the wild beasts that are ready for me! I hope they will make short work of me.

---

[72] I.e., about martyrdom, Rome being renowned for the martyrdoms of Peter and Paul.
[73] Cf. I Cor. 7:22.   [74] I Cor. 4:4.

I shall coax them on to eat me up at once and not to hold off, as sometimes happens, through fear. And if they are reluctant, I shall force them to it. Forgive me—I know what is good for 3 me. Now is the moment I am beginning to be a disciple. May nothing seen or unseen begrudge me making my way to Jesus Christ. Come fire, cross, battling with wild beasts, wrenching of bones, mangling of limbs, crushing of my whole body, cruel tortures of the devil—only let me get to Jesus Christ! Not the 6 wide bounds of earth nor the kingdoms of this world will avail me anything. "I would rather die" [75] and get to Jesus Christ, than reign over the ends of the earth. That is whom I am looking for—the One who died for us. That is whom I want—the One who rose for us. I am going through the pangs of being 2 born. Sympathize with me, my brothers! Do not stand in the way of my coming to life—do not wish death on me. Do not give back to the world one who wants to be God's; do not trick him with material things. Let me get into the clear light and manhood will be mine. Let me imitate the Passion of my God. 3 If anyone has Him in him, let him appreciate what I am longing for, and sympathize with me, realizing what I am going through.

The prince of this world wants to kidnap me and pervert my 7 godly purpose. None of you, then, who will be there, must abet him. Rather be on my side—that is, on God's. Do not talk Jesus Christ and set your heart on the world. Harbor no envy. If, 2 when I arrive, I make a different plea, pay no attention to me. Rather heed what I am now writing to you. For though alive, it is with a passion for death that I am writing to you. My Desire [76] has been crucified and there burns in me no passion for material things. There is living water [77] in me, which speaks and says inside me, "Come to the Father." I take no 3 delight in corruptible food or in the dainties of this life. What I want is God's bread, [78] which is the flesh of Christ, who came from David's line [79]; and for drink I want his blood: an immortal love feast indeed!

I do not want to live any more on a human plane. And so it 8 shall be, if you want it to. Want it to, so that you will be wanted! Despite the brevity of my letter, trust my request. Yes, Jesus 2

---

75 I Cor. 9:15.
76 A deliberate pun. Ignatius means both that Christ (on whom his love is set) is crucified, and that all earthly passion has been quelled within himself.
77 Cf. John 4:10; 7:38.   78 Cf. John 6:33.   79 Cf. Rom. 1:3.

Christ will clarify it for you and make you see I am really in earnest. He is the guileless mouth by which the Father has 3 spoken truthfully. Pray for me that I reach my goal. I have written prompted, not by human passion, but by God's will. If I suffer, it will be because you favored me. If I am rejected, it will be because you hated me.

9   Remember the church of Syria in your prayers. In my place they have God for their shepherd. Jesus Christ alone will look 2 after them[80]—he, and your love. I blush to be reckoned among them, for I do not deserve it, being the least of them and an afterthought.[81] Yet by his mercy I shall be something, if, that is, I get to God.

3   With my heart I greet you; and the churches which have welcomed me, not as a chance passer-by, but in the name of Jesus Christ, send their love. Indeed, even those that did not naturally lie on my route went ahead to prepare my welcome 10 in the different towns. I am sending this letter to you from Smyrna by those praiseworthy Ephesians.[82] With me, along 2 with many others, is Crocus—a person very dear to me. I trust you have had word about those who went ahead of me from Syria to Rome for God's glory. Tell them I am nearly there. They are all a credit to God and to you; so you should 3 give them every assistance. I am writing this to you on the twenty-fourth of August. Farewell, and hold out to the end with the patience of Jesus Christ.

[80] I.e., be their "overseer" or "bishop."
[81] Literally, an "untimely birth," an "abortion," suggested by I Cor. 15:8.
[82] I.e., who will act as postman. It would seem that some of the Ephesian delegation went ahead of Ignatius to Rome.

TO THE PHILADELPHIANS

*After leaving Smyrna, Ignatius and his guard pressed on to Troas,
where they made a halt before crossing by sea to Neapolis. It was from
Troas that Ignatius wrote his last three letters. While their themes
are the familiar ones of Church unity and heresy, their special importance
lies in the fact that they are directed to churches that Ignatius had actually
visited. (Philadelphia lay on the route he took from Laodicea to
Smyrna.) They, therefore, reflect the issues of false teaching in more
detail. The letter to the Philadelphians indicates the nature of the
Judaistic errors which had been touched upon in the letter to the Magnesians; while that to the Smyrnaeans enlarges on Docetism.*

*Two friends of Ignatius, the deacons Philo and Rheus Agathopus,
seem to have joined him in Troas after a stay in Philadelphia. They
brought news of the church there and of the fact that the dissident element had slighted them and also attacked the martyr (chs. 6:3; 11).
To answer these charges and to unmask the errors of his opponents,
Ignatius wrote his letter. An interesting feature of it is his account
of an actual debate he had with the Judaizers (ch. 8:2).*

THE TEXT

Greetings in the blood of Jesus Christ from Ignatius, the
"God-inspired," to the church of God the Father and the Lord
Jesus Christ, which is at Philadelphia in Asia—an object of the
divine mercy and firmly knit in godly unity. Yours is a deep,
abiding joy in the Passion of our Lord; and by his overflowing
mercy you are thoroughly convinced of his resurrection. You
are the very personification of eternal and perpetual joy. This
is especially true if you are at one with the bishop, and with

the presbyters and deacons, who are on his side [83] and who have been appointed by the will of Jesus Christ. By his Holy Spirit and in accordance with his own will he validated their appointment.

1 I well realize that this bishop of yours does not owe his ministry to his own efforts or to men. Nor is it to flatter his vanity that he holds this office which serves the common good. Rather does he owe it to the love of God the Father and the Lord Jesus Christ. I have been struck by his charming manner.
2 By being silent he can do more than those who chatter. For he is in tune with the commandments as a harp is with its strings. [84] For this reason I bless his godly mind, recognizing its virtue and perfection, and the way he lives in altogether godly composure, free from fitfulness and anger.

2 Since you are children of the light of truth, flee from schism and false doctrine. Where the Shepherd is, there follow like
2 sheep. [85] For there are many specious wolves who, by means of wicked pleasures, capture those who run God's race. In the
3 face of your unity, however, they will not have a chance. Keep away from bad pasturage. Jesus Christ does not cultivate it since the Father did not plant it. [86] Not that I found schism
2 among you—rather had you been sifted. [87] As many as are God's and Jesus Christ's, they are on the bishop's side; and as many as repent and enter the unity of the church, they shall be
3 God's, and thus they shall live in Jesus Christ's way. Make no mistake, my brothers, if anyone joins a schismatic he will not inherit God's Kingdom. [88] If anyone walks in the way of heresy, he is out of sympathy with the Passion.

4 Be careful, then, to observe a single Eucharist. [89] For there is one flesh of our Lord, Jesus Christ, and one cup of his blood that makes *us* one, and one altar, [90] just as there is one bishop along with the presbytery and the deacons, my

[83] The phrase seems to imply a schism, and that there were some presbyters and deacons who resisted the bishop.
[84] The meaning is not altogether clear.
[85] Cf. John 10:7 ff.   [86] Cf. Matt. 15:13.
[87] Literally, "Rather did I find filtering." The idea is that the church had gone through a purge, the heretical element being filtered or sifted out from the genuine Christians.
[88] Cf. I Cor. 6:9, 10.
[89] The implication is that the group of Judaizers held separate Eucharists, perhaps on Saturday instead of Sunday (cf. Mag. 9:1).
[90] The term "altar" implies that the Eucharistic meal had a sacrificial meaning.

fellow slaves. In that way whatever you do is in line with God's will.

My brothers, in my abounding love for you I am overjoyed 5 to put you on your guard—though it is not I, but Jesus Christ. Being a prisoner for his cause makes me the more fearful that I am still far from being perfect.[91] Yet your prayers to God will make me perfect so that I may gain that fate which I have mercifully been allotted, by taking refuge in the "Gospel," as in Jesus' flesh, and in the "Apostles," as in the presbytery of the Church.[92] And the "Prophets," let us love them too,[93] 2 because they anticipated the gospel in their preaching and hoped for and awaited Him, and were saved by believing on him. Thus they were in Jesus Christ's unity. Saints they were, and we should love and admire them, seeing that Jesus Christ vouched for them and they form a real part of the gospel of our common hope.

Now, if anyone preaches Judaism to you,[94] pay no attention 6 to him. For it is better to hear about Christianity from one of the circumcision than Judaism from a Gentile.[95] If both, moreover, fail to talk about Jesus Christ, they are to me tombstones and graves of the dead,[96] on which only human names are inscribed. Flee, then, the wicked tricks and snares of the prince 2 of this world, lest his suggestions wear you down, and you waver in your love. Rather, meet together, all of you, with a single heart. I thank my God that in my relations with you I have 3 nothing to be ashamed of. No one can brag secretly or openly that I was the slightest burden to anyone. I trust, too, that none of those I talked to will need to take what I say as a criticism of them.

Some there may be who wanted in a human way to mislead 7 me, but the Spirit is not misled, seeing it comes from God. For "it knows whence it comes and whither it goes,"[97] and exposes what is secret.[98] When I was with you I cried out,

---

91 I.e., proximity to martyrdom makes him afraid that his courage will fail him at the crucial hour.

92 A possible reference to the "Gospel" and the "Apostles" as the two divisions of the Christian writings.

93 This is an answer to the criticism of the Judaizers that Ignatius was disparaging the Old Testament.

94 It may be noted that a similar Judaizing movement in Philadelphia is attacked in Rev. 3:9.

95 Circumcision does not seem to have been included in this Judaizing movement as it had been in Galatia (Gal. 6:12).

96 Cf. Matt. 23:27.   97 Cf. John 3:8.   98 Cf. I Cor. 2:10, 11.

raising my voice—it was God's voice[99]—"Pay heed to the
2 bishop, the presbytery, and the deacons." Some, it is true,
suspected that I spoke thus because I had been told in advance
that some of you were schismatics. But I swear by Him for
whose cause I am a prisoner, that from no human channels
did I learn this. It was the Spirit that kept on preaching in
these words: "Do nothing apart from the bishop; keep your
bodies as if they were God's temple; value unity; flee schism;
imitate Jesus Christ as he imitated his Father."

8 I, then, was doing all I could, as a man utterly devoted to
unity. Where there is schism and bad feeling, God has no place.
The Lord forgives all who repent—if, that is, their repentance
brings them into God's unity and to the bishop's council. I
put my confidence in the grace of Jesus Christ. He will release
you from all your chains.[1]

2 I urge you, do not do things in cliques, but act as Christ's
disciples. When I heard some people saying, "If I don't find it
in the original documents, I don't believe it in the gospel,"
I answered them, "But it *is* written there." They retorted,
"That's just the question."[2] To my mind it is Jesus Christ who
is the original documents. The inviolable archives are his cross
and death and his resurrection and the faith that came by him.
It is by these things and through your prayers that I want to be
justified.

9 Priests are a fine thing, but better still is the High Priest[3] who
was entrusted with the Holy of Holies. He alone was entrusted
with God's secrets. He is the door to the Father.[4] Through it
there enter Abraham, Isaac, and Jacob, the prophets and
apostles and the Church. All these find their place in God's

---

[99] An instance of the "God-inspired's" prophetic utterances.

[1] Cf. Isa. 58:6.

[2] The point of the argument is that the Old Testament is the final court
of appeal. It constitutes the "original documents" which validate the
gospel. The New Testament, as a book of canonical authority, is still
in process of formation. The Bible of the primitive Church is the Septuagint. Hence a point of doctrine turns on the interpretation of Old Testament texts which are viewed as prophetically pointing to Christianity
(cf. ch. 5:2). When, however, an impasse is reached in the argument,
Ignatius makes the tradition of the gospel the final authority. He thus
opens himself to the criticism of disparaging the Old Testament (cf.
ch. 5:2).

[3] I.e., Jesus Christ. This reflects the theme elaborated in The Epistle to
the Hebrews, but Ignatius is not necessarily dependent on it. It must
have been a Christian commonplace.

[4] Cf. John 10:7, 9.

unity. But there is something special about the gospel—I 2 mean the coming of the Saviour, our Lord Jesus Christ, his Passion and resurrection. The beloved prophets announced his coming; but the gospel is the crowning achievement forever. All these things, taken together, have their value, provided you hold the faith in love.

Thanks to your prayers and to the love that you have for me 10 in Christ Jesus, news has reached me that the church at Antioch in Syria is at peace.⁵ Consequently, it would be a nice thing for you, as a church of God, to elect a deacon to go there on a mission, as God's representative, and at a formal service to congratulate them and glorify the Name. He who is privileged 2 to perform such a ministry will enjoy the blessing of Jesus Christ, and you too will win glory. If you really want to do this for God's honor, it is not impossible, just as some of the churches in the vicinity have already sent bishops; others presbyters and deacons.⁶

Now about Philo, the deacon from Cilicia. He is well spoken 11 of and right now he is helping me in God's cause, along with Rheus Agathopus—a choice person—who followed me from Syria and so has said good-by to this present life. They speak well of you, and I thank God on your account that you welcomed them, as the Lord does you. I hope that those who slighted them will be redeemed by Jesus Christ's grace. The 2 brothers in Troas send their love and greetings. It is from there that I am sending this letter to you by Burrhus.⁷ The Ephesians and Smyrnaeans have done me the honor of sending him to be with me. They in turn will be honored by Jesus Christ, on whom they have set their hope with body, soul, spirit, faith, love, and a single mind. Farewell in Christ Jesus, our common Hope.

⁵ The first indication that the persecution in Antioch, which led to Ignatius' condemnation, has blown over. The news seems to have reached him at Troas.

⁶ An indication of the deep sense of solidarity that bound together the widely scattered Christian congregations.

⁷ The Greek is ambiguous. Burrhus might be either postman or secretary.

TO THE SMYRNAEANS

At Smyrna Ignatius had come into personal contact with Docetism. To his mind this presented such an imminent danger to the church there that his letter plunges at once into the theme with a vigorous affirmation of the reality of Christ's Passion and resurrection. Only toward the end of his letter does he refer to the hospitality he had received during his stay. The number of greetings at the conclusion indicate the warm welcome he had been given.

It is worthy of notice that he adopts a harsher attitude to the Docetic heretics than to the Judaizers. The former are to be avoided altogether— he will not even mention their names (chs. 4:1; 5:3; 7:2).

Another interesting feature of this letter is the first appearance in Christian literature of the phrase "the Catholic Church" (ch. 8:2). It stands for the universal and transcendent Church in contrast to the local congregation.

THE TEXT

Heartiest greetings in all sincerity and in God's Word from Ignatius, the "God-inspired," to the church of God the Father and the beloved Jesus Christ, which is at Smyrna in Asia. By God's mercy you have received every gift; you abound in faith and love, and are lacking in no gift. [8] You are a wonderful credit to God and real saints. [9]

1　I extol Jesus Christ, the God who has granted you such wisdom. For I detected that you were fitted out with an unshak-

---

[8] Cf. I Cor. 1:7.

[9] The word literally means "bearer of sacred objects," and is taken from heathen ceremonial; cf. Ignatius, Eph. 9:2. The sacred objects here would be their virtues.

112

able faith, being nailed, as it were, body and soul to the cross of the Lord Jesus Christ, and being rooted in love by the blood of Christ. Regarding our Lord, you are absolutely convinced that on the human side he was actually sprung from David's line,[10] Son of God according to God's will and power, actually born of a virgin, baptized by John, that "all righteousness might be fulfilled by him,"[11] and actually crucified for us in 2 the flesh, under Pontius Pilate and Herod the Tetrarch. (We are part of His fruit which grew out of his most blessed Passion.)[12] And thus, by his resurrection, he raised a standard[13] to rally his saints and faithful forever—whether Jews or Gentiles—in one body of his Church.[14] For it was for our sakes 2 that he suffered all this, to save us. And he genuinely suffered, as even he genuinely raised himself. It is not as some unbelievers say, that his Passion was a sham. It's they who are a sham! Yes, and their fate will fit their fancies—they will be ghosts and apparitions.

For myself, I am convinced and believe that even after the 3 resurrection he was in the flesh. Indeed, when he came to Peter 2 and his friends, he said to them, "Take hold of me, touch me and see that I am not a bodiless ghost."[15] And they at once touched him and were convinced, clutching his body and his very breath. For this reason they despised death itself, and proved its victors. Moreover, after the resurrection he ate and drank with them [16] as a real human being, although in spirit he was united with the Father.

I urge these things on you, my friends, although I am well 4 aware that you agree with me. But I warn you in advance against wild beasts in human shapes. You must not only refuse to receive them, but if possible, you must avoid meeting them. Just pray for them that they may somehow repent, hard as that is. Yet Jesus Christ, our genuine life, has the power to bring it about. If what our Lord did is a sham, so is my being in chains. 2 Why, then, have I given myself up completely to death, fire, sword, and wild beasts? For the simple reason that near the sword means near God. To be with wild beasts means to be with God. But it must all be in the name of Jesus Christ. To

---

10 Cf. Rom. 1:3.   11 Cf. Matt. 3:15.

12 Ignatius changes his metaphors with alarming abruptness. The cross here is a tree; in the next sentence it is a military rallying standard.

13 Cf. Isa. 5:26; 11:12.   14 Cf. Eph. 2:16.

15 A possible allusion to Luke 24:39. The latter part of the saying occurs in The Preaching of Peter and in The Gospel According to the Hebrews.

16 Cf. Acts. 10:41.

share in his Passion I go through everything, for he who became the perfect man gives me the strength.[17]

5 · Yet in their ignorance some deny him—or rather have been denied by him, since they advocate death rather than the truth. The prophets and the law of Moses have failed to convince them—nay, to this very day the gospel and the sufferings of each one of us have also failed, for they class our sufferings with 2 Christ's.[18] What good does anyone do me by praising me and then reviling my Lord by refusing to acknowledge that he carried around live flesh? He who denies this has completely 3 disavowed him and carries a corpse around. The names of these people, seeing they are unbelievers, I am not going to write down. No, far be it from me even to recall them until they repent and acknowledge the Passion, which means our resurrection.

6 Let no one be misled: heavenly beings, the splendor of angels, and principalities, visible and invisible, if they fail to believe in Christ's blood, they too are doomed. "Let him accept it who can."[19] Let no one's position swell his head, for faith and love are everything—there is nothing preferable to them.

2 Pay close attention to those who have wrong notions about the grace of Jesus Christ, which has come to us, and note how at variance they are with God's mind. They care nothing about love: they have no concern for widows or orphans, for the oppressed, for those in prison or released, for the hungry or the 7 thirsty. They hold aloof from the Eucharist and from services of prayer, because they refuse to admit that the Eucharist is the flesh of our Saviour Jesus Christ,[20] which suffered for our sins and which, in his goodness, the Father raised [from the dead]. Consequently those who wrangle and dispute God's gift face death. They would have done better to love and so share 2 in the resurrection. The right thing to do, then, is to avoid such people and to talk about them neither in private nor in public. Rather pay attention to the prophets and above all to the gospel. There we get a clear picture of the Passion and see that the resurrection has really happened.

[17] Cf. Phil. 4:13.
[18] Literally, "They have the same idea about us." The sense would seem to be that Christian martyrdom is meaningless as an imitation of the Christ if he never really suffered.
[19] Matt. 19:12.
[20] It is not clear whether the Docetics abandoned the Eucharistic rite altogether, or whether they held separate Eucharists, giving them a different meaning to suit their views.

Flee from schism as the source of mischief. You should all 8
follow the bishop as Jesus Christ did the Father. Follow, too,
the presbytery as you would the apostles; and respect the
deacons as you would God's law. Nobody must do anything
that has to do with the Church without the bishop's approval.
You should regard that Eucharist as valid which is celebrated
either by the bishop or by someone he authorizes. Where the 2
bishop is present, there let the congregation gather, just as
where Jesus Christ is, there is the Catholic Church. Without
the bishop's supervision, no baptisms or love feasts are permitted. On the other hand, whatever he approves pleases God
as well. In that way everything you do will be on the safe side
and valid. It is well for us to come to our senses at last, while 9
we still have a chance to repent and turn to God. It is a fine
thing to acknowledge God and the bishop. He who pays the
bishop honor has been honored by God. But he who acts without the bishop's knowledge is in the devil's service.

By God's grace may you have an abundance of everything! 2
You deserve it. You have brought me no end of comfort; may
Jesus Christ do the same for you! Whether I was absent or
present, you gave me your love. May God requite you! If for
his sake you endure everything, you will get to him.

It was good of you to welcome Philo and Rheus Agathopus 10
as deacons of the Christ God. They accompanied me in God's
cause, and they thank the Lord on your behalf that you provided them every comfort. I can assure you you will lose
nothing by it. Prisoner as I am, I am giving my life for you— 2
not that it's worth much! You did not scorn my chains and were
not ashamed of them.[21] Neither will Jesus Christ be ashamed
of you. You can trust him implicitly!

Your prayers have reached out as far as the church at Antioch 11
in Syria. From there I have come, chained with these magnificent chains, and I send you all greetings. I do not, of course,
deserve to be a member of that church, seeing I am the least
among them. Yet it was [God's] will to give me the privilege—
not, indeed, for anything I had done of my own accord, but by
his grace. Oh, I want that grace to be given me in full measure,
that by your prayers I may get to God! Well, then, so that your 2
own conduct may be perfect on earth and in heaven, it is right
that your church should honor God by sending a delegate in
his name to go to Syria and to congratulate them on being at
peace, on recovering their original numbers, and on having

21 Cf. II Tim. 1:16.

3 their own corporate life restored to them. To my mind that is what God would want you to do: to send one of your number with a letter, and thus join with them in extolling the calm which God has granted them, and the fact that they have already reached a haven, thanks to your prayers. Seeing you are perfect, your intentions must be perfect as well.[22] Indeed, if you want to do what is right, God stands ready to give you his help.

12 The brothers in Troas send their love to you. From there I am sending this letter to you by Burrhus. You joined with your Ephesian brothers in sending him to be with me, and he has altogether raised my spirits. I wish everyone would be like him, since he is a model of what God's ministry should be. God's
2 grace will repay him for all he has done for me. Greetings to your bishop [23] (he is such a credit to God!), and to your splendid presbytery and to my fellow slaves the deacons, and to you all, every one of you, in Jesus Christ's name, in his flesh and blood, in his Passion and resurrection, both bodily and spiritual, and in unity—both God's and yours. Grace be yours, and mercy, peace, and endurance, forever.

13 Greetings to the families of my brothers, along with their wives and children, and to the virgins enrolled with the widows.[24] I bid you farewell in the Father's power. Philo,
2 who is with me, sends you greetings. Greetings to Tavia's family. I want her to be firmly and thoroughly grounded in faith and love. Greetings to Alce, who means a great deal to me, and to the inimitable Daphnus and to Eutecnus and to each one of you. Farewell in God's grace.

[22] Cf. Phil. 3:15.
[23] I.e., Polycarp, to whom the following letter is addressed.
[24] The meaning is not altogether clear. It appears, however, that the order of widows, established for works of charity (cf. I Tim. 5:9), sometimes included virgins.

TO POLYCARP

Along with the letter to the church of Smyrna, Ignatius wrote to its bishop, Polycarp. One of the most distinguished figures of the Early Church, who crowned his old age with martyrdom, Polycarp had given Ignatius a generous welcome which the latter mentions in other letters (Eph., ch. 21; Mag., ch. 15). This is an intimate and personal letter—the shortest of them all. Polycarp was the younger of the two men, perhaps in his early forties, and Ignatius is characteristically forthright in his advice. That the latter was most highly regarded by the bishop of Smyrna is clear from his own letter to the Philippians and from his making a collection of Ignatius' correspondence (Polycarp, Phil., ch. 13).

The sense of Christian solidarity which bound together the local churches is evident from the various delegations which Ignatius received in Smyrna. The suggestion, however, in the letter to the Philadelphians and repeated in this one to Polycarp, that the churches should send delegates as far as Syrian Antioch to congratulate the Christians on the cessation of persecution, is a telling witness to the universal consciousness of the local congregations. In a day when travel was neither easy nor free from danger, the dispatching of such messengers reflects the deep unity of the Christian brotherhood.

THE TEXT

Heartiest greetings from Ignatius, the "God-inspired," to Polycarp, who is bishop of the church at Smyrna—or rather who has God the Father and the Lord Jesus Christ for *his* bishop.

While I was impressed with your godly mind, which is fixed, 1 as it were, on an immovable rock, I am more than grateful that I was granted the sight of your holy face. God grant I may 2

never forget it! By the grace which you have put on, I urge you
to press forward in your race and to urge everybody to be saved.
Vindicate your position by giving your whole attention to its
material and spiritual sides.[25] Make unity your concern—there
is nothing better than that. Lend everybody a hand, as the
Lord does you. "Out of love be patient"[25] with everyone, as
3 indeed you are. Devote yourself to continual prayer. Ask for
increasing insight. Be ever on the watch by keeping your spirit
alert. Take a personal interest in those you talk to, just as God
does. "Bear the diseases"[27] of everyone, like an athlete in
perfect form. The greater the toil, the greater the gain.

2   It is no credit to you if you are fond of good pupils. Rather
by your gentleness subdue those who are annoying. Not every
wound is healed by the same plaster. Relieve spasms of pain
2 with poultices. In all circumstances be "wise as a serpent,"
and perpetually "harmless as a dove."[28] The reason you have
a body as well as a soul is that you may win the favor of the
visible world.[29] But ask that you may have revelations of
what is unseen. In that way you will lack nothing and have an
abundance of every gift.

3   Just as pilots demand winds and a storm-tossed sailor a
harbor, so times like these demand a person like you. With
your help we will get to God. As God's athlete, be sober. The
prize, as you very well know, is immortality and eternal life.
Bound as I am with chains that you kissed,[30] I give my whole
self for you—cheap sacrifice though it is!

3   You must not be panic-stricken by those who have an air of
credibility but who teach heresy.[31] Stand your ground like an
anvil under the hammer. A great athlete must suffer blows to
conquer. And especially for God's sake must we put up with
2 everything, so that he will put up with us. Show more enthusiasm
than you do. Mark the times. Be on the alert for him who is
above time, the Timeless, the Unseen, the One who became

25 The reference is to the double nature of the episcopal office in the Early
Church. The bishop was at once the guardian of the common chest fund
for the needy and the spiritual father of his congregation.
26 Eph. 4:2.   27 Matt. 8:17.   28 Matt. 10:16.
29 The idea would seem to be that having a body leads one to seek a proper
harmony with all persons and things belonging to the material world.
This sentiment is the opposite of the Docetic, which saw in matter the
source of evil.
30 It is possible that the faithful kissed the chains of the martyr, though a
more general sense ("the chains which you did not despise and in which
you delighted") may be intended.
31 Cf. I Tim. 1:3; 6:3.

visible for our sakes, who was beyond touch and passion, yet who for our sakes became subject to suffering, and endured everything for us.

Widows must not be neglected. After the Lord you must be 4 their protector. Do not let anything be done without your consent; and do not do anything without God's, as indeed you do not. Stand firm. Hold services more often. Seek out every- 2 body by name. Do not treat slaves and slave girls contemp- 3 tuously.[32] Neither must they grow insolent. But for God's glory they must give more devoted service, so that they may obtain from God a better freedom. Moreover, they must not be over-anxious to gain their freedom at the community's expense, lest they prove to be slaves of selfish passion. Flee from such 5 wicked practices—nay, rather, preach against them.

Tell my sisters to love the Lord and to be altogether con-tented with their husbands. Similarly urge my brothers in the name of Jesus Christ "to love their wives as the Lord loves the Church."[33] If anyone can live in chastity for the honor of 2 the Lord's flesh, let him do so without ever boasting. If he boasts of it, he is lost; and if he is more highly honored than the bishop, his chastity is as good as forfeited. It is right for men and women who marry to be united with the bishop's approval. In that way their marriage will follow God's will and not the prompt-ings of lust. Let everything be done so as to advance God's honor.

Pay attention to the bishop so that God will pay attention 6 to you. I give my life as a sacrifice (poor as it is) for those who are obedient to the bishop, the presbyters, and the deacons. Along with them may I get my share of God's reward! Share your hard training together—wrestle together, run together, suffer together, go to bed together, get up together, as God's stewards, assessors, and assistants. Give satisfaction to Him in 2 whose ranks you serve and from whom you get your pay.[34] Let none of you prove a deserter. Let your baptism be your arms; your faith, your helmet; your love, your spear; your endurance, your armor.[35] Let your deeds be your deposits, so that you will eventually get back considerable savings.[36]

---

[32] Cf. I Tim. 6:2.   [33] Eph. 5:25, 29.
[34] Cf. II Tim. 2:4.   [35] Cf. Eph. 6:11–17.
[36] The metaphor is taken from the custom of withholding from soldiers a part of their wages and depositing it in a savings bank, from which they were paid on their discharge. The military metaphors in this passage, and the curious number of Latin words, are due to the fact that Ignatius had a guard of ten Roman soldiers.

Be patient, then, and gentle with each other, as God is with you. May I always be happy about you!

7   News has reached me that, thanks to your prayers, the church at Antioch in Syria is now at peace. At this I have taken new courage and, relying on God, I have set my mind at rest—assuming, that is, I may get to God through suffering,

2 and at the resurrection prove to be your disciple. So, my dear Polycarp (and how richly God has blessed you!), you ought to call a most religious council and appoint somebody whom you regard as especially dear and diligent, and who can act as God's messenger. You should give him the privilege of going to Syria and of advancing God's glory by extolling your untiring gener-

3 osity. A Christian does not control his own life, but gives his whole time to God. This is God's work, and when you have completed it, it will be yours as well. For God's grace gives me confidence that you are ready to act generously when it comes to his business. It is because I am well aware of your earnest sincerity that I limit my appeal to so few words.

8   I have been unable to write to all the churches because I am sailing at once (so God has willed it) from Troas to Neapolis. I want you, therefore, as one who has the mind of God, to write to the churches ahead and to bid them to do the same. Those who can should send representatives, while the others should send letters by your own delegates. In that way you will win renown, such as you deserve, by an act that will be remembered forever.

2   Greetings to every one of you personally, and to the widow of Epitropus³⁷ with her children and her whole family. Greetings to my dear Attalus. Greetings to the one who is to be chosen to go to Syria. Grace will ever be with him and with

3 Polycarp who sends him. I bid you farewell as always in our God, Jesus Christ. May you abide in him and so share in the divine unity and be under God's care. Greetings to Alce, who means a great deal to me. Farewell in the Lord.

³⁷ It is possible that Epitropus is not a proper name but a title, so that the phrase means "the widow of the procurator."

The Letter of Polycarp,
Bishop of Smyrna,
to the Philippians

INTRODUCTION

AT THE TIME OF HIS MARTYRDOM POLYCARP, THE bishop of Smyrna, confessed that he had been a Christian for eighty-six years. Since the date of his martyrdom can be fixed with reasonable certainty as occurring in A.D. 155 or 156, his birth could therefore not have been later than the year 69 or 70. Thus his career spanned that critical era of the Church's development which witnessed, after the passing of its apostolic founders and missionaries, the menacing growth of persecution by the Roman State and the emergence of the Docetic and Gnostic heresies, and—in response to this situation —the establishment of monepiscopacy and the crystallization of the canon of New Testament writings. In these momentous issues Polycarp was destined to be intimately involved and to exercise upon them the force of his commanding personality and influence.

Yet, strange to say, our sources for the life of Polycarp are extremely meager. His own extant letter to the church in Philippi and the eyewitness account of his martyrdom reveal much about his character and his qualities of heart and mind, but they furnish us few data regarding the events of his life. There is extant in a tenth century manuscript (Cod. Parisiensis Graec., 1452) an anonymous *Vita* of Polycarp. Its historical value is much debated. All the modern editors of the work, Duchesne, Funk, Lightfoot, and the eminent Bollandist Delehaye, consider it to be fictitious, a composition of the end of the fourth century. They incline to attribute it to the Pionius who signed his name in the colophon of the Martyrdom of Polycarp. Several historical critics, on the other hand, Corssen, Schwartz, Streeter, and Cadoux, attribute the *Vita* to the presbyter and martyr Pionius of Smyrna, who suffered for his faith in the Decian persecution. However that may be, the author of the *Vita* betrays no knowledge of the traditions about Polycarp and his relations with John, the disciple of the Lord, which we have from Irenaeus and Eusebius. His own sources and traditions relate the foundation of the church in Smyrna to a disciple of Paul, one Strataeus, and name a certain Bucolus as the immediate predecessor of Polycarp as bishop of Smyrna, under whose tutelage Polycarp was prepared and trained. Inasmuch as there is so much uncertainty as to the reliability of "Pionius" with regard to his historical information, the argument for his trustworthiness rests largely upon philological and theological considerations. These tend to confirm the opinion of those who assign it to the later date and deny its usefulness in ascertaining any certain data with respect to Polycarp's life. We are on more solid ground if we rely upon the statements of those who actually knew Polycarp in person.

Our earliest testimony to Polycarp is contained in the letters that Ignatius addressed from Troas to the church in Smyrna and to Polycarp during the course of his dolorous journey to martyrdom at Rome. Ignatius' death is generally dated in the latter part of the reign of Trajan (A.D. 98–117). Hence Polycarp must have been somewhere between forty and fifty years old at the time. He was already bishop in Smyrna; but the tone of Ignatius' letter to him suggests that he had not been in this office for very long—or, at any rate, he had not as yet exerted his authority with sufficient aggressiveness. The warning given by the intrepid martyr to his younger episcopal colleague respecting the grave danger of the new Docetic heresy to the faith and unity of his flock was not without its effect.

Not long after Ignatius' departure from the Middle East— possibly before he had reached Rome—Polycarp penned his letter to the Philippians, in answer to several requests from them. One of these had to do with the collection of copies of Ignatius' letters and also with the delegation of Church representatives which Ignatius had requested his friends in Asia and Macedonia to send to Syria for assistance to his own bereaved and distressed flock he had left behind. Another concerned an unfortunate incident that had recently occurred in the church at Philippi. One of its presbyters, named Valens, and his wife, had become involved in certain dishonest money matters, and had been excommunicated. Polycarp was asked for advice in the pastoral handling of this affair. In addition there was the problem of heresy, which had so deeply concerned Ignatius.

Brief as it is, Polycarp's letter gives us the measure of the man. He was simple, humble, and direct. There was nothing subtle about him, or pretentious. He does not appear to have had much in the way of formal education. His Greek is without style, without the faintest touch of rhetoric, without learned allusion. He is not versed, as he himself admitted, in the Scriptures, i.e., the Old Testament. But he had meditated much on Christian writings; his letter is a veritable mosaic of quotation and allusion to them. Modern critics are fond of calling him "unoriginal." It is true; he shows not the slightest interest in theological or philosophical speculation. He never argues with heresy, but treats it uncompromisingly with disdain and contempt. Any deviation from the norm of "the faith once delivered" provokes him to strong language. Yet if he appears harsh and unyielding with offenders against the truth as he has received it, Polycarp can be gentle and compassionate with human failings in the moral order—as in the case, for example, of the presbyter Valens. He had the insight and the method, as it were instinctively, of the true pastor of souls. And the simplicity and honesty of his own character won him the veneration of his church and the respect of the heathen populace of Smyrna.

Of his later years, we possess only a few reminiscences of Irenaeus, who as a young lad came under Polycarp's tutelage.[1] Only a year or two before his martyrdom the aged bishop made a journey to Rome to confer with Pope Anicetus regarding the disagreement between the Asian Christians and the church of Rome over the proper date for the celebration of Easter. Though neither bishop could persuade the other to change his own tradition they both maintained in amicable unity the fellowship of communion. While in Rome, Polycarp was instrumental in converting many disciples of Marcion and the Gnostic Valentinus to orthodoxy, by his personal testimony to the apostolic faith he had received from disciples of the Lord. It was possibly during this Roman visit also that Polycarp had

---

[1] Irenaeus, *Adv. haer.* III. 3:4 (reproduced in Eusebius, *Hist. eccl.* IV. 14:3–8); his letters to Florinus and to Victor of Rome in Eusebius, *Hist. eccl.* V. 20:4–8 and V. 24:16, 17 respectively. The date of Irenaeus' birth is uncertain, but it was probably not earlier than A.D. 130 or later than 140. It is quite possible that Irenaeus was in Rome at the time of Polycarp's visit there.

his famous encounter with Marcion himself and called him "the first-born of Satan." Discussion of the Martyrdom of Polycarp will be deferred for the introduction to that work.

Irenaeus tells us that Polycarp wrote numerous letters of exhortation and admonition to churches and individuals, but the only one he cites specifically is the Letter to the Philippians. Eusebius also knows only of the Philippian letter. Its authenticity cannot be seriously questioned.[2] The original Greek text of the letter, however, has not been preserved in its entirety, but only the first nine chapters. These are contained in nine late Greek manuscripts, in which ch. 9:2 is followed immediately by an incomplete text of the Epistle of Barnabas, which begins at ch. 5:8. All these manuscripts are derived from a single archetype. The eleventh century Codex Vaticanus Graecus 859 is the best of the group. The thirteenth chapter of the letter (minus the last sentence) is preserved in Greek by Eusebius' quotation (*Hist. eccl.* III. 36: 13–15). For the remainder of the letter we are dependent upon an old Latin translation preserved with the Latin manuscripts that contain the longer recension of the Ignatian epistles. Comparison with the extant Greek pieces shows that the Latin version is a trustworthy translation of the original.

The unity of the letter has been the subject of considerable debate since the publication of Dr. P. N. Harrison's exhaustive study. According to Dr. Harrison, ch. 13, and possibly also ch. 14, was written shortly after Ignatius left Philippi and before his martyrdom at Rome. Chapters 1 to 12, on the other hand, form a separate letter, written some years later, about A.D. 135–137. The references to Ignatius in this letter would appear to assume that he was long since dead. Moreover, Dr. Harrison believes that the heresy attacked in ch. 7 is that of Marcion, and there is no evidence that Marcion had appeared on the scene so early as the end of Trajan's reign. Furthermore, the extensive use of New Testament writings in this letter would suggest a date closer to the middle of the second century.

Dr. Harrison's thesis is open to rebuttal. It was pointed out by Lightfoot long ago that the Latin phrase, "Those who are with him," in ch. 13:2, represents a Greek idiom—"those with him"—and that it cannot therefore be used as proof that Ignatius was still alive when Polycarp penned this line. The statements of ch. 7 can be applied to Marcion only with some

---

[2] Note that the opening address of the Martyrdom of Polycarp closely imitates the opening address of Polycarp's letter.

manipulation of their meaning. The fact that we know Polycarp to have called Marcion "the first-born of Satan" does not prove that Polycarp would not have used the phrase for others also—given his fondness for such exclamations about heretics, as Irenaeus attests.[3] But the principal interest of Polycarp's letter is his use of early Christian writings; yet even so it is not such as to exclude a dating of his letter in the second decade of the second century, but on the contrary it would seem to confirm the traditional view.

Polycarp was acquainted with the Synoptic Gospels and The Acts. But his citations of sayings of Jesus are often rather freely made. His conflation of quotations may be due, of course, to his citing them from memory. He is well versed in the Pauline Epistles, and his references include Hebrews and the Pastorals. His special favorite, however, is I Peter; and of the other catholic epistles he knows James and I and II John. Revelation is not cited by him, but its chiliastic point of view was not congenial to him. He makes much use of I Clement, and there are allusions to the Ignatian letters of the sort one would expect from fairly recent acquaintance with them. The surprising thing is the absence of any definite reference to the Gospel of John.[4]

Irenaeus repeatedly states that Polycarp had received his tradition of faith from John, the disciple of the Lord, and other apostles, and that "apostles in Asia" had appointed him to his bishopric.[5] For Irenaeus this was sufficient guarantee of the attribution of the corpus of "Johannine" writings in the New Testament to the apostle John, son of Zebedee. Yet he never, in so many words, states that Polycarp himself made this identification. There is certainly no reason to distrust the information that Polycarp had enjoyed personal converse, as did also his contemporary Papias, bishop of Hierapolis, with companions of Jesus, including a disciple named John; though Polycarp himself never mentions his name. But it is more than likely that Irenaeus has confused the true identity of this "John." Into the involved problem of the authorship of the Johannine writings we cannot enter here. We know from archaeological evidence (published since Dr. Harrison's book) that the Gospel of John was in circulation early in

---

[3] See his letter to Florinus in Eusebius, *Hist. eccl.* V. 20:7.
[4] Some critics have seen an allusion to John 5:21 or 6:39, 44, in ch. 5:2: "Inasmuch as he promised to raise us from the dead."
[5] See also Tertullian, *De praescr. haer.* 32. 2.

the second century.[6] There is reason to suppose that both Ignatius and Papias were familiar with it, in which case it is hardly possible that Polycarp should have been ignorant of it. We know that he used The First Epistle of John. His silence with respect to the Fourth Gospel remains an enigma.

On one other subject, namely, the monarchical episcopate, the silence of Polycarp is also problematic. This has usually been explained as due to the absence of this organizational arrangement in the church at Philippi. Even so, one would have expected Polycarp to follow the example of Ignatius in urging monepiscopacy as a safeguard of unity.

[6] See C. H. Roberts, *An Unpublished Fragment of the Fourth Gospel in the John Rylands Library* (Manchester, 1935), and the remarks of H. I. Bell, *Recent Discoveries of Biblical Papyri*, pp. 20, 21 (Oxford, 1937).

BOOKS

TEXTS

The best edition of the text, and the one used for the translation in this volume, is that of Karl Bihlmeyer, *Die apostolischen Väter*, Neubearbeitung der Funkschen Ausgabe, I Teil (Sammlung ausgewählter kirchen- und dogmengeschichtlicher Quellenschriften, II Reihe, I Heft, I Teil), Tübingen, 1924. This is a third revision of text published by F. X. Funk, *Patres apostolici*, 2 vols., Tübingen, 1901. Absolutely indispensable, however, is the monumental edition of J. B. Lightfoot, *The Apostolic Fathers*, Part 2: "S. Ignatius, S. Polycarp," Revised Texts with Introductions, Notes, Dissertations, and Translations, 3 vols., 2d ed., London, 1889. An *editio minor* of Lightfoot was edited by J. R. Harmer, *The Apostolic Fathers*, Revised Texts with Short Introductions and English Translations, London, 1912. Other texts which should be consulted are: Th. Zahn, *Ignatii et Polycarpi epistulae martyria fragmenta* (Patrum apostolicorum opera, ed. O. de Gebhardt, A. Harnack, and Th. Zahn, Vol. II), Leipzig, 1876; Adolfus Hilgenfeld, *Ignatii Antiocheni et Polycarpi Smyrnaei epistulae et martyria edidit et adnotationibus instruxit*, C. A. Schwetschke and Sons, Berlin, 1902; Kirsopp Lake, *The Apostolic Fathers*, With an English Translation (Loeb Classical Library), London, 1912, Vol. I, pp. 280–301; Auguste Lelong, Les Pères apostoliques, III, *Ignace d'Antioche et Polycarpe de Smyrne Épîtres, Martyre de Polycarpe*, pp. 108–128. Texte grec, traduction française, introduction et index (Textes et documents pour l'étude historique du Christianisme, 12, ed. H. Hemmer and P. Lejay), 2d ed., Paris, 1927; G. Bosio, *I Padri apostolici* (Corona Patrum Salesiana, Series Graeca, 14), Società editrice internazionale, Turin, 1943, Vol. II, pp. 163–201.

TRANSLATIONS AND COMMENTARIES

In addition to the translations included in the above texts by Lightfoot, Lake, Lelong, and Bosio, the following should be consulted: English: Alexander Roberts, James Donaldson, and F. Crombie, *The Writings of the Apostolic Fathers* (Ante-Nicene Christian Library, I), Edinburgh, reprinted in the American edition, The Ante-Nicene Fathers, ed. A. Cleveland Coxe, Vol. I, Buffalo, 1886. The Supplement Volume of this latter edition (1887) contains a "Bibliographical Synopsis," by E. C. Richardson, which gives copious bibliography of the older editions and works on Polycarp's Letter, pp. 7–10. Blomfield Jackson, *St. Polycarp, Bishop of Smyrna* (Early Church Classics), S.P.C.K., London, 1898, is based on Lightfoot's translation and commentary. Recent translations, all of them based on Bihlmeyer's text, are: *The Apostolic Fathers*, translated by Francis X. Glimm, Joseph M.-F. Morique, and Gerald G. Walsh, pp. 131–143 (The Fathers of the Church), Cima Publishing Company, New York, 1947; James A. Kleist, *The Didache, the Epistle of Barnabas, the Epistles and the Martyrdom of St. Polycarp, the Fragments of Papias, the Epistle to Diognetus*, Newly Translated and Annotated (Ancient Christian Writers, No. 6), pp. 69–82, Newman Press, Westminster, Maryland, 1948; Edgar J. Goodspeed, *The Apostolic Fathers: An American Translation*, pp. 237–244, Harper & Brothers, New York, 1950.

German translations: Franz Zeller, *Die apostolischen Väter*, aus dem griechischen übersetzt (Bibliothek der Kirchenväter, 35), Kempten and Munich, 1918; Walter Bauer, *Die apostolischen Väter* (Ergänzungsband, Handbuch zum Neuen Testament, ed. Hans Lietzmann), pp. 282–298, Tübingen, 1923; and G. Krüger in Edgar Hennecke, *Neutestamentliche Apokryphen*, 2d ed., pp. 518–540, Tübingen, 1924.

REFERENCE BOOKS AND DICTIONARY ARTICLES

An *index verborum* of the Greek text is included in Edgar J. Goodspeed, *Index Patristicus, sive clavis patrum apostolicorum operum*, Leipzig, 1907, based on the editions of Gebhardt, Harnack and Zahn, Funk, and Lightfoot. The New Testament citations in Polycarp's Letter are studied in *The New Testament in the Apostolic Fathers*, By a Committee of the Oxford Society of Historical Theology, pp. 84–104, Oxford, 1905. Basic introductions will be found in Adolf Harnack, *Geschichte der altchrist-lichen Literatur bis Eusebius*, I Teil, pp. 69–75, II Teil, Vol. I, pp. 381–406, Leipzig, 1893 and 1897; Th. Zahn, *Forschungen zur Geschichte des neutestamentliche Kanons und der altkirchlichen Literatur*, X Teile, Erlangen and Leipzig, 1881–1929, especially Vol. IV (1891), "Zur Biographie des Polykarpus und des Irenäus," pp. 249–283, and Vol. VI (1900), "Polykarp von Smyrna," pp. 94–109; Otto Bardenhewer, *Geschichte der altkirchlichen Literatur*, Vol. I, 2d ed., pp. 160–170, Freiburg im Breisgau, 1913. For the general history of the period, see Rudolf Knopf, *Das nachapostolische Zeitalter*, Geschichte der christlichen Gemeinden vom Beginn der Flavierdynastie bis zum Ende Hadrians, Tübingen, 1905.

Encyclopedia articles include: H. T. Andrews, in *The Encyclopædia Britannica*, 14th ed. rev., Vol. 18, pp. 180–182; George Salmon, in *A Dictionary of Christian Biography*, ed. William Smith and Henry Wace, Vol. IV (1887), pp. 423–431; N. Bonwetsch, in *The New Schaff-Herzog Encyclopedia of Religious Knowledge*, Vol. IX (1911), pp. 118–120; P. Batiffol, in *Dictionary of the Apostolic Church*, ed. James Hastings, Vol. II (1918), 242–247; and G. Fritz, in *Dictionnaire de théologie catholique*, ed. A. Vacant, E. Mangenot, and É. Amann, XII (1935), pp. 2515–2520.

BOOKS, MONOGRAPHS, AND ARTICLES

The fundamental study is that of P. N. Harrison, *Polycarp's Two Epistles to the Philippians*, Cambridge University Press, 1936. Harrison gives an exhaustive survey of the history of the criticism of Polycarp's Letter, with complete bibliography, and also furnishes an annotated text and translations. The following reviews of Harrison's book are worth consulting: K. Lake, *The Journal of Biblical Literature*, 56 (1937), pp. 72–75; C. J. Cadoux, *The Journal of Theological Studies*, 38 (1937), pp. 267–270; Claude Jenkins, *Theology*, 35 (1937), pp. 367–370; Stephen Liberty, *Church Quarterly Review*, 247 (1937), pp. 141–147; É. Amann, *Revue des sciences religieuses*, 17 (1937), pp. 344–348; H.-C. Puech, *Revue de l'histoire des religions*, 119 (1939), pp. 96–102; A. C. Headlam, "The Epistle of Polycarp to the Philippians," *Church Quarterly Review*, 281 (1945), pp. 1–25.

Brief summary introductions may be found in Otto Pfleiderer, *Primitive Christianity, Its Writings and Teachings in Their*

Historical Connections, translated by W. Montgomery, G. P. Putnam's Sons, New York, 1906–1911, Vol. III (1910), pp. 365–372; Alfred Loisy, "La Didaché et les lettres des Pères apostoliques," *Revue d'histoire et de littérature religieuses*, N. S. 7 (1921), pp. 433–480; Burnett Hillman Streeter, *The Primitive Church*, The Macmillan Company, New York, 1929, pp. 92–100, 279–285; C. P. S. Clarke, *St. Ignatius and St. Polycarp* (Little Books on Religion, No. 70), S.P.C.K., London, 1930; Cecil John Cadoux, *Ancient Smyrna, A History of the City from the Earliest Times to 324 A.D.*, Basil Blackwell, Oxford, 1938, pp. 303–367; Robert M. Grant, "Polycarp of Smyrna," *Anglican Theological Review*, 28 (1946), pp. 137–148. Polycarp's place in the development of monepiscopacy is studied by Massey H. Shepherd, Jr., "Smyrna in the Ignatian Letters: A Study in Church Order," *The Journal of Religion*, 20 (1940), pp. 141–159.

QUOTATIONS IN EUSEBIUS

The best text of Eusebius is that of Eduard Schwartz, *Eusebius Werke*, II: *Die Kirchengeschichte*, I Teil, Die Bücher I bis V (Die griechischen christlichen Schriftsteller der ersten drei Jahrhunderte), Leipzig, 1903. One should also consult the voluminous notes in the English translation of Hugh Jackson Lawlor and John Ernest Leonard Oulton, *Eusebius, Bishop of Caesarea, The Ecclesiastical History and the Martyrs of Palestine*, Translated with Introduction and Notes, 2 vols., S.P.C.K., London, 1928 (see the index under "Polycarp").

The *Vita Polycarpi*. Convenient editions of the life ascribed to Pionius may be found in Lightfoot's edition, Vol. II, 2, pp. 1005–1047, 1068–1086; and in Franciscus Diekamp, *Patres apostolici*, Editionem Funkianam novis curis in lucem emisit, Vol. II, Tübingen, 1913. Discussions of its historical worth: P. Corssen, "Die Vita Polycarpi," *Zeitschrift für die neutestamentliche Wissenschaft*, 5 (1904), pp. 266–302; A. Hilgenfeld, "Eine dreiste Fälschung in alter Zeit und deren neueste Verteidigung," *Zeitschrift für wissenschaftliche Theologie*, 48 (N.F. XIII; 1905), pp. 444–458; Hippolyte Delehaye, *Les Passions des martyrs et les genres littéraires*, Brussels, 1921, pp. 11–59 ("L'Hagiographie de Smyrne"); Streeter, *op. cit.*, pp. 271–278; and Cadoux, *op. cit.*, pp. 306–310. See also the bibliography on the Martyrdom of Polycarp in this volume.

The Letter of Saint Polycarp,
Bishop of Smyrna,
to the Philippians

THE TEXT

Polycarp and the presbyters with him, to the church of God that sojourns at Philippi; may mercy and peace be multiplied to you from God Almighty and Jesus Christ, our Saviour. [7]

I rejoice with you greatly in our Lord [8] Jesus Christ, in that [1] you have welcomed the models of true Love, [9] and have helped on their way, [10] as opportunity was given you, those men who are bound in fetters which become the saints, [11] which are indeed the diadems of the true elect of God and of our Lord. And I also rejoice because the firm root of your faith, famous [2] from the earliest times, [12] still abides and bears fruit for our Lord Jesus Christ, who endured for our sins even to face death, "whom God raised up, having loosed the pangs of Hades." [13] In him, "though you have not seen him, you believe with [3] inexpressible and exalted joy" [14]—joy that many have longed to experience—knowing that "you are saved by grace, not because of works," [15] namely, by the will of God through Jesus Christ.

"Therefore, girding your loins, serve God in fear" and in [2] truth, [16] forsaking empty talkativeness and the erroneous teaching of the crowd, [17] "believing on him who raised our Lord Jesus Christ from the dead and gave him glory" [18] and a throne

---

[7] I Peter 1:1, 2; Jude 2; I Clem., pref.; Mart. Poly., pref.

[8] Phil. 4:10; 2:17.

[9] The Love, of whom the martyrs are models, may refer either to Christ or to all those who love God and their neighbor. Cf. I John 4:16; Ignatius, Rom. 6:2; 7:3.

[10] Acts 15:3.   [11] Smyr. 11:1.   [12] Acts 15:7; Col. 1:6.

[13] Acts 2:24 (Western text).   [14] I Peter 1:8, 12.   [15] Eph. 2:5, 8, 9.

[16] I Peter 1:13; Eph. 6:14; Ps. 2:11; cf. I Clem. 19:1.

[17] I Tim. 1:6; I Clem. 9:1; 7:2; Ignatius, Phil. 1:1.   [18] I Peter 1:21.

on his right hand; "to whom he subjected all things, whether in heaven or on earth,"[19] whom "everything that breathes"[20] serves, who will come as "judge of the living and the dead,"[21] whose blood God will require from those who disobey him.[22]

2 For "he who raised him from the dead will raise us also,"[23] if we do his will and follow his commandments, and love what he loved,[24] refraining from all wrongdoing, avarice, love of money, slander, and false witness; "not returning evil for evil or abuse for abuse,"[25] or blow for blow, or curse for curse; but rather remembering what the Lord said when he taught:

3 "Judge not, that you be not judged; forgive, and you will be forgiven; be merciful, that you may be shown mercy; the measure you give will be the measure you get"[26]; and "blessed are the poor and those persecuted for righteousness' sake, for theirs is the Kingdom of God."[27]

3 I write these things about righteousness, brethren, not at my own instance, but because you first invited me to do so.

2 Certainly, neither I nor anyone like me can follow the wisdom of the blessed and glorious Paul, who, when he was present among you face to face with the generation of his time,[28] taught you accurately and firmly "the word of truth."[29] Also when absent he wrote you letters that will enable you, if you study them carefully,[30] to grow in the faith delivered to you

3 —"which is a mother of us all,"[31] accompanied by hope, and led by love to God and Christ and our neighbor.[32] For if anyone is occupied in these, he has fulfilled the commandment of righteousness; for he who possesses love is far from all sin.

4 But "the love of money is the beginning of all evils."[33] Knowing, therefore, that "we brought nothing into the world, and we cannot take anything out,"[34] let us arm ourselves "with the weapons of righteousness,"[35] and let us first of all teach ourselves to live by the commandment of the Lord.

2 Then you must teach your wives in the faith delivered to them

---

[19] Phil. 3:21; 2:10; I Cor. 15:28.   [20] Ps. 150:6; Isa. 57:16.
[21] Acts 10:42.   [22] Ezek. 3:18; Luke 11:50, 51.
[23] II Cor. 4:14; I Cor. 6:14; Rom. 8:11.   [24] I John 4:11, 12.
[25] I Peter 3:9.   [26] Matt. 7:1, 2; Luke 6:36–38; cf. I Clem. 13:2.
[27] Luke 6:20; Matt. 5:3, 10.   [28] Acts 16:12, 13.
[29] Eph. 1:13.   [30] Cf. I Clem. 45:2.
[31] Gal. 4:26. (The word "all" is not read in the best MSS. of the New Testament, but is a reading of the Textus Receptus.)
[32] Col. 1:4, 5; cf. I Thess. 1:4 for the order: faith, love, hope.
[33] I Tim. 6:10.   [34] I Tim. 6:7; cf. Job 1:21.
[35] II Cor. 6:7.

and in love and purity—to cherish their own husbands[36] in all fidelity, and to love all others equally in all chastity, and to educate their children in the fear of God.[37] And the widows 3 should be discreet in their faith pledged to the Lord, praying unceasingly on behalf of all,[38] refraining from all slander, gossip, false witness, love of money—in fact, from evil of any kind—knowing that they are God's altar, that everything is examined for blemishes,[39] and nothing escapes him whether of thoughts or sentiments,[40] or any of "the secrets of the heart."[41] Knowing, then, that "God is not mocked,"[42] we 5 ought to live worthily of his commandment and glory.

Likewise the deacons should be blameless[43] before his 2 righteousness, as servants of God and Christ and not of men; not slanderers, or double-tongued, not lovers of money, temperate in all matters, compassionate, careful, living according to the truth of the Lord, who became "a servant of all"[44]; to whom, if we are pleasing in the present age, we shall also obtain the age to come, inasmuch as he promised to raise us from the dead. And if we bear our citizenship worthy of him,[45] "we shall also reign with him"[46]—provided, of course, that we have faith.

Similarly also the younger ones must be blameless in all 3 things, especially taking thought of purity and bridling themselves from all evil. It is a fine thing to cut oneself off from the lusts that are in the world, for "every passion of the flesh wages war against the Spirit,"[47] and "neither fornicators nor the effeminate nor homosexuals will inherit the Kingdom of God,"[48] nor those who do perverse things. Wherefore it is necessary to refrain from all these things, and be obedient to the presbyters and deacons as unto God and Christ.[49] And the young women must live with blameless and pure conscience.[50]

Also the presbyters must be compassionate, merciful to all, 6 turning back those who have gone astray, looking after the sick,[51] not neglecting widow[52] or orphan or one that is poor; but "always taking thought for what is honorable in the sight

---

[36] I Clem. 1:3.   [37] I Clem. 21:6, 8.   [38] I Tim. 5:5; cf. I Thess. 5:17.
[39] I Clem. 41:2.   [40] I Clem. 21:3.   [41] I Cor. 14:25.
[42] Gal. 6:7.   [43] Cf. I Tim. 3:8–13.
[44] Mark 9:35. There is a play here on the word "deacon," which means literally "a servant."
[45] I Clem. 21:1; cf. Phil. 1:27; Col. 1:10.   [46] II Tim. 2:12; I Cor. 4:8.
[47] I Peter 2:11; Gal. 5:17.   [48] I Cor. 6:9, 10.
[49] Cf. Mag., chs. 2; 6:1; 13:2; Trall. 2:2; 3:1; Smyr. 8:1; Poly. 6:1.
[50] I Clem. 1:3.   [51] I Clem. 59:4.   [52] Cf. Poly. 4:1; Smyr. 6:2.

of God and of men,"[53] refraining from all anger, partiality,
unjust judgment, keeping far from all love of money, not hastily
believing evil of anyone, nor being severe in judgment,[54]
2 knowing that we all owe the debt of sin. If, then, we pray the
Lord to forgive us, we ourselves ought also to forgive[55]; for
we are before the eyes of the Lord and God, and "everyone
shall stand before the judgment seat of Christ and each of us
3 shall give an account of himself."[56] So then let us "serve him
with fear and all reverence,"[57] as he himself has commanded,
and also the apostles who preached the gospel to us and the
prophets who foretold[58] the coming of the Lord.

Let us be zealous for that which is good, refraining from
occasions of scandal and from false brethren, and those who
bear in hypocrisy the name of the Lord, who deceive empty-
7 headed people. For "whosoever does not confess that Jesus
Christ has come in the flesh is antichrist"[59]; and whosoever
does not confess the testimony of the cross "is of the devil"[60];
and whosoever perverts the sayings of the Lord[61] to suit his own
lusts and says there is neither resurrection nor judgment—such
2 a one is the first-born of Satan.[62] Let us, therefore, forsake the
vanity of the crowd and their false teachings[63] and turn back
to the word delivered to us from the beginning, "watching unto
prayer"[64] and continuing steadfast in fasting, beseeching fer-
vently the all-seeing God[65] "to lead us not into temptation,"[66]
even as the Lord said, "The spirit indeed is willing, but the
flesh is weak."[67]
8 Let us, then, hold steadfastly and unceasingly to our Hope[68]
and to the Pledge [69] of our righteousness, that is, Christ Jesus,
"who bore our sins in his own body on the tree, who committed
no sin, neither was guile found on his lips"[70]; but for our sakes
2 he endured everything that we might live in him. Therefore
let us be imitators of his patient endurance, and if we suffer

53 II Cor. 8:21; Rom. 12:27; Prov. 3:4.   54 Cf. I Tim. 5:19 ff.
55 Matt. 6:12, 14, 15.   56 Rom. 14:10, 12; cf. II Cor. 5:10.
57 Cf. ch. 2:1; Ps. 2:11; Heb. 12:28.   58 Acts 7:52; I Clem. 17:1.
59 I John 4:2, 3; 2:22; II John 7.   60 I John 3:8.
61 Cf. I Clem. 53:1.
62 See Irenaeus, Adv. haer. III. 3:4; Eusebius, Hist. eccl., IV, ch. 14; and
    Mart. Poly., Epilogue 3.   63 Cf. ch. 2:1; I Clem. 7:2; 9:1.
64 I Peter 4:7.   65 I Clem. 55:6; 64:1.
66 Matt. 6:13.   67 Matt. 26:41; cf. Mark 14:38.
68 Col. 1:27; I Tim. 1:1; Mag., ch. 11; Trall., pref.; ch. 2:2.
69 Eph. 1:14; II Cor. 1:22; 5:5.
70 I Peter 2:24, 22.

for the sake of his name, let us glorify him. [71] For he set us this example [72] in his own Person, and this is what we believed.

Now I exhort all of you to be obedient to the word of right- **9** eousness [73] and to exercise all patient endurance, such as you have seen with your very eyes, not only in the blessed Ignatius and Zosimus and Rufus, but also in others who were of your membership, and in Paul himself and the rest of the apostles; being persuaded that all these "did not run in vain," [74] **2** but in faith and righteousness, and that they are now in their deserved place [75] with the Lord, in whose suffering they also shared. For they "loved not this present world," [76] but Him who died on our behalf and was raised by God for our sakes. [77]

Stand [78] firm, therefore, in these things and follow the **10** example of the Lord, "steadfast and immovable" [79] in the faith, "loving the brotherhood," [80] "cherishing one another," [81] "fellow companions in the truth" [82]; in "the gentleness of the Lord preferring one another" [83] and despising no one. "Whenever you are able to do a kindness, do not put it off," [84] **2** because "almsgiving frees from death." [85] All of you submit yourselves to one another, [86] having your manner of life above reproach from the heathen, so that you may receive praise for your good works and the Lord may not be blasphemed on your account. [87] "Woe to them, however, through whom the **3** name of the Lord is blasphemed." [88] Therefore, all of you teach the sobriety in which you are yourselves living.

I have been exceedingly grieved on account of Valens, who **11** was sometime a presbyter among you, because he so forgot the office that was given him. I warn you, therefore, to refrain from the love of money and be pure and truthful. "Shun evil **2** of every kind." [89] For how shall he who cannot govern himself in these things teach another? [90] If anyone does not refrain from the love of money he will be defiled by idolatry [91] and so be judged as if he were one of the heathen, "who are ignorant of the judgment of the Lord." [92] Or "do we not know

---

[71] I Peter 4:15, 16.   [72] I Peter 2:21; I Clem. 16:17.   [73] Heb. 5:13.
[74] Phil. 2:16; cf. Gal. 2:2.   [75] I Clem. 5:4, 7.   [76] II Tim. 4:10.
[77] II Cor. 5:15; cf. I Thess. 5:10.
[78] With this chapter the original Greek text is no longer extant (except for ch. 13). The translation is from the Latin.
[79] I Cor. 15:58; Col. 1:23.   [80] I Peter 2:17.
[81] I Peter 3:8; Rom. 12:10.   [82] III John 8.
[83] II Cor. 10:1; Rom. 12:10.   [84] Prov. 3:28.   [85] Tobit 4:10 ff.
[86] I Peter 5:5.   [87] I Peter 2:12.   [88] Isa. 52:5; Trall. 8:2.
[89] I Thess. 5:22.   [90] I Tim. 3:5.   [91] Col. 3:5; Eph. 5:5.   [92] Jer. 5:4.

that the saints will judge the world," as Paul teaches?⁹³ However, I have neither observed nor heard of any such thing
among you, with whom blessed Paul labored and who were
his epistles in the beginning.⁹⁴ Of you he was wont to boast
in all the churches⁹⁵ which at that time alone knew God; for
4 we did not as yet know him. I am, therefore, very grieved
indeed for that man and his wife. "May the Lord grant them
true repentance."⁹⁶ But you, too, must be moderate in this
matter; and "do not consider such persons as enemies,"⁹⁷
but reclaim them as suffering and straying members,⁹⁸
in order that you may save the whole body of you.⁹⁹ For
in doing this you will edify yourselves.¹

12   I am confident, indeed, that you are well versed in the sacred
Scriptures and that nothing escapes you²—something not
granted to me—only, as it is said in these Scriptures, "be angry
but sin not" and "let not the sun go down on your anger."³
Blessed is he who remembers this. I believe it is so with you.
2 May God and the Father of our Lord Jesus Christ, and the
eternal High Priest himself, the Son of God, Jesus Christ,
build you up in faith and truth and in all gentleness, without
anger and in patient endurance, in long-suffering, forbearance,
and purity; and give you a portion and share⁴ among his
saints, and to us also along with you, and to all under heaven
who are destined to believe⁵ in our Lord Jesus Christ and in
3 "his Father who raised him from the dead."⁶ "Pray for all
the saints."⁷ "Pray also for emperors and magistrates and
rulers,"⁸ and for "those who persecute and hate you,"⁹ and
for "the enemies of the cross,"¹⁰ that your fruit may be manifest
in all,¹¹ so that you may be perfected in him.¹²

13   Both¹³ you and Ignatius have written me that if anyone is
leaving for Syria he should take your letter along too. I shall
attend to this if I have a favorable opportunity—either myself

---

⁹³ I Cor. 6:2.
⁹⁴ Or, "who were mentioned in the beginning of his epistle." Phil. 4:15;
    cf. II Cor. 3:2; I Clem. 47:2.
⁹⁵ Phil. 2:16; II Thess. 1:4.   ⁹⁶ II Tim. 2:25; 1:18.   ⁹⁷ II Thess. 3:15.
⁹⁸ I Clem. 59:4.   ⁹⁹ I Clem. 37:5.   ¹ I Thess. 5:11.
² I Clem. 53:1; cf. Ignatius, Eph. 14:1.   ³ Ps. 4:5, LXX; Eph. 4:26.
⁴ Acts 8:21.   ⁵ Col. 1:23; cf. I Tim. 1:16.
⁶ Gal. 1:1; Col. 2:12; I Peter 1:21.   ⁷ Eph. 6:18.
⁸ I Tim. 2:1, 2; cf. I Clem., ch. 61.   ⁹ Matt. 5:44; Luke 6:27.
¹⁰ Phil. 3:18.   ¹¹ I Tim. 4:15.   ¹² Col. 2:10; James 1:4.
¹³ The Greek original of this chapter, except for the last sentence, has been
    preserved by Eusebius (*Hist. eccl.* IV. 36: 13–15).

or one whom I shall send to represent you as well as me. We are 2
sending you the letters of Ignatius, those he addressed to us and
any others we had by us, just as you requested. They are here-
with appended to this letter. From them you can derive great
benefit, for they are concerned with faith and patient endurance
and all the edification pertaining to the Lord. Of Ignatius
himself and those who are with him, let us have any reliable
information that you know.

I am sending you this letter by Crescens, whom I recently 14
commended to you and now commend him again. He has lived
with us blamelessly, and I believe he will do so among you. [14]
I also commend to you his sister, when she arrives among you.
Farewell in the Lord Jesus Christ in grace, [15] both you and all
who are yours. Amen.

14 Cf. I Clem. 63:3.   15 Smyr., ch. 13.

THE WAY OF MARTYRDOM

The Martyrdom of Polycarp, Bishop of Smyrna, as Told in the Letter of the Church of Smyrna to the Church of Philomelium

INTRODUCTION

THE LETTER OF THE CHURCH IN SMYRNA TO THE church in Philomelium, commonly known as the Martyrdom of Polycarp, is the oldest account of the martyrdom of a Christian for his faith, outside of the pages of the New Testament, that has come down to us. It is also our earliest testimony to the cult of the martyrs in the Church, i.e., the veneration of the relics of the saints and the annual celebration of the day of martyrdom with liturgical observances. The story of the death of Polycarp and other companions is that of eyewitnesses of the tragedy. There are few pieces in the history of Christian literature that are a match for its moving pathos and edifying effect.

The writer of the narrative, who names himself Marcion, stresses the point that it was "a martyrdom conformable to the gospel." The witness unto death of Polycarp and his companions was not only a mere imitation of Christ's Passion as recorded in the New Testament Gospels—and, indeed, many details of the story recalled specifically similar details in the Passion of Christ—but more than that, it was a consummation by Christian disciples of their Lord's promise and command of suffering, if need be, for his name's sake. What distinguishes the martyrdom of a Christian from similar acts of heroism recorded of Jewish witnesses for the law, or of pagan philosophers and teachers of moral virtue, is that the Christian suffered not merely for the sake of loyalty and obedience to the beliefs and practices that he held to be true and inviolable, or because of a principle of world renunciation. Christian martyrdom was all this and more, nothing less than a mystic communion and conformation with One who died for our sins that he might raise us eternally unto a life of holiness and everlasting joy.

We do not know the exact terms whereby the profession of Christianity was proscribed by Roman law and made subject to the death penalty. But the crucial test always applied by Roman magistrates was conformity to the official worship of the Roman emperor. Failure to comply with the outward requirements of this cult was considered an overt act of treason. The Roman government was very lax, however, in enforcing the State religion. Not until the year A.D. 250 did it take the initiative and attempt a concerted action to force Christians to forswear Christ by a religious oath of allegiance to Caesar. Meanwhile the detection of Christians was left to informers or to popular outcry. Once apprehended, however, a Christian who refused to yield was subject to whatever penalty or torture a magistrate chose to employ. Very often, as in the case of Polycarp's fellow sufferers, Christian prisoners were used as victims in the bloody and cruel spectacles with which the State amused the populace in the public amphitheaters.

The occasion for the outbreak of persecution at Smyrna is not clearly indicated in our story. Much of the blame is laid upon the enmity of the Jews toward the Christians and their incitement of the mob for Christian victims, and Polycarp in particular. But certain overly zealous brethren of the Church seem to have offered themselves voluntarily—a thing that church leaders were diligent in warning their flock against, for one could never tell how extensive the fury of persecution might develop from one single instance of indiscretion. One of these volunteers, named Quintus, is described as a "Phrygian." It has been suggested that he was possibly known to the church in Philomelium, and that he belonged to the fanatical sect of Montanists, often called by the orthodox Christians "Phrygians," from the province of origin of the sect. The Montanists did not look askance at voluntary martyrdom, but rather encouraged it.[1] The Montanist movement did not arise, however, quite so early as the time of these events; though it must have drawn its initial strength from fanatical, enthusiastic elements already existing within the Phrygian Christian communities.

The life and career of Polycarp have been treated in the introduction to his letter to the Philippians. The Martyrdom is our sole testimony for the circumstances and time of his death.

[1] W. M. Calder, "Philadelphia and Montanism," *Bulletin of the John Rylands Library*, 7 (1922–1923), pp. 309–354.

Its authenticity, at least in respect to many of the miraculous details of the story, has been the subject of some learned debate. But there is no good reason to apply skeptical standards, based upon purely modern, rationalistic presuppositions, to the narrative. The story is attested by Eusebius in his Ecclesiastical History, who quotes extensive extracts from it.[2] These quotations are useful, however, in establishing the text of the Martyrdom, of which there are six Greek manuscripts of the eleventh to the thirteenth centuries. There is also a group of fragments from an encomium falsely attributed to Saint John Chrysostom. The Latin version is very careless and not trustworthy. Armenian, Coptic, and Syriac versions exist of the Eusebian extracts, all of which are witness to the widespread popularity of the story.

The prayer of Polycarp in ch. 14 has been the subject of some special study. It has many affinities with Eucharistic prayers of a later date. With a slight adjustment of the text it might be taken as a representative of the type of Eucharistic consecration prayer in use in Smyrna in the middle of the second century. Even so, there is no good reason to doubt its being a faithful recalling of what Polycarp said. It would have been most natural for him to repeat at such a solemn moment of his own life's consecration words that he had been accustomed to use in thanksgiving for his Lord's consecration to sacrifice on his behalf.

The various colophons attached to the end of the Martyrdom, including the one peculiar to the Moscow manuscript (Codex Mosquensis 159, thirteenth century), shed much light upon the way in which these stories were preserved for posterity. In ch. 20, direction is given to the church in Philomelium to send copies of the Martyrdom "to the brethren elsewhere." Among these brethren none would have valued the account more dearly than Irenaeus, who was so fond of recalling his early association as a young lad with Polycarp. The Gaius who copied the story from the papers of Irenaeus may well have been the Roman Christian mentioned by Eusebius (*Hist. eccl.* II. 25:6), a writer who seems to have an especial interest in the "trophies" of the martyrs. As for the Pionius who signs himself last in the colophon, modern critics are of two opinions. Some identify him with the Smyrnaean presbyter of that name who was martyred in the persecution of Decius in A.D. 250. Others believe that his remarks about the great age of the

[2] *Hist. eccl.*, IV, ch. 15.

copy of the Martyrdom made by Isocrates of Corinth from Gaius' copy do not fit a date so early as 250. They would identify him with the anonymous author of the *Life of Polycarp*, which comes from the end of the fourth century.

Lastly, there has been much discussion respecting the date of Polycarp's martyrdom, for although the colophon gives us the day and month, it does not give us the year in which it occurred. Eusebius guessed that it took place under Marcus Aurelius in the year A.D. 167. This became the accepted date until the year 1867, when W. H. Waddington published a study on the rhetorician Aelius Aristides, who was a friend of the proconsul L. Statius Quadratus.[3] The result of Waddington's study was to fix the date of Polycarp's martyrdom as February 23, 155. With this date the inscriptions that have come to light naming Quadratus and also the Asiarch Philip of Tralles are in accord. The complete evidence is exhaustively treated in Lightfoot's edition of Polycarp. However, C. H. Turner and Eduard Schwartz, working from the datum that the martyrdom took place on "a great Sabbath," proposed the alternative date of February 22, 156—a leap year, in which the Sabbath of Purim fell on the twenty-second. This latter date is more easily reconciled with the visit of Polycarp to Rome in the time of Pope Anicetus, who succeeded to the pontificate not earlier than the year 154. The old Syriac Martyrology of Edessa, which dates from the year 411, commemorates Polycarp on February 23, and so does the Eastern Church to this day. In the Roman Church he is commemorated on January 26, but this date is not attested earlier than the Western martyrologies of the eighth and ninth centuries.

[3] "Mémoire sur la chronologie de la vie du rhéteur Aelius Aristide," *Mémoires de l'Institut impérial de France*, Académie des Inscriptions et Belles-Lettres, XXVI (1867), pp. 203-268.

BOOKS

TEXTS

The best text, and the one used for the present translation, is that of K. Bihlmeyer, *Die apostolischen Väter*, Neubearbeitung der Funkschen Ausgabe, I Teil (Sammlung ausgewählter kirchen- und dogmengeschichtlicher Quellenschriften, II Reihe, I Heft, I Teil), Tübingen, 1924, a third revision of the text edited by F. X. Funk, *Patres apostolici*, 2 vols., Tübingen, 1901. Bihlmeyer's text was reprinted, with copious bibliography, in the collection of Acts of the Martyrs by R. Knopf, *Ausgewählte Märtyrerakten*, 3d rev. edition by G. Krüger (Sammlung ausgewählter kirchen- und dogmengeschichtlicher Quellenschriften, N. F. 3), J. C. B. Mohr, Tübingen, 1929. Indispensable, however, is the text and commentary of J. B. Lightfoot, *The Apostolic Fathers*, Part II, "S. Ignatius, S. Polycarp," Revised Texts with Introductions, Notes, Dissertations, and Translations, 3 vols., 2d ed., London, 1889. Lightfoot's text was reprinted again in the edition of J. R. Harmer, *The Apostolic Fathers*, Revised Texts with Short Introductions and English Translations, pp. 185-211, London, 1912. Lightfoot's text, collated with that of K. Lake, was published in pamphlet form, *The Martyrdom of Polycarp* (Texts for Students, No. 44), S.P.C.K., London, 1930.

Other editions of the text, and references to Eusebius and the *Vita Polycarpi* attributed to Pionius, will be found listed in the introduction to Polycarp's Letter to the Philippians, namely, those of Th. Zahn, A. Hilgenfeld, K. Lake (Vol. II, 1913, pp. 309-345), A. Lelong, and G. Bosio. Special studies of the text tradition are Hermann Müller, *Aus der Überlieferungsgeschichte des Polykarp-Martyrium, Eine hagiographische Studie*, Paderborn, 1908; and E. Schwartz, *De Pionio et Polycarpo*,

Göttingen, 1905. Both these studies are critical of the received tradition of the Greek manuscripts. Some of Schwartz's suggestions were adopted by Bihlmeyer.

TRANSLATIONS, COMMENTARIES, AND REFERENCE WORKS

Translations into English of the Martyrdom will be found in the works cited in the bibliography of Polycarp's Letter: *The Ante-Nicene Fathers*, B. Jackson, F. X. Glimm (pp. 147–163), J. A. Kleist (pp. 85–102), and E. J. Goodspeed (pp. 245–256); and also in the texts of Lightfoot and Lake, listed above. Lelong's text includes a French translation (pp. 128–161); and Bosio's, an Italian (pp. 203–247). A German translation will be found in G. Rauschen, *Frühchristliche Apologeten und Märtyrerakten* (Bibliothek der Kirchenväter, 14), Vol. II, pp. 297–308, Kempten and Munich, 1913. An English translation with notes, based on the text of Knopf, is given in E. C. E. Owen, *Some Authentic Acts of the Early Martyrs*, pp. 31-41, 129–134, Oxford, 1927.

In addition to the reference works and dictionary articles listed in the bibliography to Polycarp's Letter, one should consult the bibliography on the literature of the martyrs, in Knopf-Krüger's *Ausgewählte Märtyrerakten*, pp. vi-ix. To this list may be added Donald W. Riddle, *The Martyrs, A Study in Social Control*, University of Chicago Press, 1931; and Hans Freiherr von Campenhausen, *Die Idee des Martyriums in der alten Kirche*, Vandenhoeck und Ruprecht, Göttingen, 1936; and the thorough philological study (with copious bibliography) of the word *martus* and cognates by Hermann Strathmann in Gerhard Kittel, *Theologisches Wörterbuch zum Neuen Testament*, IV (1939), pp. 477–520.

SPECIAL STUDIES

Considerable skepticism respecting the historical trustworthiness of the Martyrdom of Polycarp was expressed by Hermann Müller, "Das Martyrium Polycarpi, Ein Beitrag zur altchristlichen Heiligengeschichte," *Römische Quartalschrift*, 22 (1908), pp. 1–16. Müller's study was effectively answered by Bernhard Sepp, *Das Martyrium Polycarpi*, Regensburg, 1911; Heinrich Baden, "Der Nachahmungsgedanke im Polykarpmartyrium," *Theologie und Glaube*, 3 (1911), pp. 115–122, and "Das Polykarpmartyrium," *Pastor bonus*, 24 (1911), pp. 705–713, 25 (1912), pp. 71–81, 136–151; and Wilhelm Reuning, *Zur Erklärung des Polykarpmartyriums*, Darmstadt, 1917. Reuning's monograph is the best single treatment of the various problems of historicity and interpretation of the work. See also Cecil John Cadoux, *Ancient Smyrna, A History of the City from the Earliest Times to* 324 A.D., pp. 303–367, Basil Blackwell, Oxford, 1938.

DATE OF POLYCARP'S MARTYRDOM

Very few scholars, since the work of Waddington, have defended the traditional Eusebian date: see J. Chapman, "La Chronologie des prémières listes épiscopales de Rome," *Revue Bénédictine*, 19 (1902), pp. 145–149 ("La Date de la mort de S. Polycarpe"); and Daniel Völter, *Polykarp und Ignatius und die ihnen zugeschriebenen Briefe* (Die apostolischen Väter neu untersucht, Vol. II, 2), Leiden, 1910. For the date February 23, 155, established by Waddington, Lightfoot's discussion is fundamental, *The Apostolic Fathers*, Part 2, Vol. I, pp. 646–722. Also for this date see T. Randall, "The Date of St. Polycarp's Martyrdom," *Studia Biblica*, By Members of the University of Oxford, I (1885), pp. 175–207; Peter Corssen, "Das Todesjahr Polykarps," *Zeitschrift für die neutestamentliche Wissenschaft*, 3 (1902), pp. 61–82; Matthew Power, "The Date of Polycarp's Martyrdom in the Jewish Calendar," *The Expository Times*, 15 (1904), pp. 330, 331; W. M. Ramsay, "The Date of Polycarp's Martyrdom," *The Expository Times*, 15 (1904), pp. 221, 222, "New Evidence on the Date of Polycarp's Martyrdom," *ibid.*, 18 (1908), pp. 188, 189, and "The Date of St. Polycarp's Martyrdom," *Jahreshefte des österreichischen archäologischen Institutes in Wien*, 27 (1932), pp. 245–258; and Bernhard Sepp, "Das Datum des Todes des hl. Polykarps," *Der Katholik* (94, Vierte Folge, XIII, 1914), pp. 135–142. For the date of February 22, 156, the basic studies are those of C. H. Turner, "The Day and Year of St. Polycarp's Martyrdom," *Studia Biblica et Ecclesiastica*, By Members of the University of Oxford, II (1890), pp. 105–155; and E. Schwartz, *Christliche und jüdische Ostertafeln* (Abhandlungen der königlichen Gesellschaft der Wissenschaften zu Göttingen, Phil.-hist. Klasse, Neue Folge, VIII, p. 6), "Die jüdische Pascharechnung und das Martyrium Polykarps," pp. 125–138, Berlin, 1905. For very recent attempts to defend a later dating see Henri Grégoire and Paul Orgel in *Analecta Bollandiana*, 69 (1951), pp. 1–38; and W. Telfer in *The Journal of Theological Studies*, New Series, 3 (1952), pp. 79-83.

THE PRAYER OF POLYCARP

Its liturgical character was first studied by J. Armitage Robinson, "Liturgical Echoes in Polycarp's Prayer," *The Expositor*, Fifth Series, IX (1899), pp. 63–72, and later by Hans Lietzmann, "Ein liturgisches Bruckstück des zweiten Jahrhunderts," *Zeitschrift für wissenschaftliche Theologie*, 54 (N.F., 19; 1912), pp. 56–61. Robinson returned to the subject in "The 'Apostolic Anaphora' and the Prayer of St. Polycarp," *The Journal of Theological Studies*, 21 (1920), pp. 97–105, to which reply was made by J. W. Tyrer, "The Prayer of St. Polycarp and Its Concluding Doxology," *ibid.*, 23 (1922), pp. 390–392; Robinson made further answer in "The Doxology in the Prayer of St. Polycarp," *ibid.*, 24 (1923), pp. 141–144. See also the comments of Reuning, *op. cit.*, pp. 31–43; and Massey H. Shepherd, Jr., "Smyrna in the Ignatian Letters: A Study in Church Order," *The Journal of Religion*, 20 (1940), pp. 150, 151.

The Martyrdom of Saint Polycarp, Bishop of Smyrna, as Told in the Letter of the Church of Smyrna to the Church of Philomelium

THE TEXT

The church of God that sojourns at Smyrna to the church of God that sojourns at Philomelium, and to all those of the holy and Catholic Church who sojourn in every place: may mercy, peace, and love be multiplied from God the Father and our Lord Jesus Christ. [4]

We write you, brethren, the things concerning those who **1** suffered martyrdom, especially the blessed Polycarp, who put an end to the persecution by sealing it, so to speak, through his own witness. For almost everything that led up to it happened in order that the Lord might show once again a martyrdom conformable to the gospel. [5] For he waited to be betrayed, just **2** as the Lord did, to the end that we also might be imitators of him, "not looking only to that which concerns ourselves, but also to that which concerns our neighbors." [6] For it is a mark of true and steadfast love for one not only to desire to be saved oneself, but all the brethren also.

Blessed and noble, indeed, are all the martyrdoms that have **2** taken place according to God's will; for we ought to be very reverent in ascribing to God power over all things. For who **2** would not admire their nobility and patient endurance and love of their Master? Some of them, so torn by scourging that the anatomy of their flesh was visible as far as the inner veins and arteries, endured with such patience that even the bystanders took pity and wept; others achieved such heroism that not one of them uttered a cry or a groan, thus showing all of us that at the very hour of their tortures the most noble martyrs of

---

[4] I Peter 1:1, 2; Jude 2; I Clem., pref.; Polycarp, Phil., pref.
[5] John 18:37; cf. Rev. 1:5; 3:14. The Passion of Christ is the pattern of that of his martyrs. Cf. Polycarp, Phil. 8:2.   [6] Phil. 2:4.

Christ were no longer in the flesh, but rather that the Lord
3 stood by them and conversed with them. And giving themselves
over to the grace of Christ they despised the tortures of
this world, purchasing for themselves in the space of one hour
the life eternal. To them the fire of their inhuman tortures was
cold; for they set before their eyes escape from the fire that is
everlasting and never quenched,[7] while with the eyes of their
heart they gazed upon the good things reserved for those that
endure patiently, "which things neither ear has heard nor eye
has seen, nor has there entered into the heart of man."[8] But
they were shown to them by the Lord, for they were no longer
4 men, but were already angels. Similarly, those condemned to
the wild beasts endured fearful punishments, being made to
lie on sharp shells and punished with other forms of various
torments, in order that [the devil][9] might bring them, if
possible, by means of the prolonged punishment, to a denial
of their faith.

3   Many, indeed, were the machinations of the devil against
them. But, thanks be to God, he did not prevail against them
all. For the most noble Germanicus encouraged their timidity
through his own patient endurance—who also fought with the
beasts in a distinguished way. For when the proconsul, wishing
to persuade him, bade him have pity on his youth, he forcibly
dragged the wild beast toward himself,[10] wishing to obtain
2 more quickly a release from their wicked and lawless life. From
this circumstance, all the crowd, marveling at the heroism of
the God-loving and God-fearing race of the Christians, shouted:
"Away with the atheists![11] Make search for Polycarp!"
4   But a Phrygian,[12] named Quintus, lately arrived from
Phrygia, took fright when he saw the wild beasts. In fact, he
was the one who had forced himself and some others to come
forward voluntarily. The proconsul by much entreaty persuaded him to take the oath and to offer the sacrifice. For this
reason, therefore, brethren, we do not praise those who come
forward of their own accord, since the gospel does not teach
us so to do.[13]

5   The most admirable Polycarp, when he first heard of it, was

[7] Matt. 3:12; Mark 9:43; Ignatius, Eph. 16:2.
[8] I Cor. 2:9; Isa. 64:4; 65:16.
[9] The subject is supplied from ch. 3:1.   [10] Cf. Ignatius, Rom. 5:2.
[11] Cf. Justin, Apol. I, chs. 6; 13; Athenagoras, Leg., chs. 3 ff.
[12] The name "Phrygian" was often given to an adherent of the Montanist
sect. See the Introduction.
[13] Cf. Matt 10:23; John 7:1; 8:59; 10:39; Acts 13:51; 17:14; 19:30, 31.

not perturbed, but desired to remain in the city. But the majority induced him to withdraw, so he retired to a farm not far from the city and there stayed with a few friends, doing nothing else night and day but pray for all men and for the churches throughout the world, as was his constant habit.[14] And while he was praying, it so happened, three days before 2 his arrest, that he had a vision and saw his pillow blazing with fire, and turning to those who were with him he said, "I must be burned alive."

And while those who were searching for him continued their 6 quest, he moved to another farm, and forthwith those searching for him arrived. And when they did not find him, they seized two young slaves, one of whom confessed under torture. For 2 it was really impossible to conceal him, since the very ones who betrayed him were of his own household.[15] And the chief of the police, who chanced to have the same name as Herod, was zealous to bring him into the arena in order that he might fulfill his own appointed lot of being made a partaker with Christ; while those who betrayed him should suffer the punishment of Judas himself.

Taking, therefore, the young slave on Friday about supper- 7 time, the police, mounted and with their customary arms, set out as though "hasting after a robber."[16] And late in the evening they came up with him and found him in bed in the upper room of a small cottage. Even so he could have escaped to another farm, but he did not wish to do so, saying, "God's will be done."[17] Thus, when he heard of their arrival, he went 2 downstairs and talked with them, while those who looked on marveled at his age and constancy, and at how there should be such zeal over the arrest of so old a man. Straightway he ordered food and drink, as much as they wished, to be set before them at that hour, and he asked them to give him an hour so that he might pray undisturbed. And when they consented, 3 he stood and prayed—being so filled with the grace of God that for two hours he could not hold his peace, to the amazement of those who heard. And many repented that they had come to get such a devout old man.

When at last he had finished his prayer, in which he remem- 8 bered all who had met with him at any time, both small and great, both those with and those without renown, and the whole Catholic Church throughout the world, the hour of

14 Cf. Polycarp, Phil. 12:3. 15 Cf. Matt. 10:36.
16 Matt. 26:55. 17 Matt. 6:10; Acts 21:14.

departure having come, they mounted him on an ass and
2 brought him into the city. It was a great Sabbath.[18] And there
the chief of the police, Herod, and his father, Nicetas, met
him and transferred him to their carriage, and tried to persuade
him, as they sat beside him, saying, "What harm is there to say
'Lord Caesar,' and to offer incense and all that sort of thing,
and to save yourself?"

At first he did not answer them.[19] But when they persisted,
he said, "I am not going to do what you advise me."

3   Then when they failed to persuade him, they uttered dire
threats and made him get out with such speed that in dis-
mounting from the carriage he bruised his shin. But without
turning around, as though nothing had happened, he proceeded
swiftly, and was led into the arena, there being such a
9 tumult in the arena that no one could be heard. But as Polycarp was entering the arena, a voice from heaven[20] came
to him, saying, "Be strong, Polycarp, and play the man."[21]
No one saw the one speaking, but those of our people who were
present heard the voice.[22]

And when finally he was brought up, there was a great
2 tumult on hearing that Polycarp had been arrested. Therefore,
when he was brought before him, the proconsul asked him if he
were Polycarp. And when he confessed that he was, he tried
to persuade him to deny [the faith], saying, "Have respect to
your age"—and other things that customarily follow this, such
as, "Swear by the fortune of Caesar; change your mind; say,
'Away with the atheists!'"

But Polycarp looked with earnest face at the whole crowd of
lawless heathen in the arena, and motioned to them with his
hand. Then, groaning and looking up to heaven, he said,
"Away with the atheists!"

3   But the proconsul was insistent and said: "Take the oath,
and I shall release you. Curse Christ."

Polycarp said: "Eighty-six years I have served him, and he
never did me any wrong. How can I blaspheme my King who
saved me?"

10   And upon his persisting still and saying, "Swear by the
fortune of Caesar," he answered, "If you vainly suppose that I
shall swear by the fortune of Caesar, as you say, and pretend
that you do not know who I am, listen plainly: I am a

[18] Cf. John 19:31.   [19] Cf. Mark 14:61; John 19:9, 10.
[20] Cf. John 12:28.
[21] Josh. 1:6, 7, 9; cf. Deut. 31:7, 23; Ps. 27:14; 31:24.   [22] Acts 9:7.

Christian. But if you desire to learn the teaching of Christianity, appoint a day and give me a hearing."

The proconsul said, "Try to persuade the people." 2

But Polycarp said, "You, I should deem worthy of an account; for we have been taught to render honor, as is befitting, to rulers and authorities appointed by God[23] so far as it does us no harm; but as for these, I do not consider them worthy that I should make defense to them."

But the proconsul said: "I have wild beasts. I shall throw 11 you to them, if you do not change your mind."

But he said: "Call them. For repentance from the better to the worse is not permitted us; but it is noble to change from what is evil to what is righteous."

And again [he said] to him, "I shall have you consumed 2 with fire, if you despise the wild beasts, unless you change your mind."

But Polycarp said: "The fire you threaten burns but an hour and is quenched after a little; for you do not know the fire of the coming judgment and everlasting punishment that is laid up for the impious. But why do you delay? Come, do what you will."

And when he had said these things and many more besides he 12 was inspired with courage and joy, and his face was full of grace, so that not only did it not fall with dismay at the things said to him, but on the contrary, the proconsul was astonished, and sent his own herald into the midst of the arena to proclaim three times: "Polycarp has confessed himself to be a Christian."

When this was said by the herald, the entire crowd of heathen 2 and Jews who lived in Smyrna[24] shouted with uncontrollable anger and a great cry: "This one is the teacher of Asia, the father of the Christians, the destroyer of our gods, who teaches many not to sacrifice nor to worship."[25]

Such things they shouted and asked the Asiarch Philip[26] that he let loose a lion on Polycarp. But he said it was not possible for him to do so, since he had brought the wild-beast sports to a close. Then they decided to shout with one accord 3 that he burn Polycarp alive. For it was necessary that the vision which had appeared to him about his pillow should be fulfilled, when he saw it burning while he was praying, and

---

[23] Rom. 13:1, 7; I Peter 2:13 ff.; I Clem., ch. 61.
[24] Cf. Rev. 2:9.   [25] Cf. Acts 16:20, 21.
[26] See note 40. The Asiarchs were officials who maintained the cult of Rome and the emperor in the province of Asia. Cf. Acts 19:31.

turning around had said prophetically to the faithful who were
with him, "I must be burned alive."[27]

13   Then these things happened with such dispatch, quicker than
can be told—the crowds in so great a hurry to gather wood
and faggots from the workshops and the baths, the Jews being
2 especially zealous, as usual, to assist with this. When the fire
was ready, and he had divested himself of all his clothes and
unfastened his belt, he tried to take off his shoes, though he was
not heretofore in the habit of doing this because [each of]
the faithful always vied with one another as to which of them
would be first to touch his body. For he had always been
3 honored, even before his martyrdom, for his holy life. Straightway then, they set about him the material prepared for the
pyre. And when they were about to nail him also, he said:
"Leave me as I am. For he who grants me to endure the fire
will enable me also to remain on the pyre unmoved, without
the security you desire from the nails."

14   So they did not nail him, but tied him. And with his hands
put behind him and tied, like a noble ram out of a great flock
ready for sacrifice, a burnt offering ready and acceptable to
God, he looked up to heaven and said:
    "Lord God Almighty,[28] Father of thy beloved and blessed
Servant Jesus Christ, through whom we have received full
knowledge of thee, 'the God of angels and powers and all
creation'[29] and of the whole race of the righteous who live
2 in thy presence: I bless thee, because thou hast deemed
me worthy of this day and hour,[30] to take my part in the
number of the martyrs, in the cup of thy Christ,[31] for
'resurrection to eternal life'[32] of soul and body in the immortality of the Holy Spirit; among whom may I be received
in thy presence this day as a rich and acceptable sacrifice,
just as thou hast prepared and revealed beforehand and
fulfilled, thou that art the true God without any falsehood.
3 For this and for everything I praise thee, I bless thee, I
glorify thee, through the eternal and heavenly High Priest,
Jesus Christ, thy beloved Servant, through whom be glory
to thee with him and Holy Spirit both now and unto the
ages to come. Amen."

15   And when he had concluded the Amen and finished his
prayer, the men attending to the fire lighted it. And when the

27 Cf. ch. 5:2.   28 Rev. 4:8; 11:17; 15:3; 16:7; 21:22.
29 Ps. 58:6, LXX; Judith 9:12, 14.   30 Cf. John 12:27.
31 Cf. Mark 10:38, 39; Matt. 20:22, 23; 26:39.   32 Cf. John 5:29.

flame flashed forth, we saw a miracle, we to whom it was given to see. And we are preserved in order to relate to the rest what happened. For the fire made the shape of a vaulted chamber, 2 like a ship's sail filled by the wind, and made a wall around the body of the martyr. And he was in the midst, not as burning flesh, but as bread baking or as gold and silver refined in a furnace. And we perceived such a sweet aroma as the breath of incense or some other precious spice.

At length, when the lawless men saw that his body could not 16 be consumed by the fire, they commanded an executioner to go to him and stab him with a dagger. And when he did this [a dove and][33] a great quantity of blood came forth, so that the fire was quenched and the whole crowd marveled that there should be such a difference between the unbelievers and the elect. And certainly the most admirable Polycarp was one of 2 these [elect], in whose times among us he showed himself an apostolic and prophetic teacher and bishop of the Catholic Church in Smyrna.[34] Indeed, every utterance that came from his mouth was accomplished and will be accomplished.

But the jealous and malicious evil one, the adversary of the 17 race of the righteous, seeing the greatness of his martyrdom and his blameless life from the beginning, and how he was crowned with the wreath of immortality and had borne away an incontestable reward, so contrived it that his corpse should not be taken away by us, although many desired to do this and to have fellowship with his holy flesh. He instigated Nicetas, the 2 father of Herod and brother of Alce,[35] to plead with the magistrate not to give up his body, "else," said he, "they will abandon the Crucified and begin worshiping this one." This was done at the instigation and insistence of the Jews, who also watched when we were going to take him from the fire, being ignorant that we can never forsake Christ, who suffered for the salvation of the whole world of those who are saved, the faultless for the sinners,[36] nor can we ever worship any other. For we 3 worship this One as Son of God, but we love the martyrs as disciples and imitators of the Lord, deservedly so, because of their unsurpassable devotion to their own King and Teacher. May it be also our lot to be their companions and fellow disciples!

[33] This is probably a late interpolation in the text.
[34] See Smyr. 8:2.
[35] Cf. the Alce mentioned in Smyr., ch. 13; Poly., ch. 8.
[36] Cf. I Peter 3:18.

18   The captain of the Jews, when he saw their contentiousness,
set it [i.e., his body] in the midst and burned it, as was their
2 custom. So we later took up his bones, more precious than
costly stones and more valuable than gold, and laid them away
3 in a suitable place. There the Lord will permit us, so far as
possible, to gather together in joy and gladness to celebrate
the day of his martyrdom as a birthday, in memory of those
athletes who have gone before, and to train and make ready
those who are to come hereafter.

19   Such are the things concerning the blessed Polycarp, who,
martyred at Smyrna along with twelve others from Philadelphia,
is alone remembered so much the more by everyone, that he
is even spoken of by the heathen in every place. He was not
only a noble teacher, but also a distinguished martyr, whose
martyrdom all desire to imitate as one according to the gospel
2 of Christ. By his patient endurance he overcame the wicked
magistrate and so received the crown of immortality; and he
rejoices with the apostles and all the righteous to glorify God
the Father Almighty and to bless our Lord Jesus Christ, the
Saviour of our souls and Helmsman of our bodies and Shepherd[37] of the Catholic Church throughout the world.

20   You requested, indeed, that these things be related to you
more fully, but for the present we have briefly reported them
through our brother Marcion. When you have informed
yourselves of these things, send this letter to the brethren
elsewhere, in order that they too might glorify the Lord, who
2 makes his choices from his own servants. To him who is able[38]
by his grace and bounty to bring us to his everlasting Kingdom,
through his Servant, the only-begotten Jesus Christ, be glory,
honor, might, majesty, throughout the ages. Greet all the
saints. Those with us greet you and also Evarestus, who wrote
this, with his whole household.

21   The blessed Polycarp was martyred on the second day of the
first part of the month Xanthicus, the seventh day before the
kalends of March, a great Sabbath, at two o'clock P.M.[39] He was
arrested by Herod, when Philip of Tralles was high priest,[40]

---

[37] I Peter 2:25.

[38] Cf. Jude 24, 25; I Clem., ch. 64.

[39] In the year 156 (a leap year) the Sabbath of Purim was on February 22.
The Syriac Martyrology commemorates Polycarp, however, on February
23. See the Introduction.

[40] Gaius Julius Philippus was appointed high priest and Asiarch sometime
between 149 and 153. The term of office was four years. See Lightfoot's
edition, I, 628-635, 666 f.; II, 241, 383-385.

and Statius Quadratus was proconsul,[41] but in the everlasting reign of our Lord Jesus Christ. To him be glory, honor, majesty, and the eternal throne, from generation to generation. Amen.

We bid you farewell, brethren, as you live by the word of **22** Jesus Christ according to the gospel, with whom be glory to God the Father and Holy Spirit, unto the salvation of his holy elect; just as the blessed Polycarp suffered martyrdom, in whose footsteps may it be our lot to be found in the Kingdom of Jesus Christ.

These things Gaius[42] copied from the papers of Irenaeus, a **2** disciple of Polycarp; he also lived with Irenaeus. And Isocrates, wrote it in Corinth from the copy of Gaius. Grace be with all.

I, Pionius,[43] again wrote it from the aforementioned copy, **3** having searched for it according to a revelation of the blessed Polycarp, who appeared to me, as I shall explain in the sequel. I gathered it together when it was almost worn out with age, in order that the Lord Jesus Christ might bring me also with his elect unto his heavenly Kingdom. To him be glory with the Father and Holy Spirit unto the ages of ages. Amen.

ANOTHER EPILOGUE FROM THE MOSCOW MANUSCRIPT

These things Gaius copied from the papers of Irenaeus. He **23** also lived with Irenaeus, who had been a disciple of the holy Polycarp. For this Irenaeus, at the time of the martyrdom of **2** Bishop Polycarp, was in Rome and taught many; and many of his excellent and orthodox writings are in circulation, in which he mentions Polycarp, for he was taught by him.[44] He ably refuted every heresy and handed down the ecclesiastical and Catholic rule, as he had received it from the saint. He says this **3** also: that once when Marcion, after whom the Marcionites are called, met the holy Polycarp and said, "Do you know us, Polycarp?" he said to Marcion, "I know you; I know the first-born of Satan."[45] And this fact is also found in the writings of **4** Irenaeus, that on the day and at the hour when Polycarp was martyred in Smyrna, Irenaeus, being in the city of Rome,

---

41 Lucius Statius Quadratus was consul in 142, but the date of his proconsulship of Asia is unknown. It could have been c. 154–156. See Lightfoot's *The Apostolic Fathers*, I, 646–677; II, 368, 369, 635–637.

42 This may be the Gaius in Eusebius, *Hist. eccl.* II. 25:6.

43 On the identity of this Pionius, see the Introduction.

44 See Irenaeus' Letter to Florinus in Eusebius, *Hist. eccl.* V. 20:6.

45 Irenaeus, *Adv. haer.* III. 3:4; cf. Polycarp, Phil. 7:1.

heard a voice like a trumpet saying, "Polycarp has suffered martyrdom."

5   From these papers of Irenaeus, then, as was said above, Gaius made a copy, and from Gaius' copy Isocrates made another in Corinth. And I, Pionius, again from the copies of Isocrates wrote according to the revelation of holy Polycarp, when I searched for it, and gathered it together when it was almost worn out with age, in order that the Lord Jesus Christ might bring me with his elect unto his heavenly Kingdom. To whom be glory with the Father and the Son and the Holy Spirit unto the ages of ages. Amen.

A CHURCH MANUAL

The Teaching of the Twelve Apostles, Commonly Called the Didache

INTRODUCTION

NO DOCUMENT OF THE EARLY CHURCH HAS PROVED so bewildering to scholars as this apparently innocent tract which was discovered by Philotheos Byrennios in 1873. The Didache or Teaching (for that is what the Greek word means) falls into two parts. The first is a code of Christian morals, presented as a choice between the way of life and the way of death. The second part is a manual of Church Order which, in a well-arranged manner, lays down some simple, at times even naïve, rules for the conduct of a rural congregation. It deals with such topics as baptism, fasting, the Lord's Supper, itinerant prophets, and the local ministry of bishops and deacons. It concludes with a warning paragraph on the approaching end of the world.

At one time this tract was viewed as a very ancient product—as early as A.D. 70 or 90. Recent study, however, has conclusively shown that, in the form we have it, it belongs to the second century. There is, nevertheless, no unanimity among scholars about its exact date or purpose. It has appropriately been called the "spoiled child of criticism"; and it will probably need a good deal more spoiling before its riddle is finally solved.

THE "TWO WAYS"

The literary problem of the Didache is extremely complex and only the bare outlines can be sketched here. As it stands, the document bears a close relationship to several other early Christian writings. The moral catechism or "Two Ways" of its opening chapters (chs. 1 to 5) appears in a rather different version at the end of the Letter of Barnabas (between A.D.

100 and 130), and has also come down to us as an independent document in a Latin translation. Much of this material, furthermore, turns up in the fourth century Apostolic Church Order (with many interpolations) and in the *Life of Schnudi* (fifth century). The connection between all these documents has been very closely studied, and differing opinions are held about it. Some claim that the author of Barnabas invented the "Two Ways."[1] Others contend that the "Two Ways" was originally an independent catechism (perhaps Jewish in origin), and that it has been incorporated in different forms by the various compilers.[2] Perhaps the most reasonable explanation to account for the many complexities is as follows:

The "Two Ways" was an independent catechism current in several versions,[3] of which three have come down to us. None represents the original in its pure form. Barnabas' is the earliest version we possess, but it suffers from displacements, and here and there the author has freely rendered his source in his own style.[4] The second form is that found (with minor variations) in the Latin, the Apostolic Church Order, and the *Life of Schnudi*. This has preserved the original order, but it displays an ecclesiastical tendency[5] and has interpolated a further section (=Did. 3:1–6, commonly called "the fences"[6]). The final form is that in the Didache. It is distinguished by the addition of yet another insertion—sayings from the Gospels and other sources (chs. 1:3 to 2:1).

DATE AND PLACE OF THE DIDACHE

The first five chapters of the Teaching, then, represent a late form of an original catechism into which the Didachist has

---

[1] So J. Armitage Robinson, J. Muilenburg, R. H. Connolly, F. C. Burkitt. See the section on Manuscripts and Books.

[2] So C. Taylor, A. Harnack (his later view), K. Kohler, B. H. Streeter, and J. M. Creed. E. Goodspeed holds that the Latin represents something like the original form.

[3] Jerome (*De Vir. Ill.* 1) and Rufinus (*In Symb. Apost.*, ch. 21) seem to have known it in some connection with Peter's name.

[4] That the version in Barnabas is secondary is clear from ch. 19:7, where he has displaced an injunction to slaves, referring it to all his readers. Furthermore, phrases that are most characteristic of Barnabas are absent from the other versions. This would hardly have happened if they all depended on him.

[5] Cf. Did. 4:1, 2; ch. 14 with Barn. 19: 9, 10, 12.

[6] From the Jewish "fences" of the law.

inserted en bloc and not very neatly[7] some distinctively Christian sayings. They betray a knowledge of Matthew and Luke, and one is clearly derived from the Shepherd of Hermas (ch. 1:5 = Man. 2:4–6), which was written about A.D. 100. Another indication of the date of the Didache is to be found in ch. 16, where a citation from the Letter of Barnabas appears (ch. 16:2 = Barn. 4:9). There can be little doubt that we are dealing with a second century document which reveals a wide canon of Scripture, including Barnabas and Hermas. The *terminus ad quem* is to be set by the quotations from the Teaching in a Syrian church order called the Didascalia. This dates from the early third century.

That the Didache comes from Alexandria[8] is suggested by several factors. The "Two Ways" was in circulation there, for the Letter of Barnabas and the Apostolic Church Order come from that locality. It is possible, but not certain, that Clement of Alexandria knew our Didache.[9] The Teaching's liberal attitude toward the New Testament canon, apparently including Barnabas and Hermas, bespeaks Alexandria. Furthermore, up to the fourth century the Teaching was highly regarded in Egypt, itself hovering on the verge of the canon, and being mentioned by Athanasius as suitable for catechetical reading (Festal Letter, ch. 39). Then again, Serapion of Thmuis (fourth century) has a quotation from the Didache in his Eucharistic prayer. In view of the conservative nature of these prayers, this is a weighty factor.

The Church Order of the Didache

The second part of the Teaching (chs. 6 to 15) is a manual of Church Order. It has generally been held that the Didachist himself wrote this section of the work, adding it to the "Two Ways." It poses, however, very difficult problems, and three main views are current about it. Some[10] claim that it faithfully reflects the subapostolic period in the rural churches of Syria.

[7] Note how the *second* command of the Teaching (2:1) has been preceded by no first command. In an Oxyrhynchus fragment of the Didache a scribe has tried to iron this out by inserting in ch. 1:3, fin.: "Hear what you must do to save your spirit. *First* of all . . ."
[8] The Egyptian origin of the Didache was held by Byrennios, Zahn, and Harnack.
[9] See F. R. M. Hitchcock's article in *The Journal of Theological Studies,* 1923, pp. 397 ff.
[10] So B. H. Streeter, J. M. Creed, T. Klauser, and J. A. Kleist.

Others [11] hold that its regulations regarding prophets betray its Montanist origin. A third opinion[12] is that the Didache is an artificial composition, aimed to recall the second century Church to greater simplicity by reconstructing an imaginative picture of primitive Christianity from apostolic sources. This third view is most unlikely. Second century literature was never purely antiquarian in mode or interest. Its reconstructions of primitive times were directed toward giving apostolic warrant to newer ideas and customs. It is the absence from the Didache of such familiar themes as virginity, episcopacy, Gnostic and anti-Gnostic tendencies, which needs explaining.

The claim that the Didache is a Montanist tract has more to be said for it. Yet this view, too, is hardly tenable. The most characteristic Montanist features are lacking from the Teaching. It reflects nothing of Montanus and his prophetesses, of the ascetic rigor of that movement, of the high place accorded women, of the lively eschatology in connection with Pepuza, or of the opposition to second marriages and second repentance. On all these questions the Didache is silent. This disturbing fact has to be met by the further assumption that all clear traces of the New Prophecy were purposely suppressed in the interests of showing "how respectable and apostolic Montanism could be." This is, in short, an admission that the Teaching is not really Montanist.[13]

It is, then, to the first view that we are driven. While it is not without difficulties, it is less unlikely than the others. Some of these difficulties, moreover, can be removed if we do not follow the general assumption that the Didachist wrote this section of the tract himself. It is much more plausible to suppose that he was a compiler, rather than an author; and that, just as he made use of the "Two Ways" at the beginning, so in the second part of his work he utilized an early source for his Church Order. That would explain why his tract has such a curious appearance. Onto the catechism he has sewn some genuinely primitive regulations about Church life. The effect is very odd, for he implies that the moral catechism sufficed for baptismal instruction (ch. 7:1), which is, of course,

[11] So R. H. Connolly and F. E. Vokes. The suggestion goes back to Hilgenfeld.

[12] So J. Armitage Robinson. See also W. Telfer's "Antioch Hypothesis" in *The Journal of Theological Studies*, 1939, revised to a "Jerusalem Hypothesis," *ibid.*, 1944.

[13] A Montanist, moreover, would never have put the prophetic ministry on a par with that of the local clergy; see ch. 15:1.

contrary to all we know of early Christianity. Only a scribe with a limited number of sources at hand could have left such an impression. He did, indeed, try to rectify things a little by adding the gospel precepts. But that was the best he could do under the circumstances. It is not possible to tell how much of the Church Order he has faithfully preserved or how much he has altered. Yet his method of handling the "Two Ways" suggests that he would be more likely to make insertions en bloc than to change his source radically.

We should assume, then, that some scribe in Alexandria about A.D. 150 edited two ancient documents which came into his hands. One was the "Two Ways"; the other was a late first century set of regulations about Church life. He made some changes in them—how many we shall never know. He certainly added a section of sayings to the "Two Ways" and probably composed the final ch. 16, which is only loosely related to the rest of the document. It is noteworthy that an interest in perfection appears in these two places (chs. 1:4; 16:2) and in one other—at the junction of the two sources (ch. 6:2). It seems a mark of the Didachist. Moreover, it is only in his addition to the catechism and in ch. 16 that a wide knowledge of New Testament Scripture is evident. In these two places he conflates Matthew with Luke and cites, among other things, Barnabas and Hermas. The rest of the work reveals only a knowledge of Matthew's Gospel.

The Didache, thus, is the first of those fictitious Church Orders which edit ancient material and claim apostolic authorship. As in many such instances (e.g., the Apostolic Church Order, the Apostolic Constitutions, the Testament of Our Lord), we cannot be sure precisely what is original and what is edited. Nor do the various regulations necessarily apply to the time of the compilation. Sometimes a scribe will brush up ancient material sufficiently to make it appear relevant to his period. More often he will change it only a little, leaving a curious combination of the ancient and the modern, which is bewildering. Hence a degree of caution is needed in citing the Didache as a witness to first century customs. Yet the main outlines of its arrangements for Church life do seem to reflect the end of the first century before the monepiscopate had finally triumphed and while the gift of prophecy was still exercised (chs. 11; 13). Moreover, the Eucharistic prayers (chs. 9; 10),[14]

[14] Some (e.g., R. H. Connolly; also G. Dix, *Shape of the Liturgy*, pp. 90 ff., London, 1944) have held that these prayers refer not to the Eucharist

so clearly modeled on the Jewish forms for grace before and after meals, betray a period when the Lord's Supper was still a real supper, and when the joyful and expectant note of the Messianic Banquet had not yet been obscured by the more solemn emphasis on the Lord's Passion.

To compile such a document must have been a congenial task for an Alexandrine scribe who adhered to the small Catholic minority in that city. Surrounded as he was by every novelty of Gnostic speculation, he would doubtless take a special delight in preserving the records of antiquity.

That the source of the Didache's Church Order (chs. 6:3 to 15) belongs to Syria and comes from the late first century may be gathered from several factors. It is clearly dependent upon Matthew's Gospel and so cannot be earlier than A.D. 90. This Gospel, it may be noted, probably comes from Syria. The Eucharistic prayers reflect an area where wheat is sown on the hillsides (ch. 9:4), and the baptismal section presupposes a vicinity where warm baths are prevalent (ch. 7:2). All these points bespeak Syria, though the Eucharistic prayers themselves may be Judean in origin. The prophets and teachers (chs. 11 and 13) forcibly recall the situation in Antioch where, according to Acts 13:1, the Church leaders were so named. We may remind ourselves that the author of The Acts is always careful about his titles.[15] The picture we gain from this source of the Didache is one of rural communities[16] periodically enjoying a visitation from the leaders of some Christian center. Indeed, a city like Antioch may well have been responsible for this primitive manual to guide the rural churches.

proper, but to the "*agapē*," or Church supper. The difficulties with this view are as follows: the supper is called "Eucharist," a term generally reserved for the Sacrament (cf. ch. 14:1); it is carefully guarded from profanation (ch. 9:5); and it follows the section on Baptism. What we anticipate is a treatment of the baptismal Eucharist such as we find in this place in other Church Orders. A description of the less significant "*agapē*" would interrupt the natural sequence in the writer's mind.

[15] That "prophets" was a title for leaders of the Church, next to the apostles, is indicated in I Cor. 12:28 and clear from Eph. 4:11. It is noteworthy that Matthew has two unique sayings about false prophets (chs. 7:15; 24:11; cf. 10:41). That Gospel evidently reflects the same problem faced by this source of the Didache (cf. ch. 11).

[16] Note the "first fruits" of ch. 13.

MANUSCRIPTS AND BOOKS

MANUSCRIPTS

Only one Greek text of the Didache has survived. It is the
Jerusalem Codex discovered by Byrennios in 1873, and published by him in Constantinople ten years later. It was written
by a scribe, Leo, in 1056. A photographic facsimile was published by J. Rendel Harris in 1887.

Two papyrus fragments of the Didache in Greek (chs. 1:3, 4
and 2:7 to 3:2) were edited by A. S. Hunt in *Oxyrhynchus Papyri*,
15, London, 1922, pp. 12–15.

The Greek texts of the Epistle of Barnabas (chs. 18 to 20)
and of the Apostolic Church Order (chs. 1 to 13) contain the
"Two Ways" material in different forms. In the latter case
there are many additions, and dependence on the "Two Ways"
breaks off at the equivalent of Did. 4:8. The Greek text of the
Apostolic Constitutions (ch. 7:1–32) contains almost the whole
of the Didache with a number of changes and many insertions.

In Syriac there are citations from the Didache in the Didascalia, edited by R. H. Connolly, Oxford University Press,
London, 1929.

In Latin there is a third century translation of the "Two
Ways." A fragment was published by B. Pez in 1723. The complete text was edited from an eleventh century manuscript
by J. Schlecht, *Doctrina XII Apostolorum*, Freiburg, 1900.

In Coptic there is a fifth century papyrus fragment of chs.
10:3b to 12:2a, edited by G. Horner in *The Journal of Theological Studies*, 25, 1924, pp. 225–231. (It is notable for adding
after the Eucharistic prayer a thanksgiving for myron, holy oil
for confirmation.)

In Arabic the "Two Ways" material is found in the fifth
century *Life of Schnudi*. A German rendering is given by L. E.

Iselin and A. Heusler in Texte und Untersuchungen, XIII, 1b, pp. 6–10, 1895.

In Ethiopic the following parts of the Didache have been preserved in the Ecclesiastical Canons: chs. 11:3–5, 7–11, 12; 12:1–5; 13:1, 3–7; 8:1, 2a, in that order. They are edited by G. Horner, *Statutes of the Apostles*, pp. 193, 194, London, 1904.

In Georgian there is a complete translation made in the fifth century by a scribe, Jeremias of Orhai. The variant readings were published by G. Peradze in *Zeitschrift für die neutestamentliche Wissenschaft*, pp. 111–116, 1932, from a copy of an eleventh century manuscript in Constantinople.

Books and Articles

The best Greek text, making use of all the available witnesses, is by Theodorus Klauser, *Doctrina Duodecim Apostolorum: Barnabae Epistula*, "Florilegium Patristicum," 1, Bonn, 1940. It has been used for this translation. Also of importance are the texts in K. Bihlmeyer, *Die apostolischen Väter*, Tübingen, 1924 (note his treatment of the Coptic evidence pp. xviii–xx), in K. Lake, *The Apostolic Fathers*, London, 1912, and in H. Hemmer, G. Oger, and A. Lamont, *Les Pères apostoliques*, Vol. I, Paris, 1907 (based on the text of F. X. Funk, *Patres apostolici*, Tübingen, 1901).

Older editions of the Didache, which contain a number of the related documents along with the text of Byrennios, are by A. Harnack, *Die Lehre der Zwölf Apostel*, Texte und Untersuchungen, II, Leipzig, 1884 (a pioneer and monumental work which includes the Greek text of the A. C. O. and the relevant parts of A. C. 7); and by Philip Schaff, *The Oldest Church Manual Called the Teaching of the Twelve Apostles*, New York, 1885 (includes the pertinent sections from Barnabas, Hermas, A. C. O., and A. C. 7).

In addition to the works of Schaff and Lake mentioned above, the following translations in English may be noted: C. Bigg, *The Doctrine of the Twelve Apostles* (revised by A. J. Maclean), London, 1922; F. X. Glimm, *The Apostolic Fathers*, in the series The Fathers of the Church, Cima Publishing Company, New York, 1947; J. A. Kleist, *The Didache, The Epistle of Barnabas*, etc., in the series Ancient Christian Writers, Newman Press, Westminster, Maryland, 1948; and E. Goodspeed, *The Apostolic Fathers: An American Translation*, New York, 1950.

In German there are renderings by F. Zeller, *Die apostolischen Väter*, Munich, 1918, in the 2d series of the Bibliothek der Kirchenväter; by R. Knopf, *Die Lehre der Zwölf Apostel: Die zwei Clemensbriefe*, Tübingen, 1920, in Handbuch zum N. T.; and by E. Hennecke, *Neutestamentliche Apocryphen*, 2d edition, Tübingen, 1924.

In French there is the translation by Hemmer, Oger, and Lamont already mentioned.

In Italian there are renderings by M. dal Pra, *La Didache*, Venice, 1938; and by G. Bosio, *I Padri apostolici*, Part I, Turin, 1940, in the series Corona Patrum Salesiana.

All these editions have introductions and notes. The most significant are by Harnack, Schaff, Hemmer, Bigg, Kleist, and Knopf. While Klauser's introduction and notes (in Latin) are most concise, they are no less important.

Studies in the Didache are extremely numerous. Of special importance are the following books: C. Taylor, *The Teaching of the Twelve Apostles with Illustrations from the Talmud*, Cambridge, 1886; J. A. Robinson, *Barnabas, Hermas, and the Didache*, London, 1920 (a revision of chs. 1 and 3 was published posthumously with a preface by R. H. Connolly in *The Journal of Theological Studies*, 1934, pp. 113–146, 225–248); J. Muilenburg, *The Literary Relations of the Epistle of Barnabas and the Teaching of the Twelve Apostles*, Ph.D. thesis, Marburg, 1929; F. E. Vokes, *The Riddle of the Didache*, S.P.C.K., London, 1938.

For many years debate about the Didache has been carried on in *The Journal of Theological Studies*. The following articles are noteworthy: J. V. Bartlet, "The Didache Reconsidered," 1921, pp. 239–249; R. H. Connolly, "The Use of the Didache in the Didascalia," 1923, pp. 147–157; F. R. M. Hitchcock, "Did Clement of Alexandria Know the Didache?" *ibid.*, pp. 397–401; R. H. Connolly, "New Fragments of the Didache," 1924, pp. 151–153; F. C. Burkitt, "Barnabas and the Didache," 1932, pp. 25–27; R. H. Connolly, "The Didache in Relation to the Epistle of Barnabas," *ibid.*, pp. 237–253; C. T. Dix, "Didache and Diatessaron," 1933, pp. 242–250, with Connolly's reply, *ibid.*, pp. 346, 347; A. L. Williams, "The Date of the Epistle of Barnabas," *ibid.*, pp. 337–346; R. D. Middleton, "The Eucharistic Prayers of the Didache," 1935, pp. 259–267; H. G. Gibbins, "The Problem of the Liturgical Section of the Didache," *ibid.*, pp. 373–386; B. H. Streeter, "The Much-belaboured Didache," 1936, pp. 369–374; R. H. Connolly, "Barnabas and the Didache," 1937, pp. 165–167;

and "Canon Streeter on the Didache," *ibid.*, pp. 364–379; J. M. Creed, "The Didache," 1938, 370–387; W. Telfer, "The Didache and the Apostolic Synod of Antioch," 1939, pp. 133–146, 258–271; J. E. L. Oulton, "Clement of Alexandria and the Didache," 1940, pp. 177–179; W. Telfer, "The 'Plot' of the Didache," 1944, pp. 141–151.

To these studies should be added K. Kohler's article "Didache" in the *Jewish Encyclopedia*, Vol. IV, 1903, pp. 585–588; Louis Finkelstein, "The Birkat Ha-Mazon," in *Jewish Quarterly Review*, 1928, pp. 211–262; C. H. Turner, "The Early Christian Ministry and the Didache" in his *Studies in Early Church History*, Oxford, 1912, pp. 1–32; B. H. Streeter's summary of his view in *The Primitive Church* (Appendix C), New York, 1929; R. H. Connolly, "The Didache and Montanism," and "Agape and Eucharist in the Didache," both in the *Downside Review*, 1937, pp. 339–347, 477–489; the treatment by H. Lietzmann in *The Beginnings of the Christian Church*, New York, 1937, pp. 270–274; and the important study by E. Goodspeed, "The Didache, Barnabas, and the Doctrina," in the *Anglican Theological Review*, 1945, pp. 228–247, reprinted in his *Apostolic Fathers: An American Translation*, New York, 1950, pp. 285–310.

Of German and French studies we may mention A. Harnack, *Die Apostellehre und die jüdischen zwei Wege*, Leipzig, 1886, 2d edition, 1896 (an expanded reprint of his article "Apostellehre" in *Realencyclopädie für protestantische Theologie und Kirche*); F. X. Funk, "Die Didache, Zeit und Verhältnis zu den verwandten Schriften," and "Zur Didache, der Frage nach der Grundschrift und ihren Rezensionen," in *Kirchengeschichtliche Abhandlungen und Untersuchungen*, 2, Paderborn, 1907, pp. 108–141, 218–229; L. Wohleb, *Die lateinische Übersetzung der Didache kritisch und sprachlich untersucht*, Paderborn, 1913; M. Dibelius, "Die Mahlgebete der Didache," in *Zeitschrift für die neutestamentliche Wissenschaft*, 1938, pp. 32–41; and H. Leclercq, "Didache," in *Dictionnaire d'archéologie chrétienne et de liturgie*, Vol. IV.1, Paris, 1920, cols. 772–798. For further notices of the literature see Leclercq; also A. Harnack, *Geschichte der altchristlichen Literatur*, Leipzig, 1893, Vol. I, pp. 86–92; O. Bardenhewer, *Geschichte der altkirchlichen Literatur*, Freiburg, 1913, Vol. I, pp. 90–103; B. Altaner, *Patrologie*, 2d edition, Freiburg, 1950, pp. 39, 40; and J. Quasten, *Patrology*, Vol. I, pp. 38, 39, Utrecht, 1950.

The Teaching of the Twelve Apostles, Commonly Called the Didache

THE TEXT

The Lord's Teaching to the Heathen by the Twelve Apostles:
There are two ways, one of life and one of death; and between 1
the two ways there is a great difference.

Now, this is the way of life: "First, you must love God who 2
made you, and second, your neighbor as yourself."[17] And
whatever you want people to refrain from doing to you, you
must not do to them.[18]

What these maxims teach is this: "Bless those who curse you," 3
and "pray for your enemies." Moreover, fast "for those who
persecute you." For "what credit is it to you if you love those
who love you? Is that not the way the heathen act?" But "you
must love those who hate you,"[19] and then you will make no
enemies. "Abstain from carnal passions."[20] If someone strikes 4
you "on the right cheek, turn to him the other too, and you
will be perfect."[21] If someone "forces you to go one mile with
him, go along with him for two"; if someone robs you "of your
overcoat, give him your suit as well."[22] If someone deprives
you of "your property, do not ask for it back."[23] (You could
not get it back anyway!) "Give to everybody who begs from 5
you, and ask for no return."[24] For the Father wants his own
gifts to be universally shared. Happy is the man who gives as
the commandment bids him, for he is guiltless! But alas for
the man who receives! If he receives because he is in need, he
will be guiltless. But if he is not in need he will have to stand
trial why he received and for what purpose. He will be thrown

17 Matt. 22:37–39; Lev. 19:18.
19 Matt. 5:44, 46, 47; Luke 6:27, 28, 32, 33.
21 Matt. 5:39, 48; Luke 6:29.
23 Luke 6:30.

18 Cf. Matt. 7:12.
20 I Peter 2:11.
22 Matt. 5:40, 41.
24 Ibid.

into prison and have his action investigated; and "he will not
6 get out until he has paid back the last cent."[25] Indeed, there
is a further saying that relates to this: "Let your donation sweat
in your hands until you know to whom to give it."[26]

2,2 The second commandment of the Teaching: "Do not
murder; do not commit adultery"; do not corrupt boys; do
not fornicate; "do not steal"; do not practice magic; do not go
in for sorcery; do not murder a child by abortion or kill a new-
3 born infant. "Do not covet your neighbor's property; do not
commit perjury; do not bear false witness";[27] do not slander;
4 do not bear grudges. Do not be double-minded or double-
5 tongued, for a double tongue is "a deadly snare."[28] Your
words shall not be dishonest or hollow, but substantiated by
6 action. Do not be greedy or extortionate or hypocritical or
malicious or arrogant. Do not plot against your neighbor.
7 Do not hate anybody; but reprove some, pray for others, and
still others love more than your own life.

3 My child, flee from all wickedness and from everything of
2 that sort. Do not be irritable, for anger leads to murder. Do not
be jealous or contentious or impetuous, for all this breeds
murder.
3 My child, do not be lustful, for lust leads to fornication. Do
not use foul language or leer, for all this breeds adultery.
4 My child, do not be a diviner, for that leads to idolatry. Do
not be an enchanter or an astrologer or a magician. Moreover,
have no wish to observe or heed such practices, for all this
breeds idolatry.
5 My child, do not be a liar, for lying leads to theft. Do not be
avaricious or vain, for all this breeds thievery.
6 My child, do not be a grumbler, for grumbling leads to
blasphemy. Do not be stubborn or evil-minded, for all this
breeds blasphemy.
7 But be humble since "the humble will inherit the earth."[29]
8 Be patient, merciful, harmless, quiet, and good; and always
"have respect for the teaching"[30] you have been given. Do not
put on airs or give yourself up to presumptuousness. Do not
associate with the high and mighty; but be with the upright
and humble. Accept whatever happens to you as good, in the
realization that nothing occurs apart from God.

---

[25] Matt. 5:26. This whole section 5 should be compared with Hermas,
    Mand. 2:4–7, on which it is apparently dependent.
[26] Source unknown.   [27] Ex. 20:13–17; cf. Matt. 19:18; 5:33.
[28] Prov. 21:6.   [29] Ps. 37:11; Matt. 5:5.   [30] Isa. 66:2.

My child, day and night "you should remember him who 4 preaches God's word to you,"[31] and honor him as you would the Lord. For where the Lord's nature is discussed, there the Lord is. Every day you should seek the company of saints to 2 enjoy their refreshing conversation. You must not start a 3 schism, but reconcile those at strife. "Your judgments must be fair."[32] You must not play favorites when reproving transgressions. You must not be of two minds about your decision.[33] 4

Do not be one who holds his hand out to take, but shuts it 5 when it comes to giving. If your labor has brought you earnings, 6 pay a ransom for your sins. Do not hesitate to give and do not 7 give with a bad grace; for you will discover who He is that pays you back a reward with a good grace. Do not turn your back 8 on the needy, but share everything with your brother and call nothing your own. For if you have what is eternal in common, how much more should you have what is transient!

Do not neglect your responsibility[34] to your son or your 9 daughter, but from their youth you shall teach them to revere God. Do not be harsh in giving orders to your slaves and slave 10 girls. They hope in the same God as you, and the result may be that they cease to revere the God over you both. For when he comes to call us, he will not respect our station, but will call those whom the Spirit has made ready. You slaves, for 11 your part, must obey your masters with reverence and fear, as if they represented God.

You must hate all hypocrisy and everything which fails to 12 please the Lord. You must not forsake "the Lord's command- 13 ments," but "observe" the ones you have been given, "neither adding nor subtracting anything."[35] At the church meeting 14 you must confess your sins, and not approach prayer with a bad conscience. That is the way of life.

But the way of death is this: First of all, it is wicked and 5 thoroughly blasphemous: murders, adulteries, lusts, fornications, thefts, idolatries, magic arts, sorceries, robberies, false witness, hypocrisies, duplicity, deceit, arrogance, malice, stubbornness, greediness, filthy talk, jealousy, audacity, haughtiness, boastfulness.[36]

Those who persecute good people, who hate truth, who love 2

31 Heb. 13:7.   32 Deut. 1:16, 17; Prov. 31:9.
33 Meaning uncertain.
34 Literally, "Do not withold your hand from . . ."
35 Deut. 4:2; 12:32.
36 Cf. Matt. 15:19; Mark 7:21, 22; Rom. 1:29–31; Gal. 5:19–21.

lies, who are ignorant of the reward of uprightness, who do not "abide by goodness"[37] or justice, and are on the alert not for goodness but for evil: gentleness and patience are remote from them. "They love vanity,"[38] "look for profit,"[39] have no pity for the poor, do not exert themselves for the oppressed, ignore their Maker, "murder children,"[40] corrupt God's image, turn their backs on the needy, oppress the afflicted, defend the rich, unjustly condemn the poor, and are thoroughly wicked. My children, may you be saved from all this!

6 See "that no one leads you astray"[41] from this way of the teaching, since such a one's teaching is godless.

2 If you can bear the Lord's full yoke, you will be perfect. But if you cannot, then do what you can.

3 Now about food: undertake what you can. But keep strictly away from what is offered to idols, for that implies worshiping dead gods.

7 Now about baptism: this is how to baptize. Give public instruction on all these points, and then "baptize" in running water, "in the name of the Father and of the Son and of the 2 Holy Spirit."[42] If you do not have running water, baptize in 3 some other. If you cannot in cold, then in warm. If you have neither, then pour water on the head three times "in the name 4 of the Father, Son, and Holy Spirit."[43] Before the baptism, moreover, the one who baptizes and the one being baptized must fast, and any others who can. And you must tell the one being baptized to fast for one or two days beforehand.

8 Your fasts must not be identical with those of the hypocrites.[44] They fast on Mondays and Thursdays; but you should fast on Wednesdays and Fridays.

2 You must not pray like the hypocrites,[45] but "pray as follows"[46] as the Lord bid us in his gospel:

"Our Father in heaven, hallowed be your name; your Kingdom come; your will be done on earth as it is in heaven; give us today our bread for the morrow; and forgive us our debts as we forgive our debtors. And do not lead us into temptation, but save us from the evil one, for yours is the power and the glory forever."

3 You should pray in this way three times a day.

---

37 Rom. 12:9.
38 Ps. 4:2.
39 Isa. 1:23.
40 Wis. 12:6.
41 Matt. 24:4.
42 Matt. 28:19.
43 Ibid.
44 I.e., the Jews. Cf. Matt. 6:16.
45 Matt. 6:5.
46 Cf. Matt. 6:9–13.

Now about the Eucharist:[47] This is how to give thanks: 9
First in connection with the cup:[48]   2

"We thank you, our Father, for the holy vine[49] of David,
your child, which you have revealed through Jesus, your child.
To you be glory forever."

Then in connection with the piece[50] [broken off the loaf]:   3
"We thank you, our Father, for the life and knowledge
which you have revealed through Jesus, your child. To you be
glory forever.

"As this piece [of bread] was scattered over the hills[51] and 4
then was brought together and made one, so let your Church
be brought together from the ends of the earth into your
Kingdom. For yours is the glory and the power through Jesus
Christ forever."

You must not let anyone eat or drink of your Eucharist 5
except those baptized in the Lord's name. For in reference to
this the Lord said, "Do not give what is sacred to dogs."[52]

After you have finished your meal, say grace[53] in this way: 10
"We thank you, holy Father, for your sacred name which 2
you have lodged[54] in our hearts, and for the knowledge and
faith and immortality which you have revealed through Jesus,
your child. To you be glory forever.

"Almighty Master, 'you have created everything'[55] for the 3
sake of your name, and have given men food and drink to
enjoy that they may thank you. But to us you have given

---

47 I.e., "the Thanksgiving." The term, however, had become a technical
one in Christianity for the special giving of thanks at the Lord's Supper.
One might render the verbal form ("give thanks"), which immediately
follows, as "say grace," for it was out of the Jewish forms for grace before
and after meals (accompanied in the one instance by the breaking of
bread and in the other by sharing a common cup of wine) that the Christian thanksgivings of the Lord's Supper developed.

48 It is a curious feature of the Didache that the cup has been displaced
from the end of the meal to the very beginning. Equally curious is the
absence of any direct reference to the body and blood of Christ.

49 This may be a metaphorical reference to the divine life and knowledge
revealed through Jesus (cf. ch. 9:3). It may also refer to the Messianic
promise (cf. Isa. 11:1), or to the Messianic community (cf. Ps. 80:8), i.e.,
the Church.

50 An odd phrase, but one that refers to the Jewish custom (taken over
in the Christian Lord's Supper) of grace before meals. The head of
the house would distribute to each of the guests a piece of bread broken
off a loaf, after uttering the appropriate thanksgiving to God.

51 The reference is likely to the sowing of wheat on the hillsides of Judea.
52 Matt. 7:6.   53 Or "give thanks." See note 47.
54 For the phrase cf. Neh. 1:9.   55 Wis. 1:14; Sir. 18:1; Rev. 4:11.

spiritual food and drink and eternal life through Jesus, your child.

4 "Above all, we thank you that you are mighty. To you be glory forever."

5 "Remember, Lord, your Church, to save it from all evil and to make it perfect by your love. Make it holy, 'and gather' it 'together from the four winds'[56] into your Kingdom which you have made ready for it. For yours is the power and the glory forever."

6 "Let Grace[57] come and let this world pass away."
   "Hosanna to the God of David!"[58]
   "If anyone is holy, let him come. If not, let him repent."[59]
   "Our Lord, come!"[60]
   "Amen."[61]

7 In the case of prophets, however, you should let them give thanks in their own way.[62]

11 Now, you should welcome anyone who comes your way and
2 teaches you all we have been saying. But if the teacher proves himself a renegade and by teaching otherwise contradicts all this, pay no attention to him. But if his teaching furthers the Lord's righteousness and knowledge, welcome him as the Lord.

3 Now about the apostles and prophets: Act in line with the
4 gospel precept.[63] Welcome every apostle on arriving, as if he
5 were the Lord. But he must not stay beyond one day. In case of necessity, however, the next day too. If he stays three days,
6 he is a false prophet. On departing, an apostle must not accept anything save sufficient food to carry him till his next lodging. If he asks for money, he is a false prophet.

7 While a prophet is making ecstatic utterances,[64] you must not test or examine him. For "every sin will be forgiven,"
8 but this sin "will not be forgiven."[65] However, not everybody

---

[56] Matt. 24:31.   [57] A title for Christ.
[58] Cf. Matt. 21:9, 15.   [59] Or perhaps "be converted."
[60] Cf. I Cor. 16:22.
[61] These terse exclamations may be versicles and responses. More likely they derive from the Jewish custom of reading verses concerning Israel's future redemption and glory, after the final benediction.
[62] I.e., they are not bound by the texts given.   [63] Matt. 10:40, 41.
[64] Literally, "speaking in a spirit," i.e., speaking while possessed by a divine or demonic spirit. This whole passage (ch. 11:7–12) is a sort of parallel to Matt. 12:31 ff. There is an interpretation of the sin against the Holy Ghost, followed by a comment on good and evil conduct (cf. Matt. 12:33–37), and concluded by the prophets' signs which are suggested by the sign of the Son of Man (Matt. 12:38 ff.).
[65] Matt. 12:31.

making ecstatic utterances is a prophet, but only if he behaves like the Lord. It is by their conduct that the false prophet and the [true] prophet can be distinguished. For instance, if a prophet 9 marks out a table in the Spirit,[66] he must not eat from it. If he does, he is a false prophet. Again, every prophet who teaches 10 the truth but fails to practice what he preaches is a false prophet. But every attested and genuine prophet who acts 11 with a view to symbolizing the mystery of the Church,[67] and does not teach you to do all he does, must not be judged by you. His judgment rests with God. For the ancient prophets too acted in this way. But if someone says in the Spirit, "Give 12 me money, or something else," you must not heed him. However, if he tells you to give for others in need, no one must condemn him.

Everyone "who comes" to you "in the name of the Lord"[68] 12 must be welcomed. Afterward, when you have tested him, you will find out about him, for you have insight into right and wrong. If it is a traveler who arrives, help him all you can. 2 But he must not stay with you more than two days, or, if necessary, three. If he wants to settle with you and is an artisan, he 3 must work for his living. If, however, he has no trade, use your 4 judgment in taking steps for him to live with you as a Christian without being idle. If he refuses to do this, he is trading on 5 Christ. You must be on your guard against such people.

Every genuine prophet who wants to settle with you "has a 13 right to his support." Similarly, a genuine teacher himself, just 2 like a "workman, has a right to his support."[69] Hence take all 3 the first fruits of vintage and harvest, and of cattle and sheep, and give these first fruits to the prophets. For they are your high priests. If, however, you have no prophet, give them to 4

---

[66] The sense is not clear, but suggests a dramatic portrayal of the Messianic banquet. It was characteristic of the Biblical prophets to drive home their teaching by dramatic and symbolic actions (cf. Jer., ch. 19; Acts 21:11; etc.).

[67] Literally, "acts with a view to a worldly mystery of the Church." The meaning is not certain, but some dramatic action, symbolizing the mystical marriage of the Church to Christ, is probably intended. The reference may, indeed, be to the prophet's being accompanied by a spiritual sister (cf. I Cor. 7:36 ff.).

[68] Matt. 21:9; Ps. 118:26; cf. John 5:43.

[69] Matt. 10:10. The provision for the prophet or teacher to settle and to be supported by the congregation implies the birth of the monarchical episcopate. Note the connection of this with the high priesthood (cf. Hippolytus, Apost. Trad. 3:4) and tithing. No provision is made for the support of the local clergy in ch. 15.

5 the poor. If you make bread, take the first fruits and give in
6 accordance with the precept.[70] Similarly, when you open a
jar of wine or oil, take the first fruits and give them to the
7 prophets. Indeed, of money, clothes, and of all your possessions,
take such first fruits as you think right, and give in accordance
with the precept.

14 On every Lord's Day—his special day[71]—come together and
break bread and give thanks, first confessing your sins so that
2 your sacrifice may be pure. Anyone at variance with his neighbor must not join you, until they are reconciled, lest your sacri-
3 fice be defiled. For it was of this sacrifice that the Lord said,
"Always and everywhere offer me a pure sacrifice; for I am a
great King, says the Lord, and my name is marveled at by the
nations."[72]

15 You must, then, elect for yourselves bishops and deacons
who are a credit to the Lord, men who are gentle, generous,
faithful, and well tried. For their ministry to you is identical
2 with that of the prophets and teachers. You must not, therefore,
despise them, for along with the prophets and teachers they
enjoy a place of honor among you.

3 Furthermore, do not reprove each other angrily, but quietly,
as you find it in the gospel. Moreover, if anyone has wronged
his neighbor, nobody must speak to him, and he must not hear
4 a word from you, until he repents. Say your prayers, give your
charity, and do everything just as you find it in the gospel of
our Lord.

16 "Watch" over your life: do not let "your lamps" go out, and
do not keep "your loins ungirded"; but "be ready," for "you
2 do not know the hour when our Lord is coming."[73] Meet
together frequently in your search for what is good for your
souls, since "a lifetime of faith will be of no advantage"[74]
3 to you unless you prove perfect at the very last. For in the final
days multitudes of false prophets and seducers will appear.
4 Sheep will turn into wolves, and love into hatred. For with the
increase of iniquity men will hate, persecute, and betray each
other. And then the world deceiver will appear in the guise of
God's Son. He will work "signs and wonders"[75] and the earth
will fall into his hands and he will commit outrages such as
5 have never occurred before. Then mankind will come to the

70 Deut. 18:3–5.
71 Literally, "On every Lord's Day of the Lord."
72 Mal. 1:11, 14.   73 Matt. 24:42, 44; Luke 12:35.
74 Barn. 4:9.   75 Matt. 24:24.

fiery trial "and many will fall away"[76] and perish, "but those
who persevere" in their faith "will be saved"[77] by the Curse
himself.[78] Then "there will appear the signs"[79] of the Truth: 6
first the sign of stretched-out [hands] in heaven,[80] then the
sign of "a trumpet's blast,"[81] and thirdly the resurrection of
the dead, though not of all the dead, but as it has been said: 7
"The Lord will come and all his saints with him. Then the
world will see the Lord coming on the clouds of the sky."[82]

[76] Matt. 24:10.   [77] Matt. 10:22; 24:13.
[78] An obscure reference, but possibly meaning the Christ who suffered
the death of one accursed (Gal. 3:13; Barn. 7:9). Cf. two other titles for
the Christ: Grace (ch. 10:6) and Truth (v. 6).
[79] Matt. 24:30.
[80] Another obscure reference, possibly to the belief that the Christ would
appear on a glorified cross. Cf. Barn. 12:2–4.
[81] Matt. 24:31.
[82] Zech. 14:5; I Thess. 3:13; Matt. 24:30.

AN EARLY CHRISTIAN SERMON

An Anonymous Sermon,
Commonly Called Clement's Second
Letter to the Corinthians

INTRODUCTION

THE DOCUMENT THAT GOES UNDER THIS MISLEADING name is neither a letter nor a genuine work of Clement of Rome. It is an anonymous Christian sermon—the earliest that has come down to us. It was written at some time before the middle of the second century; and while scholars differ widely on its place of origin, there are a number of indications that it stems from Egypt. Its importance lies in the picture it gives us of early Christian preaching.

Here is a homily that some presbyter[1] has written out with a view to reading it to a congregation immediately after the Scripture lesson (ch. 19:1). It is simple, direct, and without any claim to style or clear organization. Taking a verse from the lection (Isa. 54:1), the preacher briefly expounds it and passes on to exhort his hearers to a life of moral purity and steadfastness in persecution, emphasizing the need to repent in the light of the coming judgment. He is addressing Gentile converts (chs. 1:6; 3:1; 17:3), who are in danger of falling a prey to Gnostic teachings (ch. 10:5). In consequence, he stresses the divinity of Christ (ch. 1:1), the resurrection of the flesh (ch. 9), and the way in which the Church is the continuity of the incarnation (ch. 14). These theological emphases are sometimes tinged with Gnostic speculation (chs. 12; 14), but they are nonetheless aimed against basic Gnostic tenets which saw in Christ a being intermediary between God and man, and denied the significance of the body. By holding that the material world was the creation of an evil or impotent god who was contrasted with the good God revealed in Christ, these Gnostics

[1] It would appear from ch. 17:3 that the author associates himself with the ruling body of presbyters.

rejected the reality of the incarnation and indulged in a moral antinomianism, on the grounds that bodily life was inherently evil. Against such views our sermon is directed.

THE ORIGIN OF THE HOMILY

How this homily ever came to be associated with Clement's name and dubbed his Second Letter is something of a riddle. This had, however, occurred as early as Eusebius' time, for he mentions the fact that a second letter is ascribed to Clement, though he rejects it as unauthentic on the grounds that it is not cited by early writers.[2] Yet the sermon was held in high esteem in some areas of the Church, for it forms part of the New Testament canon in two manuscripts that have survived. In the Codex Alexandrinus (fifth century) it comes at the close of the New Testament after Clement's genuine Letter; while in a Syrian manuscript of the twelfth century the two Letters of Clement are inserted between the Catholic Epistles and the Epistles of Paul. Furthermore, the *Apostolic Canons* (a work emanating from Syria in the late fourth century) list Clement's two Letters as part of the New Testament (canon 85). It is first in Severus of Antioch[3] (sixth century) that the destination of the Second Letter to the Corinthians is made clear, though a century earlier this is probably assumed by Pseudo-Justin.[4]

Somehow or other our sermon became attached to Clement's genuine Letter. This must have happened by the middle of the second century, for by A.D. 180 the New Testament canon was sufficiently settled not to have admitted such an intruder. Indeed, it is not impossible that Irenaeus[5] knew of the homily as an addendum to Clement's Letter to the Corinthians. For in listing the contents of that work he introduces one doctrine— that of the fiery judgment—that is notably absent from it, but that plays a significant role in our sermon (chs. 16:3; 17:7). Strangely enough, this same doctrine is also attributed by Pseudo-Justin to Clement's Letter to the Corinthians.

Various attempts have been made to explain this situation. It is sometimes argued that the confusion could have originated only in Corinth. It was that church which possessed Clement's genuine Letter, and from time to time read it at worship on

---

[2] *Hist. eccl.*, III, ch. 38. So also Jerome, *De Vir. Ill.* 15.
[3] For the passage see J. B. Lightfoot, *The Apostolic Fathers*, 1890, Part 1, Vol. I, pp. 182, 183.
[4] *Ibid.*, p. 178, *Resp. ad Orthod.* 74.   [5] *Adv. haer.* III. 3:3.

Sundays.[6] What could be more likely than that some treasured but anonymous homily of that church should be bound up with Clement's Letter, and so become a part of the lectionary manuscript? Furthermore, it is claimed that one reference in our sermon makes it very clear that it stems from Corinth. In ch. 7 the preacher compares the Christian life to the Greek games, and even mentions the fact that the athletes "come by sea" to participate (ch. 7:1). Is this not a decisive indication that the local Isthmian games are in his mind?[7] The word *katapleō* literally means "sail to the shore," and it would appear that the preacher was thinking of the crowds landing on the Corinthian Isthmus.

Against this view two objections can be raised. For one thing, Corinth was not the only place where Clement's genuine Letter was prized or read in worship. Alexandria was another; for Clement of Alexandria several times cites it as Scripture,[8] apparently viewing it as an apostolic writing and identifying its author with the Clement in Phil. 4:3. It is just as likely that Alexandria should be the source of the confusion as Corinth. Moreover, the reference to the games in ch. 7 cannot be unduly pressed. The verb *katapleō* can be used in a derived sense, meaning little more than "resort to"; and the popularity of the Isthmian games was matched by that of those in other centers. Indeed, there were important games held in Alexandria.

Another theory, originally put forward by Hilgenfeld,[9] has won a good deal of acceptance, due to its elaboration by Harnack.[10] More recently it has been defended by Goodspeed.[11] It is contended that our homily is the lost letter that Bishop Soter of Rome (A.D. 166–174) wrote to the church of Corinth. This letter, as we learn from the reply by the bishop of Corinth, Dionysius,[12] was much valued, and read in public

---

[6] Eusebius, *Hist. eccl.* IV. 23:11.

[7] So Lightfoot, *op cit.*, Part 1, Vol. II, p. 197, and G. Krüger in *Studies in Early Christianity*, ed. by S. J. Case, pp. 423, 424, Zondervan, New York, 1928.

[8] For the passages see Lightfoot, *op cit.*, Part 1, Vol. I, pp. 158–160.

[9] *Novum Testamentum extra canonem receptum*, I, Leipzig, 1866, p. XXXIX. In the later ed. (1876), he argued the homily was an early work of Clement of Alexandria.

[10] *Chronologie*, 1897, Vol. I, pp. 438–450, and *Zeitschrift für die neutestamentliche Wissenschaft*, 6, 1905, pp. 67–71.

[11] *The Apostolic Fathers*, pp. 83, 84, 1950.

[12] Eusebius, *Hist. eccl.* IV. 23:11.

worship. There are two slight indications that our sermon comes from Rome. One is the curious use of a lost apocalypse (possibly that of Eldad and Modat, mentioned in Hermas, Vis. II. 3:4) by both Clement of Rome (ch. 23:3, 4) and our homily (ch. 11:2–4). The other is the similarity of our work, in its stress on repentance and the end of the world, to the Roman Shepherd of Hermas itself.

The difficulties, however, of this thesis are insuperable. A sermon is not a letter; and there could be nothing more foreign to Roman Christianity of A.D. 170 than the tone of our homily. Its semi-Gnostic phrases, despite its attack on Gnostic ideas; its speculative spirit; its lack of mention of the monepiscopate,[13] of the Logos Christology, and of tradition—all these factors tell against its Roman origin. Even more decisive is its use of an apocryphal gospel—the Gospel of the Egyptians—of which more will be said later. Here we may merely note that Hippolytus, who embodied the distinctively Roman tradition and who lived so near to Soter's time, viewed that gospel as quite heretical.[14] It is surely incredible that at a time when the fourfold gospel had triumphed, a Roman bishop should have relied on an apocryphal one for three or more citations! Then again, Dionysius does not say that Soter sent a homily with a covering letter—which we must assume on this theory. He says Soter sent a letter; and by no stretch of the imagination can our document be called that. Furthermore, the alleged similarities of our homily with the Shepherd of Hermas are not very persuasive. It is rather the marked differences between the two works that are striking. Hermas, for example, insists that only one repentance after baptism is permissible; our preacher mentions no such limit. Again, Hermas' Christology is tinged with adoptionism, while our author thinks in terms of pre-existent spirit becoming incarnate. Finally, while both Clement's genuine Letter and our homily use some lost apocalypse, we are not forced to assume that Rome was the only place where this document was current.

The only situation that really fits the temper and tone of our sermon is Alexandria. This was perceived and worked out by Vernon Bartlet as early as 1906;[15] and Streeter, quite independently, arrived at the same conclusion some twenty years later.[16] The church of Alexandria was the fountainhead of

---

[13] Only presbyters are referred to in ch. 17: 3, 5.   [14] *Ref. haer.* V. 7:9.
[15] In *Zeitschrift für die neutestamentliche Wissenschaft*, 7, 1906, pp. 123–135.
[16] *The Primitive Church*, pp. 244–253, Macmillan, 1929.

Gnostic speculation; and even the orthodox in that center cannot have been unaffected by its spirit. The strong Platonic note that underlies the discussion of the pre-existent Church in ch. 14 is thoroughly Alexandrine, and reflects the world of thought out of which Valentinus developed his "aeons." Then again, our preacher relies on an apocryphal gospel which (so far as we know) was in use only in Alexandria, and which itself shows Gnostic traces (cf. the citation in ch. 12:2). It is the Gospel of the Egyptians, some fragments of which have been preserved by Clement of Alexandria.[17] The logion in ch. 12:2 comes from that gospel (see note *ad loc.*), and we may assume that other sayings not to be found in our Gospels (chs. 4:5; 5:2-4) are similarly derived from it. Since, too, it is likely that this Egyptian gospel was a second century product based on the Synoptic tradition, other quotations in our sermon may be drawn from it, rather than from their original sources. Once more, the manuscript tradition of our homily is entirely Eastern. No Latin translation of it has turned up, nor does it seem to have been known in the West. Finally, we may emphasize the high regard shown by Clement of Alexandria for his Roman namesake's genuine Letter. If this could be treated as Scripture and publicly read in Alexandria, it is just as likely that the confusion of the documents originated there as in Corinth. Indeed, in the light of the other factors, it would seem that some local, anonymous homily was early attached in Alexandria to a lectionary manuscript that concluded with Clement's Letter. Thus our sermon came eventually to be passed off as his Second Epistle.

Religious Ideas

As we have already indicated, the purpose of this homily is to call the congregation to repentance (chs. 8:2; 9:7, 8; etc.), to urge them to steadfastness in persecution (chs. 3:1-4; 5; 19:3, 4), and to challenge some basic Gnostic ideas. There is a stress upon the divinity of Christ (ch. 1:1) and the resurrection of the flesh (ch. 9). Much is said about Christian purity, about the need to keep the seal of baptism free from defilement (chs. 6:9; 7:6), to confess Christ by our actions, and to engage in acts of charity (ch. 16:4). Such acts, it is pointed out, lighten the load of sin. This is a characteristic emphasis of the second

[17] See M. R. James, *The Apocryphal New Testament*, pp. 10-12, 1924.

century where, after the passing of the first enthusiasm of the
faith and in view of Gnostic antinomianism, the need was
always present to stress the moral life and obedience to the
commandments. Hence such un-Pauline phrases occur as:
"Fasting is better than prayer" (ch. 16:4), or, "By giving up
the soul's wicked passions we shall share in the mercy of Jesus"
(ch. 16:2). The tone of the homily is removed from Paul's
gospel of faith and justification. The accent falls rather on
repentance and good works.

The urgent note of the old eschatology is still present
(chs. 12:1; 17:4–7), and the day of judgment is already on its
way (ch. 16:3).

The most notable theological idea, however, in the sermon
is the doctrine of the Church. In a difficult passage (ch. 14),
dependent on the Platonic conception of the phenomenal
world as a copy of the immaterial forms, the author works
out a view of the Church as the continuity of the incarnation,
and connects it with the need for Christian purity. The Church,
he claims, is a pre-existent, spiritual reality which took visible
form in the flesh of Christ, and is similarly manifested in the
flesh of Christians. To abuse the flesh, therefore, is to abuse the
spiritual reality of the Church, the flesh being the copy of the
"spirit." On the other hand, to keep the flesh pure is to preserve the Church from defilement. As a result, the Christian
shares in the spiritual reality of the Church, and in return for
giving up his lustful passions, he "gets back," as it were, a
reward by sharing in "spirit." The line of thought is not
altogether clear; but the underlying conviction is that the
Church is a spiritual reality manifested in the incarnation and
also in the bodies of true Christians.

Finally, the references to Scripture may be mentioned. This
sermon is remarkable for distinguishing between the two classes
of writings in the Church—the "Bible" and the "Apostles"
(ch. 14:2). The "Bible" (literally, the "books") refers to the
Septuagint; the "Apostles" are the apostolic writings. Both were
read from in Christian worship, as Justin tells us (Apol. I, ch.
67); and these lections were immediately followed by the
sermon, as our preacher himself indicates (ch. 19:1). By his
time the apostolic writings had been elevated to the status
of "Scripture" beside the Septuagint; for in one place (ch.
2:4) he introduces a Gospel saying (Matt. 9:13) by the phrase,
"Another [passage of] Scripture says." This is the first clear
instance we have of such use of a "New Testament" on a level

with the Old.[18] Our preacher appears familiar with much of the New Testament as we know it; though some of the supposed citations are short phrases that cannot be unduly pressed.

To summarize: We have in this document the earliest Christian sermon that has been preserved. It is likely a product of the Alexandrine church before the middle of the second century. It is interesting as indicating the use of an apocryphal gospel, as evidencing certain Gnostic influences while combating basically Gnostic ideas, and as developing the view of the Church as the continuity of the incarnation.

[18] Cf. the passage in Barn. 4:14, quoting Matt. 12:14; but it may well be there that the author imagines he is citing from the Septuagint.

MANUSCRIPTS AND BOOKS

The Greek text of our homily was first known only in a defective form. The fifth century N. T. Codex Alexandrinus includes it after Clement's genuine Letter, but the manuscript breaks off at ch. 12:5a. The sermon has no heading, but in a table of contents prefixed by the scribe, it is called "Clement's Second Letter." Patrick Young (Junius) edited the first edition from this Codex in 1633.

While seventeenth century scholars, such as Henry Dodwell and J. E. Grabe, had already guessed that our work was a sermon and not a letter, it was not until 1875 that this was made plain beyond dispute. In that year Philotheos Byrennios published the eleventh century Jerusalem Codex. This contained the whole text of the sermon whose concluding chapters (chs. 18; 19) make its nature abundantly clear. A few months later the Syriac version came to light in a twelfth century manuscript of the New Testament. These are our only authorities for the text. They are described at length in Lightfoot's *Apostolic Fathers*, Part 1, Vol. I, pp. 116 ff.

The Greek text will be found in the standard editions of the Apostolic Fathers. The one used for this translation is by K. Bihlmeyer, *Die apostolischen Väter*, Part 1, Tübingen, 1924. Others are by J. B. Lightfoot, *The Apostolic Fathers*, Part 1, "S. Clement of Rome," Vol. II, pp. 211–268, revised edition, London, 1890; and by K. Lake, *The Apostolic Fathers* (Loeb Classics), Vol. I, London, 1912. The text by H. Hemmer in Hemmer and Lejay's *Les Pères apostoliques*, Part 2, Paris, 1909, is based on F. X. Funk, *Patres apostolici* of 1901.

Modern English translations will be found in the editions by Lightfoot (with introduction and copious notes) and by Lake.

There is also T. W. Crafer's *Second Epistle of Clement to the Corinthians*, S.P.C.K., London, 1921. The latest renderings are by F. X. Glimm in *The Apostolic Fathers*, New York, 1947, in the series The Fathers of the Church and by E. J. Goodspeed in his *The Apostolic Fathers: An American Translation*, New York, 1950.

There is a translation into French (with introduction and notes) in the edition by Hemmer already mentioned. In German there are renderings by R. Knopf, *Die apostolischen Väter*, Tübingen, 1920, in Handbuch zum N. T. (with full notes, many philological), and by H. von Schubert in E. Hennecke, *Neutestamentliche Apokryphen*, 2d ed., Tübingen, 1924.

Basic introductory material will be found in the standard Patrologies by Harnack, Bardenhewer, Altaner, and Quasten. Of special importance are the following studies: Harnack's chapter in his *Die Chronologie der altchristlichen Literatur bis Eusebius*, Vol. I, pp. 438–450 (Roman thesis), Leipzig, 1897, and his further article in *Zeitschrift für die neutestamentliche Wissenschaft*, 6, pp. 67–71, 1905, "Zum Ursprung des sog. zweiten Klemensbriefes"; Vernon Bartlet, "The Origin and Date of 2 Clement," in the same journal, 7, pp. 123–135 (Alexandrine thesis), 1906; and B. H. Streeter, *The Primitive Church*, pp. 244–253 (Alexandrine thesis), New York, 1929.

There are a number of studies on the religious views of II Clement: H. Windisch, "Das Christentum des zweiten Klemensbriefes" in *Harnack-Ehrung, Beiträge zur Kirchengeschichte*, pp. 119–134 (he finds in it a shallow Christianity reflecting late Judaism), Leipzig, 1921; G. Krüger, "Bemerkungen zum zweiten Klemensbrief," in *Studies in Early Christianity*, ed. S. J. Case, pp. 419–439, New York, 1928; W. Praetorius, "Die Bedeutung der beiden Klemensbriefe für die älteste Geschichte der kirchlichen Praxis," in *Zeitschrift für die Kirchengeschichte*, 33, pp. 347–363, 501–528, 1912. See also D. Völter, *Die apostolischen Väter neu untersucht*, II. 1, "Die älteste Predigt aus Rom," Leiden, 1908, where with more ingenuity than success he tries to recover an original document behind II Clement. Another attempt to dispute the literary unity of our homily will be found in W. Schüssler's "Ist der zweite Klemensbrief ein einheitliches Ganzes?" in *Zeitschrift für die Kirchengeschichte*, 28, pp. 1–13, 1907. Some interesting material has been gathered by C. Taylor in his article "The Homily of Pseudo-Clement," in *The Journal of Philology*, 28, pp. 195–208, 1901. Reference to the doctrine of penance in II Clement will be found in J. Hoh, *Die kirchliche Busse im 2 Jahrhundert*, pp. 33–40, Müller & Seiffert, Breslau, 1932, and in B. Poschmann, *Paenitentia Secunda*, pp. 124–133, Hanstein, Bonn, 1940. On the doctrine of the Church see C. Chavasse, *The Bride of Christ*, pp. 115, 116, Faber, London, 1940.

Some other articles in the *Zeitschrift für die neutestamentliche Wissenschaft* may be noted: R. Knopf, "Die Anagnose zum zweiten Klemensbriefe," 3, pp. 266–279, 1902 (the lection is Isa., chs. 54 to 66!); A. Di Pauli, "Zum sog. 2 Korintherbrief des Klemens Romanus," 4, pp. 321–329 (a refinement of Harnack's thesis, disputing the authenticity of chs. 19; 20), 1903; Rendel Harris, "The Authorship of the So-called Second Epistle of Clement," 23, pp. 193–200 (claims Julius Cassianus for its author), 1924; H. Windisch, "Julius Cassianus und die Klemenshomilie," 25, pp. 258–262 (decisively answers Rendel Harris), 1926; G. Krüger, "Zu II Klem. 14.2," 31, pp. 204, 205 (argues *ekklēsia* is the subject of *ephanerōthē*), 1932.

An Anonymous Sermon,
Commonly Called Clement's Second
Letter to the Corinthians

THE TEXT

Brothers, we ought to think of Jesus Christ as we do of God— 1
as the "judge of the living and the dead."[19] And we ought
not to belittle our salvation. For when we belittle him, we hope 2
to get but little; and they that listen as to a trifling matter, do
wrong.[20] And we too do wrong when we fail to realize whence
and by whom and into what circumstances we were called,
and how much suffering Jesus Christ endured for us. How, 3
then, shall we repay him, or what return is worthy of his gift
to us? How many blessings we owe to him! For he has given us 4
light; as a Father he has called us sons; he has rescued us
when we were perishing. How, then, shall we praise him, or 5
how repay him for what we have received? Our minds were 6
impaired; we worshiped stone and wood and gold and silver
and brass, the works of men; and our whole life was nothing
else but death. So when we were wrapped in darkness and our
eyes were full of such mist, by his will we recovered our sight
and put off the cloud which infolded us. For he took pity on 7
us and in his tenderness saved us, since he saw our great error
and ruin, and that we had no hope of salvation unless it came
from him. For he called us when we were nothing, and willed 8
our existence from nothing.

"Rejoice, you who are barren and childless; cry out and 2
shout, you who were never in labor; for the desolate woman
has many more children than the one with the husband."[21]
When he says, "Rejoice, you who are barren and childless,"

---

19 Acts 10:42.
20 The expression is characteristically loose and implies an audience
listening to a sermon on salvation, and treating it lightly.
21 Isa. 54:1; Gal. 4:27.

he refers to us; for our Church was barren before it was given
2 children. And when he says, "Shout, you who were never in
labor," this is what he means: we should offer our prayers to
God with sincerity, and not lose heart like women in labor.
3 And he says, "The desolate woman has many more children
than the one with the husband," because our people seemed to
be abandoned by God. But now that we believe, we have
become more numerous than those who seemed to have God.
4 And another Scripture says, "I did not come to call the right-
5 eous, but sinners."[22] This means that those perishing must be
6 saved. Yes, a great and wonderful thing it is to support, not
things which are standing, but those which are collapsing.
7 Thus it was that the Christ willed to save what was perishing;
and he saved many when he came and called us who were
actually perishing.

3   Seeing, then, that he has had such pity on us, firstly, in that
we who are alive do not sacrifice to dead gods or worship them,
but through him have come to know the Father of truth—what
is knowledge in reference to him, save refusing to deny him
2 through whom we came to know the Father? He himself says,
"He who acknowledges me before men, I will acknowledge
3 before my Father."[23] This, then, is our reward, if we acknowl-
4 edge him through whom we are saved. But how do we acknowledge him? By doing what he says and not disobeying his commands; by honoring him not only with our lips, but with all
5 our heart and mind.[24] And he says in Isaiah as well, "This
people honors me with their lips but their heart is far from
me."[25]

4   Let us not merely call him Lord, for that will not save us.
2 For he says, "Not everyone who says to me, Lord, Lord, will
3 be saved, but he who does what is right."[26] Thus, brothers, let
us acknowledge him by our actions, by loving one another, by
refraining from adultery, backbiting, and jealousy, and by
being self-controlled, compassionate, kind. We ought to have
sympathy for one another and not to be avaricious. Let us
acknowledge him by acting in this way and not by doing the
4 opposite. We ought not to have greater fear of men than of
5 God. That is why, if you act in this way, the Lord said, "If
you are gathered with me in my bosom and do not keep my

---

22 Matt. 9:13; Mark 2:17; Luke 5:32. This is the earliest example of a
New Testament passage being cited as "Scripture."
23 Matt. 10:32; Luke 12:8.   24 Cf. Mark 12:30.
25 Isa. 29:13; cf. Matt. 15:8; Mark 7:6.   26 Matt. 7:21.

commands, I will cast you out and will say to you: 'Depart from me. I do not know whence you come, you workers of iniquity.' "[27]

Therefore, brothers, ceasing to tarry in this world, let us do 5 the will of Him who called us, and let us not be afraid to leave this world. For the Lord said, "You will be like lambs among 2 wolves."[28] But Peter replied by saying, "What if the wolves 3 tear the lambs to pieces?" Jesus said to Peter: "After their 4 death the lambs should not fear the wolves, nor should you fear those who kill you and can do nothing more to you. But fear him who, when you are dead, has power over soul and body to cast them into the flames of hell." You must realize, brothers, 5 that our stay in this world of the flesh is slight and short, but Christ's promise is great and wonderful, and means rest in the coming Kingdom and in eternal life. What, then, must we do 6 to get these things, except to lead a holy and upright life and to regard these things of the world as alien to us and not to desire them? For in wanting to obtain these things we fall from 7 the right way.

The Lord says, "No servant can serve two masters."[29] If 6 we want to serve both God and money, it will do us no good. "For what good does it do a man to gain the whole world 2 and forfeit his life?"[30] This world and the world to come are 3 two enemies. This one means adultery, corruption, avarice, 4 and deceit, while the other gives them up. We cannot, then, 5 be friends of both. To get the one, we must give the other up. We think that it is better to hate what is here, for it is trifling, 6 transitory, and perishable, and to value what is there—things good and imperishable. Yes, if we do the will of Christ, we shall 7 find rest, but if not, nothing will save us from eternal punishment, if we fail to heed his commands. Furthermore, the Scrip- 8 ture also says in Ezekiel, "Though Noah and Jacob and Daniel should rise, they shall not save their children in captivity."[31] If even such upright men as these cannot save their children 9 by their uprightness, what assurance have we that we shall enter God's Kingdom if we fail to keep our baptism pure and undefiled? Or who will plead for us if we are not found to have holy and upright deeds?

So, my brothers, let us enter the contest, recognizing that it 7 is at hand and that, while many come by sea to corruptible

27 Source unknown, possibly the Gospel of the Egyptians.   28 *Ibid.*
29 Luke 16:13; Matt. 6:24.   30 Matt. 16:26; Mark 8:36; Luke 9:25.
31 Ezek. 14:14–20.

contests, not all win laurels, but only those who have struggled
2 hard and competed well. Let us, then, compete so that we may
3 all be crowned. Let us run the straight race, the incorruptible
contest; and let many of us sail to it and enter it, so that we too
may be crowned. And if we cannot all be crowned, let us at
4 least come close to it. We must realize that if a contestant in a
corruptible contest is caught cheating, he is flogged, removed,
5 and driven from the course. What do you think? What shall
be done with the man who cheats in the contest for the incor-
6 ruptible? For in reference to those who have not guarded the
seal,[32] it says, "Their worm shall not die and their fire shall
not be quenched, and they shall be a spectacle to all flesh."[33]
8   So while we are on earth, let us repent. For we are like clay in
2 a workman's hands. If a potter makes a vessel and it gets out
of shape or breaks in his hands, he molds it over again; but if
he has once thrown it into the flames of the furnace, he can do
nothing more with it. Similarly, while we are in this world,
let us too repent with our whole heart of the evil we have done in
the flesh, so that we may be saved by the Lord while we have a
3 chance to repent. For once we have departed this world we
4 can no longer confess there or repent any more. Thus, brothers,
by doing the Father's will and by keeping the flesh pure and by
abiding by the Lord's commands, we shall obtain eternal life.
5 For the Lord says in the Gospel: "If you fail to guard what is
small, who will give you what is great? For I tell you that he
who is faithful in a very little, is faithful also in much."[34]
6 This, then, is what he means: keep the flesh pure and the seal
undefiled, so that we may obtain eternal life.
9   Moreover, let none of you say that this flesh will not be
2 judged or rise again. Consider this: In what state were you
saved? In what state did you regain your sight, if it was not
3 while you were in this flesh? Therefore we should guard the
4 flesh as God's temple. For just as you were called in the flesh,
5 you will come in the flesh. If Christ the Lord who saved us was
made flesh though he was at first spirit, and called us in this
way, in the same way we too in this very flesh will receive our
6 reward. Let us, then, love one another, so that we may all come
7 to God's Kingdom. While we have an opportunity to be healed,
let us give ourselves over to God, the physician, and pay him
8, 9 in return. How? By repenting with a sincere heart. For he

---

[32] The reference is to preserving the seal of one's baptism from defilement.
Cf. ch. 6:9.
[33] Isa. 66:24; Mark 9:48.   [34] Luke 16:10-12.

foreknows everything, and realizes what is in our hearts. Let 10 us then praise him, not with the mouth only, but from the heart, so that he may accept us as sons. For the Lord said, "My 11 brothers are those who do the will of my Father."[35]

So, my brothers, let us do the will of the Father who called us, 10 so that we may have life; and let our preference be the pursuit of virtue. Let us give up vice as the forerunner of our sins, and let us flee impiety, lest evils overtake us. For if we are eager to 2 do good, peace will pursue us. This is the reason men cannot 3 find peace.[36] They give way to human fears,[37] and prefer the pleasures of the present to the promises of the future. For 4 they do not realize what great torment the pleasures of the present bring, and what delight attaches to the promises of the future. If they did these things by themselves, it might be 5 tolerable. But they persist in teaching evil to innocent souls, and do not realize that they and their followers will have their sentence doubled.

Let us therefore serve God with a pure heart and we shall be 11 upright. But if, by not believing in God's promises, we do not serve him, we shall be wretched. For the word of the prophet 2 says, "Wretched are the double-minded, those who doubt in their soul and say, 'We have heard these things long ago, even in our fathers' times, and day after day we have waited and have seen none of them.' You fools! Compare yourselves to a 3 tree. Take a vine: first it sheds its leaves, then comes a bud, and after this a sour grape, then a ripe bunch. So my people 4 too has had turmoils and troubles; but after that it will receive good things."[38] So, my brothers, we must not be double- 5 minded. Rather must we patiently hold out in hope so that we may also gain our reward. For "he can be trusted who prom- 6 ised"[39] to pay each one the wages due for his work. If, then, 7 we have done what is right in God's eyes, we shall enter his Kingdom and receive the promises "which ear has not heard or eye seen, or which man's heart has not entertained."[40]

Loving and doing what is right, we must be on the watch for 12 God's Kingdom hour by hour, since we do not know the day

---

[35] Matt. 12:50; Mark 3:35; Luke 8:21.
[36] The text is corrupt here and "peace" is a conjecture.
[37] Literally, "introduce human fears." The reference is possibly to avoiding persecution by sacrificing.
[38] Source unknown. The same passage is also quoted as Scripture by I Clem. 23:3, though our text adds the final sentence. The prophecy may possibly be the lost book of Eldad and Modat, referred to by Hermas, Vis. II. 3:4.   [39] Heb. 10:23.   [40] I Cor. 2:9.

2 when God will appear. For when someone asked the Lord when his Kingdom was going to come, he said, "When the two shall be one, and the outside like the inside, and the male with
3 the female, neither male nor female."[41] Now "the two" are "one" when we tell each other the truth and two bodies
4 harbor a single mind with no deception. "The outside like the inside" means this: "the inside" means the soul and "the outside" means the body. Just as your body is visible,
5 so make your soul evident by your good deeds. Furthermore "the male with the female, neither male nor female," means this: that when a brother sees a sister[42] he should not think of
6 her sex, any more than she should think of his. When you do these things, he says, my Father's Kingdom will come.

13 Right now, my brothers, we must repent, and be alert for the good, for we are full of much stupidity and wickedness. We must wipe off from us our former sins and by heartfelt repentance be saved. And we must not seek to please men or desire to please only ourselves, but by doing what is right to please even outsiders, so that the Name[43] may not be scoffed at on our
2 account. For the Lord says, "My name is continually scoffed at by all peoples"[44]; and again, "Alas for him through whom my name is scoffed at!"[45] How is it scoffed at? By your failing to do
3 what I want. For when the heathen hear God's oracles on our lips they marvel at their beauty and greatness. But afterwards, when they mark that our deeds are unworthy of the words we utter, they turn from this to scoffing, and say that it is a myth
4 and a delusion. When, for instance, they hear from us that God says, "It is no credit to you if you love those who love you, but it is to your credit if you love your enemies and those who hate you,"[46] when they hear these things, they are amazed at such surpassing goodness. But when they see that we fail to love not only those who hate us, but even those who love us, then they mock at us and scoff at the Name.

14 So, my brothers, by doing the will of God our Father we shall belong to the first Church, the spiritual one, which was created

---

41 Source unknown, probably the Gospel of the Egyptians. Both Clement of Alexandria (*Strom*. III. 13:92, citing Julius Cassianus) and the Oxyrhynchus papyri (ed. Grenfell and Hunt, Vol. IV, pp. 22 f.) have a similar saying. Clement directly attributes it to the Gospel of the Egyptians.
42 The terms refer, not to family, but to Christian, relations.
43 I.e., the name "Christian."   44 Isa. 52:5.
45 Source unknown. Possibly the Gospel of the Egyptians.
46 Luke 6:32, 35.

before the sun and the moon. But if we fail to do the Lord's will, that passage of Scripture will apply to us which says, "My house has become a robber's den."[47] So, then, we must choose to belong to the Church of life in order to be saved. I do not 2 suppose that you are ignorant that the living "Church is the body of Christ."[48] For Scripture says, "God made man male and female."[49] The male is Christ; the female is the Church. The Bible,[50] moreover, and the Apostles[51] say that the Church is not limited to the present, but existed from the beginning. For it was spiritual, as was our Jesus, and was[52] made manifest in the last days to save us. Indeed, the Church which is spiritual 3 was made manifest in the flesh of Christ, and so indicates to us that if any of us guard it in the flesh[53] and do not corrupt it, he will get it in return by the Holy Spirit.[54] For this flesh is the antitype of the spirit. Consequently, no one who has corrupted the antitype will share in the reality. This, then, is what it means, brothers: Guard the flesh so that you may share in the spirit. Now, if we say that the Church is the flesh and the 4 Christ is the spirit, then he who does violence to the flesh, does violence to the Church. Such a person, then, will not share in the spirit, which is Christ. This flesh is able to share in so 5 great a life and immortality, because the Holy Spirit cleaves to it. Nor can one express or tell "what things the Lord has prepared"[55] for his chosen ones.[56]

The advice I have given about continence is not, I think, 15 unimportant; and if a man acts on it, he will not regret it, but will save himself as well as me who advised him. For no small reward attaches to converting an errant and perishing soul, so that it may be saved. For this is how we can pay back 2 God who created us, if the one who speaks and the one who

47 Jer. 7:11; cf. Matt. 21:13.   48 Eph. 1:22, 23.   49 Gen. 1:27.
50 I.e., the sacred books of the Old Testament.
51 I.e., the Apostolic Writings, or the New Testament.
52 It is possible that the author means, "Jesus was made manifest in the last days to save us." Cf. I Peter 1:20. But the construction favors the translation given. Cf. Did. 10:2, where the vine revealed through Jesus may refer to the Church.
53 I.e., by keeping his flesh from defilement.
54 The idea is not too clear but seems to be this: By giving up lustful passions the Christian gets the spiritual Church in return, through participating in the Holy Spirit.
55 I Cor. 2:9.
56 This whole chapter is based on the Platonic distinction between immaterial reality ("spirit") and the copies of it ("flesh") in the phenomenal world.

3 hears do so with faith and love. Consequently, we must remain true to our faith and be upright and holy, so that we may petition God in confidence, who says, "Even while you are speak-
4 ing, I will say, 'See, here I am.' "[57] Surely this saying betokens a great promise; for the Lord says of himself that he is more
5 ready to give than we to ask. Let us, then, take our share of such great kindness and not begrudge ourselves the obtaining of such great blessings. For these sayings hold as much pleasure in store for those who act on them, as they do condemnation for those who disregard them.

16 So, brothers, since we have been given no small opportunity to repent, let us take the occasion to turn to God who
2 has called us, while we still have One to accept us. For if we renounce these pleasures and master our souls by avoiding
3 their evil lusts, we shall share in Jesus' mercy. Understand that "the day" of judgment is already "on its way like a furnace ablaze,"[58] and "the powers[59] of heaven will dissolve"[60] and the whole earth will be like lead melting in fire. Then men's
4 secret and overt actions will be made clear. Charity, then, like repentance from sin, is a good thing. But fasting is better than prayer, and charity than both. "Love covers a multitude of sins,"[61] and prayer, arising from a good conscience, "rescues from death."[62] Blessed is everyone who abounds in these things, for charity lightens sin.

17 Let us, then, repent with our whole heart, so that none of us will be lost. For if we have been commanded to do this too— to draw men away from idols and instruct them—how much more is it wrong for the soul which already knows God to
2 perish? Consequently we must help one another and bring back those weak in goodness, so that we may all be saved; and convert and admonish one another.
3 Not only at this moment, while the presbyters are preaching to us, should we appear believing and attentive. But when we have gone home, we should bear in mind the Lord's commands and not be diverted by worldly passions. Rather should we strive to come here more often and advance in the Lord's commands, so that "with a common mind"[63] we may all be
4 gathered together to gain life. For the Lord said, "I am coming to gather together all peoples, clans, and tongues."[64] This refers

---

[57] Isa. 58:9.   [58] Mal. 4:1.
[59] Emendation by Lightfoot. The Greek reads, "Some of the heavens."
[60] Isa. 34:4.   [61] Prov. 10:12; I Peter 4:8.   [62] James 5:20.
[63] Rom. 12:16.   [64] Isa. 66:18.

to the day of his appearing, when he will come to redeem us, each according to his deeds. And "unbelievers will see his glory" 5 and power,[65] and they will be surprised to see the sovereignty of the world given to Jesus, and they will say, "Alas for us, for you really existed, and we neither recognized it nor believed, and we did not obey the presbyters who preached to us our salvation." And "their worm will not die and their fire will not be quenched, and they will be a spectacle to all flesh."[66] He 6 refers to that day of judgment when men will see those who were ungodly among us and who perverted the commands of Jesus Christ. But the upright who have done good and patiently 7 endured tortures and hated the pleasures of the soul, when they see those who have done amiss and denied Jesus in word and act being punished with dreadful torments and undying fire, will give "glory to their God"[67] and say, "There is hope for him who has served God with his whole heart."

Consequently we too must be of the number of those who 18 give thanks and have served God, and not of the ungodly who are sentenced. For myself, I too am a grave sinner, and 2 have not yet escaped temptation. I am still surrounded by the devil's devices, though I am anxious to pursue righteousness. My aim is to manage at least to approach it, for I am afraid of the judgment to come.

So, my brothers and sisters, after God's truth[68] I am reading 19 you an exhortation to heed what was there written, so that you may save yourselves and your reader. For compensation I beg you to repent with all your heart, granting yourselves salvation and life. By doing this we will set a goal for all the young who want to be active in the cause of religion and of God's goodness. We should not, moreover, be so stupid as to be dis- 2 pleased and vexed when anyone admonishes us and converts us from wickedness to righteousness. There are times when we do wrong unconsciously because of the double-mindedness and unbelief in our hearts, and "our understanding is darkened"[69] by empty desires. Let us, then, do what is right so that we may 3 finally be saved. Blessed are they who observe these injunctions; though they suffer briefly in this world,[70] they will gather the immortal fruit of the resurrection. A religious man must not 4

---

[65] *Ibid.*   [66] Isa. 66:24; Mark 9:44.   [67] Rev. 11:13.
[68] Literally, "after the God of truth," i.e., the Scripture lesson which may possibly have come from Isa., ch. 54; see ch. 2.
[69] Eph. 4:18.
[70] Cf. I Peter 5:10.

be downcast if he is miserable in the present. A time of blessedness awaits him. He will live again in heaven with his forefathers, and will rejoice in an eternity that knows no sorrow.

20 But you must not be troubled in mind by the fact that we see the wicked in affluence while God's slaves are in straitened **2** circumstances. Brothers and sisters, we must have faith. We are engaged in the contest of the living God and are being trained by the present life in order to win laurels in the life to come. **3** None of the upright has obtained his reward quickly, but he **4** waits for it. For were God to give the righteous their reward at once, our training would straightway be in commerce and not in piety, since we would give an appearance of uprightness, when pursuing, not religion, but gain. That is why the divine judgment punishes[71] a spirit which is not upright, and loads it with chains.

5 "To the only invisible God,"[72] the Father of truth, who dispatched to us the Saviour and prince of immortality, through whom he also disclosed to us the truth and the heavenly life—to him be glory forever and ever. Amen.

[71] The aorist may be gnomic, or else the passage refers to Satan's fall.
[72] I Tim. 1:17.

IN DEFENSE OF THE FAITH

The So-called Letter to Diognetus

INTRODUCTION AND BOOKS

The History of the Text

THE SO-CALLED *Epistula ad Diognetum* IS ONE OF the most puzzling of ancient documents. While Lightfoot's description of it as "the noblest of early Christian writings"[1] expresses the common estimate, there is no agreement as to its authorship and very little as to its exact date. The Epistle is unique among patristic works of distinction, in the fact that we can find no references to it (under its present title, at least) in the writings of the scholars of the ancient Church. Moreover, the one MS. (itself medieval) in which it came to us no longer exists, so that we are dependent on later transcripts and printed editions for all that we can hope to know of the work, barring a miracle of discovery.

The unique MS. of the Epistle, *Codex Argentoratensis Graecus* 9, containing five treatises ascribed to Justin Martyr, with our Epistle in fifth place, followed by other contemporary material, was written in the thirteenth or fourteenth century. Its history is obscure, although it is known, from his annotation on the back of the codex, that it belonged to the Hebraist Reuchlin (d. 1522), who had brought it from the charterhouse of his native town. Apart from a brief appearance about 1560 at the monastery of Maursmünster in Alsace, it vanishes from sight until 1793–1795. At that time it came to the municipal library of Strasbourg (whose ancient name, Argentoratum, gave its title to the MS.), and remained there until August 24, 1870, when it was burned during the German attack on the city.

Our knowledge of the MS. comes largely from three sixteenth century transcripts. The first, which was made by H.

[1] J. B. Lightfoot, *Commentary on Colossians*, 8th edition, pp. 154 f.

Stephanus, of Paris, and served as the basis of the *editio princeps* (1592), still exists at Leyden (*Codex Graec. Voss.*, Q.30). The second, made c. 1590 by J. J. Beurer, of Freiburg, seems to have perished, but some of its readings appear in an appendix to Stephanus' edition, as well as in the edition of F. Sylburg (1593). The third copy, made in 1580 by B. Haus, was found in 1880 at Tübingen (*Codex Misc. Tübing.*, M.b.17). Most early editions relied on Stephanus, but the MS. was collated by E. Cunitz (1842) and E. Reuss (1861) for the first and third editions respectively of J. C. T. Otto's *Corpus Apologetarum* (3d edition, 1879), while F. X. Funk (*Patres apostolici*, 2d edition, 1901, later revisions by F. Diekamp and K. Bihlmeyer), on whose text this translation is based, made use of the Tübingen transcript. No major textual problems are presented by these more or less independent witnesses, but there are obvious lacunae at ch. 7:8 and ch. 10:8, and there may be a small break at ch. 10:1. While a number of readings are doubtful in detail, the emendations proposed by Lachmann and Bunsen in Bunsen's *Analecta Ante-Nicaena*, Vol. I (1854), have found favor with most editors.

Date and Authorship

Some critics have been led by the Epistle's peculiar history to regard it as a brilliant forgery, while others have looked on it as a mere showpiece, without any real relation to the experience of the Early Church. The real beauty, however, of its picture of the Christian life, the freshness of its language, and the undeveloped character of its theology all combine to suggest a date in the second or the early third century, and to guarantee the authenticity of the Epistle as an expression of early Christian piety.

To place it more precisely is another matter. Justin, to whom the MS. attributes the Epistle, is impossible. It does share with Justin's writings certain commonplaces of early apologetic, but some striking differences must be noted, such as our Epistle's disregard of Hebrew prophecy and contempt for Greek philosophy. Furthermore, the style of the work is far superior to Justin's.

A stronger candidate, whose claims have recently been revived by Dom P. Andriessen, is Quadratus of Asia Minor, who (in 123–124 or 129) addressed an "Apology" to the emperor

Hadrian.[2] Andriessen argues that the fragment dealing with Christ's healing miracles, which Eusebius quotes from Quadratus, fits very appropriately into the lacuna at Diog. 7:8. He also notes a number of passages in the Epistle that make the identification of "Diognetus" with Hadrian most plausible. The fact that Jerome was probably mistaken in identifying Quadratus, whom he describes as *discipulus apostolorum*, with the bishop of Athens of the same name, is not really relevant, and it is certainly true that the internal evidence points to the view that our Epistle, like Quadratus' Apology, originated in Asia Minor.

Before making use of this evidence, however, we must deal with the prior problem of the integrity of the Epistle and the related question of the possible common authorship of the two sections into which the lacuna at ch. 10:8 seems to divide it. It may be briefly stated that, on grounds of style alone, the critic is justified in doubting the unity of the Epistle as it stands, while differences of outlook between chs. 1 to 10 and 11; 12 (e.g., with respect to the Old Testament) decide the matter conclusively. Moreover, while the bulk of the differences might be explained by the assumption that the same author produced the two distinct sections at different times and for different purposes, the unresolved differences make the hypothesis of a common authorship untenable. At the same time, since the community of fundamental outlook is obvious enough, we can hardly doubt that the two documents stem from closely related circles. An examination of this common viewpoint may help us to place the two authors more exactly.

The Epistle as a whole is classical in style, with definite Biblical overtones. The Pauline influence is often perceptible, while the Johannine outlook dominates the work.[3] When one notes in addition the obvious influence of Ephesians and First

[2] Dom P. Andriessen, "L'Apologie de Quadratus conservée sous le titre d'Épître à Diognète," *Recherches de théologie ancienne et médiévale*, 13 (1946), pp. 5-39, 125-149, 237-260; 14 (1947), pp. 121-156.

Andriessen, "The Authorship of the *Epistula ad Diognetum*," *Vigiliae Christianae*, I (April, 1947), pp. 129 f.

Eusebius, *Hist. eccl.* IV. 3:1, 2.

Jerome, *De Vir. Ill.* 19; *Epistula* 70: 4.

[3] The following is a far from exhaustive list of parallels between the Epistle to Diognetus and the Johannine corpus:

Diognetus	Johannine Writings	Diognetus	Johannine Writings
ch. 6:3	John 16:19	ch. 7:2	John 1:1-3
	ch. 17:14-16	ch. 8:5	John 1:18
	ch. 18:36		I John 4:12

Peter on the Epistle, the case for the Asian origin of the latter becomes very strong indeed.

Among post-Biblical influences that have been detected, a number are of secondary importance for our understanding of Diognetus. J. Armitage Robinson, for example, has shown that The Preaching of Peter (c. 100–130) underlies both the Epistle and the Apology of Aristides, but some of his evidence is too general to be relevant, and none of it outweighs the divergence of outlook between the Epistle and the passages from the Preaching preserved by Clement of Alexandria, although it remains clear that our author (of Diog., chs. 1 to 10) was familiar with the latter in some form.[4] Similarly, while resemblances have been noted between the Epistle and the Apology of Aristides itself, the evidence hardly goes far enough to justify a definite assertion of the influence of either upon the other, and certainly fails to demonstrate a common authorship. Pfleiderer, indeed, argues for "the acquaintance of the author of the Epistle to Diognetus withthe earlier Apology of Aristides," but this goes beyond the data, which simply indicate *some* contact. It is not necessary, then, to play down the strongly Asian character of our Epistle, or even to rule out Quadratus as the author, simply on the ground that it must have been influenced by (and thus be later than) the work of Aristides the Athenian (c. 140).[5]

The resemblances between the Epistle and the *Protrepticus* of Clement of Alexandria (d.c. 215) are even more general, and certainly do not justify the suggestion, contrary to the indica-

Diognetus	Johannine Writings	Diognetus	Johannine Writings
ch. 10:4	I John 4:19 (as read by Codex Sinaiticus and some other MSS.)	ch.11:4	John 13:34, 35 I John 1:1–3 I John 2:7, 8 I John 5:1, 2 II John 5, 6
ch. 11:4	John 1:1, 14 John 3:3, 5	ch. 12:1	Rev. 22:2

[4] J. Armitage Robinson, *Texts and Studies*, Vol. I, No. 1, pp. 86 ff.
Clement of Alexandria, *Strom.*, I. 29: 182; VI. 5: 39 ff.; etc.
[5] H. Kihn, *Der Ursprung des Briefes an Diognet* (1882), gives the fullest statement of the case for the common authorship of Diognetus and the Apology of Aristides.
O. Pfleiderer, *Primitive Christianity* (E.T., 1911), IV, p. 482.
E. Molland, "Die literatur- und dogmengeschichtliche Stellung des Diognetbriefes," *Zeitschrift für die neutestamentliche Wissenschaft*, 33 (1934), pp. 289–312, gives a careful account of the relationship of the two works.

tions of another source and an earlier date, that the Epistle simply reflects the work of Clement. It has been argued more persuasively that it should be ascribed to Theophilus of Antioch (whose three books *Ad Autolycum* appeared c. 180), but even here the similarities are not strong enough to compel any such conclusion, particularly in view of the relatively undeveloped theology of the Epistle, although they do point to its Asian provenance and to its link with the school represented by Irenaeus.[6]

The most significant literary parallels, however, go beyond this to establish without question the association of both sections of our Epistle with that theology of Asia Minor which so ably represented the central tradition of primitive Catholicism. The work of R. H. Connolly puts the connection between Diog., chs. 1 to 10, and both Irenaeus and Hippolytus (particularly the latter's anti-Gnostic work, the so-called *Philosophumena*) beyond any reasonable doubt. As for chs. 11 and 12, Connolly has shown that they strikingly resemble certain of the acknowledged writings of Hippolytus of Rome (d. 235), while Campbell Bonner has pointed out certain interesting stylistic parallels between these chapters and the surviving fragments of the homilies of Melito of Sardis, who is known to have exerted a strong influence on Hippolytus.[7]

In the light of the evidence thus summarily presented, it is possible to offer a tentative answer to the question of date and authorship. Our answer assumes that chs. 1 to 10 were written by Quadratus in Asia Minor, as Andriessen argues, and

---

[6] The case for the connection between Diognetus and Clement's *Protrepticus*, with the possible corollary of the priority of the latter, may be studied with the aid of the following:

A. Harnack, *Geschichte der altchristlichen Literatur*, I, p. 758; II, p. 514.

J. Geffcken, *Der Brief an Diognetos*. Carl Winter, Heidelberg, 1928.

The relation of Diognetus to the work of Theophilus of Antioch is discussed by F. Ogara, "Aristidis et Epistolae ad Diognetum cum Theophilo Antiocheno cognatio," *Gregorianum*, 25 (1944), pp. 74-102.

[7] R. H. Connolly, "The Date and Authorship of the Epistle to Diognetus," *The Journal of Theological Studies*, 36 (October, 1935), pp. 347-353; "'Ad Diognetum xi-xii,'" *JTS*, 37 (January, 1936), pp. 2-15.

C. C. J. Bunsen, *Hippolytus and His Age*, E.T., I, pp. 185 ff., 193 ff., claimed Diog., chs. 11; 12 as the conclusion of the *Philosophumena*. Before Connolly, this position was also argued by J. Dräseke, in *Zeitschrift für wissenschaftliche Theologie*, 45 (1902), pp. 263 ff., and A. Di Pauli, *Theologische Quartalschrift*, 88 (1906).

E. Schwartz, *Zwei Predigten Hippolyts*, Munich (1936), argues that the same chapters belong to one of the Paschal tractates of Hippolytus.

Campbell Bonner, *Studies and Documents*, 12 (1940), *The Homily on the Passion by Melito*.

constitute the body of his Apology to Hadrian (129 ?). This will account for the strong Asian (notably Johannine) flavor of the work, and for its relatively primitive character. If this precise identification is not accepted, we must still attribute the Epistle to the same period and circle. R. H. Connolly's explanation of the relationships involved in terms of the dependence of our author (identified with Hippolytus) on Irenaeus, rather than in terms of the influence of an earlier writing on Irenaeus and through him on Hippolytus, fails to account for such significant factors as the attitude of our author toward the Old Testament, his relatively rudimentary Christology, and his failure to refer to the Church's Tradition (*paradosis*), which on the other hand played so large a part in the teaching of Irenaeus and Hippolytus.

As far as chs. 11 and 12 are concerned, the argument for Hippolytean authorship, as summed up by R. H. Connolly, seems convincing enough, although the case for the identification of the fragment as the lost tenth book of the *Philosophumena* may well be thought less persuasive, and we may prefer to regard it as a festal homily. At any rate, this over-all theory, with its ascription of chs. 1 to 10 to a predecessor of Irenaeus, and its attribution of chs. 11; 12 to one of his successors, offers a more comprehensive treatment of the evidence than any alternatives that have so far been presented.

Purpose and Content

The bulk of the Epistle (chs. 1 to 10) constitutes an apology for Christianity, based on the unique part played by Christians in society. This argument is set in the context of a "theology of history," which emphasizes the divine initiative as decisive for history, and contrasts Christianity as a supernatural factor in human relationships with the man-made religion of Gentiles and Jews alike. The attack on non-Christian religions is sometimes unfair and superficial, and must have had a very mixed effect on pagan readers, but the description of Christian life in the world comes to us across eighteen centuries with an astounding force and fragrance. To this moving statement someone possessed of a remarkable sense of fitness has added the passage from Hippolytus (chs. 11; 12), with its announcement of God's gifts of grace and truth in Christ's Church, where at this very moment Christians can renew their life at that divine source from which its unique power flows.

This vivid symbolic expression of the supernatural character of Christian life points up the fundamental theological theme of the body of the Epistle, which is concerned to present Christianity as a supernatural mystery. The writer deals with the first of Diognetus' supposed questions by affirming that the God whom Christians worship, to the contempt of all so-called gods, is the transcendent Lord of all things, who in his "Child" has revealed himself to men, destroying the divinities of human imagination. He goes on to argue that the nature of Christian life is itself a primary piece of evidence for the intrinsically supernatural basis of the Christian religion. Christians are different and mysterious, because they live by a superhuman power. The reader should note the numerous references to Christianity as a "mystery," and the realistic doctrine of sanctifying grace with which this emphasis is allied, as again and again the Christian doctrine of God and the glowing portrayal of Christian life are brought together.

The very novelty of Christianity shows its transcendent origin. The description of Christians as the "New Race" reflects, in language widely used in the Early Church, the Biblical expression of the supernatural in terms of the "New Age, Covenant, Creation." In other words, the Epistle manifests the strong historical sense characteristic of the Bible itself, and sees in the supernatural mystery of Christianity the fulfillment of the divine purpose in the creation of nature, worked out in history in accordance with the possibilities of historical situations. In the exposition of the divine *oikonomia* in history, this apprehension of the truth that the divine wisdom acts in accordance with the historical *kairos* is more effectively expressed than in any other writing before Irenaeus' magnificent picture of the workings of Providence. Some appreciation of this profound understanding of Christianity that underlies both the Epistle proper and the Hippolytean epilogue is necessary, if we are not to be led by the Epistle's tightly controlled use of its dogmatic material into overlooking its deepest roots; and the reader should always be on the watch for these fundamental theological motifs.

AIDS TO STUDY

Since this edition is intended as a simple introduction to the Epistle by way of notes on its background and central themes, accompanying a free English translation, the reader who is attracted to the study of Diognetus must go on to more adequate treatments of the Epistle. Hence this preamble should conclude with a guide (necessarily brief and selective) to the relevant literature.

Among the standard English editions, which the student will want to consult, the place of honor belongs to Lightfoot's *Apostolic Fathers* (5 vols., 1886–1890, on which all subsequent study of all these writings has in some measure depended), despite the fact that the English translations are less readable than most. Kirsopp Lake's well-known Loeb Classical Library edition (*The Apostolic Fathers*, II, 1913, reprinted, Putnam, 1930) offers a very literal (although not uniformly accurate) translation, founded on Otto's text, which is printed in parallel, and prefaced by a slight introduction. James Kleist, in Ancient Christian Writers, No. 6 (1948), gives us a useful introduction, followed by a free-flowing translation—the best in English. *The Epistle to Diognetus*, by H. G. Meecham, with its critical text, founded on that of Funk, and its exhaustive introduction and notes, is an indispensable tool for the scholarly study of the Epistle. Its (very pedestrian) translation is always reliable, while its introductory material is a mine of accurate references to other editions and to secondary material, as well as to illustrative passages from classical literature.

Reference should also be made to the standard general histories of patristic literature and thought, among which B. Altaner's *Patrologie* (2d edition, 1950) gives the most up-to-date account of the subject, with very full references to contemporary studies, both in German and in other languages. A. Harnack's *Mission and Expansion of Christianity* (E.T., 2 vols., 1908), contains the richest account of the life of the Church in the age of Diognetus, and should most certainly be read, provided that one is aware of its learned author's occasional weakness for substituting "liberal" intuitions for scholarship.

Apart from items otherwise mentioned in the introduction and notes, attention should be called to three useful discussions of the outlook of the Apologists: J. Rivière, *St. Justin et les apologistes du second siècle* (1907); P. Carrington, *Christian Apologetics of the Second Century* (1921); and A. Puech, *Les Apologistes grecs du IIe siècle de notre ère* (1912: the best comprehensive treatment of the Apologists). With the help of these works, the reader should acquire a fuller appreciation of the enterprise undertaken by the Apologists, and a better understanding of the peculiar contribution made by the Epistle to Diognetus.

The So-called Letter to Diognetus

THE TEXT: (I) AN ANONYMOUS BRIEF FOR CHRISTIANITY PRESENTED TO DIOGNETUS

THE MYSTERY OF THE NEW PEOPLE

To His Excellency, Diognetus: **1**

I understand, sir, that you are really interested in learning
about the religion of the Christians, and that you are making
an accurate and careful investigation of the subject. You want
to know, for instance, what God they believe in and how they
worship him, while at the same time they disregard the world
and look down on death, and how it is that they do not treat
the divinities of the Greeks as gods at all, although on the other
hand they do not follow the superstition of the Jews. You would
also like to know the source of the loving affection that they
have for each other. You wonder, too, why this new race or
way of life has appeared on earth now and not earlier. [8] I
certainly welcome this keen interest on your part, and I ask
God, who gives us the power to speak and the power to listen,
to let me speak in such a way that you may derive the greatest
possible benefit from listening, and to enable you to listen to
such good effect that I may never have a reason for regretting
what I have said. Now, then, clear out all the thoughts that **2**
take up your attention, and pack away all the old ways of
looking at things that keep deceiving you. You must become

---

[8] These three questions are dealt with in the text, more or less in order,
but with some overlapping. The reference to the "New [third] Race"
calls attention to an issue of great importance for the life of the Early
Church, which concerned such varied questions as the Church's understanding of its vocation in history and the Roman world's attitude
toward the Church. Cf. I Peter 2:9 f.; I Cor. 1:22–24; 10:32; The Preaching of Peter (Clement of Alexandria, *Strom.* VI. 5:39); Aristides, *Apology*
(Syriac) 16:4; Origen, *Contra Celsum*, I, ch. 26; Arnobius, *Adversus Gentes*,
II, ch. 69. There is a full discussion in Harnack, *Mission and Expansion*, I,
247 ff.

like a new man from the beginning, since, as you yourself admit, you are going to listen to a really new message.

THE STUPIDITY OF IDOLATRY

Look at the things that you proclaim and think of as gods. See with your outward eyes and with your mind what material 2 they are made of and what form they happen to have. Is not one a stone, like the stones we walk on, and another bronze, no better than the utensils that have been forged for our use? Here is a wooden one, already rotting away, and one made of silver, that needs a watchman to protect it from being stolen. Yet another one is made of iron, eaten by rust, and another of pottery, no more attractive than something provided for the 3 most ignoble purpose. Were not all these things made out of perishable material? Were they not forged by iron and fire? Surely the stonemason made one of them, and the blacksmith another, the silversmith a third, and the potter a fourth! These things have been molded into their present shapes by the arts of these craftsmen. Before they were shaped, they could just as easily have been given a different form—and would this not be possible even now? Could not vessels like them be made out of the same material, if the same craftsmen happened to be 4 available? Moreover, could not these things that you worship now be made by men into vessels like any others? They are all dumb, after all, and blind. They are without life or feeling or 5 power of movement, all rotting away and decaying. These are the things you call gods, the things you serve. You Gentiles 6 adore these things, and in the end you become like them. That is why you hate the Christians, because they do not believe that 7 these objects are gods. But is it not you yourselves who, when in your own thoughts you suppose that you are praising the gods, are in reality despising them? Surely it is mockery and insult to worship your stone and earthenware gods without bothering to guard them, while you lock up your gods of silver and gold at night, and set guards over them during the day, to keep them from being stolen.

8   Moreover, if they are not lacking in sensation, you punish them by the very honors you try to pay them, while, if they are senseless, you show them up by the mere act of worshiping 9 them with blood and sacrificial fat. Just picture one of yourselves enduring this kind of thing, or allowing it to be done to him! There is not one man who would willingly tolerate this

sort of punishment, because he has feeling and intelligence, but the stone tolerates it, because it has no feeling. Do you not then really disprove its power of feeling? I could say a good 10 deal more about the fact that Christians are not the slaves of gods like these, but if anyone cannot see the force of these arguments, I think that nothing is to be gained by arguing the matter further. [9]

THE SUPERSTITIONS OF JUDAISM

Next, I gather that you are particularly anxious to hear why 3 Christians do not worship in the same way as Jews. It is true 2 that the Jews refrain from the kind of worship that I have been describing, and on this score they are right in thinking that they adore the one God of all things and honor him as Lord; but since they offer this worship more or less in the same manner as those already mentioned, they are completely mistaken. While the Greeks provide a proof of their own lack of under- 3 standing, by making offerings to senseless and deaf objects, the Jews themselves might perhaps consider it folly rather than piety if they only recognized that they were offering gifts to God just as if he needed them. For "he who made the heaven 4 and the earth and all that is in them,"[10] and provides us with everything we need, can scarcely need any of the things that he himself supplies to those who fancy that they are giving something to him. It seems clear to me that people who 5 imagine that they are offering sacrifices to him when they give blood and fat and whole burnt offerings, and are really honoring him by these tokens of reverence, do not differ at all from people who pay the same honor to deaf images. The latter think that they are offering something to objects which in

---

[9] While this line of attack on paganism is admittedly limited in its range, it reflects very well the contemptuous attitude of the Old Testament, and is an example of how, despite the author's dislike of Judaism and his lack of overt reference to the Old Testament, the latter's outlook directs his thinking. Cf. Isa. 44:9-20; 40:18-21; Jer. 10:1-16; Ps. 115:4-8. Against most of the Apologists, who think of idols as dwellings of demons, the Epistle agrees with Justin's description of them as "lifeless and dead" (Apol. I, ch. 9). The gods of the Gentiles are so completely unreal that there is *nothing* behind the images.

[10] Cf. Acts 14:15, from which this is an almost exact quotation, and Acts 17:22-31. The emphasis on Creation is further evidence of the Old Testament's influence on Diognetus, and effectively scotches the accusations of Marcionism, brought against the author by some critics. Cf. Ps. 50:7-15, for the attack on Jewish worship.

reality cannot appropriate the honor, while the former imagine that they are giving something to him who has need of nothing.

4 As for Jewish taboos with respect to food, along with their superstition about the Sabbath, their bragging about circumcision, and their hypocrisy about fast days and new moons, I hardly think that you need to be told by me that all these 2 things are ridiculous, and not worth arguing about. How can it be anything but godlessness that makes men accept some of the things made by God for man's use as created good, 3 and reject other things as useless and superfluous? And is it not impious to pretend that God forbids a good deed on the 4 Sabbath Day? And are they not asking for ridicule when they boast of the mutilation of the flesh as a sign of their choice by God, as if for this reason they were especially beloved by him? 5 Again, when they constantly gaze at the stars and watch the moon, in order to observe months and days with scrupulous care and to distinguish the changes of the seasons which God has ordained, in order to cater to their own whims, making some into festivals, and others into times of mourning, who 6 could call this evidence of devotion rather than of folly? All this being so, I think that you have learned enough to see that Christians are right in holding themselves aloof from the aimlessness and trickery of Greeks and Jews alike, and from the officiousness and noisy conceit of the Jews. But as far as the mystery of the Christians' own religion is concerned, you cannot expect to learn that from man.

The Church in the World[11]

5 For Christians cannot be distinguished from the rest of the 2 human race by country or language or customs. They do not live in cities of their own; they do not use a peculiar form of 3 speech; they do not follow an eccentric manner of life. This doctrine of theirs has not been discovered by the ingenuity or deep thought of inquisitive men, nor do they put forward a

[11] The heading is chosen quite deliberately, despite Meecham's criticism of Puech's reference to the *"onction ecclésiastique"* of the Epistle. Cf. A. Puech, *Les Apologistes grecs*, p. 252; *Histoire de la littérature grecque chrétienne*, II, p. 219; H. G. Meecham, *The Epistle to Diognetus*, p. 31. In support of his criticism Meecham is compelled to quote an obscure upholder of the ultraspiritual doctrine of the Church (more judiciously defended by Sohm). Altogether apart, however, from the Hippolytean fragment, the whole discussion of the Christian's citizenship in the Epistle rests on those great churchly documents, Ephesians and First Peter—most notably, perhaps, on Eph. 2:19-22.

merely human teaching, as some people do. Yet, although they 4
live in Greek and barbarian cities alike, as each man's lot has
been cast, and follow the customs of the country in clothing
and food and other matters of daily living, at the same time
they give proof of the remarkable and admittedly extraordinary
constitution of their own commonwealth. They live in their 5
own countries, but only as aliens. They have a share in everything as citizens, and endure everything as foreigners. Every
foreign land is their fatherland, and yet for them every fatherland is a foreign land. They marry, like everyone else, and they 6
beget children, but they do not cast out their offspring. They 7
share their board with each other, but not their marriage bed.
It is true that they are "in the flesh," but they do not live 8
"according to the flesh."[12] They busy themselves on earth, but 9
their citizenship is in heaven.[13] They obey the established laws, 10
but in their own lives they go far beyond what the laws
require. They love all men, and by all men are persecuted. 11
They are unknown, and still they are condemned; they are 12
put to death, and yet they are brought to life. They are poor, 13
and yet they make many rich; they are completely destitute,
and yet they enjoy complete abundance. They are dishonored, 14
and in their very dishonor are glorified; they are defamed, and
are vindicated. They are reviled, and yet they bless; when they 15
are affronted, they still pay due respect. When they do good, 16
they are punished as evildoers; undergoing punishment, they
rejoice because they are brought to life. They are treated by 17
the Jews as foreigners and enemies, and are hunted down by the
Greeks; and all the time those who hate them find it impossible
to justify their enmity.[14]

12 Cf. II Cor. 10:3; 5:16; Rom. 8:4; John 17:13–19; 18:36, 37. Note this
passage's vivid contrast between the created world, in which we live, and
its corruption, which both affects our attitude toward it and conditions our
life. The Pauline-Johannine doctrine of original sin, the full meaning of
which some other Apologists failed to grasp, is here clearly implied.

13 Cf. Phil. 3:20; Eph. 2:19–22; I Peter 2:9–17. The translation of Phil.
3:20, which refers to Christians as a "colony of heaven" (Moffatt),
expresses most aptly the point of our Epistle, with its simultaneous
recognition of the transcendent destiny and the earthly responsibility
of the Christian.

14 II Cor. 6:4–10 is obviously the pattern of this passage; cf. Diog. 5:13;
II Cor. 6:10. The influence of John 15:25 should also be noted; the
parallel destiny of the Vine and the branches (John 15:1, 5), implied
in John 15:24 to 16:3, is the hidden background of our text. Here, as
so often in the Epistle, we can sense a profound theological interest which,
because of the aim of the work, must not become too obvious.

6 To put it simply: What the soul is in the body, that Christians
2 are in the world. The soul is dispersed through all the members
of the body, and Christians are scattered through all the cities
3 of the world. The soul dwells in the body, but does not belong
to the body, and Christians dwell in the world, but do not
4 belong to the world. The soul, which is invisible, is kept under
guard in the visible body; in the same way, Christians are recognized when they are in the world, but their religion remains
5 unseen. The flesh hates the soul and treats it as an enemy,
even though it has suffered no wrong, because it is prevented
from enjoying its pleasures; so too the world hates Christians,
even though it suffers no wrong at their hands, because they
6 range themselves against its pleasures. The soul loves the flesh
that hates it, and its members; in the same way, Christians love
7 those who hate them. The soul is shut up in the body, and yet
itself holds the body together; while Christians are restrained in
the world as in a prison, and yet themselves hold the world
8 together. The soul, which is immortal, is housed in a mortal
dwelling; while Christians are settled among corruptible things,
to wait for the incorruptibility that will be theirs in heaven.
9 The soul, when faring badly as to food and drink, grows better;
so too Christians, when punished, day by day increase more
10 and more. It is to no less a post than this that God has ordered
them, and they must not try to evade it.

The Christian Revelation

7 As I have indicated, it is not an earthly discovery that was
committed to them; it is not a mortal thought that they think
of as worth guarding with such care, nor have they been en-
2 trusted with the stewardship of merely human mysteries. On
the contrary, it was really the Ruler of all, the Creator of all,
the invisible God himself, who from heaven established the
truth and the holy, incomprehensible word among men, and
fixed it firmly in their hearts. Nor, as one might suppose, did
he do this by sending to men some subordinate—an angel, or
principality, or one of those who administer earthly affairs, or
perhaps one of those to whom the government of things in
heaven is entrusted. Rather, he sent the Designer and Maker
of the universe himself, by whom he created the heavens and
confined the sea within its own bounds—him whose hidden
purposes all the elements of the world faithfully carry out,
him from whom the sun has received the measure of the daily

rounds that it must keep, him whom the moon obeys when he commands her to shine by night, and whom the stars obey as they follow the course of the moon. He sent him by whom all things have been set in order and distinguished and placed in subjection—the heavens and the things that are in the heavens, the earth and the things in the earth, the sea and the things in the sea, fire, air, the unfathomed pit, the things in the heights and in the depths and in the realm between; God sent him to men.

Now, did he send him, as a human mind might assume, to 3 rule by tyranny, fear, and terror? Far from it! He sent him out 4 of kindness and gentleness, like a king sending his son who is himself a king. He sent him as God; he sent him as man to men. He willed to save man by persuasion, not by compulsion, for compulsion is not God's way of working. In sending him, God 5 called men, but did not pursue them; he sent him in love, not in judgment. Yet he will indeed send him someday as our 6 Judge, and who shall stand when he appears?[15] . . .

Do you not see how they are thrown to wild animals to make 7 them deny the Lord, and how they are not vanquished? Do you 8 not see that the more of them are punished, the more do others increase? These things do not seem to come from a human 9 power; they are a mighty act of God, they are proofs of his presence.

As a matter of fact, before he came, what man had any 8 knowledge of God at all? Or do you really accept the idle 2 nonsense talked by those plausible philosophers, some of whom asserted that God was fire—the very thing that they are on the point of going to, they call God!—while others claimed that he was water, and others said that he was yet another one of the elements created by God? And yet, if any one of these lines 3 of argument is acceptable, then each and every one of the other creatures could in the same way be shown to be God. No, this 4 is just quackery and deceit practiced by wizards. No man has 5 ever seen God or made him known, but he has manifested himself. And he manifested himself through faith, by which 6 alone it has been made possible for us to see God.

15 For the last clause, cf. Mal. 3:2. At this point there is a lacuna, indicated by a marginal note in the MS. Dom Andriessen would insert the Eusebian fragment of the Apology of Quadratus here (cf. note 2). A full statement of God's mighty acts through Christ, culminating, like many other Apologetic arguments (cf. Justin, Dialogue with Trypho, chs. 110; 121; Apol. I, ch. 39; Irenaeus, *Adv. haer.* IV. 34:3; 33:9), in a description of Christian fidelity in tribulation, would certainly not be inappropriate at this point.

7 For God, the Master and Maker of the universe, who made
all things and determined the proper place of each, showed
8 himself to be long-suffering, as well as a true friend of man. But
in fact he always was and is and will be just this—kind and
good and slow to anger and true; indeed, he alone is good.
9 And when he had planned a great and unutterable design, he
10 communicated it to his Child alone. Now, as long as he kept
back his own wise counsel as a well-guarded mystery, he seemed
11 to be neglecting us and to take no interest in us; but when he
revealed it through his beloved Child and made known the
things that had been prepared from the beginning, he granted
us all things at once. He made us both to share in his blessings
and to see and understand things that none of us could ever
have looked for.

9 And so, when he had planned everything by himself in union
with his Child, he still allowed us, through the former time, to
be carried away by undisciplined impulses, captivated by
pleasures and lusts, just as we pleased. That does not mean that
he took any delight in our sins, but only that he showed
patience. He did not approve at all of that season of wickedness, but on the contrary, all the time he was creating the present age of righteousness, so that we, who in the past had by
our own actions been proved unworthy of life, might now be
deemed worthy, thanks to God's goodness. Then, when we had
shown ourselves incapable of entering the Kingdom of God
by our own efforts, we might be made capable of doing so by
2 the power of God. And so, when our unrighteousness had come
to its full term, and it had become perfectly plain that its
recompense of punishment and death had to be expected, then
the season arrived in which God had determined to show at
last his goodness and power. O the overflowing kindness and
love of God toward man! God did not hate us, or drive us
away, or bear us ill will. Rather, he was long-suffering and for-
bearing. In his mercy, he took up the burden of our sins. He
himself gave up his own Son as a ransom for us—the holy one
for the unjust, the innocent for the guilty, the righteous one for
the unrighteous, the incorruptible for the corruptible, the im-
3 mortal for the mortal.[16] For what else could cover our sins

---

[16] Cf. Mark 10:45; I Tim. 2:6; Titus 2:14; and above all Rom. 8:32 ff.
The whole argument of Rom., chs. 5 to 8, with its exposition of our
new life in Christ who died in perfect obedience to the Father, underlies
this passage. The development of the theme in Diognetus shows how
realistically the author interpreted the Pauline doctrine of justification.

except his righteousness? In whom could we, lawless and im- 4
pious as we were, be made righteous except in the Son of God
alone? O sweetest exchange! O unfathomable work of God! 5
O blessings beyond all expectation! The sinfulness of many is
hidden in the Righteous One, while the righteousness of the
One justifies the many that are sinners. In the former time he 6
had proved to us our nature's inability to gain life; now he
showed the Saviour's power to save even the powerless, with
the intention that on both counts we should have faith in his
goodness, and look on him as Nurse, Father, Teacher, Counselor, Healer, Mind, Light, Honor, Glory, Might, Life—and
that we should not be anxious about clothing and food.

If you too yearn for this faith, then first of all you must 10
acquire full knowledge of the Father. For God loved men, and 2
made the world for their sake, and put everything on earth
under them. He gave them reason and intelligence, and to them
alone he entrusted the capacity for looking upward to him,
since he formed them after his own image. It was to them that
he sent his only-begotten Son, and to them that he promised the
Kingdom in heaven which he will give to those who love him.
And when you have acquired this knowledge, think with what 3
joy you will be filled! Think how you will love him, who first
loved you so! And when you love him, you will be an imitator 4
of his goodness. And do not be surprised to hear that a man
can become an imitator of God. He can, because God wills it.

To be happy does not, indeed, consist in lording it over one's 5
neighbors, or in longing to have some advantage over the
weaker ones, or in being rich and ordering one's inferiors
about. It is not in this way that any man can imitate God, for
such things are alien to his majesty. But if a man takes his 6
neighbor's burden on himself, and is willing to help his inferior
in some respect in which he himself is better off, and, by providing the needy with what he himself possesses because he has
received it from God, becomes a god to those who receive it—
then this man is an imitator of God. Then, while your lot is 7
cast on earth, you will realize that God rules in heaven; then
you will begin to talk of the mysteries of God; then you will
love and admire those who are being punished for their refusal
to deny God; then you will condemn the fraud and error of the
world, once you really understand the true life in heaven, once
you look down on the apparent death here below, once you
fear the real death kept for those who are condemned to the
eternal fire, which will punish to the end those that are handed

8 over to it. Then you will admire those who for righteousness'
sake endure the transitory fire, and will call them happy,
when you learn about that other fire.[17] . . .

THE TEXT: (II) A HOMILY CONCERNING THE MYSTERY OF FAITH

11 I am not speaking of things that are strange to me, nor is
my undertaking unreasonable, for I have been a disciple of
apostles, and now I am becoming a teacher of the Gentiles.
The things that pertain to the tradition I try to minister fittingly
2 to those who are becoming disciples of the truth. Can any man
who has been properly taught, and has come to love the Logos,
keep from trying to learn precisely what has been shown openly
by the Logos to those to whom he manifestly appeared and
spoke in the plainest terms? He remained, indeed, unrecognized
by unbelievers, but he gave a full explanation to his disciples
who, because he looked upon them as faithful, came to know
3 the mysteries of the Father. For this reason the Father sent the
Logos to appear to the world—the Logos who was slighted by
the chosen people, but preached by apostles and believed in
4 by the Gentiles. This is he who was from the beginning, who
appeared new and was found to be old, and is ever born young
5 in the hearts of the saints.[18] This is the eternal one, who
today is accounted a Son,[19] by whom the Church is made rich
and grace is multiplied as it unfolds among the saints—the
grace that gives understanding, makes mysteries plain,
announces seasons, rejoices in believers, is given freely to
seekers, that is, to such as do not break the pledges of their

---

[17] There is evidently a lacuna here, as a note in the MS, indicates, but it is
doubtful that the missing passage was very long. In the ten chapters as
they stand the author has pretty well accomplished what he set out to do.

[18] With this magnificent sentence the reader should compare Clement of
Alexandria, *Protrepticus*, ch. I (Loeb Classical Library, ed. G. W.
Butterworth, pp. 16–19), where the theme is bound up with the real
antiquity of the "New People" in the eternal purpose of God, and the
gospel of the incarnate Logos is proclaimed as the "New Song."

[19] This text may be a reference to the Hippolytean idea that the Logos
becomes (or is manifested as) "perfect Son" only in the incarnation. Cf.
Hippolytus, *Contra Noetum*, chs. 4; 11; 15; 17. In that case, the fragment
should probably be construed as an Epiphany homily (so Kirsopp Lake).
On the other hand, the passage could embody an allusion to Rom. 1:5,
in which case Otto's identification of these chapters as an Easter homily
must be accepted. The reference (ch. 12:9) to the "Lord's Passover"
seems to support this view. Cf. also note 7.

faith,[20] or go beyond the bounds set by the fathers. Then the 6 reverence taught by the Law is hymned, and the grace given to the Prophets is recognized, and the faith of the Gospels is made secure, and the tradition of the apostles is maintained, and the grace of the Church exults. And if you do not grieve 7 this grace, you will understand what the Logos speaks, through whom he pleases and whenever he chooses. For we simply 8 share with you, out of love for the things that have been revealed to us, everything that we have been prompted to speak out under stress, in obedience to the will and commandment of the Logos.

If you read this, and listen to it earnestly, you will discover 12 what God has prepared for those who love him as they ought, and have become a Paradise of delight, cultivating in themselves a flourishing tree, rich with all kinds of fruit, while they themselves are decked out with a variety of fruits; for in this 2 Garden a tree of knowledge and a tree of life have been planted.[21] But it is not the tree of knowledge that destroys; it is disobedience that brings destruction. Indeed, there is a deep 3 meaning in the passage of Scripture which tells how God in the beginning planted a tree of knowledge and a tree of life in the midst of Paradise, to show that life is attained through knowledge. It was because the first men did not use this knowledge with clean hearts that they were stripped of it by the deceit of the serpent. For there cannot be life without knowledge 4 any more than there can be sound knowledge without genuine life, and so the two trees were planted close together. Because 5 the apostle saw the force of this, he found fault with the knowledge that is put into effect in life without regard to the reality of the commandment, pointing out that "knowledge puffs up, but love builds up."[22] For the man who thinks he knows any- 6 thing apart from knowledge that is genuine and borne out by

20 This is presumably an allusion to the baptismal promises or profession of faith. In the rite of baptism described in Hippolytus' Apostolic Tradition, the threefold immersion follows the threefold confession of faith, step by step, and the developed creed or *symbolum* of Christianity grew out of just this baptismal invocation of the divine name as revealed to Christian faith. Cf. I Peter 3:21, which may be relevant here.

21 Cf. Gen. 2:8, 9, which is interpreted typologically in this chapter, a parallel being drawn again and again between the primordial Paradise and the Church.

22 Cf. I Cor. 8:1. The judicious approach to the question of the place of the intellect in the Christian scheme of things should be noted. The author does not let opposition to Gnostic excesses stampede him into anti-intellectualism.

life has actually learned nothing, but is deceived by the serpent, because he does not love life. But he who has gained full knowledge with reverence and seeks after life can plant in hope and look for fruit.

7 Let your heart be knowledge, and your life the true teaching
8 that your heart contains. If you bear the tree of this teaching and pluck its fruit, you will always be gathering in the things that are desirable in the sight of God, things that the serpent cannot touch and deceit cannot defile. Then Eve is not seduced,
9 but a Virgin is found trustworthy.[23] Furthermore, salvation is displayed, and the apostles are interpreted, and the Lord's Passover goes forward, and the seasons are brought together and set in order, and the Logos rejoices as he teaches the saints —the Logos through whom the Father is glorified. To him be glory forevermore. Amen.

[23] It is fairly clear that the author intends to state the common Patristic contrast (cf. Justin, Dialogue with Trypho, ch. 100; Irenaeus, *Adv. haer.* III. 22:4; V. 19:1; Tertullian, *De carne Christi,* 17) between Eve, the disobedient mother of death, and Mary, the obedient mother of life, in which case the *parthenos* of the text will be the blessed Virgin Mary.

The First Apology of Justin, the Martyr

INTRODUCTION

EARLY CHRISTIAN APOLOGIES

THE DANGER OF PERSECUTION ON THE ONE HAND, and increasing opportunities for the propagation of the gospel on the other, produced the ancient Christian writings that are known generally, from the title of some of them, as Apologies. Eusebius tells us that they began in the time of Hadrian with the Apology of Quadratus, from which he preserves only a brief fragment.[1] Early in the principate of Antoninus comes Aristides of Athens, whose Apology has been recovered from various fragments in our own time—a straightforward claim that the Christians hold the true faith and live as God commands, put forward with considerable charm. Justin comes logically next in the series; his distinguishing feature among the Apologists is the scope of what he tries to include—a reply to the legal and moral attacks and an exhibition of the Old Testament basis of the gospel.

By the middle of the second century attacks on Christianity as well as defenses of it were in circulation. A work by Marcus Aurelius' teacher, Fronto, seems to have put the legal and moral charges in a form calculated to gain the attention of Apologists connected with Rome. Somewhat later came Celsus' True Word, which was to wait two generations for Origen's massive reply. Under Marcus Aurelius, Athenagoras of Athens produced his Plea Concerning Christians, the most polished of the Apologies as a literary work. Athenagoras draws largely on Justin (though not on his Old Testament quotations), and anticipates Clement in his skillful use of Greek literary quotations. It seems fair to say that the Athenian Apologists are more interested in the religious claims of Christianity, the Roman in its civic

[1] *Hist. eccl.*, IV, ch. 3. See the Epistle to Diognetus.

status, though without neglecting its claim to present the true faith in God. Christian literature in the language of the Romans begins with the Latin Apologists of the end of the century, Tertullian and Minucius Felix. About the same time Clement of Alexandria, in his Address to the Greeks, presents Christianity as the true mystery, by which we reach the spiritual light that Eleusis fallaciously promised. The Apologists whom we may call Oriental are more concerned to maintain the claims of Christianity against rival religions. Tatian the Assyrian, after being Justin's pupil at Rome, returned to his native land and ultimately became the founder of a puritanical and dualistic sect; earlier he had shown his tendencies by attacking Greek thought and pagan practice in his Discourse to the Greeks. Theophilus of Antioch in his work To Autolycus defends prophets against philosophers with a rather narrow vigor. The most original work of Syrian Christianity deserves inclusion in the list; astrology and the slavery of fate, touched on by other Apologists, was the main topic of On Fate by Bardesanes of Edessa. Like some other Apologists in various ages, he may concede too much—the stars may control external events, he says, but not the spiritual character and moral actions of man.

Though apologetics is a permanent part of Christian writing, these writers complete the roll of the classical Apologists of the Greco-Roman world. Still close to them are Origen's Against Celsus and Cyprian's brief practical appeal To Donatus (or Epistle 1) in the middle of the third century. Finally ancient apologetic was revived by the return of somewhat similar conditions during the reign of Diocletian and the early years of Constantine. The works of Arnobius and Lactantius in the West belong to this period, and at Alexandria Athanasius' work Against the Nations ends the period of ancient apologetic while the companion piece On the Incarnation opens the classical age of conciliar Christology.

Understanding of the Apologists can be assisted by some attention to the literary forms that they employed. The first Christian writers, indeed, clearly had classical literary forms in mind, since they wrote in some hope of reaching a general audience. An Apology is by definition a speech for the defense. The use of the form for philosophic propaganda goes back to the illustrious example of Plato's Apology of Socrates. It is this surely that brings Socrates so naturally to Justin's mind in the First Apology,[2] or makes him say in the Second, "Would that

[2] Ch. 5 (references to Justin by chapter alone will be to the First Apology).

even now someone would mount on a lofty rostrum and cry out" the message of the Apologist.[3] The word and form already occur in Paul's two Apologies in Acts, chs. 22 and 26—where, like the later Apologists, Luke realizes that the best defense in these matters is attack, and that a plea for the toleration of Christianity might as well include an argument for its truth. There were also pagan parallels to both the Apology and the related form of the Acts of Martyrs, especially in the so-called "pagan Acts of the Martyrs," which represent the claims of the city of Alexandria. Since the preparation of possible or purely imaginary speeches was an important part of high education in Roman times, the use of the form in literary composition is natural. In a speech a brief exordium, aiming to please the audience or at least grasp its attention, is likely to lead to a detailed exhibition of the main point, and then subordinate points and a conclusion will follow rapidly. If a speaker (or preacher) announces three points, he knows that the second and third should be shorter than the first, or the audience will be murmuring "ten minutes more of this." Hence the difficulty of finding a balanced outline in the rhetorical Apologies— Justin, Athenagoras, and Tertullian. In each case the main point is in the center of the work—Tertullian and Athenagoras argue for belief in God, Justin for recognition of Jesus as the predicted Messiah—and there are relatively briefer introductions and conclusions.

Though in form a plea for toleration, the Apology was certainly written even more as an appeal for conversion. Here also there was a pagan parallel in the protreptic discourse or exhortation, written to commend some philosophical or ethical position. Such discourses were the stock in trade of the wandering philosophers who were the popular preachers of paganism. Literary references were specially in place in such writing; Clement's Address to the Greeks is the fullest example among the Apologists, though all exhibit some features of the form. A brief protreptic discourse could be written in the form of an epistle, such as those that make up the three books of Seneca's *Epistolae Morales*—among Christian Apologists there is the Epistle to Diognetus and Cyprian's *Ad Donatum*. Perhaps Justin's Second Apology can best be read as an Epistle to the Romans. Since the Apologists were conducting an argument,

---

[3] Ch. 12, *fin.*; this phrase has an interesting history in pagan and Christian rhetoric, always it seems with Socrates more or less in mind (see Michele Pellegrino, *Studi su l'antica Apologetica*, pp. 23-27, Rome, 1947).

the dialogue form would naturally suggest itself, if they wanted to give their opponents that much space. Justin uses it with some skill in the Dialogue with Trypho, including such minor features, familiar in the Platonic dialogue, as that the whole conversation is allegedly recounted afterward by one of the participants, and that it includes a dialogue within a dialogue. The Octavius of Minucius Felix is a more formal dialogue, or rather debate. Like some of the dialogues of Cicero, it opens with a genre picture of Roman life, which Minucius handles with considerable charm. Least of all among Apologies do we find the formal treatise, arguing and expounding various aspects of a subject, though this was also not unknown and is represented by Theophilus of Antioch. This form was especially appropriate to a work that replied point by point to the arguments of an attacker, as Josephus had done in his two books Against Apion and as Origen did in his eight Against Celsus.

Justin's Life and Work

In spite of a certain lack of polish, perhaps because of it, Justin Martyr is one of the greatest of the Apologists. His writings have the additional interest of being the most specifically Christian of the ancient Apologies. All of them deal in their various ways with the permanent and ever-changing problem of Christian apologetics—how to make contact between the claims of the gospel and the needs and interests of the age, while clearing away misunderstandings and prejudices. Most of the other Apologists lead their reader to the door of the church—Minucius Felix, indeed, does little more than point in its general direction—while Justin opens it and tells a good deal about what goes on inside. Much of the First Apology reads more like a manual for inquirers than a defense for the general public, and this feature gives it its great interest as a record of the faith and practice of the middle of the second century. Since his work was rediscovered in the sixteenth century, Justin has received more attention than at any time since his own generation. Both for the value of his own contribution to Christian thought and for the significance of his evidence as to what was believed and taught by the Christians of his time, he undoubtedly deserves it.

Justin tells us that he was the son of Priscus and grandson of Bacchius. He was a native of Flavia Neapolis (ancient Shechem and modern Nablus) in Palestine. The family were evidently Gentile citizens of a Roman colony in Samaria, a connection reflected in Justin's occasional marked interest in Samaritan affairs.[4] Though not Jewish, Justin brought from his Palestinian home a consciousness of the Jewish background of the faith that he ultimately adopted, later to be reflected in the Old Testament discussions that take up so much of the First Apology and are the subject of the Dialogue with Trypho. But his own cultural and intellectual formation was certainly Greek, and it was in philosophy that he looked for spiritual satisfaction. The "I" of the Dialogue is not strictly autobiographical, but the experience it reflects is certainly Justin's. After some contact with other schools, he was deeply attracted by Platonism, which seemed to show the way to the true knowledge of man and vision of God. But before he had gone very far on that path his attention was directed to the deeper wisdom of the prophets of Israel as expounded by the Church, and in that teaching he recognized the true philosophy which he had been looking for. The example of the martyrs moved him to give in his name to the persecuted sect of Christians.[5] Thereafter he continued, or perhaps began, to wear the philosopher's cloak, but as a professor of the divine philosophy, not of any human school.

Justin certainly ended his career as a Christian teacher at Rome, but the stages of his journey there are obscure. Our knowledge of them depends mainly on the evaluation of slight references in the Dialogue with Trypho. Eusebius tells us that the dialogue took place at Ephesus, although the only specific indication in the present text suggests Corinth. Could there be in Eusebius' MS. or ours a slip of one Pauline city for another?[6] Well-frequented lines of travel connected the Christian centers of the province of Asia with Greece and Rome, so that Justin may have lived in all three. If the evidence of the Acts is to be trusted, he had left Rome and then returned for a second stay at the time of his death.

In our own time the identification of the Apostolic Tradition of Hippolytus has provided a welcome complement to Justin's evidence about the customs of the Roman Church. Hippolytus wrote about A.D. 200, some forty or fifty years later than Justin. But since he aimed to describe customs that were already old, the difference in time is not so important as it might seem.

---

[4] Chs. 1; 26; 53; 56; Justin counts himself among the uncircumcised, Dial., ch. 92.
[5] Apol. II, ch. 12.   [6] Eusebius, *Hist. eccl.* IV. 18:6; Dial., ch. 1.

The liturgical evidence of the two writers interlocks remarkably, and a passing reference in Hippolytus to the teachers who prepared candidates for baptism doubtless gives the clue to Justin's position in the Church. Christian teaching at Rome was carried on by individuals who conducted, as it were, schools of Christianity. They were only indirectly subject to the discipline of the Church, in case they developed heresies so clear as to call for condemnation by the not very theologically minded leaders of Roman Christendom. Since services were private, and held from house to house, the residences of these teachers might be the only publicly known Christian centers—as Justin says in the Acts: "I live above one Martinus, at the Timiotinian Bath, and during the whole time (and I am now living in Rome for the second time) I have been unaware of any other meeting than this. And if anyone wished to come to me, I communicated to him the doctrines of truth."

Though freely instructing prospective converts and interested Christians, these teachers did not as such occupy any official position in the Church. Considered from another point of view, they belonged to the class of popular teachers or preachers who presented the religious claims of philosophy to the common man. So the animosity of Crescens the Cynic for Justin, which he expected would be the cause of his martyrdom,[7] had certain aspects of professional rivalry. The philosopher's cloak, one must remember, in this period was rather the habit of a begging friar than the gown of a university professor.

The chronology of Justin's life depends mainly on the references in his works. The First Apology speaks of a recent episode at Alexandria in the prefecture of Felix, who held office between A.D. 151 and 154[8]; it is addressed to Antoninus Pius and his adopted sons and colleagues, Marcus Aurelius and Lucius Verus, whose formal association in the imperial dignity dates from 147. We may date it safely about 155. The Dialogue with Trypho is placed dramatically at the time of the Jewish War of 132–135,[9] which may well be the approximate period of Justin's conversion. It is clearly, however, subsequent to the Apology, to which it refers[10]; its main theme is an enlargement of the central argument of the Apology, by more detailed exposition of Old Testament texts, to show that Christians are the true heirs of the promises made to Israel. The Second Apology also refers to the First. It was evidently written at a moment of crisis for the Christians of Rome, when martyrdoms had

[7] Apol. II, ch. 3.   [8] Ch. 29.   [9] Ch. 1.   [10] Ch. 120, *fin.*

occurred and Justin expected his own to follow shortly. Eusebius dates Justin's Second Apology and martyrdom early in the years of Marcus Aurelius, and there is no reason to doubt the correctness of that information. The Acts of Justin and other martyrs are, as they stand, considerably later, but certainly go back to a simple and authentic eyewitness account. As they describe the events, Justin and six others were arrested, probably at the house of Martinus, and brought before the prefect Rusticus. Justin's fellow martyrs were simple folk with Greek names, the most distinguished the imperial slave Euelpistus, who had first learned the faith from his parents in far-off Cappadocia. Justin had the chance to make such confession as he longed for. But as soon as he had spoken of Father, Son, and Spirit, the prefect, "who seems to have been bored at the prospect of a sermon," [11] tried in vain to get more information about Christian meeting places. Then came the fatal demand for sacrifice, after which condemnation and execution followed as a matter of course.

JUSTIN'S THOUGHT AND INTERESTS

The detailed study of Justin's ideas belongs elsewhere, but some suggestions regarding his thought are in place in this introduction.

Modern readers tend to concentrate on what seems to be unique, or what is of particular interest to us—for instance, Justin's use of the Logos concept, his attitude to philosophy, and his evidence for worship and the sacraments. But his own approach is primarily pastoral, Biblical, and traditionalist. He writes everything with a pastoral or evangelistic purpose like that of the Fourth Evangelist, "that ye might believe that Jesus is the Christ, the Son of God, and that believing, ye might have life through his name." [12] His recognition of the value of philosophy is secondary to his desire to testify and demonstrate that God has spoken through the prophets and redeemed us through his Son. He is much less interested in expounding his own ideas than in appealing for acceptance of the faith as, he believed, the Church of his day had learned it from the apostles. Phrases such as, "We have learned," "We have received," "It has been handed down," occur with surprising frequency in the First Apology. It is not too hard to distinguish

[11] E. R. Goodenough, *The Theology of Justin Martyr*, p. 75.
[12] John 20:31.

between what Justin presents as the Christian tradition and his own efforts to interpret or explain. Thus the Sacred Name that Christians venerated was clearly that of Father, Son, and Holy Spirit, into which they were baptized. Justin, doubtless not uniquely, is making an effort to interpret this when he says that Christians venerated, after God the Father and Lord of all, his Son, and thirdly the holy prophetic Spirit.[13] Similarly in the Dialogue he tries to develop a formal doctrine of the Word as a "second divine entity" (deuteros theos). To him the heart of Christianity is the Biblical message of God's care and love for man, as he found it both in the Bible (i.e., the Old Testament) and in Jesus Christ. Behind the literary form of a speech to the emperor, we are listening in the First Apology to the kind of conversation that went on between Justin and his visitors in the house of Martinus. Now he presents arguments about this or that (and the Apology could easily be thrown into dialogue form), now he brings forward quotations from the sacred text or refers to the increasingly venerated writings of the apostles. But again and again the thread of continuous argument is broken by the proclamation of the basic kerygma of the Early Church, the message of the incarnate, dying, risen, ascended Saviour and Lord.[14]

The First Apology and Dialogue with Trypho together would serve as a convert's shorter Bible, and such was doubtless one of the purposes of Justin's writing. His prospective readers were, I suspect, not the noble or learned, but intelligent members of what we may call the lower middle class. They were people who were prepared to be impressed by mysterious words of Oriental sages and who, if Justin had not taught them orthodox Christianity, would perhaps have been Marcionites or Mithraists. His references to these sects suggest that these were immediate rivals. Much of Justin's history and exegesis no longer appeals. But Christians can never renounce his central aim—to assert their claim to be legitimate heirs of "the hope of Israel."[15] In detail, Justin sometimes seems to quote from memory, sometimes to be using a collection of Biblical testimonies, one cause or the other producing the startling combinations and centos found in some of his quotations. A good example of his method is in chs. 50; 51, where he first quotes Isa. 53:12 quite loosely, doubtless from memory, and then looks up the whole passage and copies it out. The authority of the New Testament books for Justin was that of the truths they contained. They

13 Ch. 6; etc.   14 Cf. chs. 31; 42; 46; 50; 53.   15 Acts 28:20.

were records of the words and acts of Jesus; and so his references
are to the gospel story rather than to specific Gospels. For the
teachings of Christ he perhaps used a manual of instruction
(such as we find in the Didache) rather than the separate
Synoptic texts. Though the question has been disputed, he
certainly knew the Fourth Gospel, to which his references
become more frequent as he comes closer to the inner life of the
Church in the later chapters of the First Apology. He was
acquainted with the principal Pauline Epistles (probably
lesser ones too, which he does not happen to refer to); and the
Dialogue contains a specific reference to Revelation.[16] His
references to the birth and Passion of Christ contain legendary
touches such as appear in apocryphal Gospels, but whether
he derived them from written sources is uncertain.

Justin wore the philosopher's cloak, and later tradition
speaks of him as "philosopher and martyr," yet his speculative
interests were really secondary. All the more significant,
therefore, are his striking contributions to the intellectual
tradition of Christian thought. The idea of God's Logos could
be found in a variety of sources. It was floating in the air of
popular Greek philosophy and Hellenistic Judaism, and had
become naturalized in Christian circles by the Prologue of the
Fourth Gospel. (The chief thing to remember about the word
"logos" is that it means everything except a single word—
speech, design, argument, reason—therefore God's thought,
plan, utterance, and so on.) Justin's use of it is partly Biblical,
and partly apologetic. The Logos being divine, and yet not the
Father himself, accounts both for the divinity which Christians
have found in Jesus, and by retrospect for the divine appear-
ances in the Old Testament. The Reason incarnate in Christ is
also the diffused reason that speaks in every man (Justin is not
deeply interested in the cosmic action of the Logos). Hence
everything good and true really is ours by right; in the Second
Apology this thought is developed more explicitly, adopting
the term, familiar to Stoics, of the "spermatic word," the divine
force which, as it were, impregnated the universe.[17] Pregnant
as Justin's ideas were, they remained inchoate, and somewhat
crude and confused. Perhaps they are all the more suggestive
for that. It would be easy to make a long list of the points that
Justin does not clearly define because he did not have to. An
example is what kind of being the prophetic Spirit is, in view

[16] Dial., ch. 81.
[17] Apol. II, chs. 10; 13; certainly with some hint from John 1:9.

of the fact that the Logos is also a Spirit,[18] and the Spirit speaks through the prophets the Word of God. Nor again does Justin bother to state precisely how the Spirit and the Logos are distinguished from the lesser angelic powers, who follow the Son (pre-eminently God's Angel), and who in one passage are named between him and the prophetic Spirit.[19] Certainly Justin knows that God is the only Fashioner of the universe, who made it out of formless matter. But he seems to have no interest in where that came from. Perhaps he could conceive of nothing more nonexistent.[20]

A topic in which he was more interested than his modern readers was the nature and activity of demons. In later Platonism and popular Greek thought the *daimōnes* were intermediate beings. They were more than man but far beneath the supreme deity, and were often thought of as occupying the changeable heavens between the earth and the moon. The word "demon" itself was morally neutral; Justin regularly adds a qualifying adjective when he uses it in a bad sense. He shared the Jewish position that any such beings could only be fallen angels. In the Second Apology he amplifies the references in the First[21] by recounting the legend that angels who had been placed in charge of mankind had sinned with women and begotten demons.[22] That pagan worship was in fact offered to demons is an idea as old as Saint Paul.[23] But Justin develops it more in detail when he declares that demons actually appeared to men, performed some of the actions recounted in the myths, and demanded worship as gods. Part of the atmosphere of early Christianity was the sense that paganism represented invisible as well as visible foes, and that hostile forces infested even the air.[24] Justin shows much more practical interest in demons than in the good angelic powers, who, after all, were but ministering spirits of the Lord. As in the traditional baptismal service to this day, on entering the Church one renounced the devil and all his works, and in that fellowship the great serpent and the other demons were no longer to be feared.

Justin the philosopher was also, and more deeply, Justin the churchman. His description of baptism and the Eucharist is the best-known section of his work, though it is introduced

---

[18] See ch. 33 and notes.   [19] Ch. 6.
[20] Cf. ch. 59: I have translated *dēmiourgos* "Fashioner," although "Creator" would be justifiable.   [21] Ch. 5.
[22] As recounted in Gen. 6:2—an interpretation later repudiated by both Jews and Christians.   [23] I Cor. 10:20.   [24] Cf. Eph. 6:12.

rather incidentally, to assure readers that no nameless horrors are perpetrated at Christian gatherings. What strikes the reader who comes to this section from the rest of the Apology is that here he meets the Church's technical terminology, which Justin partly uses, partly explains, partly paraphrases. Hence his threefold repetition of "rebirth" in one sentence to explain that Baptism is a sacrament of regeneration. Then there are phrases like: "Those whom we call deacons," "This food we call Eucharist," and "The president of the brethren." In the last instance Justin might just as well have said "bishop."[25] The sacred language of rebirth in baptism[26] and spiritual nourishment by the body and blood of Christ was evidently already well established. Even the rather complex devotional and theological comments that Justin offers are presented as part of the received tradition. The Eucharistic teaching of the Apology is completed by that of the Dialogue. It speaks of the Christian sacrifice of the bread and cup of the Eucharist, fulfilling Malachi's prophecy of the pure offering of the Gentiles. It also gives the most complete of Justin's several summaries of the contents of the Eucharistic prayer:

"We give thanks to God for having created the world with all that is in it for the sake of man, and for having freed us from the vice in which we lived, and for having completely brought to naught the principalities and powers, through Him who became subject to suffering according to his will."[27]

Justin's religion was certainly deeper and richer than some of his formal arguments for it. The Apologist is always in danger of conceding too much for the sake of argument. Justin at times seems to say that Christ was merely on the same level as the sons of Zeus, an impression that he corrects elsewhere.[28] Nor does he really mean, I am sure, that he believed in Christ only because the prophecies fitted. Though he does not precisely describe either the need or the means of redemption, surely his faith is shown in such a simple phrase as, "For the

<hr/>

25 Certainly a permanent officer, whose functions include the administration of church finances, which by this time was episcopal; the phrase is similarly used for a bishop of Athens in Eusebius, *Hist. eccl.*, IV, ch. 23; its vagueness would also cover the case of a presbyter in a local congregation at Rome, although Justin describes Christian worship in terms of a general gathering of the church of a city and its surrounding countryside.

26 Certainly for children of believers as well as converts. Justin distinguishes the two classes in ch. 15, and the Acts states that three of his six companions in martyrdom had been Christians from childhood.

27 *Dial.*, chs. 41; 70.   28 Chs. 21; 54.

salvation of those who believe in him . . . [he] endured . . . suffering so that by dying and rising again he might conquer death."[29] Formally Justin presents a simple doctrine of free will which would suggest that the only salvation man would need is information, and the removal of the obstacles interposed by the demons. But as incidental references show, he is well enough aware that it is only by the gift of God that men are able to understand his truth. Equally does he recognize that the Christian life is a life of thanksgiving for the gifts of God.[30]

STYLE AND OUTLINE

Justin's technique is, like his theology, practical. He could pay attention to literary form, but was much more interested in what he had to say than in just how he said it. He knew how to write an oration, a dialogue, or an epistle, but did not let attention to those details stand in the way of the exposition of his message. His Greek is good, though not purist; he seems to apologize for an occasional colloquialism, even slightly for the straightforward Greek of the Gospels.[31] His sentences sometimes get out of control, either because he crowds in more ideas than he intended to or because a central point in the argument is so clearly implied that he does not pause to state it.[32] The effort to find a clear outline in the First Apology has baffled commentators, especially since the scheme apparently announced in ch. 23 is hard to follow through in detail. But the central point in any analysis is the demonstration from the Old Testament that Jesus is the promised Messiah. This theme occupies chs. 30 to 53. It is possible to see a rhetorical scheme of approach to this theme and then return from it to the point of departure, somewhat as follows:

A   Plea for a Fair Hearing, chs. 1 to 8.

    B   The Faith and Life of Christians, chs. 9 to 20.

       C   Superiority of Christianity to Paganism, chs. 21 to 29.

         D   The Argument from Prophecy, chs. 30 to 53.

       E   Paganism an Imitation of Christianity, chs. 54 to 60.

    F   Christian Worship, chs. 61 to 67.

  G   Conclusion, ch. 68.

---

[29] Chs. 53; 63, *fin.*   [30] Dial., ch. 7, *fin.*; Apol. I, chs. 13; 65.
[31] Ch. 55, "What is called the nose," ch. 14, *fin.*
[32] See examples noted in chs. 29; 51.

There are hints of the general scheme in chs. 12 and 23; the first announces that there will be not only defense, as in the opening (and closing) sections, but attack, and the three points announced in ch. 23 are approximately those of C, D, and E. The closing sections interlock with the previous ones, with a number of cross references. Several of the transitions are prepared with some care. Chapter 20, for instance, looks forward to the topic taken up in ch. 21. Chapter 53 similarly looks forward to ch. 54. As is suitable for a work in the form of a forensic speech, the Conclusion is a brief summary and plea, followed by citation of a supporting document.

The careful reader of Justin cannot call him a genius, but comes to enjoy the company of the man who appears through his writings, and to welcome his occasional moments of brilliant insight. To the history of Christian thought he made a great contribution. To him as much as to any other we may owe it that the gospel has remained rooted in the religion of the Old Testament, and on one basis or another has not been unfriendly to human thought. His influence is clear in Athenagoras and Irenaeus, as well as in his rather unworthy disciple Tatian.

MANUSCRIPTS

Eusebius seems to have had a MS. that presented the same problems as ours,[33] and to have known only the titles of other lost works. In those Justin developed the Greek, as the Dialogue develops the Jewish, elements of the First Apology.[34] Justin would be known to us only by a few spasmodic quotations had not a Byzantine scribe copied an invaluable, if defective, MS., in the year 1364. This is now *Codex Regius* 150 at Paris, and is the almost exclusive source for editions of Justin, supplemented only by the quotations of Eusebius and John of Damascus and three chapters (65 to 67) in a manuscript at Rome (*Codex Ottobonianus Graecus* 274). Consequently the editing of Justin's text is almost entirely a matter of conjectural emendation, which is necessary in places but has certainly been employed too freely by some editors. The first printed edition was that of Stephanus at Paris in 1551, since which time Justin has come into his own among the students of Christian literature.

[33] Namely, that the Second Apology precedes the First, as if a preface to it. Eusebius knew that Justin wrote two Apologies, but seems to quote from both of the preserved ones as the First. It may be that our Second Apology is a mere supplement to the First, and that Justin's Second, if there was one, is now lost. I think, however, it is more likely that the Second, which begins very abruptly, lost its opening in an early MS. and then was copied in the wrong position—rather like what is often supposed to have happened with II Corinthians.

[34] To the Greeks, another called A Refutation, and On the Sovereignty of God, which used classical quotations (the Pseudo-Justinian work with this title seems to be a feebler exercise on the theme); also *Psaltes*, perhaps a collection of hymns, and On the Soul, which might be an expansion of Dial., chs. 4; 5.

BOOKS

Background and General

Cambridge Ancient History, Vol. XII, *The Imperial Crisis and Recovery* (Cambridge University Press, Cambridge, 1939), especially Ch. 13, F. C. Burkitt, "Pagan Philosophy and the Christian Church"; Ch. 14, F. C. Burkitt, "The Christian Church in the East"; Ch. 15, H. Lietzmann, "The Christian Church in the West"; and bibliographies.

Dill, S., *Roman Society from Nero to Marcus Aurelius*, 2d ed. London, 1905.

Dix, G., *The Shape of the Liturgy*, 2d ed., London, 1905, especially Chs. 3 and 5, "The Classical Shape of the Liturgy"; Ch. 6, "The Pre-Nicene Background of the Liturgy."

Glover, T. R., *The Conflict of Religions in the Early Roman Empire*. London, 1909.

Nock, A. D., *Conversion*. Oxford University Press, Oxford, 1933.

Puech, A., *Les Apologistes grecs*. Paris, 1912.

All Church histories and histories of doctrine deal with the Apologists. See especially the histories of doctrine by Harnack, McGiffert, and Tixeront, and

Harnack, A., *The Mission and Expansion of Christianity in the First Three Centuries*, tr. J. Moffatt, 2 vols. 2d ed., Edinburgh, 1908 (from 2d German ed., Berlin, 1905).

Lietzmann, H., *The Founding of the Church Universal* (*The Beginnings of the Christian Church*, Vol. II), tr. B. L. Woolf. Charles Scribner's Sons, New York, 1938 (from German, Berlin, 1932).

Lebreton, J., and Zeiller, J., *The History of the Primitive Church*, tr. E. C. Messenger. 2 vols. (from French, Paris, 1934–1935).

EDITIONS OF THE WORKS OF JUSTIN MARTYR
Critical Editions of the Text:
Thirlby, S., London, 1722.
Maran, P., Paris, 1742 (the Benedictine edition, reprinted in
    Migne, *Patrologia Graeca*, Vol. VI. Paris, 1857).
Otto, J. C., Jena, 1842 (3d ed., 1876–1881).
Krüger, G., Leipzig, 1896 (3d ed., Tübingen, 1915).
Goodspeed, E. J., Göttingen, 1914 (in *Die ältesten Apologeten*).
Editions with Commentary:
Blunt, A. W. F., *The Apologies of Justin Martyr* (in *Cambridge
    Patristic Texts*). Cambridge, 1911.
Pfättisch, J. M., *Justinus des Philosophen und Märtyrers Apologien.*
    Munich, 1912.
Gildersleeve, B. L., *The Apologies of Justin Martyr.* New York,
    1877.
The present translation is based on Krüger's text in Blunt's
    edition.

TRANSLATIONS OF THE WORKS OF JUSTIN MARTYR
English:
Reeves, W., *The Apologies of Justin Martyr, Tertullian, and Minu-
    cius Felix.* London, 1709.
Dods, M., and Others, *The Writings of Justin Martyr and Athenag-
    oras* (in Ante-Nicene Christian Library) (genuine and spur-
    ious works, and *Acts*). Edinburgh, 1867.
Williams, A. L., *The Dialogue with Trypho.* S.P.C.K., London,
    1930.
Falls, T. B., *Saint Justin Martyr* (in The Fathers of the Church).
    Fathers of the Church Press, New York, 1948.
French:
Pautigny, L., *Justin, Apologies* (with Greek text). Paris, 1904.
Archambault, G., *Justin, Dialogue avec Tryphon* (with Greek
    text and commentary), 2 vols. Paris, 1909.
German:
Veil, H., *Justins des Philosophs und Märtyrers Rechtfertigung des
    Christentums.* Strassburg, 1904.
Rauschen, G., *Die beiden Apologien Justins des Märtyrers* (in
    Bibliothek der Kirchenväter). Kempten, 1913.

SOME STUDIES OF JUSTIN
Goodenough, E. R., *The Theology of Justin Martyr* (with an
    elaborate bibliography). Jena, 1923.

Kaye, John, *Some Account of the Writings and Opinions of Justin Martyr*, London, 1829 (reprinted under various titles; as *The First Apology of Justin Martyr*, with Reeves's translation, Edinburgh, 1912).

Martindale, C. C., *St. Justin the Martyr*. London and New York, 1921.

Pellegrino, M., *Studi su l'antica Apologetica*. Edizioni di "Storia e letteratura," Rome, 1947.

Lagrange, M. J., *Saint Justin*, 3d ed. Paris, 1914.

Seeberg, E., *Die Geschichtstheologie Justins des Märtyrers*. Ph. D. thesis, Kiel, 1939.

Hubik, K., *Die Apologien des hl. Justinus des Philosophen und Märtyrers*. Vienna, 1912.

Pfättisch, J. M., *Der Einfluss Platos auf die Theologie Justins des Märtyrers* (in *Forschungen zur christl. Literatur- und Dogmengeschichte* 10. 1). Paderborn, 1910.

The First Apology of Justin, the Martyr

THE TEXT

Plea for a Fair Hearing

1. To the Emperor Titus Aelius Hadrianus Antoninus Pius Augustus Caesar, and to Verissimus his son, the Philosopher, and to Lucius the Philosopher, son of Caesar by nature and of Augustus[35] by adoption, a lover of culture, and to the Sacred Senate and the whole Roman people—on behalf of men of every nation who are unjustly hated and reviled, I, Justin, son of Priscus and grandson of Bacchius, of Flavia Neapolis in Syria Palestina, being myself one of them, have drawn up this plea and petition.

2. Reason requires that those who are truly pious and philosophers should honor and cherish the truth alone, scorning merely to follow the opinions of the ancients, if they are worthless. Nor does sound reason only require that one should not follow those who do or teach what is unjust; the lover of truth ought to choose in every way, even at the cost of his own life, to speak and do what is right, though death should take him away. So do you, since you are called pious and philosophers and guardians of justice and lovers of culture, at least give us a hearing—and it will appear if you are really such.[36] For in these pages we do not come before you with flattery, or as if making a speech to win your favor, but asking you to give judgment according to strict and exact inquiry—not, moved by prejudice or respect for superstitious men, or by irrational

---

[35] Lucius was the son of L. Aelius Verus, Caesar under Hadrian, and after his death was adopted by Antoninus Pius, later emperor.

[36] In form at least this is the *captatio benevolentiae*, or appeal to the sympathy of the audience, with which a speech opens; the chapter plays on the emperor's surname Pius and the appellation of philosopher, loved by his family, not forgetting the etymology of the latter, "lover of wisdom."

impulse and long-established evil rumor, giving a vote which would really be against yourselves. For we are firmly convinced that we can suffer no evil unless we are proved to be evildoers or shown to be criminals. You can kill us, but cannot do us any real harm.[37]

3. But so that no one may think that this is an unreasonable and presumptuous utterance, we ask that the charges against us be investigated. If they are shown to be true, [let us] be punished as is proper.[38] But if nobody has proofs against us, true reason does not allow [you] to wrong innocent men because of an evil rumor—or rather [to wrong] yourselves when you decide to pass sentence on the basis of passion rather than judgment. Every honorable man will recognize this as a fair challenge, and only just, that subjects should give a straightforward account of their life and thought, and that rulers similarly should give their decision as followers of piety and philosophy, not with tyrannical violence. From this both rulers and subjects would gain. As one of the ancients said somewhere, "Unless both rulers and those they rule become lovers of wisdom cities cannot prosper."[39] It is for us, therefore, to offer to all the opportunity of inspecting our life and teachings, lest we ourselves should bear the blame for what those who do not really know about us do in their ignorance. But it is for you, as reason demands, to give [us] a hearing and show yourselves good judges. For if those who learn [the truth] do not do what is right, they have no defense before God.

4. The mere ascription of a name means nothing, good or bad, except for the actions connected with the name. Indeed as far as the name charged against us goes, we are very gracious people.[40] But we do not think it right to ask for a pardon because of the name if we are proved to be criminals—and on the other hand, if neither the appellation of the name nor our conduct shows us to be wrongdoers, you must face the problem whether in punishing unjustly men against whom nothing is proved you will yourselves owe a penalty to justice. Neither

---

[37] A popular Stoic thought, that no external evil can harm the virtuous man; cf. also Luke 12:4, 5.

[38] Omitting, with many editors, the confusing phrase *mallon de kolazein* ("but rather to punish") as gloss or mistaken correction.

[39] A summary of Plato, *Republic* 473 D–E.

[40] The play between *christos* and *chrēstos*, "gentle" or "kind" (cf. Luke 6:35), a more familiar Greek word often confused with it, seems impossible to represent in English; Justin may have been the first to see the apologetic value of the confusion (cf. Tertullian, *Apol.* 3:5).

reward nor punishment should follow from a name unless something admirable or evil can actually be shown about it. Among yourselves you do not penalize the accused before conviction; but with us you take the name as proof, although, as far as the name goes, you ought rather to punish our accusers. For we are accused of being Christians; and it is not right to hate graciousness. Again, if one of the accused denies the charge, saying he is not [a Christian], you dismiss him, as having no proof of misconduct against him; but if he confesses that he is one, you punish him because of his confession. You ought rather to investigate the life of the confessor and the renegade, so that it would appear from their actions what sort of person each is. There are those who, learning from Christ their teacher, when they are put to the test encourage others not to deny him—and similarly others whose bad conduct gives some excuse to those who like to accuse all Christians of godlessness and crime. This is entirely improper. There are those who assume the name and costume of philosophers, but do nothing worthy of their profession—as you know, men among the ancients who held and taught opposite views are included under the one name of philosophers. Some of them even taught godlessness, and those who became poets proclaim the impurity of Zeus, with his own children. And you do not restrain those among you who follow such teachings, but even offer prizes and honors to those who thus in beautiful words insult them [the gods].

5. What can all this mean? You do not make judicial inquiries in our case, though we are bound neither to commit crimes nor to hold such godless ideas. Instead, you punish us injudicially without deliberation, driven by unreasoning passion and the whips of evil demons. The truth must be told. In old times evil demons manifested themselves, seducing women, corrupting boys, and showing terrifying sights to men —so that those who did not judge these occurrences rationally were filled with awe. Taken captive by fear and not understanding that these were evil demons, they called them gods and gave each of them the name which each of the demons had chosen for himself. When Socrates tried by true reason and with due inquiry to make these things clear and to draw men away from the demons, they, working through men who delighted in wickedness, managed to have him put to death as godless and impious, saying that he was bringing in new divinities.[41]

[41] Part of the formal charges against Socrates (Plato, *Apol.* 24 B).

And now they do the same kind of thing to us. For these errors were not only condemned among the Greeks by reason, through Socrates, but among the barbarians, by Reason himself, who took form and became man and was called Jesus Christ. In obedience to him we say that the demons who do such things are not only not rightly called gods,[42] but are in fact evil and unholy demons, whose actions are in no way like those of men who long after virtue.

6. So, then, we are called godless. We certainly confess that we are godless with reference to beings like these who are commonly thought of as gods, but not with reference to the most true God, the Father of righteousness and temperance and the other virtues, who is untouched by evil. Him, and the Son who came from him, and taught us these things, and the army of the other good angels who follow him and are made like him, and the prophetic Spirit we worship and adore,[43] giving honor in reason and truth, and to everyone who wishes to learn transmitting [the truth] ungrudgingly as we have been taught.

7. But someone will say, "Some [Christians] have been arrested and convicted as criminals." Many at various times, perhaps, if you examine in each case the conduct of those who are accused; but do not condemn [all] because of those previously convicted. We admit in general that just as among the Greeks those who teach what seems best to them are all listed under the name of philosophy, even though their teachings are contradictory, so the name which is now being attacked is common to those among the barbarians who are and those who appear to be wise. They are all listed as Christians. So we ask that the actions of those who are denounced to you be investigated, in order that whoever is convicted may be punished as a criminal, but not as a Christian, and that whoever is shown to be innocent may be freed, committing no crime by being a Christian. We shall not ask you, however, to punish our accusers, for they suffer enough from their own wickedness and their ignorance of the good.

8. Consider that we have said these things for your sake,

---

[42] Or, as in the MS., "upright" (*orthous*); but the reading *theous*, first suggested by Thirlby in 1722, seems probable.

[43] It is barely possible to construe the sentence so that the angels are listed as subjects or recipients of Christ's teaching, along with men, rather than as objects of veneration listed in this surprising position; but this seems unnecessary, especially since Justin is here concerned to contrast the good angels who follow the Son with the evil demons who oppose him.

since when put to trial we can deny [that we are Christians]—
but we do not wish to live by telling a lie. For, longing for the
life which is eternal and pure, we strive to dwell with God,
the Father and Fashioner of all things. We are eager to confess,
being convinced and believing that those who have shown to
God by their actions that they follow him and long to dwell
with him, where no evil can disturb, are able to obtain these
things. It is this, in brief, that we look for, and have learned
from Christ, and teach. Plato similarly said that Rhadamanthus
and Minos would punish the wicked who came before them.[44]
We say that this is what will happen, but at the hands of
Christ—and to the same bodies, reunited with their souls, and
destined for eternal punishment, not for a five-hundred-year
period only, as he said. If anyone says that this is unbelievable
or impossible—at least the mistake affects us and no one else,
as long as we are not convicted of any actual crime.

The Faith and Life of Christians

9. Certainly we do not honor with many sacrifices and floral
garlands the objects that men have fashioned, set up in temples,
and called gods. We know that they are lifeless and dead and
do not represent the form of God—for we do not think of God
as having the kind of form which some claim that they imitate
to be honored—but rather exhibit the names and shapes of
the evil demons who have manifested themselves [to men].
You know well enough without our mentioning it how the
craftsmen prepare their material, scraping and cutting and
molding and beating. And often they make what they call
gods out of vessels used for vile purposes, changing and transforming by art merely their appearance. We consider it not
only irrational but an insult to God, whose glory and form
are ineffable, to give his name to corruptible things which themselves need care. You are well aware that craftsmen in these
[things] are impure and—not to go into details—given to all
kinds of vice; they even corrupt their own slave girls who work
along with them. What an absurdity, that dissolute men
should be spoken of as fashioning or remaking gods for public
veneration, and that you should appoint such people as
guardians of the temples where they are set up—not considering that it is unlawful to think or speak of men as guardians
of gods.

[44] *Gorgias* 523 E; *Phaedrus* 249 A.

Source of unformed matter?

10. But we have learned[45] [from our tradition] that God has no need of material offerings from men, considering that he is the provider of all. We have been taught and firmly believe that he accepts only those who imitate the good things which are his—temperance and righteousness and love of mankind, and whatever else truly belongs to the God who is called by no given name. We have also been taught that in the beginning he in his goodness formed all things that are for the sake of men out of unformed matter, and if they show themselves by their actions worthy of his plan, we have learned that they will be counted worthy of dwelling with him, reigning together and made free from corruption and suffering. For as he made us in the beginning when we were not, so we hold that those who choose what is pleasing to him will, because of that choice, be counted worthy of incorruption and of fellowship [with him]. We did not bring ourselves into being—but as to following after the things that are dear to God, choosing them by the rational powers which he has given us—this is a matter of conviction and leads us to faith. We hold it to be for the good of all men that they are not prevented from learning these things, but are even urged to [consider] them. For what human laws could not do, that the Word, being divine, would have brought about, if the evil demons had not scattered abroad many false and godless accusations, with the help of the evil desire that is in every man by nature [and expresses itself] in all kinds of ways.[46] None of this, however, matters to us.

11. When you hear that we look for a kingdom, you rashly suppose that we mean something merely human. But we speak of a Kingdom with God, as is clear from our confessing Christ when you bring us to trial, though we know that death is the penalty for this confession. For if we looked for a human kingdom we would deny it in order to save our lives, and would try to remain in hiding in order to obtain the things we look for. But since we do not place our hopes on the present [order], we are not troubled by being put to death, since we will have to die somehow in any case.

12. We are in fact of all men your best helpers and allies in securing good order,[47] convinced as we are that no wicked

---

45 "We have received"—the phrase proper to describe the acceptance of a sacred tradition, as in I Cor. 11:23 and 15:1.

46 A reflection perhaps of the Jewish concept of the *yetzer hara'* or evil desire in man which is the source of sin (Gen. 6:5).

47 *Eirēnē*, but obviously with reference to internal peace.

man, no covetous man or conspirator, or virtuous man either, can be hidden from God, and that everyone goes to eternal punishment or salvation in accordance with the character of his actions. If all men knew this, nobody would choose vice even for a little time, knowing that he was on his way to eternal punishment by fire; every man would follow the self-restrained and orderly path of virtue, so as to receive the good things that come from God and avoid his punishments. There are some who merely try to conceal their wrongdoing because of the laws and punishments which you decree, knowing that since you are only men it is possible for wrongdoers to escape you; if they learned and were convinced that our thoughts as well as our actions cannot be hidden from God they would certainly lead orderly lives, if only because of the consequences, as you must agree. But it seems as if you were afraid of having all men well-behaved, and nobody left for you to punish; this would be the conduct of public executioners, not of good rulers. Such things, we are convinced, are brought about by the evil demons, the ones who demand sacrifices and service from men who live irrationally; but we have not learned [to expect] any unreasonable conduct from you, who aim at piety and philosophy. But if like thoughtless men you prefer custom to truth, then go ahead and do what you can. Rulers who respect reputation rather than truth have as much power as brigands in a desert. The Word himself has shown that you will not succeed, and after God who begat him we know of no ruler more royal or more just than he. For just as all men try to avoid inheriting the poverty or sufferings or disgrace of their ancestors, so the sensible man will not choose whatever the Word forbids to be chosen. He foretold that all these things would happen—our Teacher, I mean, who is the Son and Apostle of God the Father and Master of all, that is, Jesus Christ, from whom we have received the name of Christians. We are sure that all the things taught by him are so, since we see that what he predicted is actually coming to pass. This is God's work, to announce something before it happens and then to show it happening as predicted. I might stop here and add no more, having made clear that we ask for what is just and true. But though I know that it is not easy to change over at once a mind which is bound down by ignorance, I am encouraged to add somewhat to persuade the lover of truth, being sure that one can dispel ignorance by putting truth against it.

13. What sound-minded man will not admit that we are not godless, since we worship the Fashioner of the universe, declaring him, as we have been taught, to have no need of blood and libations and incense, but praising him by the word of prayer and thanksgiving for all that he has given us? We have learned that the only honor worthy of him is, not to consume by fire the things he has made for our nourishment, but to devote them to our use and those in need, in thankfulness to him sending up solemn prayers and hymns for our creation and all the means of health, for the variety of creatures and the changes of the seasons, and sending up our petitions that we may live again in incorruption through our faith in him.[48] It is Jesus Christ who has taught us these things, having been born for this purpose and crucified under Pontius Pilate, who was procurator in Judea in the time of Tiberius Caesar. We will show that we honor him in accordance with reason, having learned that he is the Son of the true God himself, and holding him to be in the second place and the prophetic Spirit in the third rank. It is for this that they charge us with madness, saying that we give the second place after the unchanging and ever-existing God and begetter of all things to a crucified man, not knowing the mystery involved in this, to which we ask you to give your attention as we expound it.

14. We warn you in advance to be careful, lest the demons whom we have attacked should deceive you and prevent your completely grasping and understanding what we say. For they struggle to have you as their slaves and servants, and now by manifestations in dreams, now by magic tricks, they get hold of all who do not struggle to their utmost for their own salvation—as we do who, after being persuaded by the Word, renounced them[49] and now follow the only unbegotten God through his Son. Those who once rejoiced in fornication now delight in continence alone; those who made use of magic arts have dedicated themselves to the good and unbegotten God; we who once took most pleasure in the means of increasing our wealth and property now bring what we have into a common fund and share with everyone in need; we who hated and killed one another and would not associate with men of different tribes because of [their different] customs, now after the manifestation of Christ live together and pray for our enemies and

48 The reference is primarily if not exclusively to the Eucharist and the Eucharistic prayer.
49 Specifically in the baptismal renunciation of the devil and all his works.

try to persuade those who unjustly hate us, so that they, living according to the fair commands of Christ, may share with us the good hope of receiving the same things [that we will] from God, the master of all. So that this may not seem to be sophistry, I think fit before giving our demonstration to recall a few of the teachings which have come from Christ himself. It is for you then, as mighty emperors, to examine whether we have been taught and do teach these things truly. His sayings were short and concise, for he was no sophist, but his word was the power of God.

15. About continence he said this: "Whoever looks on a woman to lust after her has already committed adultery in his heart before God." [50] And: "If your right eye offends you, cut it out; it is better for you to enter into the Kingdom of Heaven with one eye than with two to be sent into eternal fire." [51] And: "Whoever marries a woman who has been put away from another man commits adultery." [52] And: "There are some who were made eunuchs by men, and some who were born eunuchs, and some who have made themselves eunuchs for the Kingdom of Heaven's sake; only not all [are able to] receive this." [53]

And so those who make second marriages according to human law are sinners in the sight of our Teacher, [54] and those who look on a woman to lust after her. For he condemns not only the man who commits the act of adultery, but the man who desires to commit adultery, since not only our actions but our thoughts are manifest to God. Many men and women now in their sixties and seventies who have been disciples of Christ from childhood have preserved their purity; and I am proud that I could point to such people in every nation. Then what shall we say of the uncounted multitude of those who have turned away from incontinence and learned these things? For Christ did not call the righteous or the temperate to repentance, but the ungodly and incontinent and unrighteous. So he said: "I have not come to call the righteous but sinners to

---

[50] Matt. 5:28; Justin's quotations from the Gospels are often somewhat free, and he summarizes or combines without hesitation; but nearly all can be referred primarily to a particular passage.

[51] Mark 9:47 (Matt. 5:29).

[52] Matt. 5:32 (Luke 16:18).

[53] Matt. 19:11, 12.

[54] The reference is mainly to remarriage after divorce, though the phrase could cover remarriage of any kind, which many early Christians disliked and some actually condemned.

repentance."[55] For the Heavenly Father wishes the repentance of a sinner rather than his punishment.

This is what he taught on affection for all men: "If you love those who love you, what new thing do you do? for even the harlots do this. But I say to you, Pray for your enemies and love those who hate you and bless those who curse you and pray for those who treat you despitefully."[56]

That we should share with those in need and do nothing for [our] glory he said these things: "Give to everyone who asks and turn not away him who wishes to borrow. For if you lend to those from whom you hope to receive, what new thing do you do? Even the publicans do this.[57] But as for you, do not lay up treasures for yourselves on earth, where moth and rust corrupt and thieves break in, but lay up for yourselves treasures in heaven, where neither moth nor rust corrupts.[58] For what will it profit a man, if he should gain the whole world, but lose his own soul? Or what will he give in exchange for it?[59] Lay up treasures therefore in the heavens, where neither moth nor rust corrupts." And: "Be kind and merciful, as your Father is kind and merciful, and makes his sun to rise on sinners and righteous and wicked.[60] Do not worry as to what you will eat or what you will wear. Are you not better than the birds and the beasts? and God feeds them. So do not worry as to what you will eat or what you will wear, for your Heavenly Father knows that you need these things. But seek the Kingdom of Heaven, and all these things will be added to you.[61] For where his treasure is, there is the mind of man."[62] And: "Do not do these things to be seen of men, for otherwise you have no reward with your Father who is in heaven."[63]

16. About being long-suffering and servants to all and free from anger, this is what he said: "To him that smites you on one cheek turn the other also, and to him that takes away your cloak do not deny your tunic either.[64] Whoever is angry is worthy of the fire. And whoever compels you to go one mile,

---

[55] Luke 5:32 (Matt. 9:13; Mark 2:17).
[56] Matt. 5:46 (Luke 6:32; like many of us, Justin finds it easy to exchange one set of Gospel characters for another—here "harlots" for Matthew's "publicans" and Luke's "sinners"); Luke 6:27, 28.
[57] Matt. 5:42 (Luke 6:34).   [58] Matt. 6:19, 20.
[59] Matt. 16:26 (Luke 9:25).   [60] Luke 6:35, 36 (Matt. 5:45).
[61] Matt. 6:25, 26, 33 (Luke 12:22, 24, 31).
[62] Matt. 6:21 (Luke 12:34); Justin properly recognizes that the Greek *nous* is a fair equivalent for the Hebraic "heart."
[63] Matt. 6:1.   [64] Luke 6:29 (Matt. 5:39, 40).

follow him for two. Let your good works shine before men, that they as they see may wonder at your Father who is in heaven." [65]

For we ought not to quarrel; he has not wished us to imitate the wicked, but rather by our patience and meekness to draw all men from shame and evil desires. This we can show in the case of many who were once on your side but have turned from the ways of violence and tyranny, overcome by observing the consistent lives of their neighbors, or noting the strange patience of their injured acquaintances, or experiencing the way they did business with them.

About not swearing at all, but always speaking the truth, this is what he commanded: "Swear not at all; but let your yea be yea and your nay nay. What is more than these is from the evil one." [66]

That God only should be worshiped he showed us when he said: "The greatest commandment is: Thou shalt worship the Lord thy God and him only shalt thou serve with all thy heart and all thy strength, the Lord who made thee." [67] And: "When one came to him and said, Good Teacher, he answered and said, There is none good, except only God who made all things." [68]

Those who are found not living as he taught should know that they are not really Christians, even if his teachings are on their lips, for he said that not those who merely profess but those who also do the works will be saved. For he said this: "Not everyone who says to me, Lord, Lord, will enter into the Kingdom of Heaven, but he who does the will of my Father who is in heaven. For whoever hears me and does what I say hears him who sent me. Many will say to me, Lord, Lord, did we not eat in your name and drink and do mighty works? And then I will say to them, Depart from me, you workers of iniquity. [69] Then there will be weeping and gnashing of teeth, when the righteous will shine as the sun, but the wicked will be sent into eternal fire. For many will come in my name clothed outwardly in sheep's clothing, but being inwardly ravening wolves; by their works you will know them. Every tree that does not bring forth good fruit is cut down and thrown into the fire." [70]

So we ask that you too should punish those who do not live

---

[65] Matt. 5:22, 41, 16.   [66] Matt. 5:34, 37.

[67] A surprising combination of Matt. 4:10 (Luke 4:8) and Mark 12:30 (Matt. 22:37).

[68] Mark 10:17, 18 (Luke 18:18, 19).   [69] Matt. 7:21–23.

[70] Matt. 13:42, 43; 7:15, 16, 19.

in accordance with his teachings, but merely say that they are Christians.

17. More even than others we try to pay the taxes and assessments to those whom you appoint, as we have been taught by him. For once in his time some came to him and asked whether it were right to pay taxes to Caesar. And he answered, "Tell me, whose image is on the coin." They said, "Caesar's." And he answered them again, "Then give what is Caesar's to Caesar and what is God's to God." [71] So we worship God only, but in other matters we gladly serve you, recognizing you as emperors and rulers of men, and praying that along with your imperial power you may also be found to have a sound mind. If you pay no attention to our prayers and our frank statements about everything, it will not injure us, since we believe, or rather are firmly convinced, that every man will suffer in eternal fire in accordance with the quality of his actions, and similarly will be required to give account for the abilities which he has received from God, as Christ told us when he said, "To whom God has given more, from him more will be required." [72]

18. Look at the end of each of the former emperors, how they died the common death of all; and if this were merely a departure into unconsciousness, that would be a piece of luck for the wicked. But since consciousness continues for all who have lived, and eternal punishment awaits, do not fail to be convinced and believe that these things are true. For the oracles of the dead and the revelations of innocent children, the invoking of [departed] human souls, the dream senders and guardians of the magi, and what is done by those who know about such things—all this should convince you that souls are still conscious after death. Then there are the men who are seized and torn by the spirits of the dead, whom everyone calls demon-possessed and maniacs, and the oracles so well-known among you, of Amphilochus and Dodona and Pytho, and any others of that kind, and the teaching of writers, Empedocles and Pythagoras, Plato and Socrates, and the ditch in Homer and the descent of Odysseus to visit the dead, [73] and other stories like this. Treat us at least like these; we believe in God not less than they do, but rather more, since we look forward to

71 Matt. 22:20, 21 (Mark 12:14–17; Luke 20:22–25).   72 Luke 12:48.
73 *Odyssey* 11:25 ff.; this chapter is mainly an *argumentum ad hominem*—Justin's opponents ought not to object to the idea of survival after death, since they had much of the same in their own traditions.

receiving again our own bodies, though they be dead and buried in the earth, declaring that nothing is impossible to God.

19. Indeed, what would seem more incredible to an observer than if we were not in the body and someone should say that from a single drop of human seed it were possible for the form that we see to come into being, with bones and nerves and flesh? Consider this hypothesis; if you were not such as you are, born of such parents, and someone were to show you the human seed and a picture of a man, and assure you that the one could grow into the other, would you believe it before you saw it happening? No one would dare to deny [that you wouldn't]. In the same way unbelief prevails about the resurrection of the dead because you have never seen an instance of it. But as you at first would not have believed that from a little drop such beings [as men] could develop, yet you see it happening, so consider that it is possible for human bodies, dissolved and scattered in the earth like seeds, to rise again in due time by God's decree and be clothed with incorruption. [74] I cannot imagine how any adequate concept of divine power can be held by those who say that everything returns into that from which it came and that not even God can do anything more than this. But I may remark that they would not have believed it possible for such creatures as they are to have come into being, yet they see themselves as they are, and indeed the whole world [as it is], and what they were made from. We have learned that it is better to believe things impossible to our own nature and to men than to disbelieve like others, since we know that our Teacher Jesus Christ said, "The things that are impossible with men are possible with God." [75] And: "Fear not those who put you to death and after that can do no more, but fear him who after death is able to cast both body and soul into Gehenna." [76] Gehenna is the place where those who live unrighteously will be punished, and those who do not believe that these things will come to pass which God has taught through Christ.

20. Both Sybil and Hystaspes declared that there will be a destruction of corruptible things by fire. [77] Those who are called

[74] Cf. I Cor., ch. 15, especially vs. 35–50.
[75] Luke 18:27 (Matt. 19:26; Mark 10:27).
[76] Luke 12:4, 5 (Matt. 10:28).
[77] *Teste David cum Sibylla*; the reference is to the Sibylline Books (Jewish but thought to be Gentile), and the legendary Persian sage Hystaspes, of whom more may have been told in Mithraic circles than preserved records show.

Stoic philosophers teach that God himself will be resolved into fire, and the universe come into being again by return. We think that God, the Maker of all, is superior to changeable things. But if on some points we agree with the poets and philosophers whom you honor, and on others [teach] more completely and more worthily of God, and are the only ones who offer proof, why are we above all hated unjustly? When we say that all things have been ordered and made by God we appear to offer the teaching of Plato—in speaking of a coming destruction by fire, that of the Stoics; in declaring that the souls of the unrighteous will be punished after death, still remaining in conscious existence, and those of the virtuous, delivered from punishments, will enjoy happiness, we seem to agree with [various] poets and philosophers; in declaring that men ought not to worship the works of their hands we are saying the same things as the comedian Menander and others who have said this, for they declared that the Fashioner is greater than what he has formed. [78]

SUPERIORITY OF CHRISTIANITY TO PAGANISM

21. In saying that the Word, who is the first offspring of God, was born for us without sexual union, as Jesus Christ our Teacher, and that he was crucified and died and after rising again ascended into heaven we introduce nothing new beyond [what you say of] those whom you call sons of Zeus. You know how many sons of Zeus the writers whom you honor speak of— Hermes, the hermeneutic Word and teacher of all [79]; Asclepius, who was also a healer and after being struck by lightning ascended into heaven—as did Dionysus who was torn in pieces; Heracles, who to escape his torments threw himself into the fire; the Dioscuri born of Leda and Perseus of Danaë; and Bellerophon who, though of human origin, rode on the [divine] horse Pegasus. [80] Need I mention Ariadne and those who like her are said to have been placed among the stars? and what of your deceased emperors, whom you regularly think worthy of being raised to immortality, introducing a witness who swears that he saw the cremated Caesar ascending into heaven

[78] A fair statement of Platonic ideas, somewhat less so of Stoic; Menander is quoted somewhat to this effect in Pseudo-Justin, De Monarchia 5.

[79] By allegorical interpretation of his mythological function as messenger of Zeus.

[80] Legends cited correctly except that Bellerophon's ride on Pegasus did not take him to heaven.

from the funeral pyre? [81] Nor is it necessary to remind you what kind of actions are related of each of those who are called sons of Zeus, except [to point out] that they are recorded for the benefit and instruction of students—for all consider it a fine thing to be imitators of the gods. [82] Far be it from every sound mind to entertain such a concept of the deities as that Zeus, whom they call the ruler and begetter of all, should have been a parricide and the son of a parricide, and that moved by desire of evil and shameful pleasures he descended on Ganymede and the many women whom he seduced, and that his sons after him were guilty of similar actions. But, as we said before, it was the wicked demons who did these things. We have been taught that only those who live close to God in holiness and virtue attain to immortality, and we believe that those who live unjustly and do not reform will be punished in eternal fire.

22. Now if God's Son, who is called Jesus, were only an ordinary man, he would be worthy because of his wisdom to be called Son of God, for all authors call God father of men and gods. When we say, as before, that he was begotten by God as the Word of God in a unique manner beyond ordinary birth, this should be no strange thing for you who speak of Hermes as the announcing word from God. If somebody objects that he was crucified, this is in common with the sons of Zeus, as you call them, who suffered, as previously listed. Since their fatal sufferings are narrated as not similar but different, so his unique passion should not seem to be any worse—indeed I will, as I have undertaken, show, as the argument proceeds, that he was better; for he is shown to be better by his actions. If we declare that he was born of a virgin, you should consider this something in common with Perseus. When we say that he healed the lame, the paralytic, and those born blind, [83] and raised the dead, we seem to be talking about things like those said to have been done by Asclepius.

23. In order to make this clear to you I will present the evidence that the things we say, as disciples of Christ and of the prophets who came before him, are the only truths and older than all the writers who have lived, and we ask to be accepted,

---

[81] As reported in the cases of Julius Caesar and Augustus (Suetonius, *Augustus*, ch. 100); it may have become a form on later occasions.

[82] To be understood ironically, and so not requiring emendation.

[83] Following the suggested reading *pērous*, "blind" (or "maimed") for *ponērous*, "wicked."

not because we say the same things as they do, but because we are speaking the truth—[second] that Jesus Christ alone was really begotten as Son of God, being his Word and First-begotten and Power, and becoming man by his will he taught us these things for the reconciliation and restoration of the human race—and [third] that before he came among men as man, there were some who, on account of the already mentioned wicked demons, told through the poets as already having occurred the myths they had invented, just as now they are responsible for the slanders and godless deeds alleged against us, of which there is neither witness nor demonstration. [84]

24. The first point is that though we say the same as do the Greeks, we only are hated, because of the name of Christ. We do no wrong but are put to death as offenders [because of our worship, though] others everywhere worship trees and rivers, mice and cats and crocodiles and many kinds of irrational animals, [85] and the same objects are not honored by all, but different ones in different places, so that all are impious to each other, because of not having the same objects of worship. Yet this is the one complaint you have against us, that we do not worship the same gods that you do, and do not bring libations and offerings of fat to the dead, crowns for their statues, and sacrifices. Yet, as you know well, the same beings are gods to some and wild animals to others, while still others think of them as sacred victims.

25. Secondly, out of every race of men we who once worshiped Dionysus the son of Semele and Apollo the son of Leto, who in their passion for men did things which it is disgraceful even to speak of, or who worshiped Persephone and Aphrodite, who were driven mad by [love of] Adonis and whose mysteries you celebrate, or Asclepius or some other of those who are called gods, now through Jesus Christ despise them, even at the cost of death, and have dedicated ourselves to the unbegotten and impassible God. We do not believe that he ever descended in mad passion on Antiope or others, nor on Ganymede, nor was he, receiving help through Thetis, delivered by that hundred-handed monster, nor was he, because of this, anxious

---

[84] As this section stands, Justin distinguished between mythmakers and poets, which seems unduly complex, and several emendations have been suggested that would identify them; it may be that after referring to the demons Justin continues as if they were the subject of the sentence, which is in any case clumsily phrased.

[85] A reference primarily to the animal deities of Egypt, which amused pagan as well as Jewish and Christian observers.

that Thetis' son Achilles should destroy so many Greeks for the sake of his concubine Briseis. [86] We pity those who believe [such stories], for which we know that the demons are responsible.

26. A third point is that after Christ's ascent into heaven the demons put forward various men who said that they were gods, and you not only did not persecute them, but thought them worthy of honors. One was a certain Simon, a Samaritan from the village of Gitta, who in the time of Claudius Caesar, through the arts of the demons who worked in him, did mighty works of magic in your imperial city of Rome and was thought to be a god. He has been honored among you as a god by a statue, which was set up on the River Tiber, between the two bridges, with this inscription in Latin, SIMONI DEO SANCTO. [87] Almost all the Samaritans, and a few in other nations, confess this man as their first god and worship him as such, and a woman named Helena, who traveled around with him in those days, and had formerly been a public prostitute, they say was the first Concept produced from him. Then we know of a certain Menander, who was also a Samaritan, from the village of Capparetaea, who had been a disciple of Simon's, and was also possessed by the demons. He deceived many at Antioch by magic arts, and even persuaded his followers that he would never die; there are still some who believe this [as they learned] from him. Then there is a certain Marcion of Pontus, who is still teaching his converts that there is another God greater than the Fashioner. By the help of the demons he has made many in every race of men to blaspheme and to deny God the Maker of the universe, professing that there is another who is greater and has done greater things than he. As we said, all who derive [their opinions] from these men are called Christians, just as men who do not share the same teachings with the philosophers still have in common with them the name of philosophy, thus brought into disrepute. Whether they commit the shameful deeds about which stories are told— the upsetting of the lamp, promiscuous intercourse, and the meals of human flesh, [88] we do not know; but we are sure that

---

[86] *Iliad* 2:3, 4.

[87] "To Simon the holy god"; it is commonly assumed that Justin saw and misinterpreted the dedication to the Sabine god Semo Sancus, *Semoni Sanco Deo*, which was discovered on the island in the Tiber at Rome in 1574.

[88] A reference to the charges of incest (facilitated by darkness) and cannibalism which other Apologists (Athenagoras, Tertullian, Minucius Felix) treat at length.

they are neither persecuted nor killed by you, on account of their teachings anyway. I have compiled and have on hand a treatise against all the heresies which have arisen, which I will give you if you would like to consult it.

27. That we may avoid all injustice [89] and impiety, we have been taught that to expose the newly born is the work of wicked men—first of all because we observe that almost all [foundlings], boys as well as girls, are brought up for prostitution. As the ancients are said to have raised herds of oxen or goats or sheep or horses in their pastures, so now [you raise children] just for shameful purposes, and so in every nation a crowd of females and hermaphrodites and doers of unspeakable deeds are exposed as public prostitutes. You even collect pay and levies and taxes from these, whom you ought to exterminate from your civilized world. [90] And anyone who makes use of them may in addition to [the guilt of] godless, impious, and intemperate intercourse, by chance be consorting with his own child or relative or brother. Some even prostitute their own children and wives, and others are admittedly mutilated for purposes of sodomy, and treat this as part of the mysteries of the mother of the gods—while beside each of those whom you think of as gods a serpent is depicted as a great symbol and mystery. You charge against us the actions that you commit openly and treat with honor, as if the divine light were overthrown and withdrawn—which of course does no harm to us, who refuse to do any of these things, but rather injures those who do them and then bring false witness [against us].

28. Among us the chief of the evil demons is called the serpent and Satan and the devil, as you can learn by examining our writings. Christ has foretold that he will be cast into fire with his host and the men who follow him, [all] to be punished for endless ages. God delays doing this for the sake of the human race, for he foreknows that there are some yet to be saved by repentance, even perhaps some not yet born. In the beginning he made the race of men endowed with intelligence, able to choose the truth and do right, so that all men are without excuse before God, for they were made with the powers of reason and observation. Anyone who does not believe that God cares for these things either manages to profess that he does not

---

[89] Following the emendation *mēden adikōmen* for *mēdena diōkōmen* ("that we may persecute no one") proposed by Stephanus in 1551.

[90] *Oikoumenē*, the inhabited or civilized world, assumed by Greeks and Romans to be identical with the Empire.

exist, or makes out that he exists but approves of evil or remains [unaffected] like a stone, and that virtue and vice are not realities, but that men consider things good or bad by opinion alone; this is the height of impiety and injustice.

29. And again [we do not expose children] lest some of them, not being picked up, should die and we thus be murderers. But to begin with, we do not marry except in order to bring up children, or else, renouncing marriage, we live in perfect continence. [91] To show you that promiscuous intercourse is not among our mysteries—just recently one of us submitted a petition to the Prefect Felix in Alexandria, asking that a physician be allowed to make him a eunuch, for the physicians there said they were not allowed to do this without the permission of the Prefect. When Felix would by no means agree to endorse [the petition], the young man remained single, satisfied with [the approval of] his own conscience and that of his fellow believers. [92] I think it proper in this connection to remind you of the recent case of Antinoüs, whom everybody, through fear, hastened to worship as a god, though knowing perfectly well who he was and where he came from. [93]

The Argument from Prophecy

30. But lest someone should argue against us, What excludes [the supposition] that this person whom you call Christ was a man, of human origin, and did these miracles you speak of by magic arts, and so appeared to be God's Son?—we will bring forward our demonstration. We do not trust in mere hearsay, but are forced to believe those who prophesied [these things] before they happened, because we actually see things that have happened and are happening as was predicted. This will, as we think, be the greatest and surest demonstration for you too.

31. There were among the Jews certain men who were prophets of God, through whom the prophetic Spirit announced in advance events that were to occur. The successive rulers of the Jews carefully preserved their prophecies, as they were spoken when they prophesied, in their own Hebrew language,

---

[91] And hence no unwanted children are born.

[92] An overliteral following of Matt. 19:12, paralleled by "Origen's rash act" in the following century.

[93] Hadrian's favorite, drowned in the Nile in A.D. 130, who was made the presiding deity of the new city of Antinoöpolis.

[and] as arranged in books by the prophets themselves. When Ptolemy, king of Egypt, was founding a library, and set out to gather the writings of all mankind, he learned about these prophecies and sent to Herod, then king of the Jews, asking him to send him the prophetic books. King Herod sent them, written in the aforementioned Hebrew language. Since their contents were not intelligible to the Egyptians, he again sent and asked him to send men who could translate them into Greek. [94] This was done, and the books remain in the hands of the Egyptians down to the present; the Jews everywhere have them too. But though they read them, they do not understand what they say, but consider us their enemies and opponents, putting us to death or punishing us, as you do, whenever they can, as you can realize—for in the Jewish War recently past Bar-Cochba, the leader of the revolt of the Jews, ordered Christians only to be subjected to terrible punishments, unless they would deny Jesus the Christ and blaspheme [him]. [95] We find it predicted in the books of the prophets that Jesus our Christ would come, born of a virgin, grown to manhood, healing every sickness and every disease and raising the dead, hated and unacknowledged and crucified, dying and rising again and ascending into heaven, both really being and being called Son of God. [We find also that] men sent by him would proclaim these things to every race of mankind, and that men of the Gentiles especially would believe in him. This was prophesied over five thousand years before he appeared, then three thousand, and two thousand, and again one thousand, and once more eight hundred [years before]. [96] For there were new prophets again and again as the generations passed.

32. Thus Moses, who was the first of the prophets, said in these very words: "The ruler shall not depart from Judah, nor the governor from his thighs, until he come for whom it is reserved; and he shall be the expectation of the nations, binding his colt to the vine, washing his robe in the blood of the grape." [97] You can inquire precisely and learn up to whose time the Jews had their own ruler and king. [It was] until

---

[94] A brief summary of the legend of the origin of the Septuagint, with a surprising substitution of King Herod for the high priest contemporary with Ptolemy Philadelphus(285–247 B.C.).

[95] The Second Jewish Revolt, A.D. 132–135.

[96] 5000 B.C. may be intended for the promises in Gen., ch. 3; the other dates do not seem to refer to any particular prophets; in general Justin gives high figures for Old Testament chronology (1500 B.C. for David, ch. 42).   [97] Gen. 49:10, 11.

the manifestation of Jesus Christ, our teacher and the ex-
pounder of the unrecognized prophecies, as was predicted by
the divine and holy prophetic Spirit through Moses, that a
ruler would not depart from the Jews until he should come for
whom the Kingdom is reserved. For Judah was the forefather
of the Jews, after whom they are called Jews; and after his
[Christ's] appearance you began to rule over the Jews and
gained control of their whole land. The saying, He shall be
the expectation of the nations, is a testimony that men of
every nation will look forward to his coming again, as you can
clearly see and be convinced by the fact, for men of every race
are looking for him who was crucified in Judea, immediately
after which the land of the Jews fell to you as spoil of war.
Binding his foal to the vine and washing his robe in the blood
of the grape is a symbolic exhibition of the things that would
happen to Christ, and his actions. For an ass's foal was standing
at the entrance of a village, bound to a vine,[98] which he then
ordered his companions to bring to him; when it was brought
he mounted and sat on it and entered into Jerusalem, where
was the great Temple of the Jews which you afterward overthrew. After this he was crucified, so as to fulfill the rest of the
prophecy. For washing his robe in the blood of the grape was
predictive of the Passion which he was to suffer, cleansing by
his blood those who believe on him. For the men who believe
on him in whom dwells the seed of God, the Word, are what the
divine Spirit through the prophet calls a garment. The blood
of the grape that was spoken of was a sign that he who was to
appear would have blood, though not from human seed but
by divine power. The first Power after God the Father and
Master of all, even [his] Son, is the Word—how he was made
flesh and became man we shall describe below. As the blood of
the grape was not made by man, but by God, so it was testified,
that [his] blood should not come from human seed, but from
divine power, as we said before. Isaiah, another prophet,
prophesying the same things in other words, said: "A star shall
rise out of Jacob, and a flower will come forth from the root
of Jesse, and upon his arm will the nations hope."[99] The

[98] The prophecy has in this detail influenced Justin's version of the Gospel
story (this is not followed in the treatment of the same passage in Dial.,
ch. 53).

[99] Isa. 11:1 and 51:5, combined with Num. 24:17; Justin's Old Testament
quotations combine the Prophets as freely as his Gospel quotations
mingle the Evangelists.

shining star has risen and the flower has grown from the root of Jesse—this is Christ. For he was by the power of God conceived by a virgin of the seed of Jacob, who was the father of Judah, the father of the Jews, as has been explained; Jesse was his ancestor, according to the oracle, and he was the son of Jacob and Judah by lineal succession.

33. And again, hear how it was literally prophesied by Isaiah that he would be born of a virgin. He said, "Behold, the Virgin shall conceive and bear a son, and they will call his name, God with us."[1] For God testified in advance through the prophetic Spirit that things which are unbelievable and thought impossible among men would happen, so that when this should occur it would not be disbelieved, but received with faith because it had been predicted. Lest some, not understanding the prophecy which has been referred to, should bring against us the reproach that we bring against the poets who say that Zeus came upon women for the sake of sexual pleasure, we will try to explain these words clearly. For "Behold, the Virgin shall conceive" means that the Virgin would conceive without intercourse. For if she had had intercourse with anyone, she would not have been a virgin; but God's power, coming upon the Virgin, overshadowed her, and caused her to conceive while still remaining a virgin. The angel of God who was sent to this Virgin at the time brought her this good news, saying, "Behold, you will conceive in the womb by a Holy Spirit and will bear a son, and he will be called Son of the Highest and you shall call his name Jesus, for he will save his people from their sins,"[2] as those who recorded everything about our Saviour Jesus Christ have taught us. We believe them, since the prophetic Spirit through the above-mentioned Isaiah said that this would happen, as we noted before. The Spirit and the Power from God cannot rightly be thought of as anything else than the Word, who is also the First-born of God, as Moses the above-mentioned prophet testified. So this [Spirit], coming upon the Virgin and overshadowing her, made her pregnant— not by intercourse, but by [divine] power.[3] The name Jesus in Hebrew means the same as Saviour in Greek, and so the angel said to the Virgin, "And you shall call his name Jesus, for he will save his people from their sins." Even you will

---

[1] Isa. 7:14 (Matt. 1:23).
[2] Luke 1:31, 32; Matt. 1:21.
[3] I.e., the Spirit here referred to is not the prophetic Spirit, but the Word, causing his own incarnation.

agree, I think, that those who prophesied were inspired by none other than the divine Word.

34. Hear also in what part of the earth he was to be born, as another prophet, Micah, foretold. He said, "And you Bethlehem, land of Judah, are by no means the least among the rulers of Judah; for out of you will come a Ruler who will shepherd my people."[4] This is a village in the land of the Jews, thirty-five stadia from Jerusalem, in which Jesus Christ was born, as you can learn from the census which was taken under Quirinius, who was your first procurator in Judea.[5]

35. How the Christ after his birth was to live hidden from other men until he grew to manhood, as also happened—hear the predictions that refer to this. There is this: "A child is born to us, and a young man is given to us, and the government will be upon his shoulders—"[6] testifying the power of the cross, which when crucified he took upon his shoulders, as will be shown more clearly as the argument proceeds. Again the same prophet Isaiah, inspired by the prophetic Spirit, said: "I have stretched out my hands over a disobedient and contradicting people, over those who walk in a way that is not good. They now ask judgment of me and dare to draw near to God."[7] Again in other words he says through another prophet: "They pierced my hands and feet, and cast lots for my clothing."[8] Now David, the king and prophet, who said this, suffered none of these things. But Jesus Christ stretched out his hands when he was crucified by the Jews, who contradicted him and denied that he was Christ. As the prophet said, "They placed him in mockery on the judgment seat and said, Judge us."[9] "They pierced my hands and feet," was an announcement of the nails that were fastened in his hands and feet on the cross. After fastening him to the cross, those who crucified him cast lots for his clothing and divided it among themselves. That these things really happened, you can learn from the Acts of what was done under Pontius Pilate. And that it was distinctly prophesied that he would take his seat on the foal of an ass

---

[4] Micah 5:2 (Matt. 2:6).

[5] Luke 2:2, but with Quirinius thought of as a predecessor of Pontius Pilate.

[6] Isa. 9:6; with a more systematic writer one would assume that something was missing early in this chapter; but probably the reference to the cross leads Justin to that topic, and what might be expected here appears in ch. 48.

[7] Isa. 65:2; 58:2.   [8] Ps. 22 (LXX, 21): 16, 18.

[9] Mark 15:18 and parallels; the apocryphal Gospel of Peter corresponds closely to Justin's wording.

and so enter Jerusalem, we will quote the words of the prophecy of another prophet, Zephaniah, as follows: "Rejoice greatly, O daughter of Zion; shout for joy, O daughter of Jerusalem; behold your King comes to you, meek, and riding upon an ass and a colt the foal of a donkey."[10]

36. When you hear the words of the prophets spoken as in a particular character, do not think of them as spoken by the inspired men themselves, but by the divine Word that moved them. For sometimes he speaks as predicting the things that are to happen, sometimes he speaks as in the character of God the Master and Father of all, sometimes as in the character of Christ, sometimes in the character of the people answering the Lord or his Father. You can see the same thing in your own writers, where one man is the author of the whole work but introduces different characters in dialogue. Not understanding this, the Jews who are in possession of the books of the prophets did not recognize Christ even when he came, and they hate us who declare that he has come and show that he was crucified by them as had been predicted.

37. So that you may see this clearly, here is the kind of words spoken in the character of the Father through the above-mentioned prophet Isaiah: "The ox knows his owner, and the ass his master's crib, but Israel knows me not and my people does not understand. Woe, sinful nation, people full of sins, wicked seed, lawless children, you have forsaken the Lord."[11]

Again in another place, where the same prophet speaks similarly for the Father: "What kind of house will you build for me? says the Lord. Heaven is my throne and the earth is my footstool."[12] And again elsewhere: "My soul hates your new moons and sabbaths, I cannot endure the great day of the fast, and [your] idleness; nor when you come to appear before me will I hear you. Your hands are full of blood, and if you bring offerings of fine flour, [and] incense, it is an abomination to me; the fat of lambs and blood of bulls I do not wish. For who demanded this at your hands? But loose every bond of iniquity, tear apart the knots of the contracts of violence, cover the homeless and naked, deal out your bread

---

[10] Zech. 9:9 (Matt. 21:5); the prophet is named correctly in Dial., ch. 53. Justin may refer to the *Acta Pilati*, which contain mainly the material indicated here and in ch. 48; on the other hand these references may be to the Gospels, or to a report of Pilate's assumed to exist, and have given the hint for the apocryphal *Acta*.   [11] Isa. 1:3, 4.   [12] Isa. 66:1.

to the hungry." [13] You can now notice the kind of things that were taught by the prophets as from God.

38. When the prophetic Spirit speaks in the character of the Christ, he says, "I stretched out my hands over a disobedient and contradicting people, over those who walk in a way that is not good." [14] And again: "I have offered my back to scourges and my cheeks to blows, and I did not turn away my face from the shame of spittings. And the Lord became my helper, therefore I was not confounded, but set my face as a hard rock, and I knew that I would not be put to shame, for he who justifies me is at hand." [15] Again when he says: "They cast lots for my clothing, and pierced my feet and hands. I lay down and slept and rose up again, for the Lord supported me." [16] Again when he says, "They spoke with their lips, they shook their heads, saying, Let him deliver himself." [17] All these things were done by the Jews to Christ, as you can learn. For when he was crucified they stuck out their lips and shook their heads, saying, "He who raised the dead, let him now save himself." [18]

39. When the prophetic Spirit speaks as prophesying things to come, he says: "For the law will go forth from Zion and the Word of the Lord from Jerusalem, and he shall judge in the midst of the nations and rebuke much people; and they shall beat their swords into plowshares and their spears into pruning hooks, and nation will not lift up sword against nation, neither shall they learn to war any more." [19] We can show you that this has really happened. For a band of twelve men went forth from Jerusalem, and they were common men, not trained in speaking, but by the power of God they testified to every race of mankind that they were sent by Christ to teach to all the Word of God; and [now] we who once killed each other not only do not make war on each other, but in order not to lie or deceive our inquisitors we gladly die for the confession of Christ. For it would be possible for us to follow the saying, "The tongue has sworn, the mind remains unsworn." [20] But it would be ridiculous when the soldiers whom you have recruited and enrolled stick to their loyalty to you [21] before their own

---

[13] Isa. 1:11–15 (abridged and out of order); ch. 58:6, 7.   [14] Isa. 65:2.
[15] Isa. 50:6–8.   [16] Ps. 22 (21): 18, 16 and Ps. 3:5.
[17] Ps. 22 (21): 7, 8.   [18] Cf. Mark 15:29–32.
[19] Micah 4:2, 3 (Isa. 2:3, 4).
[20] A familiar quotation from Euripides, *Hippolytus* 612.
[21] Literally "your confession," suggesting a parallel between military loyalty following on the soldier's oath (*sacramentum*) and Christian loyalty, following the baptismal promises.

life and parents and native land and all their families, though you have nothing incorruptible to offer them, for us, who desire incorruption, not to endure all things in order to receive what we long for from Him who is able to give it.

40. Hear now how predictions were made about those who were to proclaim his teaching and testify to his manifestation; for the above-mentioned prophet and king said this through the prophetic Spirit: ." Day to day utters speech, and night to night shows forth knowledge. There is no language or speech where their words are not heard. Their sound went out into all the earth, and their words to the end of the inhabited world. He set his tabernacle in the sun, and he himself, as a bridegroom coming out of his chamber, will rejoice like a giant to run his course." [22] In addition to these I have thought it good and appropriate to mention some other prophetic words spoken through the same David, from which you may learn how the prophetic Spirit exhorts men to live, and how he testifies of the conspiracy which was formed by Herod the king of the Jews and the Jews themselves and Pilate, who was your procurator among them, with his soldiers, against Christ. [He also testifies] that he would be believed in by men of every race, and that God calls him his Son and has declared that he will subject his enemies to him, and how the demons try as far as they can to escape the power of God the Father and Master of all and that of his Christ, and how God calls all men to repentance before the day of judgment comes. These words were as follows: [23]

"Blessed is the man who has not walked in the council of the ungodly, nor stood in the way of sinners, nor taken his seat upon the seat of pestilence, but his will is in the law of the Lord, and in his law will he meditate day and night. And he shall be like the tree which is planted by the watercourses, which will give its fruit in its season, and his leaf will not wither, and whatever he does will be prospered. Not so are the ungodly, not so, but rather like the chaff which the wind blows away from the face of the earth. Therefore the ungodly will not arise in judgment, nor sinners in the council of the righteous, because the Lord knows the way of the righteous, and the way of the ungodly will be destroyed.

"Why have the nations raged and the peoples imagined new things? [24] The kings of the earth stood up, and their rulers

[22] Ps. 19 (18): 2–5 (cf. Rom. 10:18).   [23] Ps. 1; 2.
[24] Several LXX MSS. read "*kaina*," "new," for "*kena*," "vain," as does Justin.

assembled together against the Lord and against his Christ, saying, Let us break their bonds and let us cast away from us their yoke. He that dwells in heaven will laugh them to scorn, and the Lord will mock at them. Then will he speak to them in his wrath and vex them in his anger. I have been set up by him as king on Zion his holy mountain, proclaiming the Lord's decree. The Lord said to me, You are my Son, today have I begotten you; ask of me and I will give you nations for your inheritance, and the ends of the earth for your possession; you will shepherd them with a rod of iron, you will break them like potter's vessels. And now, O kings, understand; be instructed, all you who judge the earth. Serve the Lord with fear and rejoice before him with trembling. Accept discipline, lest the Lord should be angry, [and] wrathful, and you be destroyed from the right way when his anger is kindled in haste. Blessed are all those who have put their trust in him."

41. And again in another prophecy the prophetic Spirit, testifying through the same David that after being crucified Christ would reign, said: "O sing to the Lord, all the earth, and proclaim his salvation from day to day; for great is the Lord and highly to be praised, terrible beyond all the gods. For all the gods of the nations are images of demons, but God made the heavens. Glory and praise are before him, and strength and pride in the place of his sanctification. Give glory to the Lord, the Father of the ages. Receive favor and go in before his face and worship in his holy courts. Let all the earth fear before him, and be set upright and not shaken. Let them exult among the nations; the Lord has reigned from the tree."[25]

42. Now when the prophetic Spirit speaks of things to come as already having happened, as is illustrated in the passages quoted—I will explain this too so that those who come on it will have no excuse [for not understanding]. Things he fully knows are to happen he speaks of in advance as if they had already occurred. Give careful attention to the passages

---

[25] Ps. 96 (95): 1, 2, 4–10, also in I Chron. 16:23, 25–31. Justin's variations from the LXX include "images of demons" where LXX has "demons" in Ps. 95, "images" in I Chron.; "Father of the ages" for "families of the nations"; "receive favor" (*charin*) for "take offerings"; and the addition "from the tree," otherwise known only to Latin Christian writers whose acquaintance with it may derive from him; he defends this reading in Dial., ch. 73, arguing that the Jews have deliberately omitted it (although in the MS. the psalm is then quoted as in LXX, perhaps due to collation by a copyist; it seems that Justin knew an eccentric text, possibly from liturgical use.

quoted [and you will see] that this is the way they must be taken. David uttered the words quoted above fifteen hundred years before Christ, made man, was crucified, and none of those who were crucified before him gave joy to the nations, nor of those [crucified] after him either. But in our time Jesus Christ, who was crucified and died, rose again and, ascending into heaven, began to reign; and on account of what was proclaimed by the apostles in all nations as [coming] from him, there is joy for those who look forward to the incorruption which he has promised.

43. So that none may infer from what we have said that the events we speak of, because they were foreknown and predicted, took place according to inevitable destiny—I can explain this too. We have learned from the prophets, and declare as the truth, that penalties and punishments and good rewards are given according to the quality of each man's actions. If this were not so, but all things happened in accordance with destiny, nothing at all would be left up to us. For if it is destined that one man should be good and another wicked, then neither is the one acceptable nor the other blameworthy. And if the human race does not have the power by free choice to avoid what is shameful and to choose what is right, then there is no responsibility for actions of any kind. But that [man] walks upright or falls by free choice we may thus demonstrate. We [often] observe the same man in pursuit of opposite things. If he were destined to be either wicked or virtuous, he would not be thus capable of opposites, and often change his mind. Nor would some be virtuous and others wicked, for then we would have to declare fate to be the cause of evils and [at the same time] to act in opposition to itself [26]—or to accept as true the opinion referred to above, that there is no real virtue or vice, but only by opinion are things considered good or bad; which, as the true Reason shows us, is the greatest impiety and wickedness. But we do say that deserved rewards are irrevocably destined for those who have chosen the good, and likewise their just deserts for those [who have chosen] the opposite. But God did not make man like other [beings], such as trees and animals, which have no power of choice. For he would not be worthy of rewards or praise if he did not choose the good of himself, but was so made, nor if he were evil would he justly

[26] I.e., by also being the cause of good—Otto conjectures "goods and" before evils, which is certainly the sense, though I doubt whether one can be sure that Justin was so clear.

deserve punishment, if he were not such of himself, but was unable to be anything different from that for which he was formed.

44. The holy prophetic Spirit taught us these things, saying through Moses that God said to the first-formed man, "Behold I have set before you good and evil, choose the good."[27] And again through Isaiah, another prophet, this was said to the same purpose, as from God the Father and Master of all things: "Wash yourselves, be clean, take away wickednesses from your souls, learn to do good, give judgment for the orphan and defend the cause of the widow, and come and let us reason together, says the Lord. And though your sins be as scarlet, I will make them as white as wool, and though they be like crimson, I will make them as white as snow. And if you are willing and listen to me, you will eat the good of the land; but if you will not listen to me, the sword will devour you; for the mouth of the Lord has spoken these things." [28] The phrase, "The sword will devour you," does not mean that the disobedient will be slain by swords, but the sword of God is the fire, of which those who choose to do what is evil are made the fuel. Because of this he says, "A sword will devour you, for the mouth of the Lord has spoken it." For if he were speaking of a sword that cuts and at once destroys, he would not have said, "Will devour."

So when Plato said, "The blame belongs to him who chooses, and God is free from blame,"[29] he took this from the prophet Moses. For Moses was earlier than Plato and all the Greek writers. And everything that philosophers and poets said about the immortality of the soul, punishments after death, contemplation of heavenly things, and teachings of that kind—they took hints from the prophets and so were able to understand these things and expounded them. So it seems that there were indeed seeds of truth in all men, but they are proved not to have understood them properly since they contradict each other.

So when we say that things yet to happen have been prophesied, we do not say that they take place by inevitable destiny, but since God foreknows what all men are to do, and it is his decree that each will be rewarded according to the quality of his actions, he foretells by the prophetic Spirit what he will do in accordance with the quality of what they do. So he is ever leading the human race to reflection and remembrance, showing

---

[27] Deut. 30:15—cf. Gen. 2:17 and Ecclus. 15:11–17.
[28] Isa. 1:16–20.   [29] *Republic* 617 E.

that he cares for it and provides for men. But by the working of the wicked demons death has been decreed against those who read the books of Hystaspes or Sybil or the prophets,[30] so that they might frighten people away from receiving the knowledge of good things by consulting them, and keep them in slavery to themselves. But they did not succeed in this forever, for we not only boldly consult these books, but also as you see offer them for your inspection, being sure that what they declare will be welcome to all. Even if we only persuade a few, this will be a great gain for us; for as good husbandmen we will receive our reward from our Master.[31]

45. Now hear how it was said through David the prophet, that God the Father of all would take up Christ into heaven after raising him from the dead, and then wait to smite the demons who are his enemies, until the number be completed of those whom he foreknows will be good and virtuous,[32] for whose sake he has not yet brought about the destruction of the world by fire. The words are these: "The Lord said to my Lord, Sit on my right hand until I make your enemies your footstool. The Lord will send forth the rod of power from Jerusalem; and dominate in the midst of your enemies. The beginning is with you in the day of your power, in the splendors of your holy ones; I have begotten you from the womb before the morning star."[33] The phrase, "He will send forth the rod of power for you from Jerusalem," is a prediction of the mighty word which his apostles, going forth from Jerusalem, preached everywhere, and which, although death is decreed against those who teach or even confess the name of Christ, we everywhere both receive and teach. If you respond to these words with hostility, you can do no more, as we said before, than to kill us, which will not do harm to us, but will lead to eternal punishment through fire for you and all who unjustly are enemies [to the gospel] and do not repent.

46. Lest some should unreasonably object, in order to turn men away from what we teach, that we say that Christ was born a hundred and fifty years ago under Quirinius, and taught what we say he taught still later, under Pontius Pilate, and

30 A reference, somewhat exaggerated, to Roman law against divination of coming political events by private individuals, and the periodic restrictions on Jewish proselytism.
31 Apparently a confusion between the parable of the Talents (Matt. 25: 14–23) and that of the Wicked Husbandmen (Matt. 21:33–41).
32 Parallel clauses in Greek, but probably to be taken together.
33 Ps. 110 (109):1–3.

should accuse us [as supposing] that all men born before that time were irresponsible, I will solve this difficulty in advance. We have been taught that Christ is the First-begotten of God, and have previously testified that he is the Reason of which every race of man partakes. Those who lived in accordance with Reason are Christians, even though they were called godless, such as, among the Greeks, Socrates and Heraclitus and others like them; among the barbarians, Abraham, Ananiah, Azariah, and Mishael,[34] and Elijah, and many others, whose deeds and names I forbear to list, knowing that this would be lengthy. So also those who lived without Reason were ungracious and enemies to Christ, and murderers of those who lived by Reason. But those who lived by Reason, and those who so live now, are Christians, fearless and unperturbed. For what cause a man was conceived of a virgin by the power of the Word according to the will of God, the Father and Master of all, and was named Jesus, and after being crucified and dying rose again and ascended into heaven, an intelligent man will be able to comprehend from the words that were spoken in various ways. But since the further demonstration of this does not seem necessary at the moment, I will pass on to more needed demonstrations.

47. Hear how the prophetic Spirit said that the land of the Jews would be ravaged. The words are spoken as in the character of the people, wondering at what had happened, as follows: "Zion has become a wilderness, Jerusalem has become like a wilderness, the house of our sanctuary [is made] a curse, and the glory which our fathers praised is burned with fire, and all its glorious things are fallen. And you abide these things, and have kept silence, and have humbled us greatly."[35] You are well aware that Jerusalem was laid waste, as it was predicted would happen. That it would be laid waste, and no one permitted to dwell there, was said through Isaiah the prophet: "Their land is a desert, their enemies eat it up before them, and none of them will dwell in it."[36] You certainly know that under your guard there is no one in it, and that death has been decreed against any Jew caught entering.[37]

48. How it was prophesied that our Christ would heal all

---

[34] The original names of the "three holy children" (Dan. 1:7) are the ones commonly used in Greek.   [35] Isa. 64:10–12.

[36] Isa. 1:7 and Jer. 50:3.

[37] Judea was ravaged when the revolt of Bar-Cochba was suppressed under Hadrian, and Jews were excluded from the new city built on the site of Jerusalem (not, as Justin suggests, from the whole country).

diseases and raise the dead, hear what was spoken, as follows: "At his coming the lame will leap like a hart, and the stammering tongue will be clear; blind will see and lepers be cleansed, and the dead will arise and walk." [38] That he did these things, you can learn from the Acts of what took place under Pontius Pilate. How it was testified by the prophetic Spirit that he would be put to death, together with the men who hoped in him, hear what was said through Isaiah, as follows: "See how the Just One perishes and no one takes it to heart, and just men are slain and none consider it. The Just One is taken away from the presence of wickedness, and his burial will be in peace; he is taken away from the midst [of us]." [39]

49. Here again is how it was said through the same Isaiah, that the peoples of the Gentiles who were not looking for him would worship him, and the Jews who were constantly looking for him would not recognize him when he came. These words are spoken as in the character of the Christ himself, as follows: "I became manifest to those who asked not after me, I was found by those who sought me not. I said, Here am I, to a nation who did not call upon my name. I stretched out my hands over a disobedient and contradicting people, over those who walked in a way that was not good, but after their sins, a people who rouse me to anger." [40] For the Jews, having the prophecies, and constantly looking for the Christ, failed to recognize him when he came—more than that, they even mistreated him. But men of the Gentiles, who had never even heard about Christ until his apostles who came forth from Jerusalem testified to the things about him and gave them the prophecies, were filled with joy and faith, turned away from their idols, and dedicated themselves to the unbegotten God through Christ. That the slanders which would be spoken against those who confess Christ were foreknown, and how those would be afflicted who slander him and say that it is better to keep the ancient customs, hear what was briefly spoken through Isaiah as follows: "Woe to those who call sweet bitter and bitter sweet." [41]

50. How, being made man for us, he endured suffering and dishonor, and will come again with glory—hear the prophecies which were spoken to this effect, as follows:

"Because they delivered his soul to death, and he was counted with the wicked, he has borne the sins of many, and

---

[38] Isa. 35:5, 6 (cf. Matt. 11:5, which adds the lepers).
[39] Isa. 57:1, 2.　　　　[40] Isa. 65:1–3.　　　　[41] Isa. 5:20.

will make propitiation for the wicked.[42] For behold, my
servant will understand and be exalted and greatly glorified.
As many will be astonished at you, so your form will be dishonored from [among] men and your glory from men, so that
many nations will wonder, and kings will shut their mouths;
because those who were not told about him will see, and those
who have not heard will understand. O Lord, who has believed
our report, and to whom has the arm of the Lord been revealed?
We have spoken before him as a child, as a root in thirsty
ground. He has no form nor glory; and we saw him and he
had no form nor beauty, but his form was dishonored and
despised beyond [any of] mankind. He was a stricken man,
knowing how to bear infirmity, because his face was turned
away, and he was dishonored and not esteemed. It is he who
bears our sins and undergoes travail for us, and we thought
him to be in distress, smitten and afflicted. But he was wounded
for our wickednesses and suffered infirmity for our sins; the
chastisement of [our] peace was upon him, and by his bruises
we are healed. We have all as sheep gone astray, [every]
man has gone astray in his own way. And he gave himself up
for our sins, and did not open his mouth because of affliction.
He was led as a sheep to slaughter, and as a lamb before its
shearer is dumb, so he opened not his mouth. In his humiliation
his judgment was taken away."[43] For after he was crucified
even all his acquaintances deserted him, denying him. But
later, when he rose from the dead and appeared to them, and
taught them to consult the prophecies, in which it was predicted that all these things would happen; and when they had
seen him ascending into heaven, and believed on him, and
received the power which he sent them from there, and went
into every race of men, they taught these things and were
known as apostles.

51. In order to testify to us that he who suffered these things
is of ineffable origin and reigns over his enemies, the prophetic
Spirit spoke thus:

"Who will declare his generation? For his life was taken away
from the earth; on account of their wickednesses he goes to
death. And I will give the wicked for his burial and the rich
for his death, for he did no wickedness nor was guilt found
in his mouth. And the Lord wills to cleanse him from the
blow. If you give an offering for sin, your soul will see a long-

[42] Isa. 53:12 (perhaps here from memory and in ch. 51 from the text).
[43] Isa. 52:13 to 53:8a.

lived seed. And the Lord wills to remove his soul from sorrow, to show him light and to form him with understanding, to justify the Just One who is a good servant to many. And he shall bear away our sins. Because of this he will inherit many and divide the booty of the strong, for that his soul was delivered to death, and he was numbered among the wicked, and he himself bore the sins of many, and because of their wickednesses he was betrayed."[44]

Hear how he was to go up to heaven, as it was prophesied. This was spoken: "Lift up the gates of heaven, be opened, that the King of glory may come in. Who is this King of glory? The Lord of might and the Lord of power."[45] And that he is to come from heaven with glory, hear what was spoken to this effect through Jeremiah the prophet, as follows: "Behold how the Son of Man comes on the clouds of heaven, and his angels with him."[46]

52. Since we have shown that all these things that have already happened were proclaimed in advance through the prophets before they happened, it must similarly be believed that those things which were similarly prophesied and are yet to happen will certainly take place. Just as these things which have already happened came true, proclaimed in advance and [yet] unrecognized, so in the same way the remainder, even if unacknowledged and disbelieved, will come to pass. For the prophets foretold two comings of Christ—one, which has already happened, as that of a dishonored and passible man, and the second, when as has been foretold he will come from heaven in glory with his angelic host, when he will raise the bodies of all the men who have ever lived, and will clothe the worthy with incorruption, but send those of the wicked, eternally conscious, into eternal fire with the evil demons. How it was predicted that these things will happen we will show. This was spoken through the prophet Ezekiel: "Joint will come together with joint and bone with bone, and flesh will grow again. And every knee will bow to the Lord and every tongue will confess him."[47] That the wicked will be punished, still conscious, hear what was similarly spoken on this topic, as follows: "Their worm shall not rest, and their fire shall not be extinguished."[48] And then they will repent, when it will no longer do them any good. What the peoples of the Jews will

44 Isa. 53:8b–12. 45 Ps. 24 (23):7, 8.
46 Dan. 7:13; Matt. 24:30; 26:64; Mark 14:62.
47 Ezek., ch. 37; Isa. 45:23. 48 Isa. 66:24.

say and do, when they see him coming in glory, was thus prophesied through the prophet Zechariah:

"I will command the four winds to bring together the scattered children; I will command the north wind to carry them, and the south wind not to keep them back. [49] And then there will be great lamentation in Jerusalem, not a lamentation of mouths or lips, but a lamentation of the heart, and they shall rend not their garments but their minds. Tribe after tribe will lament, and then they will see him whom they pierced, [50] and will say: Why, O Lord, did you make us wander astray from thy way? The glory which our fathers praised has become our disgrace." [51]

53. I could cite many other prophecies too, but pause, thinking that these are sufficient to convince those who have ears to hear and understand, and considering that such people can understand that we do not, like those who tell the mythical stories about the so-called sons of Zeus, merely talk, without having proofs. For why should we believe a crucified man that he is First-begotten of the Unbegotten God, and that he will pass judgment on the whole human race, unless we found testimonies proclaimed about him before he came, and was made man, and see that things have thus happened? For we have seen the desolation of the land of the Jews, and the men of every nation who have been persuaded by the teaching that comes from his apostles, and have turned away from the old customs in which they lived, wandering astray—that is ourselves, since we know that the Gentile Christians are more numerous and truer than those from among the Jews and Samaritans. For all the other nations of mankind are called Gentiles by the prophetic Spirit, while the Jewish and Samaritan tribes are called Israel and House of Jacob. How it was prophesied that more of the Gentiles would be believers than of the Jews and Samaritans—I will cite what was prophesied. It was spoken thus: "Rejoice, O barren and bearing not, break forth and shout, you who did not travail, for the children of the desolate are more than those of her who had a husband." [52] For all the Gentiles were desolate of the true God, serving the works of [men's] hands. But Jews and Samaritans, having the word from God given them through the prophets and constantly looking for the Christ, did not recognize him when he came, except only for a few, whose salvation the holy prophetic

49 Isa. 43:5, 6 (the four winds in Zech. 2:6).
50 Zech. 12:10–12 (cf. John 19:37).   51 Isa. 63:17; 64:11.   52 Isa. 54:1.

Spirit predicted through Isaiah. For he said, speaking as in their character, "Except the Lord had left us a seed, we should have been as Sodom and Gomorrha."[53] Moses tells the story of Sodom and Gomorrha, cities of godless men which God overthrew, burning them with fire and brimstone, none of the people in them being saved except a certain stranger of Chaldaean race, Lot by name, with whom his daughters were saved also. Those who want to can see their whole countryside, desolate and burned and still unproductive. That it was foreknown that those of the Gentiles would be truer and more faithful, we will cite what was said through Isaiah the prophet. He spoke thus, "Israel is uncircumcised in heart, and the Gentiles are the uncircumcision,"[54] seeing such things should reasonably bring conviction and faith to those who welcome the truth, and are not vainglorious or controlled by their passions.

PAGANISM AN IMITATION OF CHRISTIANITY

54. But those who hand on the myths invented by the poets offer no demonstration to the youngsters who learn them—indeed I [am prepared to] show that they were told at the instigation of the wicked demons to deceive and lead astray the human race. For when they heard it predicted through the prophets that Christ was to come, and that impious men would be punished by fire, they put forward a number of so-called sons of Zeus, thinking that they could thus make men suppose that what was said about Christ was a mere tale of wonders like the stories told by the poets. These stories were spread among the Greeks and all the Gentiles, where, as they heard the prophets proclaiming, Christ would especially be believed in. But, as I will make clear, though they heard the words of the prophets they did not understand them accurately, but made mistakes in imitating what was told about our Christ. The prophet Moses was, as I said before, older than all [Greek] writers, and this prophecy was made through him, as previously cited: "The ruler shall not depart from Judah, nor the governor from his thighs, until he come for whom it is reserved; and he shall be the expectation of the nations, binding his colt to the

---

53 Isa. 1:9.
54 Jer. 9:26, quoted more fully and expounded in Dial., ch. 28; a verse which has for Justin the associations of Rom., ch. 4, and suggests that those circumcised in the flesh are uncircumcised in heart, and vice versa (Jer. 4:4).

vine, washing his robe in the blood of the grape." [55] So when
the demons heard these prophetic words they made out that
Dionysus had been a son of Zeus, and handed down that he
was the discoverer of the vine (hence they introduce wine in his
mysteries), and taught that after being torn in pieces he ascended
into heaven. Now the prophecy given through Moses did not
precisely indicate whether he who was to come would be the
Son of God, and whether, mounted on a colt, he would remain
on earth or ascend into heaven; and the word "colt" can indicate the colt of an ass or a horse. So not knowing whether the
predicted one would bring the colt of an ass or of a horse as the
symbol of his coming, and, as said above, whether he was the
Son of God or of a man, they said that Bellerophon, a man
and born of men, had gone up to heaven on the horse Pegasus.
Then when they heard it said through that other prophet
Isaiah that he was to be born of a virgin and would ascend into
heaven by his own [power], they put forward what is told about
Perseus. When they learned that it was said, as has been quoted,
in the ancient prophecies, "Strong as a giant to run his
course," [56] they said that Heracles was strong and had traveled
over the whole earth. Again when they learned that it was
prophesied that he would heal every disease and raise the dead,
they brought forward Asclepius. [57]

55. But never was the crucifixion imitated in the case of
any of the so-called sons of Zeus; for they did not understand
it since, as has been explained, everything said about it was
expressed symbolically. Yet, as the prophet predicted, it [the
cross] is the greatest symbol of his power and authority, as
[can be] shown from things you can see. Reflect on all things
in the universe [and consider] whether they could be governed
or held together in fellowship without this figure. For the sea
cannot be traversed unless the sign of victory, which is called
a sail, [58] remain fast in the ship; the land is not plowed without
it; similarly diggers and mechanics do not do their work except
with tools of this form. The human figure differs from the irrational animals precisely in this, that man stands erect and
can stretch out his hands, and has on his face, stretched down
from the forehead, what is called the nose, through which goes
breath for the living creature—and this exhibits precisely the

---

[55] Gen. 49:10, 11.   [56] Ps. 19 (18):5.   [57] Cf. ch. 21.
[58] Curiously phrased; is it possible that sailors in Justin's time called the
mainmast the "trophy," which he takes as a tribute to its form suggestive
of the cross, the trophy of the victory of Christ?

figure of the cross. So it was said through the prophet, "The breath before our face is Christ the Lord." [59] Even your own symbols display the power of this figure—on the standards and trophies, with which you make all your solemn processions, using these [cross-shaped objects] as signs of authority, even though without understanding what you're doing. Then you set up the images of your deceased emperors on this figure, and in the inscriptions call them gods. So now since I have done my best to persuade you, both by argument and by [appealing to] a visible figure, I am free from reproach even if you disbelieve; my part is done and finished.

56. The wicked demons were not satisfied with saying before the appearance of Christ that there had been the so-called sons of Zeus. After he had appeared and lived among men, when they learned how he had been predicted by the prophets, and saw how he was believed on and looked for in every race, they again, as we showed before, put forward others, Simon and Menander of Samaria, who by doing mighty works of magic deceived and are still deceiving many. For as I said before, Simon lived in your own imperial city of Rome under Claudius Caesar, and so impressed the Sacred Senate and the Roman people that he was thought to be a god and was honored with a statue like the other gods whom you honor. We ask you therefore to join the Sacred Senate and your people as joint judges of this petition of ours, so that if any are ensnared by his teachings they may be able to learn the truth and flee from this error. And, if you will, destroy the statue.

57. Nor can the wicked demons persuade men that there will be no burning for the punishment of the impious, just as they were not able to keep Christ hidden when he came. All they can do is to make men who live contrary to reason, having been brought up in bad habits of passion and prejudice, kill and hate us. Yet we do not hate them, but, as is evident, pity them and try to persuade them to reform. For we are not afraid of death, admitting that we are certainly going to die, and [since] there is nothing new [for unbelievers], but things continue the same in this dispensation—if boredom seizes those who share in such things even for a year,[60] then in order to be

---

[59] Lam. 4:20.
[60] Here and in the following chapter, Justin indicates briefly, and somewhat obscurely, what he thought was the real spiritual condition of his pagan contemporaries—the reference here seems to be to the *taedium vitae* expressed in many funeral inscriptions.

free from suffering and want they should pay attention to our
teachings. If they do not believe that there is anything after
death, but declare that those who die pass into unconsciousness,
then they are our benefactors in delivering us from the sufferings
and needs [of life] here. But they still show themselves to be
wicked, misanthropic, and prejudiced. For they do not kill us
in order to set us free, but rather murder us in order to deprive
us of life and its pleasures.

58. As I said before, the wicked demons have also put forward Marcion of Pontus, who is even now teaching men to
deny that God is the Maker of all things in heaven and earth
and that the Christ predicted by the prophets is his Son. He
preaches another God besides the Fashioner of the universe,
and likewise another Son. Many are persuaded by him, as if
he alone knew the truth, and make fun of us, though they have
no proof of the things they say, but are irrationally snatched
away, like lambs by a wolf,[61] and become the prey of
godless teachings and of demons. For those who are called
demons strive for nothing else than to draw men away
from God who made [them] and from Christ his First-
begotten. Those who cannot rise above the earth they have
nailed down by [the worship of] earthly things and the works
of men's hands. They even push back those who aim at the
contemplation of things divine, unless their thinking is prudent
and pure and their life free from passion, and drive them into
ungodliness.

59. So that you may learn that Plato borrowed from our
teachers, I mean from the Word [speaking] through the prophets, when he said that God made the universe by changing
formless matter, hear the precise words of Moses, who as declared above was the first of the prophets and older than the
Greek writers. The prophetic Spirit testified through him how
in the beginning God fashioned the universe, and out of what,
saying: "In the beginning God made the heaven and the earth.
And the earth was invisible and unfurnished, and darkness
[was] over the abyss; and the Spirit of God was borne over
the waters. And God said, Let there be light. And it
was so." [62] So by God's word the whole universe was
made out of this substratum, as expounded by Moses, and
Plato and those who agree with him, as well as we, have
learned it [from him], and you can be sure of it too. We also

61 Cf. John 10:12.
62 Gen. 1:1–3.

know that Moses had already spoken of what the poets call Erebus.[63]

60. In the discussion of the nature of the Son of God in Plato's *Timaeus*, when he says, "He placed him like an X in the universe,"[64] this was similarly borrowed from Moses. For it is recorded in the writings of Moses that in his time, when the Israelites had gone out of Egypt and were in the wilderness, they encountered poisonous beasts, vipers and asps and every kind of snake which were killing the people. By an inspiration and influence that came from God, Moses took brass and made the form of a cross, and placed it over the holy tent, saying to the people, "If you look on this form and believe on it, you will be saved." And he records that when this was done, the snakes died, and so, he tells us, the people escaped death.[65] Plato, reading this and not clearly understanding, nor realizing that it was the form of a cross, but thinking it was [the letter] *Chi*, said that the Power next to the first God was placed X-wise in the universe. And he spoke of a third, since he read what I have quoted from Moses, that the Spirit of God was borne over the waters. For he gives the second place to the Word who is with God, who, he says, was placed X-wise in the universe, and the third to the Spirit which was said to be borne over the water, saying, "The third [order of] beings around the third."[66] And hear how the prophetic Spirit has testified through Moses that there will be a destruction by fire. He said, "Everliving fire will descend and will devour even to the abyss below."[67] So it is not that we hold the same opinions as others, but that what all others say is an imitation of ours. Among us you can hear and learn these things from those who do not even know the letters of the alphabet—uneducated and barbarous in speech, but wise and faithful in mind—even from cripples and the blind. So you can see that these things are not the product of human wisdom, but are spoken by the power of God.

[63] Commentators speculate inconclusively whether this suggestion, which Justin touches on lightly, was based on the "evening" (Hebrew *'erev*) of the days of creation.

[64] *Tim.*, 36 B–C, a reference to the soul of the universe which is as it were folded together; the Greek letter *Chi* has the form (not of course the sound) of *X*.

[65] Num. 21:6–9 with some legendary additions; cf. John 3:14.

[66] Plato, 2 *Epist.* 312 E (with singular and plural reversed), an undeniably obscure passage, though scarcely meaning what Justin supposed.

[67] Deut. 32:22; Justin here passes from Platonic to Stoic ideas, as in ch. 20.

CHRISTIAN WORSHIP

61. How we dedicated ourselves to God when we were made new through Christ I will explain, since it might seem to be unfair if I left this out from my exposition. Those who are persuaded and believe that the things we teach and say are true, and promise that they can live accordingly, are instructed to pray and beseech God with fasting for the remission of their past sins, while we pray and fast along with them. Then they are brought by us where there is water, and are reborn by the same manner of rebirth by which we ourselves were reborn; for they are then washed in the water in the name of God the Father and Master of all, and of our Saviour Jesus Christ, and of the Holy Spirit. For Christ said, "Unless you are born again you will not enter into the Kingdom of heaven." [68] Now it is clear to all that those who have once come into being cannot enter the wombs of those who bore them. But as I quoted before, it was said through the prophet Isaiah how those who have sinned and repent shall escape from their sins. He said this: "Wash yourselves, be clean, take away wickednesses from your souls, learn to do good, give judgment for the orphan and defend the cause of the widow, and come and let us reason together, says the Lord. And though your sins be as scarlet, I will make them as white as wool, and though they be as crimson, I will make them as white as snow. If you will not listen to me, the sword will devour you; for the mouth of the Lord has spoken these things." [69] And we learned from the apostles this reason for this [rite]. At our first birth we were born of necessity without our knowledge, from moist seed, by the intercourse of our parents with each other, and grew up in bad habits and wicked behavior. So that we should not remain children of necessity and ignorance, but [become sons] of free choice and knowledge, and obtain remission of the sins we have already committed, [70] there is named at the water, over him who has chosen to be born again and has repented of his sinful acts, the name of God the Father and Master of all. Those who lead to the washing the one who is to be washed call on [God by] this term only. [71] For no one may give a proper

---

[68] John 3:3, 4. [69] Isa. 1:16–20.

[70] The second birth is also connected with moisture, but is otherwise contrasted with the first in all respects.

[71] Thirlby and later editors emend the plurals in this sentence to the singular, unnecessarily—Justin is writing from the point of view of the

name to the ineffable God, and if anyone should dare to say that there is one, he is hopelessly insane. [72] This washing is called illumination, since those who learn these things are illumined within. The illuminand is also washed in the name of Jesus Christ, who was crucified under Pontius Pilate, and in the name of the Holy Spirit, who through the prophets foretold everything about Jesus.

62. When the demons heard this washing proclaimed through the prophets, they arranged that those who go into their temples and are about to approach them to offer libations and burnt offerings should sprinkle themselves—and further they have them wash themselves completely as they pass on into the sanctuaries where they are enshrined. The order given by the priests to devotees to remove their shoes as they enter the temples and approach them [73] [the demons] is an imitation devised by the demons when they learned what happened to Moses, the above-mentioned prophet. For at the time when Moses was ordered to go down to Egypt and bring out the people of the Israelites who were there, as he was pasturing in the land of Arabia the sheep of his maternal uncle, our Christ addressed him in the form of fire out of a bush, and said, "Unloose your sandals and come near and hear." When he had taken them and approached, he heard [that he was] to go down into Egypt, and lead out the people of the Israelites there, and received great power from Christ, who spoke to him in the form of fire. [74] He went down and led out the people after he had done great miracles—if you want to learn about them, you may learn in detail from his writings.

63. Even now the Jews all teach that the unnamed God himself spoke to Moses. Wherefore the prophetic Spirit said in condemnation of them through Isaiah the above-mentioned prophet, as was quoted before: "The ox knows his owner and

individual convert, but slips into the plural here, either because the occasion was one regularly repeated, or (more likely) because he was accustomed to group baptisms with a number of officiants, and not to the medieval and modern custom of baptism of a single candidate by a single minister.

72 Justin was aware that the Old Testament divine name was used for magical purposes (as *Iao* and the like), and hence his vigorous condemnation of a practice he considers not only wrong (as all Jews would) but impossible.

73 Accepting Gildersleeve's suggestion of *prosiontas autois* for *tois autois*; the general sense is clear but the text confused.

74 Ex., ch. 3; Justin calls Jethro Moses' uncle instead of father-in-law, perhaps by confusion with Jacob and Laban.

the ass his master's crib, but Israel does not know me and my people does not understand." [75] Likewise Jesus the Christ, because the Jews did not know what the Father is and what the Son, himself said in condemnation of them: "No one knows the Father except the Son, nor the Son except the Father and those to whom the Son will reveal it." [76] Now the Word of God is his Son, as I said before. He is also called "Angel" and "Apostle," for [as Angel] he announces what it is necessary to know, and [as Apostle] is sent forth to testify to what is announced, [77] as our Lord himself said, "He that hears me hears him that sent me." [78] This can be made clear from the writings of Moses, in which this is to be found: "And the Angel of God spoke to Moses in a flame of fire out of the bush and said, I am he who is, God of Abraham, God of Isaac, God of Jacob, the God of your fathers; go down to Egypt and bring out my people." [79] Those who wish to can learn what followed from this; for it is not possible to put down everything in these [pages]. But these words were uttered to demonstrate that Jesus Christ is the Son of God and Apostle, who was first the Word, and appeared, now in the form of fire, now in the image of the bodiless creatures. Now, however, having become man by the will of God for the sake of the human race, he has endured whatever sufferings the demons managed to have brought upon him by the senseless Jews. For they have it clearly said in the writings of Moses, "And the Angel of God spoke to Moses in a flame of fire in the bush and said, I am he who is, the God of Abraham, the God of Isaac, and the God of Jacob," [79] yet they say that he who said these things was the Father and Fashioner of the universe. Jesus again, as we cited, when he was with them said, "No one knows the Father except the Son, nor the Son except the Father and those to whom the Son may reveal it." [76] So the Jews, continuing to think that the Father of the universe had spoken to Moses, when it was the Son of God, who is called both Angel and Apostle, who spoke to him, were rightly censured both by the prophetic Spirit and by Christ himself, since they knew neither the Father nor the Son. For those who identify the Son and the Father are condemned, as neither knowing the Father nor recognizing that the Father of the universe has a Son,

[75] Isa. 1:3.   [76] Luke 10:22; Matt. 11:27; cf. John 8:19; 16:3.

[77] Angel, reference below—the angel in the bush, who said, "I am the God of Abraham," and Isa. 9:6; Apostle, Heb. 3:1.

[78] Cf. Luke 10:16 (Matt. 10:40); cf. John 14:24.   [79] Ex. 3:14, 15.

who being the Word and First-begotten of God is also divine. Formerly he appeared in the form of fire and the image of a bodiless being to Moses and the other prophets. But now in the time of your dominion he was, as I have said, made man of a virgin according to the will of the Father for the salvation of those who believe in him, and endured contempt and suffering so that by dying and rising again he might conquer death. What was said out of the bush to Moses, "I am he who is, the God of Abraham and the God of Isaac and the God of Jacob and the God of your fathers," was an indication that they though dead still existed and were Christ's own men. For they were the first of all men to devote themselves to seeking after God, [80] Abraham being the father of Isaac, and Isaac of Jacob, as Moses also recorded.

64. From what has been said you can understand why the demons contrived to have the image of the so-called Kore erected at the springs of waters, saying that she was a daughter of Zeus, imitating what was said through Moses. For Moses said, as I have quoted: "In the beginning God made the heaven and the earth. And the earth was invisible and unfurnished, and the Spirit of God was borne over the waters." [81] In imitation of the Spirit of God, spoken of as borne over the water, they spoke of Kore, daughter of Zeus. With similar malice they spoke of Athena as a daughter of Zeus, but not as a result of intercourse—since they knew that God designed the creation of the world by the Word, they spoke of Athena as the first Concept. This we consider very ridiculous, to offer the female form as the image of an intellectual concept. And similarly the other so-called sons of Zeus are condemned by their actions.

65. We, however, after thus washing the one who has been convinced and signified his assent, lead him to those who are called brethren, where they are assembled. They then earnestly offer common prayers for themselves and the one who has been illuminated and all others everywhere, that we may be made worthy, having learned the truth, to be found in deed good citizens and keepers of what is commanded, so that we may be saved with eternal salvation. On finishing the prayers we

[80] Cf. Mark 12:26, 27 and parallels; Justin's comment is also suggestive of the Philonic allegorization of the journey to Canaan as the journey to the spiritual realm.

[81] Gen. 1:1, 2; the suggestion that the pagan goddess of springs was in some way parallel to the Spirit brooding over the waters would seem to come from someone in Syria (probably not Justin originally) with a background of Semitic languages, in which the word "spirit" is feminine.

greet each other with a kiss. Then bread and a cup of water and mixed wine are brought to the president of the brethren and he, taking them, sends up praise and glory to the Father of the universe through the name of the Son and of the Holy Spirit, and offers thanksgiving at some length that we have been deemed worthy to receive these things from him. When he has finished the prayers and the thanksgiving,[82] the whole congregation present [83] assents, saying, "Amen." "Amen" in the Hebrew language. means, "So be it." When the president has given thanks and the whole congregation has assented, those whom we call deacons give to each of those present a portion of the consecrated [84] bread and wine and water, and they take it to the absent.

66. This food we call Eucharist, of which no one is allowed to partake except one who believes that the things we teach are true, and has received the washing for forgiveness of sins and for rebirth, and who lives as Christ handed down to us. For we do not receive these things as common bread or common drink; but as Jesus Christ our Saviour being incarnate by God's word took flesh and blood for our salvation, so also we have been taught that the food consecrated by the word of prayer which comes from him, from which our flesh and blood are nourished by transformation, is the flesh and blood of that incarnate Jesus. [85] For the apostles in the memoirs composed by them, which are called Gospels, thus handed down what was commanded them: that Jesus, taking bread and having given thanks, said, "Do this for my memorial, this is my body"; and likewise taking the cup and giving thanks he said, "This is my blood"; and gave it to them alone.[86] This also the wicked

[82] Or, one could equally well say "the Eucharistic prayer."

[83] Literally, "all the people present," i.e., those present as being a gathering of the people of God (*laos*), the laity in the positive sense; cf. Neh. 8:5, 6.

[84] Literally, "eucharistized," i.e., blessed by the solemn prayer of thanksgiving, in accordance with the Jewish form of prayer, in which offering thanks to God for his gifts also blesses them for human use (cf. Mark 14:22, 23 and I Tim. 4:4, 5); but *eucharisteo* as a transitive verb in this connection seems to be Christian and Gentile.

[85] "Eucharistized food," see note 84; "by the word of prayer which comes from him" (*di' euchēs logou tou par' autou*) refers to the pattern of the Eucharistic prayer as instituted by Christ—*para* for the source of a tradition also, e.g., in ch. 42, *fin.*, and in ch. 61—the *logos* of baptism learned from the apostles, which probably means its rationale, but may mean the threefold formula.

[86] Mark 14:22–24 and I Cor. 11:23–25; quoted as from the Gospels, but perhaps representing in brief what Justin was used to hearing recited at the celebration of the Eucharist.

demons in imitation handed down as something to be done in the mysteries of Mithra; for bread and a cup of water are brought out in their secret rites of initiation, with certain invocations which you either know or can learn.

67. After these [services] we constantly remind each other of these things. Those who have more come to the aid of those who lack, and we are constantly together. Over all that we receive we bless the Maker of all things through his Son Jesus Christ and through the Holy Spirit.[87] And on the day called Sunday there is a meeting in one place of those who live in cities or the country, and the memoirs of the apostles or the writings of the prophets are read as long as time permits. When the reader has finished, the president in a discourse urges and invites [us] to the imitation of these noble things. Then we all stand up together and offer prayers. And, as said before, when we have finished the prayer, bread is brought, and wine and water, and the president similarly sends up prayers and thanksgivings to the best of his ability, and the congregation assents, saying the Amen; the distribution, and reception of the consecrated [elements] by each one, takes place and they are sent to the absent by the deacons. Those who prosper, and who so wish, contribute, each one as much as he chooses to.[88] What is collected is deposited with the president, and he takes care of orphans and widows, and those who are in want on account of sickness or any other cause, and those who are in bonds, and the strangers who are sojourners among [us], and, briefly, he is the protector of all those in need. We all hold this common gathering on Sunday, since it is the first day, on which God transforming darkness and matter made the universe, and Jesus Christ our Saviour rose from the dead on the same day. For they crucified him on the day before Saturday, and on the day after Saturday,[89] he appeared to his apostles and

---

[87] Not merely a general statement, but a reference to the custom, binding on Christians as on Jews, of giving thanks to God before receiving his gifts, which makes every meal a sacred act; cf. Chapter 13.

[88] The emphasis on the purely voluntary character of these contributions may have a legal purpose, to stress that the unlicensed Christian societies did not profess to collect dues (cf. Tertullian, *Apol.* 39:5).

[89] Justin may be avoiding using the term "day of Aphrodite" for Friday, or referring to the Sabbath and its preparation-day (*paraskeuē*) without using Jewish technical terms; he certainly wishes to disclaim, without dignifying with formal mention, any idea that the Christians were worshipers of the sun, as Jews were sometimes supposed to be devotees of Saturn (Cronus).

disciples and taught them these things which I have passed on to you also for your serious consideration.

Conclusion

68. If what we say seems to you reasonable and true, treat it with respect—if it seems foolish to you, then despise us as foolish creatures and do not decree the death penalty, as against enemies, for those who do no wrong. I have said before that you will not escape the future judgment of God if you continue unjust, while we will cry out, What God desires, let that be done.[90] On the ground of a letter of your father, the great and illustrious Caesar Hadrian, we could demand that you order judgment to be given as we have asked. Yet we do not ask [for this] on the basis of Hadrian's judgment, but since we know that what we ask is just, we have made this petition and explanation. I have subjoined a copy of the letter of Hadrian, so that you may know that I speak the truth in this matter. Here is the copy:[91]

Hadrian to Minucius Fundanus. I have received the letter addressed to me by your predecessor the Honorable Serenius Granianus, and it does not seem right to me to pass over this report in silence, lest innocent people should be molested and false accusers given the opportunity of doing harm. So if the people of your province can formally support their petition against the Christians by accusing them of something before [your] tribunal, I do not forbid their following this course; but I do not permit them to make use of mere requests and clamorous demands in this matter. It is much more proper, if anyone wishes to bring an accusation, for you to take cognizance of the matters brought forward. Therefore if anyone brings an accusation and proves that the men referred to have

[90] A familiar quotation from Plato, *Crito* 43 D—used probably with reference both to the *Deo Gratias* with which Christians accepted martyrdom and to their readiness for the final judgment.

[91] Translated from the Latin given by Rufinus in his translation of Eusebius, *Hist. eccl.*, IV, ch. 8, which probably represents the Latin that Eusebius says was attached to his copy of Justin, but which is replaced by Eusebius' Greek version in the MS. The rescript is probably genuine, and as such means no more than that proceedings against Christians must be taken by due process of law—and Christians could always be turned into criminals in Roman eyes by calling on them to perform any of the religious acts of loyalty which were civic duties to the Romans, but idolatry for Christians as for Jews. Minucius Fundanus was proconsul of Asia about A.D. 125.

done anything contrary to the laws, you will assign penalties in accordance with the character of the offenses. But you must certainly [92] take the greatest care, that if anyone accuses any of these people merely for the sake of calumny, you will punish him with severe penalties for his offense. [93]

[92] Latin *mehercule*, which is the mildest form of oath, scarcely worth translation; the imperial rescript, though having the effect of law, was still in form a private letter.

[93] It does not seem proper to include the items which follow in the present MS.—a letter from Antoninus Pius (according to Eusebius, of Marcus Aurelius) to the provincial council of Asia, in which Hadrian's principle is carried farther in the sense Justin desired; and an alleged letter of Marcus Aurelius recounting the incident of the Thundering Legion, whose prayers brought down rain for the army in Germany and hail on their enemies. Neither can be part of Justin's work; the second is certainly fictitious, and the first, though perhaps based on an imperial letter, has at least been adapted and enlarged.

A Plea Regarding Christians
by Athenagoras,
the Philosopher

INTRODUCTION

I T IS AN ODD FACT THAT THE AUTHOR OF WHAT IN
many ways is the ablest of the Greek Apologies remained
almost unknown in Christian antiquity. Apart from a
citation in a third century writer, Methodius of Tyre,[1] and a
misleading reference in a most unreliable historian of the fifth
century, Philip of Side, Athenagoras' work is passed over in
silence by the Church Fathers. Philip's *Christian History* is lost,
but fragments have been preserved by the fourteenth century
compiler Nicephorus Callistus.[2] Athenagoras is there stated
to have been the first head of the catechetical school of Alexandria, to have had Clement as his pupil, to have flourished
in the time of Hadrian and Antoninus, and, while bent on
attacking Christianity, to have been converted through study-
ing Scripture. No weight can be given to any of these statements: the first three are without question wrong. Again, it is
vaguely possible (one can hardly say more) that our Athenagoras is the one to whom the second century philosopher
Boethos addressed his work, *On Obscure Expressions in Plato*.[3]
In any case, neither Eusebius nor Jerome mentions him, and
we are left to deduce what we can about him from his writings.

Of these but two have survived: his Plea Regarding Christians and his Treatise on the Resurrection. From their titles we

---

[1] *De Resurrectione* I. 37:1, Ed., Bonwetsch, Leipzig, 1917. The citation is
from ch. 24 of the Plea. There are a sufficient number of similarities
between the Plea and Minucius Felix' Octavius to suggest that the latter
might have known Athenagoras' work. He does not, however, mention
him.

[2] For the reference to Athenagoras, see Migne, P.G. 6.182 (reprinting
Dodwell's text).

[3] Photius, *Bibliotheca*, 155.

gather that Athenagoras was a Christian philosopher of Athens. We owe these titles, it is true, to a tenth century manuscript, the Aretas Codex, and they may not be reliable. Yet the moderation of Athenagoras' Plea, its clarity and sense of order along with its suggestions of Attic style, give them a certain credence.

DATE

The date of the Plea can be determined with reasonable certainty. It is addressed to the emperors Marcus Aurelius and Lucius Aurelius Commodus. The latter is doubtless Marcus Aurelius' son, who was raised to the purple in A.D. 176. Later on in the Plea, Athenagoras refers directly to the relationship of father and son which existed between the two emperors (chs. 18 and 37). Another indication of date is the mention of the profound peace which the Empire is enjoying (ch. 1). The only period between A.D. 176 and the date of Marcus Aurelius' death in A.D. 180 that would adequately fit this reference is 176–177. These dates mark the suppression of the insurrection of Avidus Crassus on the one hand, and the outbreak of the Marcomannic War on the other. Since, too, Athenagoras makes no mention of the violent, though local, outbreak of persecution in Lyons and Vienne,[4] which occurred in the latter part of A.D. 177, we may safely assume that the Plea was written between the end of A.D. 176 and the early part of A.D. 177.

To these calculations two objections have been raised. It has been questioned whether Marcus Aurelius' son is intended by the name Lucius Aurelius Commodus, and it has been suggested that the Plea betrays a faint reflection of the persecution of Lyons and Vienne.

To appreciate the discussion of the first objection, the exact words of Athenagoras' inscription must be borne in mind. He writes, "To the Emperors Marcus Aurelius Antoninus and Lucius Aurelius Commodus, conquerors of Armenia and Sarmatia, and—what is more important—philosophers." Who is Lucius Aurelius Commodus? The title "conqueror of Armenia" properly belongs to Marcus Aurelius' adopted brother, Lucius Aurelius Verus Commodus, not to his son. But the adopted brother can scarcely be meant. He dropped the name Commodus on sharing the government with Marcus Aurelius, and he never bore the title "conqueror of Sarmatia," since this conquest occurred only after his death in A.D. 169. The fact

4 See Eusebius, *Hist. eccl.*, V, ch. 1.

of the matter seems to be that Athengoras associates the son with the father in his honors. This is clear from the fact that both are styled "philosophers." Neither the son nor the adopted brother, for that matter, could have any personal claim to such a title.

The second objection is equally tenuous. It has been urged[5] that, because the same charges of cannibalism and incest are mentioned by Athenagoras and by the letter of the churches of Lyons and Vienne, recording their persecution,[6] and because one other slight similarity can be detected,[7] Athenagoras reflects a knowledge of this letter. In reply it must be observed that such charges were too widespread to indicate Athenagoras' dependence upon that particular document, while the other supposed similarity is too meager to be taken into account. Moreover, had Athenagoras had that letter in mind, he would scarcely have claimed (in ch. 35) that slaves of Christians had never denounced their masters for cannibalism. For at Lyons and Vienne it was slaves who had preferred this very accusation.[8] It may be noted too that the charge of atheism, which forms the main burden of the Plea, does not happen to be mentioned in the letter.

STYLE

Of all the Apologists, Athenagoras is the most eloquent. The arrangement of his material is clear and his argument moves with cogency. His rhythmic style, patterned after that of the Atticists, betrays the self-conscious rhetorician. He has some notable descriptions, and his detailed references to mythology and history, which at times seem irrelevant to his central point, are quite purposeful. They aim to hold the reader's attention by providing interesting information. On the other hand, his style suffers from ellipses, parentheses (of which there are many), and anacolutha. This is partly to be explained by his intention to give his Apology the air of a speech which was actually delivered. This fiction underlies the reference in ch. 11

---

[5] See the edition by P. Ubaldi, pp. xvii, xviii.
[6] Athenagoras, Plea, ch. 3; cf. Eusebius, *Hist. eccl.* V. 1:14.
[7] Athenagoras in ch. 34 retorts to the charge of incest that it is really the immoral accusers of Christians who "outrage human flesh." In the letter (Eusebius, *Hist. eccl.* V. 1:52) a burning martyr cries out, "What you are doing is to eat men."
[8] Eusebius, *Hist. eccl.* V. 1:14.

(see note 35). Athenagoras did not, of course, give his Apology as a public oration in the emperor's presence.

CONTENTS AND PURPOSE

The Plea answers three current charges brought against Christianity—atheism, incest, and cannibalism. It is the first of these with which the large body of the work is concerned (chs. 3 to 30). The others are treated rather summarily at the end (chs. 31 to 36). The case against atheism is the central point, for, with this proved, the moral calumnies are in principle disposed of. This division of material, moreover, reflects the rhetorical skill of Athenagoras. He realized that the attention of his audience would be better held by expanding the first point, while correspondingly contracting the second and third.

The charges themselves were a natural result of the Christian message. To deny the traditional gods, to stand in opposition to the syncretic temper of the age, and above all to claim to practice a religion which dispensed with the most essential mark of ancient religion, viz., sacrifice, could not but have provoked the accusation of atheism. Furthermore, the close association, in the ancient mind, of gods with race and soil must have made it extremely hard for the pagan to take the Christian case seriously. The Christians were not a racial or national group venerating the traditions of their forefathers. The new religion seemed to be undermining every religious sanction of antiquity.

The charges of incest and cannibalism arose from the fact that only the baptized were permitted to attend the Eucharist. What, therefore, was done in secret by such people was quite likely, in the pagan's mind, to be immoral. Moreover, the fragmentary knowledge which the pagan gained by hearsay about the meaning of the Lord's Supper—eating and drinking the body and blood of Christ—quickly led to the suspicion of cannibalism; while the Christian emphasis on love and brotherhood was easily distorted into a cloak for incest.

Athenagoras' aim in the Plea is to show that Christianity is a respectable philosophy, distinguished by a peculiarly high standard of moral conduct. He urges that Christians should be given the same fair treatment accorded other philosophers (ch. 2, *fin.*). They should not be persecuted because of a name. Rather should each be tried on his own merits, and only punished if a real offense is proved. The emphasis laid by Christian

Apologists on their being persecuted because of a name is not so foolish as is sometimes imagined. The name was primary. It had become a symbol of social opprobium, and around it there had gathered a host of wild and unsubstantiated charges. It is true, of course, that what basically underlay the opposition to the name was the Christian refusal to sacrifice to the pagan gods, and notably to the imperial genius. But the Apologists felt that it was the absurd rumors and emotionalism which the name engendered, that prevented their case from being heard with reason. Hence their emphasis on the irrationality of opposing a mere name.

On the question of the imperial cult Athenagoras is shrewdly silent. He has many protestations of loyalty to the emperor, and perhaps hints at his view of the imperial genius in his reference to Antinoüs (ch. 30) and to the gods' having originally been kings (ch. 28). But he naturally refrains from making a clear issue of this point, lest he should endanger the strength of his apology. His intention is to gain a hearing for the Christian case for monotheism. Only then could the current manner of showing loyalty to the Empire be successfully challenged.

To answer the charge of atheism Athenagoras shows that the Christians share their conviction of the unity of God with the great Greek philosophers and poets. Here was the point at which Christianity could relate itself to the finest spirit of antiquity, and so win a hearing. Proceeding from this, Athenagoras demonstrates the unique elements in the new faith, viz., the doctrine of the Trinity and the high moral life of the Christians; and he continues by showing the weaknesses in the traditional religion with its sacrifices and mythology.

Philosophy and Theology

Neither as a philosopher nor as a theologian did Athenagoras possess a creative mind. Nor can he be said to be a profound scholar. He was a Christian rhetorician, combining a graceful style with some originality and considerable knowledge.

He was well acquainted with the leading ideas of the current philosophies and his outlook betrays the essential spirit of the age—eclecticism. Doubtless he had read Homer, Plato, and Herodotus. But the majority of his many citations come (as he himself confesses) from florilegia (see chs. 6 and 33). This was a current practice of rhetoricians. In some cases, where the context was not clear, it could not fail to lead to misconstruction of the original. Notable examples are the first two citations from Euripides in ch. 5. A good deal of ch. 28, along with other notices of pagan theology, is taken from a work by Apollodorus, *On the Gods.* The list of gods in ch. 1 may go back to the same book, though Athenagoras may here have obtained his information secondhand through some skeptical writer who used the references in Apollodorus for polemical purposes. Athenagoras may also be dependent on Plutarch's *Placita* for some of his material. There are a number of similarities, but no exact citations.[9]

Athenagoras shows his originality in several ways. His rational argument for the unity of God (ch. 8) has no parallel in ancient literature, and the references sometimes cited from Cicero and Philo[10] serve only to indicate his independent mind. Again, while he is dependent upon Justin's Apology for many of his ideas, his line of approach is rather different. He does not elaborate the argument from Old Testament prophecy with the endless details and citations we find in Justin. Such references, which consume about a third of Justin's work, were scarcely calculated to convince pagans. Nor does he indulge in Justin's fanciful ideas of Plato's prediction of the cross or of his dependence on Moses. His references to the Old Testament are few, and he has better sensed the temper of his readers by dealing more thoroughly with the current religious notions and their essential weaknesses.

Philosophically Athenagoras is an eclectic. From Plato he derives his ideas of God's essential goodness (ch. 24) and of the primacy of the immaterial (ch. 36). From the Stoics he takes his emphasis on the harmony and order of the world as a proof of God (chs. 4; 5; 16); his contrast of man's unnatural vice with the natural life of beasts (ch. 3); and his psychological explanation of visions (ch. 27). From the Neo-Pythagoreans comes his view of the cosmos, as an enclosed sphere moving in rhythm (ch. 16). He is dependent on the Skeptics for his account of the prolific number and contradictory nature of the cults (chs. 1; 14), and for his conviction that the many conflicting doctrines of philosophy indicate that reason has its limits (ch. 7). In this hospitable attitude toward Greek philosophy and culture Athenagoras shares Justin's view, which stands in marked contrast with that of his Syrian contemporary, Tatian.

[9] Cf. *Placita* 1:8 with Plea, chs. 5 ff.
[10] Cicero, *De nat. Deorum* 1. 37:103, and Philo, *De conf. ling.* 1:425, etc.

Athenagoras owes his theological ideas largely to Justin. From him come the Logos doctrine, his views of prophetic inspiration, resurrection, demonology, angelology, and so on. Unique with Athenagoras, however, is his clear exposition of the Trinity (ch. 10), his careful avoidance of subordinating the Son, his emphasis on chastity, and his condemnation of second marriages (ch. 33). Regarding this latter, it has been contended that Athenagoras here shows the influence of Montanism. But it must be noted that Athenagoras' moral attitudes are not so severe as those of the Montanists, and that an increasing veneration of asceticism was characteristic of the second century.

Apart from a vague and passing reference in ch. 21, Athenagoras makes no mention of the incarnation. This may seem strange to us, for whom this doctrine is central. But we must remember that Athenagoras' purpose is *apologetic*. He is not writing a systematic theology, but defending the faith against certain calumnies. Hence Athenagoras' Christianity cannot be completely reconstructed from his Apology. It is a mistake to imagine that, because the fullness of the faith is not apparent in their works, the Apologists attenuated Christianity by accommodating it to Greek culture. Their first aim was the same as that of the modern missionary—to defend monotheism. That was the prerequisite to establishing the truth of Christianity, and the basis upon which the gospel rested. Hence the Apologists narrowed their sights to concentrate on this fundamental issue, and they leaned on Greek philosophy to make a contact with their readers. If one compares Tertullian's apologetic works with those addressed specifically to Christians, one notes the same approach. The apologetic treatises do not give a whole account of Christianity. Thus, in reading Athenagoras, one must not seek for a full exposition of the faith, or imagine that this one tract contains all that he believed. In short, Athenagoras' Plea should be read for what it claims to be—a defense of practical monotheism. By setting Christianity almost exclusively in this light, the author proved himself a somewhat more astute Apologist than Justin. He sought to show that the new faith corresponded to the best philosophic schools of the day.

MANUSCRIPTS AND BOOKS

The text of Athenagoras' Plea, like that of other Greek Apologies, is far from satisfactorily preserved. All the manuscripts, of which there are many, go directly or indirectly back to the famous Aretas Codex (Paris. Graec. 451[11]). This was written by a scribe, Baanes, in A.D. 914 for the archbishop of Caesarea, Aretas. The archbishop himself corrected the Codex as carefully as possible, adding the accents and breathings, and separating the words that were undistinguished in the original uncial copied by Baanes. This uncial must have contained many errors, and Aretas made numerous emendations which can be differentiated from those of later humanists.

From this manuscript there directly derive Codex Mutinensis III D 7 and Codex Parisinus Graec. 174, both of the eleventh century. From the first of these the Strassburg Codex (Argentoratensis 9), destroyed in the fire of 1870, was copied.

The first edition of the Plea was published by C. Gesner in Zurich, 1557. The text reprinted in Migne, P.G. 6, cols. 887–1024, was by P. Maran, Paris, 1742. Critical notes were added by J. H. Nolte. The edition by J. K. Theodor von Otto, in his *Corpus Apologetarum Saeculi Secundi*, Vol. 7, Jena, 1858, has extensive prolegomena, notes, and indexes.

Modern critical study of the text is dependent on the work of E. Schwartz, "Athenagorae Libellus pro Christianis," in Texte und Untersuchungen, Vol. IV. 2, Leipzig, 1891. The three most

---

11 For this see O. Gebhart, "Der Arethascodex," in Texte und Untersuchungen, Vol. I. 3, Leipzig, 1883. See also Harnack's study, "Die Überlieferung der griechischen Apologeten des II Jahrhunderts in der alten Kirche und im Mittelalter," in Texte und Untersuchungen, Vol. I. 1, 2, Leipzig, 1882.

recent editions are by Johannes Geffcken, *Zwei griechischen Apologeten* (Aristides and Athenagoras), Leipzig, 1907; E. Goodspeed in his *Die ältesten Apologeten*, Göttingen, 1914; and P. Ubaldi, *Athenagoras, La Supplica Per I Christiani, Testo Critico e Commento*, Turin, 1920, second edition, 1933. This was the basis for the edition published by Michele Pellegrino in the Greek series of the Corona Patrum Salesiana, Vol. XV, 1947.

For the translation offered here, Goodspeed's text has been followed. I have not, however, felt obliged to accept all his emendations. At times I have relied on other texts as well as on suggestions in modern translations.

The Plea has been rendered into English by B. P. Pratten in the Ante-Nicene Christian Library, Vol. II, pp. 123–148, Buffalo, 1885. The first English translation was by D. Humphreys, London, 1714. In German there is a translation by P. A. Eberhard in *Frühchristliche Apologeten*, in the second series of the Bibliothek der Kirchenväter, Vol. XII, Kempten and Munich, 1913 (with introduction and useful notes). Most recent is the French rendering by Gustave Bardy, *Athénagore, supplique au sujet des Chrétiens*, Éditions du Cerf, Paris, 1943, in the series Sources chrétiennes. This has excellent introductory material and comprehensive notes. In Italian there is the edition by Michele Pellegrino already mentioned.

Invaluable material for the study of Athenagoras will be found in Johannes Geffcken's edition. While far from sympathetic, it is rich and often incisive in its handling of parallel literature, both pagan and Christian. The article "Athenagoras," by Spenser Mansel in the *Dictionary of Christian Biography*, Vol. I., pp. 204–207, London, 1877, should be consulted, as also the study by G. Bareille in the *Dictionnaire de la théologie catholique*, Vol. I, cols. 2210–2214, Paris, 1903, and especially the one by P. Keseling in the *Reallexikon für Antike und Christentum*, Hiersemann Verlag, Leipzig, 1943, cols. 881–888. An earlier but fundamental work is that by L. Arnould, *De Apologia Athenagorae*, Paris, 1898; while Aimé Puech has devoted a lucid chapter to Athenagoras in his *Les Apologistes grecs*, Paris, 1912. An introductory summary of the general field will be found in Philip Carrington's *Christian Apologetics of the Second Century*, New York, 1921.

There are several special studies dealing with the theology and philosophy of Athenagoras: F. Schubring, *Die Philosophie des Athenagoras*, Berlin, 1882; K. F. Bauer, *Die Lehre des Athenagoras von Gottes Einheit und Dreieinigkeit*, Bamberg, 1902; L. Richter,

Philosophisches in der Gottes- und Logoslehre des Apologeten Athenagoras aus Athen, Mainz, 1905; H. A. Lucks, *The Philosophy of Athenagoras: Its Sources and Value,* Catholic University of America, Washington, 1936.

The following briefer essays may be mentioned: G. Lösche, "Minucius Felix' Verhältnis zu Athenagoras," in *Jahrbücher für protestantische Theologie,* Vol. VIII, pp. 168–178, 1882; A. Pommrich, *Die Gottes und Logoslehre des Theophilus von Antiocheia und Athenagoras von Athen,* pp. 43–61, Leipzig, 1904; J. Lortz, "Das Christentum als Monotheismus in den Apologien des zweiten Jahrhunderts," in *Beiträge zur Geschichte des christlichen Altertums und der Byzantinischen Literatur,* edited by A. M. Köninger, pp. 301–327, Leipzig, 1922; K. von Preysing, "Ehezweck und 2 Ehe bei Athenagoras," in *Theologische Quartalschrift,* pp. 85–110, 1929; and the chapter by V. Spence Little in his *Christology of the Apologists,* pp. 210–228, Duckworth, London, 1934.

A Plea Regarding Christians
by Athenagoras, the Athenian
a Philosopher and a Christian [12]

THE TEXT

To the Emperors Marcus Aurelius Antoninus and Lucius Aurelius Commodus, conquerors of Armenia and Sarmatia, and—what is more important—philosophers:

PREFACE

1. In your Empire, Your Most Excellent Majesties, different peoples observe different laws and customs; and no one is hindered by law or fear of punishment from devotion to his ancestral ways, even if they are ridiculous. A citizen of Troy calls Hector a god, and worships Helen, taking her for Adrasteia. The Lacedaemonian venerates Agamemnon as Zeus, and Phylonoë, the daughter of Tyndareus, under the name of Enodia. The Athenian sacrifices to Erechtheus as Poseidon. The Athenians also perform religious rites and celebrate mysteries in honor of Agraulus and Pandrosus, whom they imagine guilty of impiety for opening the box.[13] In brief, among every nation and people, men perform whatever

---

[12] The word "plea" in the title is sometimes wrongly translated (as by the Latin) "legation" or "embassy." While this is the original meaning of the Greek word *presbeia*, it is used here in the derived sense of a "plea" or "apology." *Owing to the difficulties of the text it has seemed inappropriate to mark every emendation. Only where the text and meaning are in serious doubt has this been noted. Where, moreover, a significant lacuna appears it has been indicated thus*: . . . .

[13] According to the myth, Athena hid the child Erichthonius in a chest, which she gave to Agraulus and her sisters, instructing them not to open it. Stirred by curiosity, they opened the box; whereupon they were driven mad by the sight of Erichthonius' serpentine body.

sacrifices and mysteries they wish.[14] The Egyptians reckon among their gods even cats, crocodiles, serpents, asps, and dogs. And to all these cults both you and the laws grant toleration. For you think it impious and wicked to believe in no god at all; and you hold it necessary for everyone to worship the gods he pleases, so that they may be kept from wrongdoing by fear of the divine. [With us, on the contrary, although you yourselves are not, like the crowd, led astray by rumors, our name is the object of hatred. But names do not deserve to be hated. It is wrongdoing which merits penalty and punishment.] [15]

Accordingly, while everyone admires your mildness and gentleness and your peaceful and kindly attitude toward all, they enjoy equal rights under the law. The cities, according to their rank, share in equal honor, and the whole Empire through your wisdom enjoys profound peace.

But you have not cared for us who are called Christians in this way. Although we do no wrong, but, as we shall show, are of all men most religiously and rightly disposed toward God and your Empire, you allow us to be harassed, plundered, and persecuted, the mob making war on us only because of our name. We venture, therefore, to state our case before you. From what we have to say you will gather that we suffer unjustly and contrary to all law and reason. Hence we ask you to devise some measures to prevent our being the victims of false accusers.

The injury we suffer from our persecutors does not concern our property or our civil rights or anything of less importance. For we hold these things in contempt, although they appear weighty to the crowd. We have learned not only not to return blow for blow, nor to sue those who plunder and rob us, but to those who smite us on one cheek to offer the other also, and to those who take away our coat to give our overcoat as well. But when we have given up our property, they plot against our bodies and souls, pouring upon us a multitude of accusations which have not the slightest foundation, but which are the stock in trade of gossips and the like.

2. If, indeed, anyone can convict us of wrongdoing, be it trifling or more serious, we do not beg off punishment, but are prepared to pay the penalty however cruel and unpitying.

---

[14] The point is that each city worshiped its local heroes and divinities, some of whom were universalized by identification with the Olympian gods.
[15] This section appears to be out of place.

But if the accusation goes no farther than a name—and it is clear that up to today the tales about us rest only on popular and uncritical rumor, and not a single Christian has been convicted of wrongdoing—it is your duty, illustrious, kind, and most learned Emperors, to relieve us of these calumnies by law. Thus, as the whole world, both individuals and cities, shares your kindness, we too may be grateful to you, rejoicing that we have ceased to be defamed.

It does not befit your sense of justice that others, accused of wrongdoing, are not punished before they have been convicted, while with us the mere name is of more weight than legal proof. Our judges, moreover, do not inquire if the accused has committed any wrong, but let loose against the name as if *it* were a crime. But no name in and of itself is good or bad. It is by reason of the wicked or good actions associated with names that they are bad or good. You know all that better than anyone, seeing you are versed in philosophy and thoroughly cultured.

That is why those who are tried before you, though arraigned on the most serious charges, take courage. For they know that you will examine their life and not be influenced by names if they mean nothing, or by accusations if they are false. Hence they receive a sentence of condemnation on a par with one of acquittal. We claim for ourselves, therefore, the same treatment as others. We should not be hated and punished because we are called Christians, for what has a name to do with our being criminals? Rather should we be tried on charges brought against us, and either acquitted on our disproving them or punished on our being convicted as wicked men, not because of a name (for no Christian is wicked unless he is a hypocrite), but because of a crime.

It is in this way, we know, that philosophers are judged. None of them before the trial is viewed by the judge as good or bad because of his system or profession, but he is punished if he is found guilty. (No stigma attaches to philosophy on that account, for he is a bad man for not being a philosopher lawfully, and philosophy is not responsible.) On the other hand, he is acquitted if he disproves the charges. Let the same procedure be used in our case. Let the life of those who are accused be examined, and let the name be free from all reproach.

I must at the outset of my defense beg you, illustrious Emperors, to hear me impartially. Do not prejudge the case through being influenced by popular and unfounded rumor, but apply your love of learning and of truth to our cause. Thus you will not be led astray through ignorance, and we, disproving the uncritical rumors of the crowd, shall cease to be persecuted.

STATEMENT OF THE CHARGES

3. Three charges are brought against us: atheism, Thyestean feasts,[16] and Oedipean intercourse.[17] If these are true, spare no class; proceed against our crimes; destroy us utterly with our wives and children, if anyone lives like a beast. Beasts, indeed, do not attack their own kind. Nor for mere wantonness do they have intercourse, but by nature's law and only at the season of procreation. They recognize, too, those who come to their aid. If, then, anyone is more savage than brutes, what punishment shall we not think it fitting for him to suffer for such crimes?

But if these charges are inventions and unfounded slanders, they arise from the fact that it is natural for vice to oppose virtue and it is in accord with God's law for contraries to war against each other. You yourselves, moreover, are witness to the fact that we are guilty of none of these things, since it is only the confession of a name that you forbid. It remains for you, then, to examine our lives and teachings, our loyalty and obedience to you, to your house, and to the Empire. By doing so you will concede to us no more than you grant to our persecutors. And we shall triumph over them, giving up our very lives for the truth without any hesitation.

REPLY TO THE CHARGE OF ATHEISM

4. We are of course not atheists (I will meet the charges one by one)—and I hope it does not sound too silly to answer such an allegation. Rightly, indeed, did the Athenians accuse Diagoras[18] of atheism, since he not only divulged the Orphic doctrine as well as the mysteries of Eleusis and of the Cabiri and chopped up a statue of Heracles to boil his turnips, but he proclaimed outrightly that God simply did not exist. In our case,

---

16 I.e., cannibalistic feasts, from the legendary banquet where Atreus, in order to avenge the rape of his wife by his brother Thyestes, slew the latter's children and served them to him.

17 I.e., incest, from the legend of Oedipus Rex, who unwittingly killed his father and married his mother.

18 Melian poet of the fifth century B.C.

however, is it not mad to charge us with atheism, when we distinguish God from matter, and show that matter is one thing and God another, and that there is a vast difference between them? For the divine is uncreated and eternal, grasped only by pure mind and intelligence, while matter is created and perishable.

If we shared the views of Diagoras when we have so many good reasons to adore God—the order, harmony, greatness, color, form, and arrangement of the world—we should rightly be charged with impiety and there would be due cause to persecute us. But since our teaching affirms one God who made the universe, being himself uncreated (for what exists does not come into being, only what does not exist), and who made all things through his Word, on two scores, then, we are treated unreasonably—by being slandered and by being persecuted.

WHAT POETS AND PHILOSOPHERS HAVE TAUGHT

5. The poets and philosophers have not been viewed as atheists because they speculated about God. In connection with those whom popular opinion ignorantly calls gods, Euripides expresses his embarrassment thus:

> "If Zeus dwells in heaven
> He should not deal out misfortunes." [19]

But when he gives his view about him who can intelligently be known as God, he says:

> "Do you see him above who embraces
> The boundless sky and the earth with his humid arms?
> Consider him Zeus: regard him as God." [20]

In the case of the former gods he recognized no underlying reality to which the title "god" might be applied. "For who Zeus is, is only a matter of words." [21] He saw too that they were not given their divine names because of real deeds they

[19] Literally, "He should not make the same man unfortunate."

[20] The Greek is ambiguous, and Athenagoras doubtless misconstrued Euripides who meant: "Do you see the boundless ether above, embracing the earth with its humid arms? Consider this Zeus: regard this as divine." The epithet "humid" refers to the ancient belief that the universe was surrounded by water.

[21] A fragment from Euripides. This seems to be what Athenagoras understood by the line. It is more generally translated, "Who Zeus is I know only from hearsay."

had done; and, since they lack reality, what are they more than names?

But the latter God he recognized from his works, understanding that what is seen points to what is invisible. . . . Him, then, who is the source of creation and who governs it by his Spirit, he grasped was God. And Sophocles agrees with him, saying:

"In truth there is one God, one alone,
Who made the heaven and the wide earth." [22]

Hence, with regard to God's nature, which fills the universe with his beauty, Euripides teaches both the necessity of his existence and his unity.

6. Philolaus too, when he says that everything is enclosed by God as in a prison, teaches his unity and his superiority over matter. Lysis and Opsimus [23] define God thus: the former says he is an ineffable number, the latter that he is the difference between the greatest number and the one below it. Since, then, according to the Pythagoreans, the greatest number is ten, that is, the tetractys which contains all the relations of arithmetic and harmony, [24] and the number next to it is nine, God is a unit, that is, one. For the greatest number exceeds that next to it by one. . . .

And now regarding Plato and Aristotle. But first let me note that in going through what the philosophers have said about God, I do not intend to give a full review of their opinions. For I know that as you excel all men in intelligence and imperial power, so you surpass all in your grasp of every branch of learning, mastering them all with more success than those who devote themselves exclusively to one. But as it is impossible without mentioning names to show that we are not alone in limiting the number of the gods to one, I shall rely on collections of maxims.

This is what Plato says: "To discover the creator and father of the universe is difficult, and when you have discovered him it is impossible to tell everybody about him." [25] In speaking thus, Plato views God as uncreated and eternal. And if he recognizes other gods, such as the sun, the moon, and the stars, he recognizes them as created, saying: "Gods that are sons of

22 Not a genuine fragment of Sophocles.
23 The three were Pythagorean philosophers.
24 I.e., by being the sum of one, two, three, and four.
25 *Tim.* 28 C.

gods, I am their creator. I am the father of works which are indissoluble only so far as I will it, for all things which are composed are corruptible." [26] If, then, Plato is not an atheist when he considers the one uncreated maker of the universe to be God, neither are we atheists when we recognize and affirm him to be God by whose Word all things were created and by whose Spirit they are held together.

Aristotle and his followers introduce a single principle, a sort of compound being, composed of body and soul, and say that he is God. They imagine that his body is the ether, the planets, and the sphere of the fixed stars that are propelled in circles. His soul, on the other hand, is the principle whereby the body is set in motion. Though itself unmoved, the soul becomes the cause of the body's moving.

The Stoics, too, actually think God is one, though they multiply names for the divine by the terms they use for the variations of matter, which they say is permeated by God's spirit. For if God is a creative fire, methodically fashioning the world and embracing in himself all the seminal principles by which each thing is produced in accordance with fate, and if his Spirit pervades the universe, then in their doctrine he is one. He is called Zeus with regard to the fervid part of matter, and Hera with regard to the air; while his other titles similarly refer to each special part of matter which he pervades.

7. All philosophers, then, even if unwillingly, reach complete agreement about the unity of God when they come to inquire into the first principles of the universe. We too affirm that he who arranged this universe is God. Why, therefore, are they allowed to speak and write freely about God as they wish, while against us, who can adduce true proofs and reasons for our idea and right conviction of the unity of God, a law is put in force?

Here as elsewhere the poets and philosophers have proceeded by conjecture. They were driven each by his own soul and through a sympathy with the divine spirit to see if it were possible to find out and to comprehend the truth. They were able, indeed, to get some notions of reality, but not to find it, since they did not deign to learn about God from God, but each one from himself. For this reason they taught conflicting doctrines about God, matter, forms, and the world.

We, on the contrary, as witnesses of what we think and believe, have prophets who have spoken by the divine Spirit

[26] *Tim.*, 41 A.

about God and the things of God. And you, who excel others in intelligence and in devotion to the true God, would surely admit that we should be acting unreasonably were we to abandon our belief in God's Spirit, which moved the mouths of the prophets like instruments, and to cling to human opinions.

RATIONAL PROOF FOR GOD'S UNITY

8. To grasp the rational basis of our faith, that from the beginning there was one God who made this universe, look at the matter thus. If there were originally two or more gods, they would share in one and the same being or else each would have an independent being. But for them to share in one and the same being is impossible, since, if they shared the same godhead, they would be alike; but because gods are uncreated they cannot be alike. For it is created things which resemble their patterns, but uncreated things are dissimilar, as they are not created by anyone or for anyone. And if, moreover, it is claimed that, just as hand, eye, and foot are constituent parts of a single body, so God's unity is made up from two or more gods, this is equally false. Socrates, indeed, was compounded and divided into parts, for the very reason that he was created and perishable. But God is uncreated, impassible, and indivisible. He does not, therefore, consist of parts.

But if, on the other hand, each god has an independent being, and the creator of the world is higher than created things and above what he made and arranged, where can a second god or other gods be? For if the world, being made spherical, is confined within the circles of the heaven, and if the creator of the world, though above created things, retains the world in his providence, what place is there for a second god or for others? For such a second god is not in the world since it belongs to another. Nor does he surround the world, since the God who is the creator of the world is above it. If, then, he neither is in the world nor surrounds it, seeing that all space around it is occupied by the creator, where can he be? Is he higher than the world and God: is he in and around another world? If so, then he is no concern of ours, for he does not control this world; nor does he have great power, for he dwells in a limited space. And if he is neither in another world (for all things are filled by the creator), nor around another world (for all space is occupied by the creator), then he does not exist; for there is nowhere where he can be.

What, moreover, would this second god have to do, seeing that another owns the world and that, while he is above the creator of the world, he is neither in the world nor around it? [Is there, then, some other place where he can stand—this god who has arisen in opposition to the true God? But God and what belongs to God are above him. And what place shall he have, seeing that the creator fills the regions above the world?] [27] Would he perhaps exercise providence? Certainly not, unless he were the creator. If, therefore, he does not create or exercise providence, and if there is no place where he can dwell, then from the beginning there has been one God and one alone, the creator of the world.

PROOF FROM SCRIPTURE

9. Were we satisfied with such reasoning, one would think our doctrine was human. But prophetic voices confirm our arguments. Seeing how learned and well-informed you are, I suppose that you are not unaware of Moses, Isaiah, Jeremiah, and the rest of the prophets. Under the impulse of the divine Spirit and raised above their own thoughts, they proclaimed the things with which they were inspired. For the Spirit used them just as a flute player blows on a flute. What, then, did they say? "The Lord is our God: no other can be compared with him." [28] Or again, "I am God the first and the last; and apart from me there is no god." [29] Similarly: "Before me there was no other god, and after me there shall be none. I am God, and there is none besides me." [30] Then, concerning his greatness: "Heaven is my throne and earth is my footstool. What kind of house will you build for me, or in what place shall I rest?" [31] But I leave it to you, when you come on their books, to examine their prophecies in more detail, so that you will have good reason to dispel the false accusations brought against us.

THE TRINITY

10. I have sufficiently shown that we are not atheists since we acknowledge one God, who is uncreated, eternal, invisible, impassible, incomprehensible, illimitable. He is grasped only by mind and intelligence, and surrounded by light, beauty,

---

[27] The sequence of thought is broken by this sentence which repeats the argument of the preceding paragraph and seems out of place here.
[28] Ex. 20:2, 3.   [29] Isa. 44:6.   [30] Isa. 43: 10, 11.   [31] Isa. 66:1.

spirit, and indescribable power. By him the universe was created through his Word, was set in order, and is held together. [I say "his Word"], for we also think that God has a Son.

Let no one think it stupid for me to say that God has a Son. For we do not think of God the Father or of the Son in the way of the poets, who weave their myths by showing that gods are no better than men. But the Son of God is his Word in idea and in actuality; for by him and through him all things were made, the Father and the Son being one. And since the Son is in the Father and the Father in the Son by the unity and power of the Spirit, the Son of God is the mind and Word of the Father.

But if, owing to your sharp intelligence, it occurs to you to inquire further what is meant by the Son, I shall briefly explain. He is the first offspring of the Father. I do not mean that he was created, for, since God is eternal mind, he had his Word within himself from the beginning, being eternally wise.[32] Rather did the Son come forth from God to give form and actuality to all material things, which essentially have a sort of formless nature and inert quality, the heavier particles being mixed up with the lighter. The prophetic Spirit agrees with this opinion when he says, "The Lord created me as the first of his ways, for his works." [33]

Indeed we say that the Holy Spirit himself, who inspires those who utter prophecies, is an effluence from God, flowing from him and returning like a ray of the sun. Who, then, would not be astonished to hear those called atheists who admit God the Father, God the Son, and the Holy Spirit, and who teach their unity in power and their distinction in rank? Nor is our theology confined to these points. We affirm, too, a crowd of angels and ministers, whom God, the maker and creator of the world, appointed to their several tasks through his Word. He gave them charge over the good order of the universe, over the elements, the heavens, the world, and all it contains.

CHRISTIAN MORAL TEACHING

11. Do not be surprised that I go into detail about our teaching. I give a full report to prevent your being carried away by popular and irrational opinion, and so that you may know the truth. Moreover, by showing that the teachings themselves,

[32] *Logikos*, corresponding to *Logos*, "Word."   [33] Prov. 8: 22.

to which we are attached, are not human, but were declared and taught by God, we can persuade you not to hold us for atheists. What, then, are these teachings in which we are reared? "I say to you, love your enemies, bless those who curse you, pray for those who persecute you, that you may be sons of your Father in heaven, who makes his sun to shine on the evil and on the good, and sends his rain on the just and on the unjust." [34]

Although what I have said has raised a loud clamor, [35] permit me here to proceed freely, since I am making my defense to emperors who are philosophers. Who of those who analyze syllogisms, resolve ambiguities, explain etymologies, or [teach] homonyms, synonyms, predicates, axioms, and what the subject is and what the predicate—who of them do not promise to make their disciples happy through these and similar disciplines? And yet who of them have so purified their own hearts as to love their enemies instead of hating them; instead of upbraiding those who first insult them (which is certainly more usual), to bless them; and to pray for those who plot against them? On the contrary, they ever persist in delving into the evil mysteries of their sophistry, ever desirous of working some harm, making skill in oratory rather than proof by deeds their business. With us, on the contrary, you will find unlettered people, tradesmen and old women, who, though unable to express in words the advantages of our teaching, demonstrate by acts the value of their principles. For they do not rehearse speeches, but evidence good deeds. When struck, they do not strike back; when robbed, they do not sue; to those who ask, they give, and they love their neighbors as themselves.

12. If we did not think that a God ruled over the human race, would we live in such purity? The idea is impossible. But since we are persuaded that we must give an account of all our life here to God who made us and the world, we adopt a temperate, generous, and despised way of life. For we think that, even if we lose our lives, we shall suffer here no evil to be compared with the reward we shall receive from the great Judge for a gentle, generous, and modest life.

Plato, indeed, has said that Minos and Rhadamanthus [36] will judge and punish the wicked; but we say that, even if a man

---

[34] Matt. 5:44, 45; Luke 6: 27, 28.
[35] Following a rhetorical device, Athenagoras imagines that his speech has been met by hostile gibes.
[36] Sons of Zeus, and just men who judged the dead.

were Minos or Rhadamanthus or their father, he could not
escape God's judgment.

Then there are those who think that life is this: "Eat and
drink, for tomorrow we shall die." [37] They view death as a
deep sleep and a forgetting—"sleep and death, twin brothers" [83]
[as the saying goes]. And men think them religious! But there
are others who reckon this present life of very little value. They
are guided by this alone—to know the true God and his Word,
to know the unity of the Father with the Son, the fellowship of
the Father with the Son, what the Spirit is, what unity exists
between these three, the Spirit, the Son, and the Father, and
what is their distinction in unity. These it is who know that the
life for which we look is far better than can be told, if we arrive
at it pure from all wrongdoing. These it is whose charity
extends to the point of loving not only their friends, for, the
Scripture says, "If you love those who love you, and lend to
those who lend to you, what credit is it to you?" [39] Since we
are such and live this way to escape condemnation, can anyone
doubt that we are religious?

These points, however, are trifles from a great store, a few
taken from many, lest we should trouble you further. For
those who test honey and whey judge by a taste if the whole is
good.

The Problem of Pagan Sacrifices

13. Since many of those who charge us with atheism do not
have the vaguest idea of God, being unversed in, and ignorant
of, physics and theology, they measure religion by the observance of sacrifices, and charge us with not having the same gods
as the cities. Heed what I have to say, Your Majesties, on both
these counts. And first about our not sacrificing.

The creator and Father of the universe does not need blood
or the smell of burnt offerings or the fragrance of flowers or
incense. He himself is perfect fragrance. He lacks nothing and
has need of nothing. But the greatest sacrifice in his eyes is
for us to realize who stretched out the heavens in a sphere,
who set the earth in the center, who gathered the water into
seas and separated the light from darkness, who adorned the
sky with the stars and made the earth bring forth all kinds of
seed, who made the animals and fashioned man. When, therefore, we recognize God the creator of the universe, who preserves it and watches over it with the wisdom and skill he does,

[37] Isa. 22:13.   [38] *Iliad* 16: 672.   [39] Luke 6: 32, 34.

and lift up holy hands to him, what need has he then of a hecatomb?

"It is with sacrifices and humble prayer,
  With libation and burnt offering that men implore [the
    gods]
And turn [their wrath], when any has offended or sinned." [40]

What need have I of burnt offerings, when God does not need them? Rather is it needful to present a bloodless sacrifice, to offer a "spiritual worship." [41]

BELIEF IN THE TRADITIONAL GODS

14. Regarding their other charge, that we neither accept nor venerate the same gods as the cities, it is quite senseless. The very ones who accuse us of atheism for not acknowledging the same gods that they believe in are not agreed among themselves about the gods. The Athenians have set up Celeus and Metanira as gods; the Lacedaemonians, Menelaus—they sacrifice to him and keep his festival; the Trojans cannot bear his name,[42] and worship Hector; the Ceans adore Aristaeus, imagining he is identical with Zeus and Apollo; the Thasians worship Theagenes, who committed a murder at the Olympian games; the Samians, Lysander for all his slaughter and wickedness! . . . [43] The Cilicians worship Niobe; the Sicilians, Philip the son of Boutacides; the Amathusians, Onesilus; the Carthaginians, Hamilcar.[44] The day is too short to enumerate the rest.

When, then, they fail to agree among themselves about their gods, why do they charge us with disagreeing with them? Take the case of the Egyptians, is it not ridiculous? On their high feasts in the temples they strike their breasts as if lamenting the dead and then sacrifice to them as if they were gods. And it is no wonder. They worship the brutes as gods, shave themselves when they die, bury them in their temples, and appoint days of public mourning. If we are irreligious for not worshiping the same gods as they, then every city and people is irreligious, for they do not all revere the same gods.

[40] *Iliad* 9: 499–501.   [41] Rom. 12:1, or "reasonable service" (K.J.V.).
[42] Because, being the husband of Helen and king of Lacedaemon, he led the Greek forces in the Trojan War.
[43] The text which here includes the three names Alcman, Hesiod, and Medea is corrupt. The first two are a gloss on the story of Niobe.
[44] Hector, Lysander, Philip, Onesilus, and Hamilcar were military heroes. Aristaeus delivered the Ceans from a drought by erecting an altar to Zeus; hence the identification.

IDOLS AND IDOLATRY

15. But grant that they worship the same gods. What then? Since the populace cannot distinguish between matter and God or appreciate the chasm that separates them, they have recourse to idols made of matter. Shall we, then, who can distinguish and differentiate between uncreated and created, between being and nonbeing, between the intelligible and the sensible, and who call these things by their proper names— shall we, just because of the populace, come and worship statues? If matter and God are identical, two names for the same thing, we are surely irreligious for not thinking that stones, wood, gold, and silver are gods. But if there is a vast difference between them, as great as separates the craftsman and his materials, why are we called to account?

It is like the potter and the clay. The clay is matter, the potter is an artist. So is God the creator an artist, while matter is subject to him for the sake of his art. But as clay cannot by itself become pottery without art, so matter, which is altogether pliable, cannot receive distinction, form, or beauty apart from God the creator. We do not, moreover, reckon pottery of more value than the potter, or bowls or vessels of gold than the artisan. If they have artistic merit, we praise the artist. It is he who reaps the renown for making them. So it is with matter and God. It is not matter which justly receives praise and honor for the arrangement and beauty of the world, but its creator, God. If, then, we were to worship material forms as gods, we should seem to be insensitive to the true God, identifying what is eternal with what is subject to dissolution and corruption.

16. Beautiful, indeed, is the world in its all-embracing grandeur, in the arrangement of the stars, both those in the circle of the ecliptic and those at the Septentrion, and in its form as a sphere. Yet it is not the world, but its maker, who should be worshiped.

For when your subjects come to you, they do not fail to pay their homage to you, their lords and masters, from whom they may obtain what they need. They do not have recourse to the magnificence of your palace. When they come upon the royal residence, they admire it in passing for its beauty and splendor; but it is you whom they honor in every possible way. You emperors, moreover, adorn your palaces for yourselves; but God did not make the world as if he were in need of it. For he is complete in himself, unapproachable light, perfect beauty, spirit, power, reason.

If, then, the world is an instrument in tune, moving in rhythm, I will worship not the instrument but him who makes the harmony, strikes the notes, and sings the accompanying melody. For the judges at contests do not disregard the lute players and crown the lutes. If, as Plato says, the world is God's artistry, I admire its beauty and am directed to the artist. Or if, as the Peripatetics say, the world is a substance and a body, we do not bow down to "the wretched and weak elements,"[45] neglecting to worship God who is the cause of the body's motion, and adoring passible matter instead of "impassible spirit" (as they call it). Or again, if someone thinks the parts of the world are powers of God, we do not worship and adore the powers, but their maker and Lord.

I will not beg of matter what it cannot give; I will not pass God by to worship the elements, which can do no more than they are bidden. For even if they are beautiful to behold as the work of their maker, yet are they by the nature of matter corruptible. Plato too bears witness to this view when he says: "For the being we have called heaven and earth shares in many blessings from the Father, but it still partakes of a body. Hence it cannot possibly be free from change."[46] If, then, I admire the heaven and the elements for their artistry, I do not worship them as gods, for I know they are subject to dissolution. How much less can I call those objects gods, whose makers I know were men?

RECENCY OF THE NAMES AND STATUES OF THE GODS

17. Hear me briefly on this question. In making my defense I must give more detailed arguments to show that the names of the gods are quite recent, and their statues are, so to say, only of yesterday. You yourselves are thoroughly versed in these things since more than all others and in all details you are familiar with ancient writers.

I say, then, that it was Orpheus, Homer, and Hesiod who gave both genealogies and names to those who are called gods. Herodotus testifies to this: "I think that Hesiod and Homer lived four hundred years before me, no more. It was they who devised a theogony for the Greeks, gave the gods their names, assigned them honors and functions, and described their

[45] Gal. 4:9.   [46] *Politics* 269 D.

forms." [47] Statues of gods, moreover, were unthought of
before the plastic arts, painting and sculpture, were invented.

These arts came in later with Saurias the Samian, Crato
the Sicyonian, Cleanthes the Corinthian, and a Corinthian
girl. Drawing was invented by Saurias when he sketched a
horse in the sun; [48] and painting by Crato when he traced the
outline of a man and a woman in oils on a white surface. It
was the girl who invented relief sculpture. When she fell in
love with a certain man, she traced his outline on a wall while
he was asleep. Her father was so delighted by the extraordinary
resemblance that, being a potter, he embossed the sketch by
filling up the outline with clay. The figure is still preserved in
Corinth. After them Daedalus, Theodorus, and Smilis invented
sculpture and the plastic arts.

Thus images and statuary are of such recent date that we can
name the artist of each god. The image of Artemis in Ephesus,
the one of Athena (or rather of Athela, [49] for that is what those
who speak in a more mystic fashion call her, and that was the
name of the ancient statue made of olive), and another of
Athena seated, are the work of Endoeus, a pupil of Daedalus.
The Pythian god was made by Theodorus and Teleches. The
Delian god and Artemis were fashioned by Tectaeus and
Angelio. The Hera in Samos and the one in Argos are the
handiwork of Smilis. The other images were made by Phidias. [50]
The Aphrodite in Cnidus is a product of Praxiteles, while the
Asclepius in Epidaurus is the work of Phidias.

In a word, there is not one of these statues but has been
made by a man. If, then, these are gods, why did they not
exist from the beginning? Why are they more recent than those
who made them? Why did they need the aid of man and of
art to come into existence? They are nothing but earth, stones,
matter, and paltry art.

THE GODS WERE CREATED

18. Some, however, say that these are only statues, but that
the gods, in whose honor they are made, are real. To them the
processions to the images and the sacrifices have reference.
These actions are directed toward the gods, since there is no
other way of approaching them.

[47] Herodotus, *Hist.* 2:53.　　　　[48] I.e., drew its outline from a shadow.
[49] I.e., "unsuckled," for she sprang without a mother and in full armor
from Zeus's head.　　　　[50] Text and meaning doubtful.

"The direct vision of the gods is hard to bear." [51]

As a proof that this is so these people bring forward the powers which some of the images have. Come then, let us look into the power of their names. But before I proceed I would beg Your Most Excellent Majesties to excuse me if I adduce convincing arguments. It is not my first intention to unmask the idols; rather is it to refute the slanders brought against us. It is for that reason that I set forth the rationale of our principles. Would that you might by yourselves search out the heavenly Kingdom! For to you, father and son, all things are subject, since you have received the kingdom from above. For "the soul of the king is in God's hand," as the prophetic Spirit says. [52] In the same way all things are subject to the one God and to his Word—to his Son, that is—whom we think of as inseparable from him.

This, then, I especially ask you to heed. The gods, as it is generally held, did not exist from the beginning. Each of them was created, just as we were. With this view everyone agrees. Homer, for instance, says,

"Oceanus, the father of the gods and Tethys their mother." [53]

Then take Orpheus. [54] He was the first to give the gods names. He recounted their genealogies and their several exploits, and is viewed by our accusers as a rather reliable theologian. Homer mostly follows him, especially in his references to the gods. He asserts that they owed their origin to water: "Oceanus, who is the origin of everything." For, according to him, water was the beginning of everything.

From water mud was formed; and from these an animal was produced, a dragon that had on it a lion's head and a bull's head, and in between the face of a god. It was called Heracles and Kronos. This Heracles gave birth to an enormous egg, which through the power of its father got bigger and bigger and by friction was burst into two. The top part came to be the Heaven (Ouranos); the lower became Earth (Gē). Thus there came forth a divine being with two bodies. Ouranos had intercourse with Gē and begat the females, Clotho, Lachesis, and Atropos, [55] and the males, Cottys, Gyges, and Briareus, all hundred-handed, [56] and the Cyclopes—Brontes,

---

[51] *Iliad* 20: 131.   [52] Prov. 21:1.

[53] *Iliad* 14: 201, 302.

[54] Legendary musician and prophet of Thrace, to whom is ascribed the verse comprising the doctrines and myths of Orphism.

[55] I.e., the Fates.   [56] I.e., the Giants.

Steropes, and Arges. These he bound and hurled to Tartarus, because he had learned from the beginning that he would be dethroned by his children. Whereupon Earth in her rage gave birth to the Titans.

" The godlike Gaia bore sons to Heaven,
  Who bear the name of Titans,
  Because they took vengeance on the great starry
    Heaven."[57]

19. Such is the origin of their gods and of the universe. Now what are we to make of this? For each of the beings to whom they attribute divinity has had a beginning.[58] If they did not exist before they were created (as those claim who attribute divinity to them), then they do not exist now. For either a thing is uncreated and eternal, or it is created and corruptible.

What I am saying is not at variance with what the philosophers say. "What is that which is eternal and has no origin; or what is that which is created and never truly existed?"[59] Plato is here discussing the intelligible and the sensible. He teaches that the eternal, the intelligible, is uncreated, while the sensible has a beginning and an end. In the same way the Stoics contend that the universe will be burned up and exist all over again; and so the world will have a new beginning.

Moreover, suppose we grant their thesis of two principles, one active and governing, which is providence, the other passive and changeable, which is matter. Then the world, even though subject to providence, cannot remain unchanging, because it is created. How, then, can the nature of the gods remain unaltered, when they do not have essential being but are created? And wherein are the gods superior to matter, since they derive their nature from water? But not even water, according to them, is the origin of everything. For what could be constituted from simple and homogeneous elements? Moreover, matter requires an artisan, and an artisan matter. Or how could statues exist without both matter and artisan? On the other hand, it is unreasonable that matter should be older than God: for the efficient cause must necessarily precede what is created.

[57] Fragment of Orpheus. There is a pun on "Titans" (*Titēnas*) and "took vengeance" (*tisasthēn*).
[58] The text of this sentence and the preceding one is corrupt. This is roughly the sense.
[59] Plato, *Tim.* 27 D.

THE FORMS AND EXPLOITS OF THE GODS

20. I would pass on to the other charges [our accusers bring against us], did the absurdity of their theology reach no farther than the statement that the gods derive their nature from water; for I have already shown that there is nothing created which is not subject to dissolution. But they go farther and describe their bodies. They speak of Heracles as a god in the form of a coiled-up dragon. Others are hundred-handed. The daughter of Zeus, born of his mother Rhea who is also named Demeter, has two eyes in their natural place and two others in her forehead. In addition, she has the face of an animal on the back part of her neck, and horns as well. Hence Rhea, terrified at such a monster for a child, fled from her and withheld her breast. For this reason she is mystically called Athela,[60] though more usually Persephone and Kore. She must not, however, be confused with Athena, who is named "Kore" from her virginity.[61]

They have, furthermore, described their exploits with a wealth of supposed detail. They say that Kronos castrated his father, and hurled him out of a chariot. They tell, too, how he murdered his children and swallowed the male ones. Zeus bound his father and cast him into Tartarus, just as Ouranos did to his sons. He warred against the Titans for supremacy, and persecuted his mother Rhea for refusing to marry him. When, indeed, she became a dragon, he changed himself into one, bound her with the so-called Herculean knot, and raped her. The rod of Hermes is a symbol of that union. Then he raped his daughter Persephone, this time also taking the shape of a dragon. From her he had the child Dionysus.

In the light of these fables, I must say just this: what is so noble or valuable in these tales as to make us believe that Kronos or Zeus or Kore or the rest of them were gods? Is it the descriptions of their bodies? What man of judgment and reflection would believe a snake was begotten by a god? Yet Orpheus writes:

"Phanes begat another fearful offspring
   From the sacred womb, a viper terrible to see,
   With hairs on its head and with a face of beauty;
   But the rest of its body was like a dreadful snake
   From the top of the neck."

[60] I.e., unsuckled.   [61] "Kore" means girl, damsel.

Or who would admit that Phanes himself, the first-born god who sprang from the egg, had the shape of a dragon or was swallowed by Zeus so that Zeus might be illimitable? If these so-called gods differ in no way from the vilest animals, then they are not gods, for it is obvious that the divine must be distinguished from what is earthly and derived from matter. And how could we pay them homage when they have the same origin as cattle, are shaped like the brutes, and are ugly as well?

THE PASSIONS OF THE GODS

21. Were they content to say that flesh, blood, procreation, and the passions of wrath and lust belonged to the gods, even then their opinions would have to be regarded as silly and ridiculous. For wrath, lust, passion, and procreation are not appropriate to God. Let them be corporeal; but they should at least be above rage and anger, so that Athena will not be seen:

"Angry with father Zeus, and a wild rage seizes her;"[62]

or Juno appear thus:

"Juno's breast could not contain her rage, and she spoke thus. . . ."[63]

They should surely be above this kind of grief:

"O shame! It is a man dear to me that with my eyes I see
Pursued around the rampart, and my heart grieves."[64]

For even men who give way to rage and grief I call dense and stupid.

When the father of men and of gods bewails his son thus:

"Woe, woe is me, that fate decrees that Sarpedon,[65] most
dear to me of men,
Should be slain by Patroclus, the son of Menetius,"[66]

and when he cannot by his lament ward off the danger:

"Sarpedon, son of Zeus; but Zeus does not defend his son,"[67]

who would not accuse them of ignorance, who by such myths pretend to love God, but are rather atheists?

---

[62] *Iliad* 4:23. [63] *Ibid.*, 4:24.
[64] *Ibid.*, 22:168, 169. The reference is to Hector.
[65] A commander in the Trojan war, who was killed by Patroclus and mourned by his father Zeus.
[66] *Iliad* 16:433, 434. [67] *Ibid.*, 16:522.

Or again, let the gods be corporeal; but surely Aphrodite
should not be wounded in the body by Diomedes:
"Diomedes, the daring son of Tydeus, has struck me." [68]
[Nor should Hephaestus be wounded] in the heart by Ares:

"Because I am lame, Aphrodite the daughter of Zeus
Ever dishonors me, and loves Ares the destroyer." [69]

[Or again, should Ares whom Diomedes wounded]—he

"tore through the beautiful flesh" [70] —

[should Ares,] fierce in battle, and the ally of Zeus against the
Titans, be weaker than Diomedes?
[Or again,]

"He raged, like Ares brandishing his spear." [71]

Hush, Homer! Gods do not rage. You tell me, too, this god is
bloodstained and the bane of men:

"Ares, Ares, bane of mortals, stained with blood." [72]

You describe his adultery and his bonds:

"Scarcely had they reached the bed and gone to sleep, when
          round them both
The ingenious net of cunning Hephaestus fell
So that they could not move a limb." [73]

Do they not pour out at length such impious nonsense about
the gods? Ouranos is castrated, Kronos is bound and hurled
down to Tartarus, the Titans revolt, Styx dies in battle (they
even represent the gods as mortal!), they fall in love with
each other and with men:

"Aeneas, born of Anchises and divine Aphrodite,
When the goddess lay witha mortal in the gorges of Ida." [74]

Are they not in love? Do they not suffer? If they were truly
gods, desire would not touch them. . . . But even if a god takes

[68] *Iliad* 5:376.
[69] *Odyssey* 8:308, 309. To clarify the text the name of Hephaestus has
been inserted.
[70] *Iliad* 5: 858. A lacuna in the text has been filled out with the reference
to Diomedes.   [71] *Ibid.*, 15:605.   [72] *Ibid.*, 5:31.
[73] *Odyssey* 8: 296–298. Two stories are interwoven. Diomedes, who took
a prominent part in the Trojan War, wounded both Aphrodite, daughter
of Zeus, and Ares, ally of Zeus, by the help of Athena. Hephaestus, the
lame god of the forge, set a trap about his couch, capturing Aphrodite,
his unfaithful wife, and Ares, her lover.   [74] *Iliad* 2:820, 821.

flesh for a divine purpose, must he become a slave of lust like this:

> "Never has such love for goddess or for woman
> Filled my breast or overcome my soul.
> Not even when I loved the wife of Ixion,
> Or Danaë with beautiful ankles, the daughter of Acrisius,
> Or the daughter of the far-famed Phoenix,
> Or Semele, or Alcmena in Thebes,
> Or Demeter, the queen with the lovely tresses,
> Or glorious Leto, or even thyself." [75]

He is a creature. He is corruptible. There is nothing divine about him.

These gods even hire themselves out to men:

> "O halls of Admetus, where I endured
> To be content with a menial table, though I was a god." [76]

They even feed cattle:

> "On coming to the land, I tended cattle for my host,
> And looked after this house." [77]

Admetus, thus, was superior to the god. O prophet, [78] you who are wise and who foresee the future for others, you did not predict the murder of your beloved. But with your own hand you slew him, dear as he was: [79]

> "And I had hoped that the divine mouth of Apollo
> Had been full of truth and poured forth oracles." [80]

Thus Aeschylus ridicules Apollo for being a false prophet:

> "This god who sings, who is here at the feast,
> Who says these things, it is he who has murdered
> My son." [81]

---

[75] *Ibid.*, 14:315-327, a speech of Zeus to Hera.

[76] Euripides, *Alcestis* 1, 2. As punishment for killing the Cyclopes, Apollo was banished from heaven and made to serve the table and tend the cattle of the mortal Admetus.

[77] *Ibid.*, 8, 9. [78] The reference is to Apollo.

[79] The boy Hyacinthus, loved by both Apollo and Zephyrus, was struck on the head and killed by a discus, hurled by Apollo at play. Out of jealousy Zephyrus (the West Wind) had diverted it to this end.

[80] A fragment of Aeschylus.

[81] *Ibid.* The lines are put into the mouth of Thetis and refer to Apollo's responsibility for the death of Achilles. See Plato, *Republic* 2. 383B.

The Natural Theology of the Myths

22. But perhaps this sort of thing is poetic license, and there is a natural explanation of it, such as this by Empedocles:

"Zeus is brightness, and Hera source of life, along with Aïdoneus
And Nestis who bathes with tears the eyes of mortals."

If, then, Zeus is fire, Hera the earth, Aïdoneus the air, and Nestis water, and these (fire, water, and air) are elements, then none of them—Zeus, Hera, or Aïdoneus—is a god. For the nature and origin of these elements is derived from God's separating matter into its different parts:

"Fire and water and earth and the gentle height of the air,
And love along with them. . . ."

How can anyone call those things gods which need love in order to exist and which collapse through discord? According to Empedocles, love is primary. Compounds are derived from it, and it is the governing principle. In this way, if we identify the power of the principle with the power of what is derived from it, we unintentionally equate God, who is uncreated, eternal, and ever self-harmonious, with matter, which is corruptible, fluctuating, and changeable.

According to the Stoics, Zeus is the fiery substance, Hera the air (you get this by doubling the name), and Poseidon is water.[82] Others give different natural explanations. Some hold that Zeus is the air and has a double nature, masculine and feminine. Others contend that he is the time of year which brings mild weather, whence he alone escaped from Kronos.[83]

To the Stoics, however, we may reply as follows: You think that there is one God above, uncreated and eternal, and that there are a number of compounds into which matter is changed. You say, furthermore, that the spirit of God pervades matter and takes on different names in accordance with its variations. Hence the forms of matter constitute God's body. These forms and the names of God with them must eventually be done away with, since the elements will be destroyed by fire. Only the spirit of God will then remain. But who, in the light of this,

[82] There are puns on all these names: Zeus from *zeō* (boil), Hera from *aēr* (air: if the name Hera is doubled [*ēraēra*] *aēr* appears in the middle), and Poseidon from *posis* (drink).

[83] There is a play on the word for "time" (*chronos*).

would believe those bodies to be gods whose material changes end in destruction?

Then, again, there are those who say that Kronos is time and Rhea earth. (The myth goes that she became pregnant by Kronos and gave birth, and so is viewed as the mother of all; and that he bore children and devoured them.) They explain the castration [in the myth] as intercourse between male and female, which cuts off the sperm and casts it into the womb and begets a human being who has sexual desire (i.e., Aphrodite) in himself. They further expound the madness of Kronos as the change of season, which brings destruction to animate and inanimate things alike. The bonds [of Kronos] and Tartarus [84] are time which changes with the seasons and disappears. To all this we reply: if Kronos is time, he changes. If he is the seasons, he alternates. If he is darkness or ice or moisture, they all pass away. But the divine is immortal, immovable, and immutable. Hence neither Kronos nor his idol is God.

And concerning Zeus again, if he is the air created by Kronos whose male part is Zeus as Hera is his female part (whence she is both his sister and his wife), then he is subject to change. If he is the seasons, he varies. But the divine never changes or alters.

But why should I trouble you further with such accounts? You are well acquainted with the views of those who adduce these natural explanations. You know what the different writers have thought about the nature of the gods. About Athena, whom they consider to be the wisdom which pervades all things. Or about Isis, who they say is eternal being from which all are derived and through which they continue to exist. Or about Osiris, who was murdered by his brother Typhon, . . . and whose limbs Isis searched for with her son Horus. On finding them, she buried them in a tomb which is still called "Osiriake."

Since these thinkers are forever concentrating on the forms of matter, they miss the God who is known only by reason. They make gods out of the elements or parts of them, at different times giving them different names. Osiris, for instance, is the sowing of the wheat. For this reason, so they say, when his members or the ears of wheat are discovered in the course of the mysteries, Isis is thus addressed: "We have found, we

[84] The reference is to Kronos, whom his son, Zeus, bound and hurled into Tartarus.

rejoice." Again, Dionysus is the fruit of the vine. . . . Semele is the vine itself, while the thunderbolt [of Zeus] is the sun's warmth. [85]

In fact, those who make real gods out of the myths do everything rather than form a true theology. For they fail to realize that by the very defense they make of their gods, they only confirm the reproaches brought against them. For what have Europa, the Bull, the Swan, and Leda to do with the earth and the air, so that Zeus's foul intercourse with these women should represent the relation of the earth to the air? The greatness of God escapes them and they are incapable of exercising their reason, for they have no sympathy for the heavenly realm. Bound to the forms of matter, they fall so low as to deify the changes of the elements. They resemble a passenger who would take the place of the helmsman and steer the boat in which he sailed. And as a ship without its helmsman is no longer serviceable, no matter how well it is fitted out, so the elements, though set in careful order, are of no avail without God's providence. For a ship does not sail by itself, and the elements are not set in motion apart from the creator.

Why Some Statues Have Power

23. Since you surpass all men in understanding, you may ask, "Why is it that some of the idols have power, if the gods to whom these statues are erected do not exist?" For it is unlikely that lifeless and motionless images should have any power by themselves without someone being responsible.

We do not deny that in different places, cities, and nations, some mighty acts have been done in the name of idols. We do not, however, imagine that they are gods who bring about these effects, whether for the benefit of some or for the harm oɩ others. Rather have we made a careful inquiry why it is that you think the idols have power, and who it is that do these things, masquerading under the names of the gods. In proceeding to show who they are that act in the name of the idols, and that they are not gods, I will have to avail myself of some testimonies from the philosophers.

The first of these is Thales. According to those who have studied him thoroughly, he distinguishes between God, demons, and heroes. God he recognizes as the cosmic Intelligence. By demons he understands beings with living souls. He thinks

[85] I.e., that ripens the vine.

that heroes are separated souls of men, the good ones being good souls and the bad ones evil souls.

Plato, for his part, while not agreeing in other respects, also distinguishes between the uncreated God, the beings created by the uncreated to adorn the heaven (the planets and the fixed stars, that is), and the demons. Concerning the latter he does not himself claim a right to speak, but thinks it proper for us to heed what others have said about them.

"Concerning the other demons," he writes, "to tell and to know their origin is beyond our capacity. But we should trust those who have spoken about them before us, and who, they say, are descendants of the gods. For they obviously must have been well acquainted with their parents. We cannot, therefore, disbelieve the sons of gods even though they speak without plausible and convincing proofs. Rather must we, in accordance with custom, believe them, since they profess to speak about their family affairs. Let us then, hold their view of the origin of these gods, which we will now propound. Oceanus and Tethys were the offspring of Gē and Ouranos. From them came Phorcus, Kronos and Rhea, and the rest. From Kronos and Rhea came Zeus, Hera, and all those who are said to be their brothers. From them in turn came other descendants." [86]

Now Plato understood that God was eternal and to be grasped by intelligence and reason. He declared his attributes, how he is essential being, how he has a single nature and is the source of goodness, which is truth. He discoursed about the primal power, . . . [and said:] "All things encircle the King of the universe. They exist because of him and he is the cause of everything." He told further about a second and third cause, "the second surrounding the second realm, the third surrounding the third." [87]

Would such a man imagine that to learn the truth of those beings which are said to be derived from sensible things, i.e., from the earth and the heaven, was something beyond his capacity? Certainly not. He was unable to admit or to teach that gods were born; and for two reasons he said that it was beyond his capacity to know or express anything about the origin of the other demons. It was impossible for him to imagine that the gods either begat or were begotten, since everything created comes to an end. It was even more impossible to change the opinions of the multitude who accepted the myths uncritically.

[86] *Tim.* 40 D–E. [87] Plato, 2 *Epist.* 312 E.

Plato makes this further statement: "Zeus, the great sovereign in heaven, driving his winged chariot, is the first to go forth, setting all things in order and giving heed to them. There follows him a host of gods and demons." [88] This does not have reference to the Zeus who is said to be born of Kronos. For in this passage the name is used of the Creator .of the universe. Plato himself makes this clear. As he had no other way of addressing him, he used the popular title, not as if it were really appropriate for God, but for the sake of clarity. For it is not possible to explain fully about God to everyone. He also added the epithet "great," so as to distinguish the heavenly Zeus from the earthly, the uncreated from the created. The latter is younger than heaven and earth, and younger even than the Cretans who stole him away so he would not be slain by his father. [89]

The Christian View of Demons

24. Since you have looked into all such arguments, why should I mention the poets or review other opinions? But let this suffice. Even if the poets and philosophers had not recognized the unity of God and explained these so-called gods sometimes as demons, sometimes as matter, and sometimes as men who once lived, would there be any good reason for persecuting us, because we distinguish between God and matter and between their essences?

We speak of God, of the Son, his Word, and of the Holy Spirit; and we say that the Father, the Son, and the Spirit are united in power. [90] For the Son is the intelligence, reason, and wisdom of the Father, and the Spirit is an effluence, as light from fire. In the same way we recognize that there are other powers which surround matter and pervade it. Of these there is one in particular which is hostile to God. We do not mean that there is anything which is opposed to God in the way that Empedocles opposes strife to love and night to day in the phenomenal world. For even if anything did manage to set itself up against God, it would cease to exist. It would fall to pieces by the power and might of God. Rather do we mean that the spirit which inhabits matter is opposed to God's goodness,

[88] *Phaedr.* 246 E.
[89] According to a Cretan myth, the child Zeus was hidden in a cave in order that Kronos might not swallow him.
[90] Text and meaning doubtful.

which is an essential quality with him and coexists with him as color is inseparable from a body and cannot exist without it. I do not mean it is a part of him, but it is a necessary accompaniment which is united and fused with him as red is with fire and blue is with the sky. This opposing spirit was created by God, just as the other angels were created by him and entrusted with administering matter and its forms.

For God made these angels to exercise providence over the things he had set in order. Thus, while he reserved for himself the universal and general providence over everything, the angels exercise a particular providence over the parts entrusted to them.

Just as men have free will to choose good or evil (for you would not praise the good and punish the wicked, if vice and virtue were not in their power), and some turn out diligent in the tasks you give them and others faithless, so it is with the angels. Some—and God created them with free will—remained obedient in the tasks for which they were made and appointed. But others violated their very nature and office. Among them was this prince of matter and its forms, and others who were set in the first firmament. (You will note that we say nothing without authority and speak only of what the prophets have told).[91] These latter angels fell into lusting after virgins and became slaves of the flesh, while the prince of matter became negligent and wicked in managing what was entrusted to him. From those who had intercourse with the virgins were begotten the so-called giants. That even the poets have something to say of the giants should not surprise you. For worldly wisdom differs [from divine][92] just to the measure that truth differs from plausibility. While the one is of heaven, the other is of earth; yet, according to the prince of matter himself, "We know how to tell many lies that resemble the truth."[93]

25. Those angels, then, which fell from the heavens, haunt the air and the earth and are no longer able to rise to heavenly things. Along with the souls of the giants, they are the demons which wander about the world. Of these there are two classes: the demons proper,[94] who act in accordance with the natures they have received; and the angels, who act in accordance

---

[91] The reference is to Gen. 6:1–4.
[92] Text and meaning doubtful.
[93] Hesiod, *Theog.* 27. The point is that the poets say some things about the giants which resemble the truth.
[94] I.e., the giants.

with the lusts they indulged. The prince of matter, moreover, as is clear from what happened, rules and governs in opposition to the goodness of God.

> "Often has the thought crossed my mind
> That either fate or a demon rules human affairs.
> Beyond hope and beyond justice
> It brings some to banishment from their homes,
> But others to enjoy prosperity." [95]

If Euripides is left speechless by the fact that prosperity and adversity are beyond hope or justice, who, then, so runs earthly affairs that a poet can say:

> "How then, when we see these things, can we say
> That a race of gods exists or laws should be obeyed?" [96]

It was this which led Aristotle to deny that the things below heaven are subject to providence. God's eternal providence, however, is equally over us all:

> "Of necessity the earth, willing or unwilling,
> Brings forth her produce and fattens my cattle." [97]

And in fact, not in fancy, God's particular providence is directed toward the deserving, while everything else is subject to God's providential law of reason according to the common nature of things. It is, however, the demonic movements and operations, coming from the opposing spirit, which produce these chaotic onslaughts. They affect men, some in one way, some in another. They influence them within and without, individually and by nations, separately and in common, both according to the principle of matter and to the principle of harmony with the divine.

For this reason some, who have no small reputation, have imagined that this universe was not constituted in an orderly manner, but is impelled by blind fate. They failed to recognize that there is nothing in the constitution of the whole world which is disorderly or neglected. Each part has its origin in reason, and hence none of them violates its appointed order. Man too, so far as his Maker goes, is a well-ordered being. With regard to the way he is born, it is one and the same for all. With regard to the constitution of his body, it does not overstep its appointed bounds. With regard to the end of his life, he

[95] A fragment of Euripides. The final line is corrupt.
[96] A fragment of an unknown tragedy.   [97] Euripides, *Cyclop.* 332, 333.

shares this in common with all. But so far as their individuality goes, and in view of the influence exerted by the prince [of matter] and his demonic cohorts, men are driven in various directions, although they all share in a common reason.

26. It is, then, these demons we have been talking about that draw men to idols. They are eager for the blood of sacrifices and lick them up. But the gods in whom the crowd delights and after whom the statues are named were really men, as you can tell from the stories about them. The fact, however, that the demons operate under their names is clear from their individual acts. For some engage in castration, as the devotees of Rhea; others stab and slash, as those of Artemis. (Artemis of Tauris even murders all strangers!) But I will pass over those who lacerate themselves with knives and scourges of bones, and the various kinds of demons.

It does not belong to God to prompt acts contrary to nature. Rather,

"When the demon plots against a man,
    He first impairs the mind." [98]

God, on the other hand, is perfect goodness and is always doing good.

But the greatest proof that other beings are at work here than those to whom the statues are erected is afforded by Troas and Parium. The former place has statues of Neryllinus, a contemporary of ours. Parium has statues of Alexander and Proteus. Both the tomb and the statue of Alexander are still in the forum. The other statues of Neryllinus are public ornaments, if indeed you can ornament a city in that way. But one of them is thought to utter oracles and to heal the sick. It is for these reasons that the people of Troas make sacrifices to the statue, anoint it, and set a golden crown on it.

Regarding the statues of Alexander and of Proteus, the latter is also said to utter oracles. This Proteus, you know, is the one who threw himself into the fire near Olympia. In honor of the statue of Alexander ("O luckless Paris, so fair of form but slave of woman!" [99]), public sacrifices and festivals are held as if to a god who heeds prayer. Are we then to say that Neryllinus, Proteus, and Alexander are responsible for these things that

---

[98] An unknown fragment.
[99] *Iliad* 3:39. This verse, referring to the Trojan Alexander or Paris, is mockingly introduced with Alexander of Abonuteichus (described by Lucian) in view.

occur at their statues? Or shall we say the constitution of matter is responsible? But the matter is bronze. What can bronze do by itself—bronze which can be changed into another shape, as Amasis did with his foot pan according to the story in Herodotus? [1] And what can Neryllinus, Proteus, and Alexander do for the sick? For whatever the statue is said to do now, it does while Neryllinus is living and even when *he* gets sick. [2]

27. What then? In the first place, the irrational powers of the soul, which produce fantasies, bring forth all kinds of images. Some they derive from matter. Others they form and project by themselves. The soul experiences this especially when it partakes of the spirit of matter and is mingled with it. It then ceases to fix its eyes on heavenly things and on its creator. It lowers its vision to earthly things. In a word, it becomes just blood and flesh, and is no longer a pure spirit.

These irrational powers and fantasies of the soul produce visions marked by a passion for idols. A tender and susceptible soul which is ignorant of sound teaching and has no experience in it, having neither contemplated the truth nor reflected upon the Father and Maker of the universe, is easily impressed with false notions of itself. Hence the demons which haunt matter, eager for the smell and blood of sacrifices, and ready to lead men astray, avail themselves of these capacities for fantasy in the souls of the multitude. Occupying their minds, they pour visions into them, making it seem as if these came from the idols and statues. Moreover, in whatever ways the soul, because of its immortality, is moved by reason to foretell the future or to heal the present, the demons reap the glory of them all.

THE GODS WERE ORIGINALLY MEN

28. Perhaps it is necessary, in the light of what we have been saying, to add a word about the names of the gods. Herodotus and Alexander the son of Philip, in his letter to his mother, say that they learned from the Egyptian priests that the gods had once been men. Each of these authors, by the way, is said to have interviewed the priests in Heliopolis, Memphis, and Thebes. This is what Herodotus writes:

[1] Herodotus, *Hist.* 2. 172.
[2] It would seem that Neryllinus (whoever he was) was still alive. That is evidently the meaning of the phrase, "A contemporary of ours," used above. Proteus and Alexander had died around A.D. 170.

"They indicated, then, that those beings whom the statues represented were of such a nature that they were far from being gods. But before these men, they said, the Egyptians had gods for their rulers. They dwelt with men and one of them was always supreme. The last of these kings was Horus, the son of Osiris, whom the Greeks call Apollo. He deposed Typhon and became the last god to rule over Egypt. Osiris is called Dionysus by the Greeks."[3]

The others, then, as well as Osiris, were kings of Egypt; and it is from them that the Greeks got the names of their gods. Apollo is the son of Dionysus and Isis. The same Herodotus writes, "They say that Apollo and Artemis were the children of Dionysus and Isis, and that Leto became their nurse and savior."[4]

These heavenly beings they had for their first kings. Partly because they were ignorant of true piety toward the divine, and partly in gratitude for their rule, they took them, along with their wives, for gods. "All the Egyptians sacrifice the steers if they are without blemish and the male calves. But they are not allowed to sacrifice the cows, as they are sacred to Isis. The statue of Isis is that of a woman with the horns of a cow, similar to the way the Greeks depict Io."[5]

Who could be more worthy of credence when they make such statements than those in the family succession? For they received, son from father, not only the priesthood but the history of it. It is not likely that the very priests who reverence the idols would be lying when they say the gods were originally men. Herodotus, indeed, might perhaps be put down as a romancer where he tells us that the Egyptians record their gods were once men, since he also said, "I do not intend to relate all that I heard of their sacred history, but only the names of the gods."[6] But since Alexander and Hermes, surnamed Trismegistus, and plenty of others whom I will not mention individually, claim a divine origin for their family, there is no reason whatever to dispute that the Egyptian kings were considered gods.

That the gods were originally men the most learned of the Egyptians indicate. While they regard the air, the earth, the sun, and the moon as gods, they consider the rest of the gods to have been mortal men and think of the temples as their tombs. Apollodorus takes this view in his work entitled *On the*

---

[3] Herodotus, *Hist.* 2. 144.   [4] *Ibid.*, 2. 156.
[5] *Ibid.*, 2. 41.   [6] *Ibid.*, 2. 3.

Gods. Herodotus, furthermore, refers to their sufferings as mysteries. "I have already spoken of the way they celebrate the feast of Isis in the city of Busiris. After the sacrifice all the men and women—vast crowds of them—lament; but in what connection they do this, it would not be right for me to disclose." [7] Had they been gods, they would have been immortal. But if people lament for them, and it is their sufferings which constitute mysteries, then they are men.

This same Herodotus further remarks: "In Sais, in the temple of Athena, there is a tomb erected in honor of the god whose name religious scruples forbid me to mention in this connection. It stands behind the sanctuary and extends the whole length of its wall. There is a lake there, which is beautifully encircled with a stone edging. Its size, I imagine, is that of the lake in Delos which we call The Circle. It is in this lake that the Egyptians at night perform representations of his passion, which they refer to as mysteries." [8] They show you there not only the tomb of Osiris, but also his mummy. "When a corpse is brought to them, they show the bearers wooden images of corpses, realistically painted. The most perfect of them is said to be that of the god whose name I must not, for religious reasons, disclose in this connection." [9]

29. The Greek poets and historians have this to say about Heracles:

"In his cruelty, respecting neither the vengeance of the
    gods nor the table
His host proffered him, he slew him forthwith," [10]

i.e., Iphitus. Such a person deserved to go mad, and appropriately lighted a funeral pyre and burned himself to death.

Of Asclepius, Hesiod writes:

"The father of men and of gods
    Was wroth, and hurling the dear son of Leto from Olympus
He slew him with the smoking thunderbolt,
    Arousing anger . . . " [11]

---

[7] Herodotus, *Hist.* 2. 61. The reference here and in the two following citations is to Osiris.

[8] *Ibid.*, 2. 170.

[9] *Ibid.*, 2. 86.

[10] *Odyssey* 21:28, 29.

[11] A fragment of Hesiod. The end is corrupt.

And Pindar:

"But even wisdom is tied to gain.
The gold seen in the hand perverted even him with its
    splendid bribe.
Therefore the son of Kronos hurled from his two hands the
    thunderbolt
That destroyed forthwith the breath of his lungs.
The flaming thunderbolt brought death." [12]

Had they been gods, they would not have hankered after gold:

"O gold, the fairest prize of mortals!
For neither mother nor children can offer equal delights;" [13]

for the divine is in need of nothing and is above desire. Nor would they have died.

But if they are not gods, then they were originally men—and bad ones at that, being ignorant and slaves of money. Why should I speak at length recalling Castor or Pollux or Amphiaraus? They are thought to be gods; yet they were men, born of men, so to say, only the other day. Why should I mention them when Ino, despite her madness and the sufferings consequent upon it, is taken for a goddess?[14] Of her they say, "Wanderers on the sea invoke her as Leucothea." [15] And of her son, "By sailors he is called holy Palaemon." [16]

30. These people, then, detestable as they were and hating God, nonetheless got the reputation of being gods. The daughter of Derceto,[17] Semiramis,[18] a lascivious and blood-stained wench, was hailed as a Syrian goddess. The Syrians even worship fishes because of Derceto, and pigeons because of Semiramis. (For according to the myth in Ctesias the impossible happened, and a woman was changed into a pigeon!) What

---

[12] *Pyth.* 3. 54, 55, 57, 58. Upon the death of her lover, Hippolytus, Artemis bribed Asclepius with gold to restore him. In succeeding, Asclepius was slain by Zeus for interfering with the established order of nature.

[13] A fragment of Euripides.

[14] Because Ino had nursed Dionysus, Hera drove her mad. Whereupon she leaped into the sea with Melicertes, her son.

[15] An unknown fragment.   [16] An unknown fragment.

[17] A Syrian fertility goddess who, according to the myth, fell into a lake and was changed into a fish.

[18] An Assyrian queen of the ninth century B.C. She was renowned for military exploits and for building Babylon. Tended by doves at her birth, she was finally metamorphized into one.

wonder, then, that some should be called gods by their people on the ground of their rule and sovereignty? Hence the Sibyl (and Plato [19] mentions her) says:

> "This was the tenth generation of mortal men
> Since the flood came upon the first men.
> Kronos and Titan and Japetus then ruled.
> They were the excellent offspring of Earth and Heaven;
> And men gave them these names when they named Earth and Heaven,
> Because they were the first of mortal men." [20]

What wonder, too, that others, such as Heracles and Perseus, should be called gods on the ground of their strength? and yet others, as Asclepius, on the ground of their skill?

Either their subjects accorded them this honor or else the rulers themselves seized it. Some got the title from fear, others from reverence. Thus Antinoüs [21] had the good fortune to be thought of as a god because of the kindness of your predecessors toward their subjects. And those who lived later accepted these deifications uncritically.

> "The Cretans always lie; for they, O King,
> Have built your tomb, and you are not yet dead." [22]

While you, Callimachus, believe in the birth of Zeus, you disbelieve in his tomb. While you imagine you are hiding the truth, you actually proclaim, even to those who do not realize it, that Zeus is dead. If you see the cave, you call to mind the childbirth of Rhea; while if you see the coffin, you try to obscure the truth that he is dead. For you will not recognize that the only eternal God is uncreated.

CONCLUSION ON THE CHARGE OF ATHEISM

Thus, if the myths about the gods, which the populace and the poets repeat, are false, to reverence them is superfluous. For these gods do not exist if the tales about them are untrue.

---

[19] *Phaedrus* 244 B.   [20] *Orac. Sibyll.* 3. 108–113.

[21] Hadrian's favorite who was tragically drowned in the Nile and deified.

[22] Callimachus, *Hymn. Jov.* 8, 9. The first part of the first line is attributed to Epimenides the Cretan (cf. Titus 1: 12, 13). The verse refers to the tomb of Zeus, the Cretan Zeus being the personification of the cycle of the seasons.

If on the other hand, all these stories about the gods are true—their births, loves, murders, thefts, castrations, thunderbolts—then they no longer exist, since they have ceased to be, just as they originally had no being before they were created. And what good reason is there to believe some of the tales and to disbelieve others, since the poets told them in order to idealize their heroes? For surely those who so magnified them by their stories that they were taken for gods would not have invented their sufferings.

That, therefore, we are not atheists, since we worship God the creator of this universe, and his Word, I have proved as best I can, even if I have not done the subject justice.

Two Further Charges

31. Our accusers have made up the further charges against us of impious feasts and intercourse. They do this to convince themselves that they have grounds for hating us. They imagine, moreover, that by fear they will either draw us away from our present mode of life or else, by the enormity of the accusations, render our princes harsh and implacable. But this is a foolish approach toward those who realize that of old, and not merely in our time, wickedness has a habit of warring against virtue, in obedience to some divine law and principle. Thus, for instance, Pythagoras with three hundred companions was put to the flames. Heraclitus and Democritus were banished, the one from the city of Ephesus, the other, charged with insanity, from Abdera. Finally, the Athenians condemned Socrates to death. And just as the virtue of these men suffered no whit from the opinions of the mob, so our uprightness of life is in no way obscured by the reckless calumnies of some persons. For we are in good standing with God.

Nonetheless, I will meet these charges too, although I am very confident that I have made my case by what I have already said. You, who are more intelligent than others, know that those who faithfully regulate their lives by reference to God, so that each of us stands before him blameless and irreproachable, will not entertain even the thought of the slightest sin. Were we convinced that this life is the only one, then we might be suspected of sinning, by being enslaved to flesh and blood and by becoming subject to gain and lust. But since we realize that God is a witness day and night of our thoughts and our speech, and that by being pure light he can see into our very hearts, we are convinced that when we depart this present life we shall live another. It will be better than this one, heavenly, not earthly. We shall live close to God and with God, our souls steadfast and free from passion. Even if we have flesh, it will not seem so: we shall be heavenly spirits. Or else, if we fall along with the rest, we shall enter on a worse life and one in flames. For God did not make us like sheep and oxen, a bywork to perish and be done away with. In the light of this it is not likely that we would be purposely wicked, and deliver ourselves up to the great Judge to be punished.

The Charge of Incest

32. It is nothing surprising that our accusers should invent the same tales about us that they tell of their gods. They present their sufferings as mysteries; and, had they wanted to judge shameless and indiscriminate intercourse as a frightful thing, they should have hated Zeus. For he had children from his mother, Rhea, and his daughter Kore, and married his own sister. Or else, they should have detested Orpheus, who invented these tales, because he made Zeus even more unholy and wicked than Thyestes. For the latter had intercourse with his daughter in pursuance of an oracle, and because he wanted to gain a throne and avenge himself.

But we, on the contrary, are so far from viewing such crimes with indifference [23] that we are not even allowed to indulge a lustful glance. For, says the Scripture, "He who looks at a woman lustfully, has already committed adultery in his heart." [24] We may look only on those things for which God created the eyes to be our light. For us a lustful glance is adultery, the eyes being made for other purposes. How, then, in the light of this and of the fact that we shall be called to account for even our thoughts, can it be doubted that we exercise self-control?

We do not have to reckon with human laws, which a wicked man may evade. (At the outset I assured you, Your Majesties, that our teaching came from God.) Rather do we have a law which requires us to have right relations with ourselves and with our neighbors. [25] Hence, according to their age, we think of some as sons and daughters. Others we regard as brothers and sisters, while we revere those who are older as we would

[23] Text and meaning doubtful.   [24] Matt. 5:28.
[25] The text here is corrupt and obscure.

fathers and mothers. We feel it a matter of great importance that those, whom we thus think of as brothers and sisters and so on, should keep their bodies undefiled and uncorrupted. For the Scripture says again, " If anyone kisses a second time because he found it enjoyable . . ." [26] Thus the kiss, or rather the religious salutation,[27] should be very carefully guarded. For if it is defiled by the slightest evil thought, it excludes us from eternal life.

33. Having, therefore, the hope of eternal life, we despise the enjoyments of the present, even the pleasures of the soul. According to our laws, each of us thinks of the woman he has married as his wife only for the purpose of bearing children. For as the farmer casts his seed on the soil and awaits the harvest without sowing over it, so we limit the pleasure of intercourse to bearing children.

You would, indeed, find many among us, both men and women, who have grown to old age unmarried, in the hope of being closer to God. If, then, to remain virgins and eunuchs brings us closer to God, while to indulge in wrong thoughts and passions drives us from him, we have all the more reason to avoid those acts, the very thought of which we flee from. For we center our attention not on the skill of making speeches but on the proof and lessons of actions. We hold that a man should either remain as he is born or else marry only once. For a second marriage is a veiled adultery. The Scripture says, "Whoever puts away his wife and marries another, commits adultery." [28] Thus a man is forbidden both to put her away whose virginity he has ended, and to marry again. He who severs himself from his first wife, even if she is dead, is an adulterer in disguise. He resists the hand of God, for in the beginning God created one man and one woman. But the adulterer breaks the fellowship based on the union of flesh with flesh for sexual intercourse.[29]

34. Since we are such (and why should I speak of such degrading things?), our situation resembles that of the proverb, "The harlot reproves the chaste." Our accusers have set up a market for fornication, have established infamous houses of every sort of shameful pleasure for the young, and do not even spare the males, "males committing shocking acts with

---

26 The source is unknown and the conclusion is wanting.
27 The reference is probably to the kiss of peace in the liturgy.
28 Matt. 19:9; Mark 10:11.
29 Text and meaning doubtful.

males." [30] In all sorts of ways they outrage those with the more graceful and handsome bodies. They dishonor God's splendid creation, for beauty on earth is not self-made, but has been created by the hand and mind of God. It is these people who revile us with the very things they are conscious of in themselves and which they attribute to their gods. They boast of them indeed, as noble acts and worthy of the gods. Adulterers and corrupters of boys, they insult eunuchs and those once married. They even live like fish. For they gulp down whatever comes their way. The stronger chase the weaker. That means they outrage human flesh, even while the laws are in force which you and your forefathers carefully enacted in view of all that is right. To these very laws they do such violence that the governors appointed by you over the provinces are not able to keep order. We, however, cannot refrain from turning the cheek when we are struck, nor from blessing when we are reviled. For it is not enough to be just—justice consisting in returning blows—but we have to be generous and to put up with evil.

The Charge of Cannibalism

35. Since this is our character, what man of sound judgment would say that we are murderers? For you cannot eat human flesh until you have killed someone. If their first charge against us is a fiction, so is the second. For if anyone were to ask them if they had seen what they affirm, none of them would be so shameless as to say he had.

Moreover, we have slaves: some of us more, some fewer. We cannot hide anything from them; yet not one of them has made up such tall stories against us. Since they know that we cannot endure to see a man being put to death even justly, who of them would charge us with murder or cannibalism? Who among our accusers [31] is not eager to witness contests of gladiators and wild beasts, especially those organized by you? But we see little difference between watching a man being put to death and killing him. So we have given up such spectacles. How can we commit murder when we will not look at it, lest we should contract the stain of guilt? What reason would we have to commit murder when we say that women who induce abortions are murderers, and will have to give account of it to God? For the same person would not regard the fetus in the womb as a living thing and therefore an object of God's

[30] Rom. 1:27.   [31] Text and meaning doubtful.

care, and at the same time slay it, once it had come to life.
Nor would he refuse to expose infants, on the ground that those
who expose them are murderers of children, and at the same
time do away with the child he has reared. But we are altogether consistent in our conduct. We obey reason and do not
override it.

Relevance of the Doctrine of the Resurrection

36. What man, moreover, who is convinced of the resurrection would make himself into a tomb for bodies that will
rise again? The same persons would surely not believe that our
bodies will rise again and then eat them as if there were no
resurrection. They would not think that the earth will give back
its dead and then imagine that it will fail to demand those
entombed in them.

On the contrary, those who deny they will have to give
account of the present life, be it wicked or good, who reject
the resurrection and who count on the soul's perishing along
with the body and, so to say, flickering out, are likely to stop
at no outrage. But those who are convinced that God will
look into everything and that the body which has aided the
soul in its unreasonable lusts and passions will be punished
along with it, they have no good reason to commit even the
slightest sin.

But suppose someone thinks it sheer nonsense that the body
which has rotted, decomposed, and been reduced to nothing,
should again be put together. Those who do not believe this
would be wrong in accusing us of wickedness. They should
rather accuse us of folly. For we do not harm anyone by having
mistaken opinions.

It would be out of place here to show that we are not alone
in believing bodies will rise again. Many of the philosophers
have taught this. But we do not want to seem to introduce
matters beyond the scope of our present task. We will not discuss
the intelligible and the sensible and their natures. Nor the
fact that the incorporeal is prior to the corporeal, and the
intelligible precedes the sensible. It is true, of course, that we
first experience the sensible; but the corporeal owes its origin
to the incorporeal by being combined with the intelligible.
The sensible similarly owes its origin to the intelligible.[32]
Even according to Pythagoras and Plato the dissolution of the

[32] Text and meaning doubtful.

body does not prevent it from being reconstructed with the very elements of which it originally consisted.

Conclusion

37. But we must defer our discussion of the resurrection. Now that I have disposed of the charges brought against us and shown that we are religious, kindly, and gentle in spirit, I beg you, grant your royal approval to my request. For in every possible way, by nature as well as education, you are kind, temperate, generous, and worthy of the imperium. And who, indeed, are more justified in getting what they ask than we? For we pray for your authority, asking that you may, as is most just, continue the royal succession, son from father, and receive such increase and extension of your realm that all men will eventually be your subjects. This is to our interest too, "so that we may lead a quiet and peaceable life," [33] and be ready to do all we are commanded.

[33] I Tim. 2: 2.

AN EXPOSITION OF THE FAITH

Selections from the Work Against Heresies by Irenaeus, Bishop of Lyons: "The Refutation and Overthrow of the Knowledge Falsely So Called"

INTRODUCTION

THE GENERAL CHARACTER OF HIS WORK

IRENAEUS OF LYONS OCCUPIES A PARADOXICAL position in the modern study of the Fathers of the Church. Since his great work was first published by Erasmus in 1526, no Christian writer of the age before Augustine has been so frequently called to enter directly into our modern controversies. The result is that his ideas are discussed as ideas and not simply as historical relics of early Christian teaching. This is partly due to his significant, though not wholly clear, references to topics of Church order and New Testament history, and his statements about the authority of Scripture and tradition, matters that have been of current interest ever since the sixteenth century. His evidence for the Eucharistic devotion and liturgical practice of his time is so valuable, and yet so tantalizing, that an eighteenth century scholar was led to amplify this source of information by publishing a few fragments of Irenaeus which he seems to have constructed himself.[1] Yet all these are matters rather incidental in Irenaeus' discussion, introduced as buttresses to his main argument. His main purpose in writing is to establish in clear simplicity the belief in one God which Christianity inherited from Judaism, and the faith in the redemption of the human race through Jesus Christ his only Son. These constitute the specifically Christian gospel, whether in the twentieth century or in the second. It is not surprising that modern theologians invite Irenaeus to give them his support in our modern discussions. One of the works that has been a turning point of modern

[1] The "Pfaffian Fragments"; see A. Harnack, *Die Pfaff'schen Irenäus-Fragmente als Fälschungen Pfaffs nachgewiesen* (Texte und Untersuchungen XX. 3). Leipzig, 1900.

theology calls for a return to the "classic doctrine" of the atonement which he expounded.[2] Again, a recent writer looks to him for a sound statement of the structure of revelation.[3] It is not unnatural that all claim him for their own—a Swedish bishop finds his teaching in harmony with that of Luther,[2] a French Church historian speaks of him as a truly Catholic soul,[4] and an English editor modestly observes that one could easily find in his writings all the articles of the Church of England.[5]

Yet when the student first turns from modern citations of Irenaeus to the actual writings of the bishop of Lyons he is likely to be puzzled and even repelled. Weird systems of fantastic speculation, almost as difficult to understand as to sympathize with, are given careful if not favorable exposition. Moreover, they are refuted by arguments which, when they get beyond general principles, seem often to be based on eccentric interpretations of the Bible, or on attempts at reasoning in which rhetoric is stronger than logic. The profound insights which commentators have found in Irenaeus appear as islands of brilliance in a work which pursues its turgid way, following a general outline to be sure, but often seeming to lose sight of it when the author descends to details.

The greatness of Irenaeus appears all the more clearly when one realizes how fully it was by concentration on the problems of his own day that he made his permanent contribution to Christian thought. The title under which he wrote his great work, The Refutation and Overthrow of the Knowledge Falsely So Called, is both more impressive and a truer reflection of his approach than the prosaic label Five Books Against the Heresies, by which the manuscripts generally describe it. Irenaeus may be considered as the first great systematic theologian of the Church, but he did not write a systematic theology. As his preface indicates, he wrote as a pastor and teacher of the Church, and addressed himself to other pastors to assist them in protecting their flocks from teachings that seriously perverted the gospel or replaced it by a jumble of speculations and encouraged either laxity of conduct or serious misbehavior.

[2] G. Aulén, Christus Victor, tr. A. G. Hebert. S.P.C.K., London, 1931.
[3] L. S. Thornton, Revelation and the Modern World. Black, London, 1950.
[4] J. Lebreton, in J. Lebreton and J. Zeiller, The History of the Primitive Church, tr. E. C. Messenger, 2 vols., Vol. II, p. 690. New York, 1949.
[5] W. W. Harvey, Sancti Irenaei Libros Quinque Adversus Haereses, 2 vols., Vol. I, p.clxxiii. Cambridge, 1857.

The systems that we call Gnostic have this in common, that they found orthodox Christianity, with its straightforward creed, too simple. (Our use of the term "Gnostic" is not exactly Irenaeus', since he seems to use it for the earlier phases of the movement, although it is not clear precisely to what systems he limited it.) They professed at least to give a more complex answer to the riddle of the universe. It might be in terms of a vague world of divine beings, the Fullness or *Plērōma* of deity, the least and feeblest of whom had, as a result of some fatal error, departed from the bright world above and brought into being this physical universe, from which the goal of true wisdom is to escape. Or it might be in terms of dualism, explaining the ambiguities of mortal existence by telling of the conflict of two independent powers, good and evil, or perhaps merely perfect and imperfect. The first of these answers produces the system of Valentinus, the second that of Marcion, and most of the rest may be classified as variations of one or the other. Marcion is of all the leading Gnostics the one who is most definitely a heretic, that is, the leader of a divergent movement within the Christian tradition itself. He is indeed the first founder of a denomination or sect among Christians; in various parts of the Near East Marcionite Churches confronted Catholic for some centuries. In spite of his rejection of the Old Testament, his teaching had a strong Puritan note. His followers became one of the sects, of which the Manichaeans were the most lasting, in which the ascetic was considered to be the only real Christian and the ordinary believer, who had not wholly broken with the world and its affairs, was either denied baptism or treated as little more than a catechumen. Gnostics of the Valentinian type, on the other hand, are scarcely to be listed as Christians, although the names of Jesus Christ, the Father, the Spirit, and other Christian or Jewish terms might be the most concrete elements in otherwise shadowy systems of speculation. They were more likely to be concerned with the difference between matter and spirit than with that between good and evil—or, if they were trichotomists, with a distinction between the physical, the psychic, and the spiritual. Only the higher order mattered, and hence the body was perhaps to be abused, or perhaps to be indulged—in any case it was not to be redeemed. Hence one could not believe that even a lesser deity had really entered into human nature. Christ was perhaps a high power (how much higher, different teachers would express differently) who came upon Jesus at his baptism and left him before his death, thus avoiding the double scandal of the birth from a woman and the death on the cross. Their closest approach to the idea of God present in the man Christ Jesus would be in such words as these:

"The invisible Christ was incorporeal, whereas Jesus was a corporeal or bodily existence. The dual personality, of the seen and the unseen, the spiritual and material, the Christ and Jesus, continued until the Master's ascension, when the human, the corporeal concept, or Jesus, disappeared, while his invisible self, or Christ, continued to exist in the eternal order of Divine Science," [6] though this quotation is from a modern writer.

To Irenaeus the refutation of Gnosticism was primarily a practical and pastoral matter. The background of his writings is the rivalry between sound religion and the vagaries of the esoteric and the occult for the souls of men and also of women. The latter are represented by the good ladies of Irenaeus' own congregation on the banks of the Rhone, who were attracted by the impressive if meaningless ceremonies of a Gnostic conventicle, in which when grace was called down upon the water it visibly turned pink—by some chemical trick, as Irenaeus was sure. [7] Gnostics could not really believe in the incarnation. Therefore they could not really believe in the extension of divine power into human life by sacraments celebrated within this physical order. Least of all could they hope in the resurrection, which proclaimed that the eternal promise of life with God belonged to the body as well as to the soul. In replying to them Irenaeus develops in some detail the interrelation of incarnation, Eucharist, and resurrection. His general line of thought, if not any particular phrase, seems to be the justification for the sentiment which English writers since the seventeenth century have ascribed rather vaguely to the Fathers, that the sacraments are the extension of the incarnation.

THE LIFE OF IRENAEUS

Only a few episodes from the life of Irenaeus are recorded. He first appears as the bearer of a letter from the confessors of Lyons to the church of Rome at the time of the persecution of A.D. 177. He was then already a respected leader of the

[6] Mary Baker Eddy, *Science and Health with Key to the Scriptures*, 52d ed., (Boston, 1891), ch. 5, no. 15 of platform, p. 229.
[7] Irenaeus, I, ch. 13 (unless otherwise noted, refs. are to *Adversus Haereses*).

Church, holding the office of presbyter.[8] He himself tells us that he had personal memories of the great Polycarp, the "blessed and apostolic presbyter" who for many years headed the church of Smyrna. As quoted by Eusebius from a lost letter, they seem more like the memories of a bright boy, vividly recalling the scenes of his childhood, than of a pupil of a theologian. He could remember where Polycarp used to sit and stand, what he looked like, and what he used to say in his sermons.[9] Polycarp could say at his martyrdom in 155 that he had served the Lord for six-and-eighty years; his reminiscences of John and others who had seen the Lord made him for Irenaeus an invaluable link in tradition, since thus only two stages separated him from the days of Jesus. Whether family, personal, or missionary motives led to his going to Rome and then to Lyons we cannot say. He was probably at Rome when Polycarp visited the city in the time of Bishop Anicetus, shortly before his death, although Irenaeus' references to that visit do not stress his personal knowledge.[10] He derives enough of both ideas and phrases from Justin Martyr to make it probable that he had been a pupil of Justin's as well as a reader of his books, though his own interests are considerably different. When he wrote the Refutation and Overthrow he had probably long since left the capital, except for the visit of 177. But it was still for him the natural center of the Christian as of the civilized world. The heresies that he attacked were primarily those that had either sprung from, or spread to, the imperial city, although he improved his information about them by personal inquiries at Lyons.

Second century Lyons was a lesser Rome. A commercial city at the head of navigation on the Rhone, center of the Roman road system for Gaul, it was the seat of a garrison, and the capital of one of the Gallic provinces. Through the *concilium Galliarum* it was the headquarters of the imperial cult for three provinces, and a metropolis in its own right as well as a gateway between the Mediterranean world and the provinces north of the Alps. Like Rome, it had a large Greek-speaking element in its population, and among this element Christianity was first established. The martyrs of Lyons included several of Asiatic origin, and the account of their martyrdom notes as

---

[8] Eusebius, *Hist. eccl.*, V, ch. 4.

[9] *Ibid.*, V, ch. 20; cf. Irenaeus, III. 3:4; and Irenaeus as a disciple of Polycarp preserving the letter that recorded his martyrdom (Mart. Poly., ch. 22).   [10] Eusebius, *Hist. eccl.* V. 24:14–17.

exceptional that the deacon Sanctus of the nearby town of Vienne confessed his faith in Latin, answering to all questions only *Christianus sum*.[11] Irenaeus felt a human homesickness at times for the Greek cities of his youth. He registers a real sorrow as well as making a formal rhetorical apology, when he notes that he is an exile among the Celts, accustomed to speaking a barbarous tongue. By this I am not at all sure that he does not mean Latin, although local Celtic dialects are also in view. His later contacts with the rest of the Christian world are by letter. In spite of his love for personal tradition, he learned about earlier days largely from the same literary sources that are known to us.

On return from his visit to Rome, Irenaeus succeeded the martyr Pothinus as bishop at Lyons, and Eusebius speaks of him as leader of Christians in Gaul. Certainly his interest, perhaps also his missionary responsibility, extended to such congregations as existed in northern parts of Gaul and in Germany (that is, in the Roman provinces along the Rhine). In the Refutation and Overthrow, Irenaeus continues the list of Roman bishops down to Eleutherus, who was succeeded by Victor about 189 or 190. He thus dates approximately the composition of that work. His other preserved work, The Demonstration of the Apostolic Preaching, refers to the Refutation and is therefore later. Irenaeus last appears in history when he addresses a respectful but firm letter of protest to Pope Victor for his threatened excommunication of the Asiatic churches on account of their loyalty to the observance of the paschal feast on the Jewish date, the fourteenth of Nisan, instead of the following Sunday. Eusebius takes leave of him with the note that he was indeed a promoter of the peace of the Church, as his name suggested, both in this and in his other letters on the subject.[12] Having been more than an infant when he knew Polycarp, Irenaeus was probably over sixty by the end of the second century. He would scarcely have been silent in the controversies that arose after the death of Victor (A.D. 198), and probably passed away himself at about the same time. No authentic tradition credits him with a martyr's death, although a general sense of the fitness of things led to his inclusion as bishop and martyr in medieval martyrologies, and he is so honored in the calendar of saints today. He was certainly a martyr in the broader sense, a steadfast witness for the truth of the gospel.

[11] Eusebius, *Hist. eccl.* V. 1:20.   [12] *Ibid.*, V. 24:18.

IRENAEUS' WORK AND THOUGHT

In general the Refutation and Overthrow follows a logical order, although it is not always clear in detail. Book I describes the heresies in question, sometimes sarcastically, and Book II shows their absurdity. In Book III the basis of Christian doctrine in Scripture and tradition is laid down, and its essential points, the unity of God and redemption through Christ, are enlarged on in detail. Book IV defends against Marcion the unity of the two covenants, and Book V resumes the discussion of redemption and passes on to the last things and the hope of the world to come. The Demonstration, which seems to represent Irenaeus' teaching to catechumens, follows the order of the baptismal formula, adducing Scripture proof for belief in Father, Son, and Holy Spirit. It avoids the literal millenarianism of the Refutation, which suggests that Irenaeus had either changed his views on the subject or thought best to pass over the matter more lightly.[13] Eusebius mentions several other works now lost, but they seem to be smaller essays on topics discussed in the Refutation and Overthrow.

Irenaeus was profoundly a churchman and a pastor, and he writes as such. He was not desirous of originality, and had no more hesitation than the Biblical writers in reproducing material derived from different sources. From this there perhaps derive the slightly confusing shift in numbering the list of bishops at Rome, in which the apostles are sometimes counted and sometimes not, and some repetition with variations in his treatment of particular heresies. The latter is doubtless due to notes taken from different sources, and does not simplify the already complex problem of what Gnosticism really was. One important source is certainly the work of Justin Martyr on the history of heresies, whether the collection of material on that subject referred to in Justin's First Apology should be thought of as a published work or as a collection of notes available for people like Irenaeus who were interested in the subject.[14] The formal prominence of Simon Magus as the father of Gnosticism is certainly due to Justin, whose interest in another native of Samaria was further stimulated by what he took to be a statue of the heresiarch on the banks of the Tiber. The systems with which Irenaeus was actively concerned were the Valentinian, with its variations, and the Marcionite. On

[13] *Demonstration*, ch. 61.   [14] Justin, Apol. I, ch. 26.

these he doubtless collected information from a number of sources, supplementing it by some personal contacts with such representatives of the sects as had come to Lyons and were causing confusion in his own congregation. A recent study has shown Irenaeus' use of works of Theophilus of Antioch, and also some of the blocks of Eastern Christian tradition which he employed.[15]

But though Irenaeus was dependent on a variety of sources, it is a great mistake to think of him merely as a compiler. Even on that level we have to ask why he compiled precisely this collection of facts and arguments. He did not aim at originality, but this did not prevent his achieving a considerable amount of it. He was, to be sure, a man of tradition, *paradosis*. To him, however, what was handed down was not a collection of formal beliefs, but a means of living contact with the sources of life, indeed with the Life himself. He felt to the full what a modern writer has called "the thrill of tradition."[16] His highest aim was to state clearly what the Church believed and taught, and to preserve that teaching from corruption. Indeed in his various statements of faith there appear all the essentials of the Creed of Nicaea except its technical terms. Yet in his repeated outlines and comments he presented the essence of Christian theology. Preaching to Gentiles, he was conscious that the firm belief in one God, Creator of all things, from which Jews began their introduction to Christianity, needed to be stressed with others. His view of mankind is neither unduly dark nor merely optimistic. God has led man through history to his final revelation, especially by the Law and the Prophets, whose standing it was necessary to defend against the Marcionite rejection of them. But on the other hand much of that history is the record of the great rebellion of angels and men, the apostasy, which God finally countered by the incarnation of his only Son.[17]

Irenaeus' view of redemption is rich, and indeed may have gained something from his dealing with Gnostic thought. Vague as was the basis of Gnostic mythology, it certainly described the moral and metaphysical structure of the universe

[15] F. Loofs, *Theophilus von Antiochien Adversus Marcionem und die andere theologische Quellen bei Irenaeus* (Texte und Untersuchungen, 46, 2), Leipzig, 1930; cf. Thornton's comment, *Revelation and the Modern World*, pp. 118, 119.

[16] James Moffatt, *The Thrill of Tradition*, p. 71. The Macmillan Company, New York, 1944 (though he misunderstands Irenaeus, III. 2:1).

[17] Cf. Irenaeus, IV, chs. 14; 37 to 38.

in dramatic terms. Irenaeus sticks to the simplicity of the faith, but gives it some of the thrill that enables one to describe the Creed as an epic and the dogma as the drama. The Son of God worsted the ancient enemy in fair fight, thus redeeming mankind from its slavery. (It is most unfair to read into the one word "redeemed" the idea of a ransom paid to the devil.) [18] We were bought with a great price; but it was the price of the victor's toils endured that we might be free, not a price paid by omnipotence to any lesser power. In Christ there is a new creation, a new source of higher life, overcoming the defects of the basically good yet weakened first creation. There is a new Adam and also, as Irenaeus observes in passing, a new Eve, since the obedience of Mary began to repair the damage done by the disobedience of the mother of all living. Is this a piece of unwritten apostolic tradition, as has been suggested,[19] or was Irenaeus here stimulated by Gnostic ideas about the mother to start a chain of speculation on the dignity of the mother of Christ, which was later to have remarkable developments? In any case, the new life is primarily life in Christ, of whom Irenaeus anticipates an Alexandrian epigram when he says that he became what we are so that we might become what he is.[20] This new life is a life of faith, which certainly for Irenaeus means the acceptance of sound belief, but in the sense of joyful turning to God, not simply of correct information about him. In the circle of the new life God's world, created good, returns once more to its right relation to him. In contrast to all Gnostic or falsely spiritual depreciation of the material universe, Irenaeus stresses the significance of the offerings of bread and wine which the Church, as the priest of creation, offers to God. They are the gifts of thanksgiving which become the body and blood of Christ, and as such preserve our bodies and souls to everlasting life.[21] God redeems nature by nature and through nature. We can best understand Irenaeus' tendency to even a literal eschatology of the earthly millennium as part of his insistence that God has redeemed his own dear universe and not simply provided a way of escape from it. And so at the end of the drama the world which came from God will visibly return to him again.

[18] V, ch. 1; cf. H. Rashdall, *The Idea of Atonement in Christian Theology*, pp. 233–248 (the interpretation here criticized on p. 244, n.1). London, 1919.
[19] Charles Gore, *The Holy Spirit and the Church*, p. 280. London, 1924.
[20] V, pref.   [21] IV, chs. 17; 18; V, chs. 1; 2.

Irenaeus did not want to speculate, but he could not help it. He was a practical theologian and not a formal philosopher. After all, he was a missionary and pastor in Lyons, and did not move in the sophisticated circles to which some of the Apologists tried to commend the gospel. But he provided the framework of formal theology and indicated the topics that later theology and Christian philosophy would have to take up. How the Son of God and the Spirit are related to the Father he never discusses, but he lays down the terms of that discussion by treating both as in the sphere of deity, while writing on the precise subject of Christian monotheism. That question was to come up immediately, in fact, was already the subject of controversy at Rome before the death of Irenaeus. On other topics, like the atonement and sacraments, he threw out hints that were not to be taken up for some time. His credal assertions, however, about God and his world waited for philosophical development only for the next Christian who was also a philosopher—in other words, for the bright boy who was already reading books at Alexandria when the old bishop finished his task at Lyons. Irenaeus closes the first age of the formulation of tradition, and opens the way for Origen, who is his logical successor in the general movement of Christian thought.

The great interest of the study of Irenaeus' sources for his knowledge of Christian truth is that they are also ours. In other words, he is the first Christian writer who worked with the New Testament much as we do. It is for him as for us part of the Bible, although he does not put it exactly that way. He reveres the Old Testament and vigorously asserts its authority for Christians; but the Apostolic Writings can be quoted for themselves, and Irenaeus does not have to attempt, like Justin or the Apostolic Fathers, to base the gospel on the Old Testament if he is to use arguments from a sacred book. He refers to all the New Testament books except two or three of the shortest epistles,[22] although the authority of the Writings is still that of each of its parts taken separately rather than of the collection as a whole. Tradition brought him the creed and the rites of the Church; but it was not, except perhaps for one or two minor items, a great source of further information. On the whole he was dependent on the books available to him at Lyons, including already venerated works of the early Fathers,

[22] Philemon, III John, and perhaps Jude; cf. F. R. Montgomery Hitchcock, *Irenaeus of Lugdunum*, ch. 12, Cambridge, 1914.

like I Clement and the Shepherd of Hermas, which are admirable Writings too, though not on the level of the apostolic compositions. In writing about the New Testament Scriptures and interpreting them, Irenaeus is an exegete and even a higher critic. He collects external and internal evidence for the authorship and character of the Gospels. His essays in exegesis are sometimes startling, as when he argues that Jesus had a long ministry of two decades, since otherwise there would be no point in the phrase, "You are not yet fifty years old." [23] As an interpreter of the Christian tradition, Irenaeus had about the same resources that were available to later Patristic scholars.

Irenaeus could already look back to an early Church and even to a middle period, the age of men like Polycarp who connected his generation with that of the apostles. Through them he could almost join hands with Jesus himself, and in effect say to his Gallic converts, "What our eyes have seen . . . and our hands have handled of the Word of life." [24] Life in Christ is ever new and directly received, but its connection with the historic Jesus is already dependent on links; hence the importance of a sound succession in the Church. This must be taken in no narrow sense. Irenaeus finds it in the traditions of elders, and points it out in the series of directors in a great Church like the Roman (so we might translate *episkopos*, since the term had not yet become primarily a technical one by translation). But the great succession which Irenaeus stresses is the succession of faith and life from generation to generation of believers, bound together in the fellowship of the Body of Christ.

The Latin Translation of Irenaeus

Irenaeus has suffered the strange fate that none of his works are preserved complete in the language in which they were written. This is partly because he wrote so definitely for the problems of his own age, partly because the hints he offered for Greek theology were so completely taken up by later writers as to make reference to him superfluous. Doubtless also local situations contributed. Lyons was the natural center of interest in Irenaeus, and the Greek tradition in the church there did not long survive him. Eusebius still knew Irenaeus in Greek; like many modern students, he was mainly interested in the

23 II, ch. 22; Jesus thus, it occurs to Irenaeus, sanctifying every age of human life.　　　　　24 I John 1:1.

incidental historical evidence that he preserves. Treatises on heresies rapidly became a form of Christian antiquarianism. This kind of interest is responsible for the preservation of much of Book I by the fourth century heresiologist, Epiphanius of Salamis, who lifted into his collection Irenaeus' account of Valentinus and other Gnostics. Hippolytus of Rome had already made use of him, and there are a few later quotations.

Happily a Latin translation of the Refutation and Overthrow was produced, probably not very long after Irenaeus' time, and as further fragments of the Greek are identified they can be checked into their proper place in it. Where the original is available, the translation seems to be almost woodenly literal, and on the whole the student of Irenaeus is grateful for this, since it gives him reasonable confidence in depending on the general sense of the translation elsewhere. A point on which the translator gives us comfort rather than help is the question of those Gnostic terms that are also Greek words. Are they to be treated as personal names or personifications, and so in English should it be Bythos or Depth, Sophia or Wisdom, Monogenes or Only-begotten, and so on? The Latin translator evidently felt that they were sometimes one and sometimes the other, and used his discretion as to whether to translate or transliterate, not always consistently; the English translator seems justified in following his example without always being bound by his authority. The first printed edition was edited by Erasmus in 1526, and ever since then the study of Irenaeus has been pursued with vigor. Seventeenth century scholars identified two families among the Latin manuscripts; critical editions begin with the eighteenth. W. W. Harvey's edition of 1857 prints a full collection of Greek fragments along with the Latin, and is adequate for most practical purposes. More recently an Armenian version has come to light (Books 4 and 5 and fragments) and will have to be employed in any future critical edition. It is also to an Armenian version that we owe the modern recovery of the Demonstration.

BOOKS

The Works of Irenaeus

A. *Refutation and Overthrow of the Knowledge Falsely So Called* (*Adversus Haereses*)

Latin:

Erasmus. Basel, 1526.
Feuardent. Cologne, 1596.

Latin and Greek:

Grabe, J. E., Oxford, 1702.
Massuet, R., Paris, 1710 (the Benedictine edition, reprinted in Migne, *Patrologia Graeca*, Vol. VII, Paris, 1857).
Stieren, A. Leipzig, 1848–1853.
Harvey, W. W., Cambridge, 1857.
A. Harnack's judgment is worth quoting: "In the year 1702 appeared Grabe's good edition, in 1710 . . . the outstanding one of Massuet" (*Die Pfaff'schen Irenäus-Fragmente*, Texte und Untersuchungen, Vol. XX. 3, p. 11, Leipzig, 1900). The present translation is based on Harvey's edition, but the chapter and section divisions are given as in Massuet (and the Roberts and Rambaut translation).

Armenian:

Irenaeus gegen die Häretiker . . . Buch IV und V in armenischer Version, entdeckt von Lic.Dr.Karapet Ter-Mekerttschian, hrsgeg. von Lic.Dr.Erwand Ter-Minassiantz, Texte und Untersuchungen, Vol. XXXVI. 3. Leipzig, 1913.
Holl, K. *Armenische Irenaeusfragmente*, mit deutscher Übersetzung nach Dr. W. Lüdtke, Texte und Untersuchungen, Vol. XXXVI. 3. Leipzig, 1913.

Modern Translations—English:

Roberts, Alexander, and Rambaut, W. H., *The Writings of Irenaeus* (Ante-Nicene Christian Library, Vols. V and IX) (careful and literal). Edinburgh, 1868–1869.

Hitchcock, F. R. Montgomery, *The Treatise of Irenaeus of Lugdunum Against the Heresies*, 2 vols. (extracts and summaries). London, 1912.

French:

Saint Irénée (*Pensée chrétienne*) (extracts and summaries). Paris, 1905.

German:

Klebba, E., *Der hl. Irenaeus* (in Bibliothek der Kirchenväter), 2 vols. Kempten, 1912.

B. *The Demonstration of the Apostolic Preaching*

Armenian:

Ter-Mekerttschian, K., and Ter-Minassiantz, E., *Des heiligen Irenaeus Schrift zum Erweise der apostolischen Verkündigung*, Texte und Untersuchungen, Vol. XXXI. 1 (with German translation). Leipzig, 1907.

Modern Translations:

Faldati, U., *Esposizione della predicazione apostolica* (*Scrittori cristiani antichi* 6). Rome, 1923.

Robinson, J. Armitage, *St. Irenaeus, The Demonstration of the Apostolic Preaching* (an unpretentious but outstanding piece of scholarship, with an introduction valuable for some easily neglected aspects of Irenaeus such as his doctrine of the Holy Spirit). London, 1920.

Weber, S., *Sancti Irenaei demonstratio apostolicae praedicationis*. Freiburg, 1917.

WORKS ON IRENAEUS

Beuzart, P., *Essai sur la théologie d'Irénée*. Paris, 1908.

Bonwetsch, N., *Die Theologie des Irenaeus*. Gütersloh, 1925.

Dodwell, Henry, *Dissertationes in Irenaeum* (still valuable, especially for the life of Irenaeus). Oxford, 1689.

Dufourcq, A., *St. Irénée* (*Les Saints*) (a helpful brief introduction). Paris, 4th ed., 1926.

Hitchcock, F. R. Montgomery, *Irenaeus of Lugdunum, A Study of His Teaching* (a careful if somewhat pedestrian account). Cambridge, 1914.

Klebba, E., *Die Anthropologie des hl. Irenaeus.* Münster, 1894.

Lawson, J., *The Biblical Theology of Saint Irenaeus,* Epworth, London, 1948.

Loofs, Friedrich, *Theophilus v. Antiochien Adversus Marcionem und die anderen theologischen Quellen bei Irenaeus,* Texte und Untersuchungen, Vol. XLVI. 2. Leipzig, 1930.

Lundström, Sven, *Neue Studien zur Lateinischen Irenäusübersetzung, Lund Universitets Arsskrift,* XLIV. 8, Lund, 1948.

SOME REFERENCES ON IRENAEUS AND GNOSTICISM

Aulén, G., *Christus Victor,* tr. A. G. Hebert. S.P.C.K., London, 1931.

Burkitt, F. C., *Church and Gnosis, A Study of Christian Thought and Speculation in the Second Century.* Cambridge University Press, Cambridge, 1932.

More, Paul Elmer, *Christ the Word* (*The Greek Tradition,* Vol. IV) (Ch. II, "The Setting of Gnosticism"). Princeton, 1927.

Thornton, L. S., *Revelation and the Modern World.* Black, London, 1950.

See general references in bibliography for Justin Martyr, and Bardenhewer, O., *Geschichte der altkirchlichen Literatur,* Vol. I, 3d ed., Freiburg, 1913 (Irenaeus, pp. 399–430), and Quasten, J., *Patrology,* Vol. I, pp. 287–313.

Selections from the Work Against Heresies by Irenaeus, Bishop of Lyons: "The Refutation and Overthrow of the Knowledge Falsely So Called"

THE TEXT: (BOOK I) THE HERETICS

PREFACE

1 Certain men, rejecting the truth, are introducing among us false stories and vain genealogies, which serve rather to controversies, as the apostle said,[25] than to God's work of building up in the faith. By their craftily constructed rhetoric they lead astray the minds of the inexperienced, and take them captive, corrupting the oracles of the Lord, and being evil expounders of what was well spoken. For they upset many, leading them away by the pretense of knowledge from Him who constituted and ordered the universe, as if they had something higher and greater to show them than the God who made the heaven and the earth and all that is in them. By skillful language they artfully attract the simple-minded into their kind of inquiry, and then crudely destroy them by working up their blasphemous and impious view about the Demiurge. Nor can their simple hearers distinguish the lie from the truth.

2 For their error is not displayed as what it is, lest it should be stripped naked and shown up; it is craftily decked out in an attractive dress, and made to seem truer than the truth itself to the inexperienced because of the outer appearance. As one better than I am has said about these matters, a precious stone like emerald, which many value greatly, can be put to shame by a clever imitation in glass, unless there is someone on hand who can test it, and show what was done deceptively by art; and when brass is mixed with silver, what untrained person can easily prove it? So then, lest some should be made prey of through my fault, like sheep by wolves, not recognizing them because of their outwardly wearing sheep's clothing—whom the Lord warned us to guard against[26]—and because they

[25] 1 Tim. 1:4.   [26] Matt. 7:15.

358

talk like us, though thinking very differently, I thought it necessary, my dear friend, after reading the Commentaries, as they call them, of the disciples of Valentinus, and having met some of them and so become familiar with their point of view, to expound to you those portentous and profound mysteries, which not all accept, since not all have sufficiently purged their brains.[27] Then you, being informed about these things, may be able to make them clear to all your people, and to warn them to be on their guard against this abysmal folly and blasphemy against Christ. As well as I can, then, I will briefly and clearly describe the position of the present false teachers, I mean the followers of Ptolemaeus, who is an offshoot of the school of Valentinus. I will further provide, as far as my modest ability extends, the means of overthrowing it, showing how absurd and foreign to the truth are the things they say. I am neither practiced in writing nor trained in rhetoric, but my love for you and yours encourages me to bear my witness about these teachings which have been hidden till the present, but have now by the grace of God come to light. "For there is nothing hidden that shall not be revealed, nor secret, that shall not be made known."[28]

You will not expect from me, a resident among the Celts, [3] and mostly accustomed to a barbarous language, rhetorical skill, which I have never learned, nor power in writing, which I have not acquired, nor beauties of language and style, which I am not acquainted with.[29] But what I write to you out of love, plainly and truly and simply, you will surely receive in love, and you can then amplify for yourself, having greater ability than mine, what I have given you, as it were, in basic principles. With your breadth of mind you will be able to make much more fruitful what I have said to you in brief, and will be able to present powerfully to your people what I have feebly expounded to you. As I have endeavored, in response to your long-held desire to know their position, not only to make it plain to you, but also to give you the necessary means of showing its falsity, so do you perform a similar service for the rest, according to the grace which the Lord has given you, so that men may no longer be ensnared by their plausibilities, which are as follows.

27 These phrases are of course meant satirically.
28 Matt. 10:26; Luke 12:2.
29 Irenaeus is not the only author to use the best resources of his rhetoric to protest his lack of it.

THE FAITH OF THE CHURCH

10 Now the Church, although scattered over the whole civilized world to the end of the earth, received from the apostles and their disciples its faith in one God, the Father Almighty, who made the heaven, and the earth, and the seas, and all that is in them, and in one Christ Jesus, the Son of God, who was made flesh for our salvation, and in the Holy Spirit, who through the prophets proclaimed the dispensations of God— the comings, the birth of a virgin, the suffering, the resurrection from the dead, and the bodily reception into the heavens of the beloved, Christ Jesus our Lord, and his coming from the heavens in the glory of the Father to restore all things, and to raise up all flesh, that is, the whole human race, so that every knee may bow, of things in heaven and on earth and under the earth, to Christ Jesus our Lord and God and Saviour and King, according to the pleasure of the invisible Father, and every tongue may confess him,[30] and that he may execute righteous judgment on all. The spiritual powers of wickedness, and the angels who transgressed and fell into apostasy, and the godless and wicked and lawless and blasphemers among men he will send into the eternal fire. But to the righteous and holy, and those who have kept his commandments and have remained in his love, some from the beginning [of life] and some since their repentance, he will by his grace give life incorrupt, and will clothe them with eternal glory.

2 Having received this preaching and this faith, as I have said, the Church, although scattered in the whole world, carefully preserves it, as if living in one house. She believes these things [everywhere] alike, as if she had but one heart and one soul, and preaches them harmoniously, teaches them, and hands them down, as if she had but one mouth. For the languages of the world are different, but the meaning of the [Christian] tradition is one and the same. Neither do the churches that have been established · in Germany believe otherwise, or hand down any other tradition, nor those among the Iberians, nor those among the Celts, nor in Egypt, nor in Libya, nor those established in the middle parts of the world. But as God's creature, the sun, is one and the same in the whole world, so also the preaching of the truth shines everywhere, and illumines all men who wish to come to the knowledge of

30 Phil. 2:10, 11.

the truth. Neither will one of those who preside in the churches who is very powerful in speech say anything different from these things, for no one is above [his] teacher,[31] nor will one who is weak in speech diminish the tradition. For since the faith is one and the same, he who can say much about it does not add to it, nor does he who can say little diminish it.

This matter of having more or less understanding does not 3 mean that men change the basic idea, and imagine another God above the Demiurge and Maker and Nourisher of this universe, as if he were not enough for us, or another Christ or another Only-begotten. But it consists in working out the things that have been said in parables, and building them into the foundation of the faith: in expounding the activity and dispensation of God for the sake of mankind; in showing clearly how God was long-suffering over the apostasy of the angels who transgressed, and over the disobedience of men; in declaring why one and the same God made some things subject to time, others eternal, some heavenly, and some earthly; in understanding why God, being invisible, appeared to the prophets, not in one form, but differently to different ones; in showing why there were a number of covenants with mankind, and in teaching what is the character of each of the covenants; in searching out why God shut up all in disobedience that he might have mercy on all; in giving thanks that the Word of God was made flesh, and suffered; in declaring why the coming of the Son of God [was] at the last times, that is, the Beginning was made manifest at the end; in unfolding what is found in the prophets about the end and the things to come; in not being silent that God has made the despaired-of Gentiles fellow heirs and of the same body and partners with the saints; and in stating how this mortal and fleshly [body] will put on immortality, and this corruptible incorruption; and in proclaiming how he says, "What was not a people, is a people, and what was not beloved, is beloved," and, "Many more are the children of the desolate than of her who has a husband." [32] With reference to these things and others like them the apostle exclaimed, "O depth of the riches and wisdom and knowledge of God; how unsearchable are his judgments and his ways past finding out!" [33] But [this greater skill] does not consist in imagining beyond the Creator and Demiurge the Mother of these

[31] Matt. 10:24; Luke 6:40.
[32] Eph. 2:19; I Cor. 15:54; Rom. 9:25 (Hos. 2:23); Gal. 4:27 (Isa. 54:1).
[33] Rom. 11:33.

things and of him, the Desire of a wandering Aeon, and coming
to such a point of blasphemy, nor in falsely conceiving of the
Pleroma above her, now with thirty, now with an innumerable
crowd of Aeons, as these teachers who are indeed void of divine
understanding say. But as I said before, the real Church has
one and the same faith everywhere in the world.

VALENTINUS

11   Let us now look at the inconsistent views of these men, since
there are two or three of them anyway, how they do not even
agree on the same topics, but vary from each other both about
things and about names. The first of these, Valentinus, who
adapted the principles of the so-called Gnostic heresy to the
individual character of his school, thus expounded it, defining
that there is an unnamable Dyad, of which one is called
Ineffable and the other Silence. Then from this Dyad a second
Dyad was produced, of which he calls one part Father and the
other Truth. From the Tetrad were produced Logos and Zoë,
Anthropos and Ecclesia,[34] and this is the first Ogdoad. From
Logos and Zoë he says that ten Powers were produced, as I
said before, but from Anthropos and Ecclesia twelve, one of
which, falling away and suffering a lack, brought about the
rest of the business. He postulated two Boundaries, one between
the depth and the rest of the Pleroma, dividing the begotten
Aeons from the unbegotten Father, and the other separating
their Mother from the Pleroma. Christ was not produced from
the Aeons within the Pleroma, but was conceived by the
Mother who was outside, according to her knowledge of better
things, but with a kind of shadow. He, being male, cast off
the shadow from himself and returned into the Pleroma. Then
the Mother, being left with the shadow, and emptied of spiritual
substance, brought forth another Son, and this is the Demiurge,
whom he also calls almighty over things subject to him. He
taught that there was also produced with him a left-hand
Ruler, as do those falsely called Gnostics whom we shall
speak of. He sometimes says that Jesus was produced by him
who was separated from their Mother and reunited with the
others, that is, the Desired; sometimes from him who returned
to the Pleroma, that is, from Christ; sometimes from Anthropos
and Ecclesia. And he says that the Holy Spirit was produced
by the Truth to inspect and fructify the Aeons, entering into

[34] Or Word and Life, Man and Church.

them invisibly, through whom the Aeons produced the plants of truth.

SECUNDUS

Secundus [35] says that there is a first Ogdoad, a right-hand 2 and a left-hand Tetrad, as he would have them called, one light, the other darkness; and the Power that fell away and suffered lack was not begotten of the thirty Aeons, but of their fruits. There is another distinguished teacher among them, 3 who, striving after something more sublime, and an even greater knowledge, speaks thus of the first Tetrad: There is a certain Proarche before all things, beyond any thought or speech or name, whom I call Monotes; with this Monotes is another Power, whom I call Henotes. [36] This Henotes, and this Monotes, being the One, sent forth, but not as causing an emanation, the intelligible Arche over all things, which Arche is known in speech as Monad. With this Monad there also reigns a Power of one substance with him, which I also call the One. These powers, Monotes and Henotes, Monad and the One, sent forth the other productions of the Aeons.

Iu, iu, and *pheu, pheu!* Truly we may utter these exclamations 4 from tragedy at such bold invention of ridiculous nomenclature, and at the audacity that made up these names without blushing. For when he says, "There is a certain Proarche before all things, above all thought, which I call Monotes," and again, "With this Monotes there reigns a Power, which I call Henotes," it is obvious that he admits that he is talking about his own inventions, and that he has given names to his inventions which no one else had given them before. It is clear also that he himself dared to make up these names, and unless he had been on hand the Truth would have had no name. There is no reason why someone else shouldn't assign names like these on the same basis: There is a royal Proarche above all thought, a Power above all substance, indefinitely extended. Since this is the Power which I call the Gourd, there is with it the Power which I call Superemptiness. This Gourd and Superemptiness, being one, emitted, yet did not emit, the fruit, visible, edible, and delicious, which is known to language as the Cucumber. With this Cucumber there is a Power of like quality with it, which I call the Melon. These Powers, the Gourd, Superemptiness,

---

[35] Or just possibly "the second," if the Latin translation was sufficiently well-known to have corrupted the Greek extracts.
[36] That is, Beginning, Uniqueness, and Oneness.

the Cucumber, and the Melon, sent forth the remaining crowd of the delirious Melons of Valentinus.[37] For if the language which is used about all kinds of things is to be transferred to the first Tetrad, and anyone can assign names as he pleases, who would prohibit [our using] these names, which are much more credible, and in common use and generally known?

OTHER GNOSTICS AND THEIR RITES

5   Others again have called their first and self-begotten Ogdoad by these names—first Proarche, then Inconceivable, the third Ineffable, and the fourth Invisible; and from the first Proarche proceeded in the first place [of the second Tetrad], and fifth [of the whole] Arche, from Inconceivable in the second and sixth place Incomprehensible, from Ineffable in the third and seventh place Unnamable, and from Invisible in the fourth and eighth place Unbegotten, the Pleroma of the first Ogdoad. They would have these Powers anterior to Depth and Silence, so that they may appear as more perfect than the perfect and more knowing than the Gnostics—to whom one might properly say, "What babbling sophists!" And even about Depth there are many different opinions among them. Some make him out to be unmated, being indeed neither male nor female— in fact, not being anything. Others say that he is both male and female, assigning him the nature of a hermaphrodite. Others again assign him Silence as a consort, that there may be the first conjunction.

21   Their [i.e., the Marcosian] tradition about redemption[38] is obscure and incomprehensible, as being the mother of things that cannot be grasped or clearly seen. Because it is fluctuating, it cannot be described simply or in one account, as each one of them hands it down as he chooses. Each of these mysta-gogues has his own ceremony of redemption. That this pattern has been instigated by Satan to lead them to renounce the baptism of rebirth to God, indeed to deny the whole faith, I

---

[37] Satire, indeed sarcasm, although there are hints that the sacredness of cucumbers and melons, as the least material kinds of fruit, was a not unknown idea. Cf. the prohibition against offering them in church (Hippolytus, Apost. Trad. 28), and their later use by Manichaeans as food for the elect.

[38] The tradition, *paradosis*, here is that of a rite, such as the *paradosis* of the Eucharist in I Cor., ch. 11; Irenaeus contrasts the simple Christian *paradosis* of baptism with Gnostic attempts at outdoing that rite and the anointings that followed it.

will show in the proper place when I refute them. They say that 2
it is necessary for those who have received perfect knowledge
to be reborn into the power which is above all things—otherwise one cannot enter the Pleroma, since this is what leads them
to the Depth. The baptism of Jesus who appeared [on earth]
was [they say] for remission of sins, but the redemption of the
Christ who came down upon him, for perfection, and they
allege that the former is animal, the latter spiritual. Baptism
was preached by John for repentance, but redemption was
added by Jesus for perfection; and it is with reference to this
that he says, "I have another baptism to be baptized with,
and I press on eagerly towards it." [39] So they also say that the
Lord propounded this redemption to the sons of Zebedee,
when their mother asked that they might sit on his right and
left in the Kingdom, and he said, "Can you be baptized with
the baptism that I am to be baptized with?" [40] Paul too, they
claim, often testifies of the redemption in Christ Jesus, and this
is [the rite] which they hand down in diverse and discordant
forms.

For some of them prepare a nuptial couch and perform a 3
sacred rite for those who are "perfected," with certain invocations, saying that they have performed a spiritual marriage,
according to the likeness of the conjunctions above. Some bring
[the candidates] to the water, and baptize them with these
words: "In the Name of the unknowable Father of all things—
in Truth the mother of all—in him who came down upon
Jesus—into union and redemption and the fellowship of the
Powers." Others invoke certain Hebrew names, in order to
impress the initiates even more, thus, "*Basema chamosse baaiabora
mistadia ruada kousta babophor calachthei.*" [41] The interpretation
of these is as follows: "Above every Power of the Father I
invoke the light which is named, and the good Spirit and Life,
for you have reigned in the body." Others use this invocation
for redemption: "The name which is hidden from all godhead,
and lordship, and truth, which Jesus of Nazareth put on in the
regions of the light of Christ, of Christ who lives by the Holy
Spirit, for angelic redemption—the name of restoration, *Messia
ouphareg namempsaiman chaldaian mosomedaea acphranai psaoua,*

---

[39] Luke 12:50 with an interesting (not necessarily Gnostic) variant.
[40] Mark 10:38.
[41] *Basema* suggests "in the Name" in some Semitic language; the ultimate
source of this gibberish, as it now is, might be the Trinitarian formula
in Aramaic.

Jesus Nazaria." The interpretation of these is as follows: "I do not divide the Spirit of Christ, the heart, and the supercelestial power, the merciful; may I name your name, O Saviour of Truth." This is what those who initiate invoke, while he who is initiated replies, "I am strengthened and redeemed, and I redeem my soul from this age, and from all things connected with it in the name of Iao, who redeemed his soul to full redemption in the living Christ." Then those present respond, "Peace to all on whom this name rests." Then they anoint the initiate with balsam, for they say that this ointment is a type of the sweetness which is above all things.

4   Some of them say that it is superfluous to lead men to the water, but mixing oil and water together, with utterances like those which I have quoted, they pour it on the head of those being initiated; and this they make out to be the redemption. They also anoint them with balsam. Others omit all these things, and say that the mystery of the ineffable and invisible should not be performed by means of visible and corruptible things, and [that of] the inconceivable and incorporeal, by sensible and bodily; but the perfect redemption is the knowledge of the ineffable Greatness itself. For weakness and suffering were brought about by ignorance, and everything that has come from ignorance is destroyed by knowledge, and knowledge is the redemption of the inner man. This is not bodily, since the body is corruptible; nor is it psychic, since the soul came from deficiency, and is as it were a mere dwelling place of the spirit—therefore redemption must be spiritual. So the inner spiritual man is redeemed by knowledge, and they need nothing more than the knowledge of all things—and this is true redemption.

5   There are others who keep on "redeeming" the dying up to the moment of death, pouring oil and water on their heads, or the ointment mentioned above mixed with water, and with the invocations mentioned above, that they may not be grasped or seen by the principalities and powers, and that their inner man may ascend even above the invisible things, while their body is left among the things of the world and the soul abandoned to the Demiurge. [42] And they tell them to say this when they come to the Powers after they have died: "I am the son of the Father, the Father who pre-existed, a son in the pre-existent; I came to see both alien things, and my own, yet they

---

[42] Among sources for this rite would be the Christian anointing of the sick (James 5:14), and the formulas with which Egyptians equipped the dead for their last journey.

are not wholly alien, but belong to Achamoth, who is female, and made them for herself; for I derive my race from the pre-existent, and I go again to my own, from which I came forth." And they claim that he who says this will avoid and escape the powers; he will come to those who surround the Demiurge, and say to them: "I am a precious vessel, more than the female being who made you. Though your mother does not know her origin, I know myself, and I know whence I am, and I call on the incorrupt Wisdom, who is in the Father, who is the Mother of your mother, and has no Father nor any male consort; for a female, made of a female, made you, not knowing her own Mother, and thinking that she was alone; but I call upon her Mother." When they hear this, those who surround the Demiurge will be greatly troubled, and revile their origin, and the race of their Mother; but he will go to his own, casting off his chain, that is, the [animal] soul. This is what has come to me about the redemption. Since their teachings and traditions are different, and the newer ones among them claim to be constantly finding something new, and working out what no one ever thought of before, it is hard to describe their views.

CERDON AND MARCION

Cerdon, who took his start from the followers of Simon, and **27** settled at Rome under Hyginus, who held the ninth place in the episcopal succession from the apostles,[43] taught that the God preached by the Law and the Prophets was not the Father of our Lord Jesus Christ. For the former was known and the latter unknown, the former righteous and the latter good.

After him came Marcion of Pontus, who developed his **2** teaching, shamelessly blaspheming the God whom the Law and the Prophets proclaimed, describing him as the author of evils, desirous of wars, changing his opinions, and [at different times] contrary to himself. But Jesus [was] from the Father who is above the God that formed the world, and came into Judea in the time of Pontius Pilate, who was procurator of Tiberius Caesar; manifest in human form to those who were in Judea, he abolished the Prophets and the Law, and all the works of that God who made the world, whom he calls the World Ruler.[44] In addition to this he mutilated the Gospel According to Luke, removing everything about the birth of the Lord,

[43] Here the apostles are included in the series, while in III. 3: 3 they are not.　　　　[44] The Cosmocrat. Cf. Eph. 6:12.

and much of the teaching of the words of the Lord, in which the Lord is recorded as clearly confessing the creator of this universe as his Father. He persuaded his disciples that he was more veracious than the apostles who handed down the gospel, giving them not a gospel but a mere fragment of a gospel. He also similarly cut up the Epistles of Paul, removing whatever the apostle said clearly about the God who made the world, that he is the Father of our Lord Jesus Christ, and whatever the apostle teaches by referring to the prophetic writings that predict the coming of the Lord.

3   Only the souls [he says] of those who have learned his teaching will come to salvation; the body, since it is taken from the earth, cannot be saved. To his blasphemy against God he adds this, speaking diabolically indeed and in direct opposition to the truth: that Cain and those like him—the men of Sodom and the Egyptians, and other such, and in general all the nations that walked in all kinds of wickedness—were saved by the Lord when he descended into the lower regions, and came running to him and received him into their realm; but Abel and Enoch and Noah and the other righteous, and the patriarchs such as Abraham, with all the prophets and those who were pleasing to God, did not share in the salvation which the serpent who was in Marcion preached. For, he says, since they knew that their God was always testing them, they thought he was testing them then, and so did not come to Jesus or believe his proclamation, and therefore their souls remained in Hades.

4   But since this man alone has dared publicly to mutilate the Scriptures, and more than any others to malign God shamelessly, I will refute him separately, convicting him from his own writings, and from the words of the Lord and the apostles which he preserves and uses I will overthrow him, with the help of the Lord.[45] But here it is necessary only to mention him, that you may know that all those who corrupt the truth and injure the teaching of the Church are the disciples and successors of Simon Magus the Samaritan. Although, in order to deceive others, they do not confess the name of their teacher, yet they teach his views. Setting up the name of Christ Jesus as a kind of decoy, but in one way or another introducing the impiety of Simon, they bring many to destruction, spreading their evil teachings under a good name, and by the sweetness and beauty of the name [of Christ] offering them the bitter and evil poison of the serpent, the prince of the apostasy.

[45] A topic taken up, though not quite in this manner, in Book IV.

THE TEXT: (BOOK III) THE FAITH IN SCRIPTURE AND TRADITION

PREFACE

It was your command, my dear friend, that I should bring out into the open the teachings of the Valentinians, which they consider to be hidden, showing their diversity, and developing an argument against them. So I undertook to exhibit the succession of their teachings, maintaining that they derive from Simon the father of all heretics, and to reply to them all. Since it is in many respects part of one work to explain and to refute them, I have sent you these books, of which the first contains the opinions of all of them, and shows their habits and the nature of their behavior. In the second their evil teachings are destroyed and overthrown, and shown up nakedly for what they are. Now in this third book I introduce the arguments from the Scriptures, thus leaving out nothing that you asked for. Indeed, I will have given you, beyond what you had expected, the means of reasoning with and refuting those who offer any kind of evil teaching. For the love which is in God, being rich and ungrudging, gives more than one asks from it. Keep in mind therefore what I have said in the two previous books; and by adding this to them you will have from me a full reply against all heretics, and will be able to resist them faithfully and boldly on behalf of the one true and life-giving faith, which the Church has received from the apostles and imparts to her children. For the Lord of all gave to his apostles the power of the gospel, and by them we also have learned the truth, that is, the teaching of the Son of God—as the Lord said to them, "He who hears you hears me, and he who despises you despises me, and him who sent me." [46]

[46] Luke 10:16.

THE TRADITIONS OF THE GOSPELS

1 For we learned the plan of our salvation from no others than from those through whom the gospel came to us. They first preached it abroad, and then later by the will of God handed it down to us in Writings,[47] to be the foundation and pillar of our faith. For it is not right to say that they preached before they had come to perfect knowledge, as some dare to say, boasting that they are the correctors of the apostles. For after our Lord had risen from the dead, and they were clothed with the power from on high when the Holy Spirit came upon them, they were filled with all things and had perfect knowledge. They went out to the ends of the earth, preaching the good things that come to us from God, and proclaiming peace from heaven to men, all and each of them equally being in possession of the gospel of God. So Matthew among the Hebrews issued a Writing of the gospel in their own tongue, while Peter and Paul were preaching the gospel at Rome and founding the Church. After their decease Mark, the disciple and interpreter of Peter, also handed down to us in writing what Peter had preached. Then Luke, the follower of Paul, recorded in a book the gospel as it was preached by him. Finally John, the disciple of the Lord, who had also lain on his breast, himself published
2 the Gospel, while he was residing at Ephesus in Asia. All of these handed down to us that there is one God, maker of heaven and earth, proclaimed by the Law and the Prophets, and one Christ the Son of God. If anyone does not agree with them he despises the companions of the Lord, he despises Christ the Lord himself, he even despises the Father, and he is self-condemned, resisting and refusing his own salvation, as all the heretics do.

THE APOSTOLIC TRADITION

2 But when they are refuted from the Writings they turn around and attack the Writings themselves, saying that they are not correct, or authoritative, and that the truth cannot be found from them by those who are not acquainted with the tradition. For this [they say] was not handed down in writing, but orally, which is why Paul said, "We speak wisdom among

[47] *In scripturis*, doubtless representing "*En graphais*," not yet quite as technical as "Scripture."

the perfect, but not the wisdom of this world." [48] Each of them utters a wisdom which he has made up, or rather a fiction, so that according to them the truth was once to be found in Valentinus, then at another time in Marcion, at another time in Cerinthus, then later in Basilides, or was also in that opponent, who has no saving message to utter. [49] Each one of them is wholly perverse, and is not ashamed to preach himself, corrupting the rule of faith.

But when we appeal again to that tradition which has come 2 down from the apostles and is guarded by the successions of elders [50] in the churches, they oppose the tradition, saying that they are wiser not only than the elders, but even than the apostles, and have found the genuine truth. For the apostles [they say] mixed matters of the Law with the words of the Saviour, and not only the apostles, but even the Lord himself, spoke sometimes from the Demiurge, sometimes from the middle power, sometimes from the highest, while they know the hidden mystery without doubt or corruption, and in its purity. This is in nothing less than shameless blasphemy against their Maker. What it comes to is that they will not agree with either Scripture or tradition. It is such people, my dear friend, that 3 we have to fight with, who like slippery snakes are always trying to escape us. Therefore we must resist them on all sides, hoping that by cutting off their escape we may be able to bring them to turn to the truth. For although it is not easy for a soul which has been seized by error to turn back, still it is not absolutely impossible to put error to flight by putting the truth beside it. [51]

The tradition of the apostles, made clear in all the world, 3 can be clearly seen in every church by those who wish to behold the truth. We can enumerate those who were established by the apostles as bishops in the churches, and their successors down to our time, none of whom taught or thought of anything like their mad ideas. Even if the apostles had known of hidden mysteries, which they taught to the perfect secretly and apart

---

[48] I Cor. 2:6.
[49] Probably the unnamed heretic of I. 11:3, whom Irenaeus or his source may have left nameless as a recent and therefore familiar (or painful) defection; attempts to identify him by conjectural restoration of misunderstood Greek do not seem convincing.
[50] *Presbuteroi* in Irenaeus are sometimes holders of an office in the Church, but often, as probably here, the grand old men who were links in the chain of tradition.
[51] Apparently a citation of Justin, Apol. I, ch. 12, *fin.*

from others, they would have handed them down especially to those to whom they were entrusting the churches themselves. For they certainly wished those whom they were leaving as their successors, handing over to them their own teaching position, to be perfect and irreproachable, since their sound conduct would be a great benefit [to the Church], and failure 2 on their part the greatest calamity. But since it would be very long in such a volume as this to enumerate the successions of all the churches, I can by pointing out the tradition which that very great, oldest, and well-known Church, founded and established at Rome by those two most glorious apostles Peter and Paul, received from the apostles, and its faith known among men, which comes down to us through the successions of bishops, put to shame all of those who in any way, either through wicked self-conceit, or through vainglory, or through blind and evil opinion, gather as they should not.[52] For every church must be in harmony with this Church because of its outstanding pre-eminence, that is, the faithful from everywhere, since the apostolic tradition is preserved in it by those from everywhere.[53]

3   When the blessed apostles had founded and built up the Church, they handed over the ministry of the episcopate to Linus. Paul mentions this Linus in his Epistles to Timothy. Anencletus succeeded him. After him Clement received the lot of the episcopate in the third place from the apostles. He

[52] I.e., assemble apart from the gatherings in communion with the Church (cf. Ignatius, Eph., ch. 5); or perhaps more generally, do not gather the harvest with the Lord, and so scatter (Luke 11:23; Matt. 12:30; cf. Lebreton, *The History of the Primitive Church*, p. 676).

[53] *Ad hanc enim ecclesiam propter potentiorem principalitatem necesse est omnem convenire ecclesiam, hoc est, eos qui sunt undique fideles, in qua semper ab his qui sunt undique conservata est ea quae est ab apostolis traditio.* This sentence, preserved only in Latin, deserves to be quoted more because of the many discussions of it than for its own importance. Eusebius tantalizingly begins a quotation immediately afterward with what he considered of real interest in this passage. Irenaeus' solid reasons for selecting the Roman Church as his chief sample of the preservation of tradition in all churches have just been given; he seems here to mix them rather confusingly with the thought that as the city of Rome was a microcosm of the Empire, so was the Roman Church a microcosm of the Christian world, and the confluence of Christians there preserved the faith by representing all local traditions; *convenire* might mean simply "meet," but is probably best translated as above; for recent discussion see W. L. Knox, "Irenaeus *Adv. Haer.* III. 3:2." *Journal of Theological Studies*, Vol. 47, 1946, pp. 180–184, and P. Galtier, " '. . . Ab his qui sunt undique. . .' Irénée, *Adv. Haer.* III. 3:2," *Revue d'histoire ecclésiastique*, Vol. 44, 1949, pp. 411–428.

had seen the apostles and associated with them, and still had their preaching sounding in his ears and their tradition before his eyes—and not he alone, for there were many still left in his time who had been taught by the apostles. In this Clement's time no small discord arose among the brethren in Corinth, and the Church in Rome sent a very powerful letter to the Corinthians, leading them to peace, renewing their faith, and declaring the tradition which they had recently received from the apostles, which declared one almighty God, maker of heaven and earth and fashioner of man, who brought about the Deluge, and called Abraham; who brought out the people from the land of Egypt; who spoke with Moses; who ordained the Law and sent the Prophets; and who has prepared fire for the devil and his angels. Those who care to can learn from this Writing that he was proclaimed by the churches as the Father of our Lord Jesus Christ, and so understand the apostolic tradition of the Church, since this Epistle is older than those present false teachers who make up lies about another God above the Demiurge and maker of all these things that are.[54] Evarestus succeeded to this Clement, and Alexander to Evarestus; then Xystus was installed as the sixth from the apostles, and after him Telesphorus, who met a glorious martyrdom; [55] then Hyginus, then Pius, and after him Anicetus. Soter followed Anicetus, and Eleutherus now in the twelfth place from the apostles holds the lot of the episcopate. In this very order and succession the apostolic tradition in the Church and the preaching of the truth has come down even to us. This is a full demonstration that it is one and the same life-giving faith which has been preserved in the Church from the apostles to the present, and is handed on in truth.

Similarly Polycarp, who not only was taught by apostles, 4 and associated with many who had seen Christ, but was installed by apostles for Asia, as bishop in the church in Smyrna— I saw him myself in my early youth—survived for a long time, and departed this life in a ripe old age by a glorious and magnificent martyrdom. He always taught what he learned from the apostles, which the Church continues to hand on, and

---

54 Irenaeus properly recognizes the Old Testament emphasis of I Clement; evidently, like us, he derived his knowledge about it entirely from the document itself, except for the tradition of some connection with Clement.

55 "Gloriously bore his witness"; the verb is doubtless used technically, as is the noun in the next section.

which are the only truths. The churches in Asia all bear witness to this, as do those who have succeeded Polycarp down to the present time; he is certainly a much more trustworthy and dependable witness than Valentinus and Marcion and the other false thinkers. When he visited Rome under Anicetus, he converted many of the above-mentioned heretics to the Church of God, proclaiming that he had received from the apostles the one and only truth, the same which is handed on by the Church. There are those who have heard him tell how when John the disciple of the Lord went to bathe at Ephesus, and saw Cerinthus inside, he rushed out of the bath without washing, but crying out, "Let us escape, lest the bath should fall while Cerinthus the enemy of the truth is in it." Polycarp himself, when Marcion once met him and said, "Do you know us?" answered, "I know you, the first-born of Satan." The apostles and their disciples took such great care not even to engage in conversations with the corrupters of the truth, as Paul also said, "A heretical man after a first and second warning avoid, knowing that such a man has fallen away and is a sinner, being self-condemned."[56] There is also a very powerful letter of Polycarp addressed to the Philippians, from which those who care to, and are concerned for their own salvation, can learn the character of his faith and [his] preaching of the truth. The church in Ephesus also, which was founded by Paul, and where John survived until the time of Trajan, is a true witness of the tradition of the apostles.

4 ⌊Since there are so many clear testimonies, we should not seek from others for the truth which can easily be received from the Church. There the apostles, like a rich man making a deposit, fully bestowed upon her all that belongs to the truth, so that whoever wishes may receive from her the water of life.⌉She is the entrance to life; all the others are thieves and robbers.[57] Therefore we ought to avoid them, but to love with the greatest zeal the things of the Church, and so to lay hold of the tradition of the truth. What if there should be a dispute about some matter of moderate importance? Should we not turn to the oldest churches, where the apostles themselves were known, and find out from them the clear and certain answer to the problem now being raised? Even if the apostles had not left their Writings to us, ought we not to follow the rule of the tradition which they handed down to those to whom they 2 committed the churches? Many barbarian peoples who believe

---

[56] Titus 3:10, 11.   [57] Cf. Rev. 22:17; John 10:7, 8.

in Christ follow this rule, having [the message of their] salvation written in their hearts by the Spirit without paper and ink. Diligently following the old tradition, they believe in one God, maker of heaven and earth and of all that is in them, through Christ Jesus the Son of God, who on account of his abundant love for his creation submitted to be born of a virgin, himself by himself uniting man to God, and having suffered under Pontius Pilate, and risen, and having been received up into splendor, is to come in glory as the Saviour of those who are saved, and the judge of those who are judged, and will send into eternal fire those who alter the truth, and despise his Father and his coming. Those who believe in this faith without written documents are barbarians in our speech, but in their convictions, habits, and behavior they are, because of their faith, most wise, and are pleasing to God, living in all righteousness and purity and wisdom. If anyone should preach to them the inventions of the heretics, speaking in their own language, they would at once stop their ears and run far, far away, not enduring even to listen to such blasphemous speech. So by that old tradition of the apostles they do not even take into their minds whatever their impressive words may mean.

Nor do they have any proper congregation or established teaching. For there were no Valentinians before Valentinus, or 3 Marcionites before Marcion; nor were there any of these perverse thinkers whom I have listed above before the founders and inventors of their perversity. For Valentinus came to Rome under Hyginus; he. flourished under Pius and remained until [the time of] Anicetus. Cerdon, who was Marcion's predecessor, used to come into the Church under Hyginus and make his confession,[58] reaching the point where he would now give his secret teaching, now make his confession in public, and then was convicted of his evil teachings and was separated from the assembly of the brethren. Marcion, who followed him, flourished under Anicetus, who held the tenth place in the series of bishops. As we have shown, the others who are called Gnostics began with Menander, the disciple of Simon, and each has as his father and chief the one whose opinions he followed. All of these rebelled in their apostasy much later [than the founding of the Church], in the midst of the Church's history.

58 *Exomologoumenos* probably confession of sins, as in I.13:7 (and the regular term for public penance, *exomologēsis*), though possibly confession of the faith.

5   So the apostolic tradition is preserved in the Church and has come down to us. Let us turn, then, to the demonstration from the Writings of those apostles who recorded the gospel, in which they recorded their conviction about God, showing that our Lord Jesus Christ is the Truth, and in him is no lie—as also David said when he prophesied his birth of a virgin and the resurrection of the dead, "Truth has come forth from the earth." [59] The apostles, being disciples of the truth, are apart from every lie. For a lie has no fellowship with the truth, any more than light with darkness, but the presence of one excludes the other. [60] So our Lord, being the Truth, did not lie, and he would never have confessed one whom he knew to be the result of a defect as God and God of all, supreme King and his Father, the perfect [acknowledging] the imperfect, a spiritual being one who was natural, one who was in the Pleroma one outside it. Nor did his disciples name any other being as God, or call any other Lord, except him who is the true God and Lord of all—though it be said by these vainest of sophists that the apostles hypocritically adjusted their teaching to the capacity of their hearers, giving answers according to the presumptions of inquirers, telling blind fables to the blind according to their blindness, to the sick according to their sickness, and to those who were going astray according to their error, and to those who thought that the Demiurge was the only God declaring that this was the case, but to those who can understand the ineffable Father expounding the unspeakable mystery by parables and riddles. So [they allege] the Lord and the apostles did not exercise their teaching office in strict accordance with the truth, but hypocritically in accordance with what differ-

2   ent individuals could grasp. This is not the behavior of those who heal and give life, but rather of those who aggravate disease and increase ignorance. The Law shows itself much truer than such people, when it says that whoever leads a blind man astray in the way is accursed. [61] The apostles were sent to find those who were lost, and to bring sight to those who did not see, and healing to the sick, and so they did not speak to them in accordance with their previous opinions but by

---

[59] Ps. 85 (84):11; "truth" is used practically as a name of Christ, as later not uncommonly by Latin Fathers (especially Augustine and Gregory the Great).

[60] II Cor. 6:14; I John 1:6; Irenaeus' combinations of passages from either Testament or both in such allusive references are an interesting aspect of his use of the Bible.

[61] Deut. 27:18.

manifestation of the truth. For no men of any kind would be acting rightly if they told blind men who were already beginning to fall over the precipice to continue in their very dangerous way, as if it were a sound one and as if they would come through all right. What doctor, when wishing to cure a sick man, would act in accordance with the desires of the patient, and not in accordance with the requirements of medicine? The Lord himself testified that he came as the physician of the sick, saying, "The well have no need of a physician but the sick; I came not to call the righteous but sinners to repentance." [62] How, then, are the sick to be made strong? and how are sinners to repent? Is it by persevering as they are? or on the contrary, by undergoing a great change and reversal of their previous behavior, by which they brought upon themselves serious illness, and many sins? Ignorance, the mother of these things, is driven out by knowing the truth. Therefore the Lord imparted knowledge of the truth to his disciples, by which he cured those who were suffering, and restrained sinners from sin. So he did not speak to them in accordance with their previous ideas, nor answer in accordance with the presumptions of inquirers, but in accordance with the sound teaching, without any pretense or respect for persons.

This can be shown by the words of the Lord. He displayed 3 the Son of God to those of the circumcision, the Christ who was predicted by the prophets—that is, he showed himself, who restored freedom to men and gave them the heritage of incorruption. Then the apostles taught the Gentiles that they should leave the vain sticks and stones which they thought of as gods, and worship the true God, who had established and made the whole human race, and by his ordinance nourished, increased, and preserved them, and gave them their being; and that they should look for his Son Jesus Christ—who redeemed us from the apostasy by his blood, that we also might be made a holy people—who is to come down from heaven in the power of the Father, and who is to execute judgment upon all, and give the good things that come from God to those who have kept his commandments. He appeared in these last times and gathered and united into one those who were far off and those who were near, enlarging Japheth and establishing him in the dwelling of Shem. [63]

62 Mark 2:17; Luke 5:31, 32; Matt. 9:12, 13.
63 Gen. 9:27; Eph. 2:13, 17.

John's Refutation of Gnosticism

11 John, the disciple of the Lord, proclaimed this faith and wished by the proclamation of the gospel to destroy the error which had been planted among men by Cerinthus, and much earlier by those who are called Nicolaitans, who are an offshoot of the knowledge which is falsely so called, [writing] to confound them and show that there is one God who made all things by his Word. It is not true, as they say, that the Fashioner is one and the Father of the Lord another, and the Son of the Fashioner one being, the Christ from on high another, who remained free from suffering, descending on Jesus the Son of the Fashioner and returning again to his Pleroma; [they allege] that the Beginning was the Only-begotten, and Logos the true Son of the Only-begotten,[64] and that this world order in which we live was not made by the supreme God but by some power far inferior to him and cut off from contact with those things which are invisible and ineffable.

The disciple of the Lord wished to cut off all such ideas and to establish the rule of truth in the Church, that there is one God Almighty who made all things by his Word, both visible and invisible, and also to indicate that through the same Word through whom God made this world order he also bestowed salvation on the men who belong to this order. So he starts off with the teaching according to the Gospel, thus: "In the beginning was the Word and the Word was with God and the Word was God; this was in the beginning with God. All things were made through him, and without him nothing was made. What was made was life in him, and the life was the light of men, and the light shines in the darkness and the darkness has not seized hold of it."[65] All things, he says, were made through him; this word "all" therefore includes this world order of ours. It must not be conceded to them that "all" means what is within that Pleroma of theirs. For if this Pleroma of theirs contains everything, then this order is not outside it, as I have shown in the Book before this. But if these things are outside the Pleroma, which really does not seem possible, then this Pleroma of theirs does not comprise "all things," and so [in any case] this vast created order is not merely "outside."

---

[64] A Gnostic interpretation of the Prologue to the Fourth Gospel, which takes Beginning (Arche) and Only-begotten (Monogenes) as entities in a Gnostic system.   [65] John 1:1–5.

John himself indeed takes away all our disputes on this matter 2
when he says: "He was in this world, and the world was made
by him, and the world knew him not. He came to his own
[things] and his own [people] did not receive him." [66] Now
according to Marcion and those who are like him, neither was
the world made by him, nor did he come to his own things, but
rather to alien. According to some of the Gnostics, this world
was made by angels and not through the Word of God. According to the followers of Valentinus again, it was not made
through him, but through the Demiurge. For he, as they say,
made certain images in imitation of the things above, but the
Demiurge carried out the forming of the creation. For they say
that the Lord and Demiurge of this created order of things,
by whom they say this world was made, was sent forth by the
Mother—when the Gospel clearly states that all things were
made through the Word, who was in the beginning with God,
which Word, he says, was made flesh and dwelt among us.

Now according to them neither was the Word made flesh, 3
nor Christ, nor the Saviour who was made out of all [the
Aeons]. For they allege that the Word and Christ never came
into this world, and that the Saviour was neither incarnate nor
suffered, but that he descended as a dove upon that Jesus
who was made by [higher] dispensation, and when he had
proclaimed the unknown Father, ascended again into the
Pleroma. Some of them indeed say that this Jesus who was by
dispensation was incarnate and suffered, and that he had passed
through Mary like water through a tube; others say that it
was the son of the Demiurge, on whom the Jesus who was by
dispensation descended; others again say that Jesus indeed
was born of Joseph and Mary, and that Christ who came from
above descended on him, being without flesh and free from
suffering. But according to none of the views of the heretics
was the Word of God made flesh. If one should read over all
their credal statements, he would find that they always bring
in the Word of God and the Christ who is from above as without
flesh and free from suffering. Some think that he was manifested as a transfigured man, but say that he was neither born
nor incarnate. Others say that he did not even take the form of
a man, but descended like a dove on that Jesus who was
born of Mary. So the disciple of the Lord shows them all to be
false witnesses when he says, "And the Word was made flesh,
and dwelt among us." And so that we should not query what 4

[66] John 1:11.

God it was whose Word was made flesh, he further taught, saying, "There was a man sent from God, his name was John; he came for witness, to bear witness of the light. He was not himself the light, but [came] that he might bear witness of the light." [67] What God was it who sent John the Forerunner, who bore witness of the light? He whose angel Gabriel is, who brought the good news of his birth, he who also promised through the prophets that he would send his angel before the face of his Son, and that he would prepare his way, that is, would bear witness of the light, in the spirit and power of Elijah. [68] And whose servant and prophet was Elijah? His who made the heaven and the earth, as he also confessed. So how could John, who was sent by the Creator and Fashioner of this world, testify of that light which descended from things that are unnamable and invisible? For all the heretics have taught that the Demiurge was ignorant of the power above him, as witness and pointer-out of whom John appeared. [69] Because of this, the Lord said that he ranked as more than a prophet. For all the other prophets proclaimed the coming of the Father's light, and longed to be worthy to see him whom they foretold; John, however, both predicted him like the others, and also saw and pointed him out when he came, and persuaded many to believe in him, so that he ranks as both prophet and apostle. [70] This is something more than a prophet —first apostles, then prophets [71]—but all came from one and the same God.

5   It was a good thing which was made by God's creation in the vineyard, and was first drunk as wine. [72] None of those who drank of it spoke badly of it, and the Lord also took some of it. But better wine was that which was made by the Word directly and simply out of water for the use of those who were invited to the wedding. Although the Lord could have provided wine for the feasters and satisfied the hungry with food without using any object of the created order, he did not do so; but taking loaves which came from the earth, and giving thanks, and again making water into wine, he satisfied those who lay

[67] John 1:6–8.   [68] Luke 1:17 (Mal. 4:5).
[69] John must therefore have come from the highest power, not from an inferior ignorant of him; yet John belonged to the God of the Old Testament.
[70] Matt. 11:9; Luke 7:26; cf. John 1:19–37.   [71] I Cor. 12:28.
[72] An abrupt but not ineffective transition; we seem to come here on notes of a sermon in which the two kinds of wine drunk at Cana are treated as symbols of the two covenants.

down to eat, and he gave drink to those who were invited to the wedding. [73] Thus he showed that God who made the earth, and commanded it to bring forth fruit, and established the waters, and brought forth the springs, also in these last times through his Son gives to the human race the blessing of food and the favor of drink, the incomprehensible [acting] through the comprehensible and the invisible through the visible, since there is none beyond him, but he is in the bosom of the Father. For, he says, no man ever saw God, unless the only-begotten 6 Son of God, who is in the bosom of the Father, himself declared him. For the Father who is invisible is declared to all by his Son who is in his bosom. Because of this he is known by those to whom the Son has revealed him, and again the Father through the Son gives knowledge of his Son to those who love him. [74] So Nathaniel learned from him and knew him, to whom the Lord bore witness, "This is a true Israelite, in whom is no guile." The Israelite knew his King, in that he said to him, "Rabbi, you are the Son of God, you are the King of Israel." [75] Peter was taught by him and knew the Christ, the Son of the Living God, who said: "Behold my beloved Son, in whom I am well pleased; I will put my Spirit upon him and he will proclaim judgment to the nations. He will not strive, nor shout, nor will anyone hear his voice in the streets; he will not break the shaking reed, and will not extinguish the smoking flax, until he send forth judgment into strife, and the nations will hope in his name." [76]

THE UNITY AND NUMBER OF THE GOSPELS

These, then, are the principles of the gospel. They declare 7 one God, the maker of this universe, who was proclaimed by the Prophets, and who through Moses established the dispensation of the Law, the Father of our Lord Jesus Christ, and besides him they know no other God, nor any other Father. So firmly established is this position in the Gospels that the heretics themselves bear witness to them, and starting from them each one of them tries to establish his teaching. So the Ebionites, who use only the Gospel According to Matthew, are shown by that very document not to have right views about the Lord.

---

[73] John 6:11 (and parallels) and 2:9.
[74] John 1:18; Matt. 10:27; Luke 10:22.   [75] John 1:47, 49.
[76] Matt. 12:18–20 (Isa. 42:1–3); apparently from a Greek text that read *neikos*, "strife," for *nikos*, "victory."

Marcion cut up that According to Luke, yet is clearly, by the passages which he still keeps, shown to be a blasphemer of the one existing God. Those who separate Jesus from Christ and say that Christ remained impassible while Jesus suffered, and try to bring forward the Gospel According to Mark, can be corrected out of that, if they will read it with a love of the truth. The followers of Valentinus, who make a great use of that According to John to demonstrate their conjunctions, can be demonstrated from that to be wholly mistaken, as I have demonstrated in the first Book. Since [even] our opponents bear witness to us and make use of these [works], our demonstration based on them is firm and true.

8 The Gospels could not possibly be either more or less in number than they are. Since there are four zones of the world in which we live, and four principal winds, while the Church is spread over all the earth, and the pillar and foundation of the Church is the gospel, and the Spirit of life, it fittingly has four pillars, everywhere breathing out incorruption and revivifying men. From this it is clear that the Word, the artificer of all things, he who sits upon the cherubim and sustains all things, being manifested to men gave us the gospel, fourfold in form but held together by one Spirit. As David said, when asking for his coming, "O sitter upon the cherubim, show yourself." [77] For the cherubim have four faces, and their faces are images of the activity of the Son of God. For the first living creature, it says, was like a lion, signifying his active and princely and royal character; the second was like an ox, showing his sacrificial and priestly order; the third had the face of man, indicating very clearly his coming in human guise; and the fourth was like a flying eagle, making plain the giving of the Spirit who broods over the Church. Now the Gospels, in which Christ is enthroned, are like these. [78] For that According to John expounds his princely and mighty and glorious birth from the Father, saying, "In the beginning was the Word, and the Word was with God, and the Word was God," and, "All things were made by him, and without him was nothing made." Therefore this Gospel is deserving of all confidence, for such indeed is his person. That According to Luke, as having a priestly character, began with the priest Zacharias offering incense to God. For

[77] Ps. 80(79):1.
[78] The first appearance of the creatures of Ezek., ch. 1, and Rev. 4:7, 8, as symbols of the Evangelists; later the lion is assigned to Saint Mark and the eagle to Saint John.

the fatted calf was already being prepared which was to be
sacrificed for the finding of the younger son.⁷⁹ Matthew proclaims his human birth, saying, "The book of the generation
of Jesus Christ, son of David, son of Abraham," and, "The birth
of Jesus Christ was in this manner," for this Gospel is manlike,
and so through the whole Gospel [Christ] appears as a man of a
humble mind, and gentle. But Mark takes his beginning from
the prophetic Spirit who comes on men from on high, saying,
"The beginning of the gospel of Jesus Christ, as it is written in
Isaiah the prophet," showing a winged image of the gospel.
Therefore he made his message compendious and summary,
for such is the prophetic character. Again, the Word of God
himself used to speak to the patriarchs before Moses, in a divine
and glorious manner, but for those under the Law he established a priestly and liturgical order; after this, becoming man,
he sent out the gift of the Holy Spirit into the whole earth,
guarding us by his own wings. As is the activity of the Son of
God, such is the form of the living creatures; and as is the form
of the living creatures, such is also the character of the Gospel.
For the living creatures were quadriform, and the gospel and
the activity of the Lord is fourfold. Therefore four general
covenants were given to mankind: one was that of Noah's
deluge, by the bow; the second was Abraham's, by the sign of
circumcision; the third was the giving of the Law by Moses;
and the fourth is that of the Gospel, through our Lord Jesus
Christ.

Since this is the case, they are foolish and uninstructed, even 9
audacious, who destroy the pattern of the gospel, and present
either more or less than four forms of the gospel—the former,
because they claim to have found more than the truth, the
latter because they annul the dispensations of God. So Marcion,
rejecting the whole gospel, rather indeed cutting himself off
from the gospel, still boasts of having a share in the gospel.
Others frustrate the gift of the Spirit, which in these last
times has been poured out on the human race according to the
Father's decree, refusing to admit that aspect [of the gospel]
which is according to John's Gospel, in which the Lord promised that he would send the Paraclete; but they reject together
both the gospel and the prophetic Spirit. Unhappy men, who
want to be some kind of false prophets, but deny the gift of
prophecy to the Church, suffering what those do who, because
of those who come in insincerity, separate themselves from the

⁷⁹ An allegorical interpretation of Luke 15:23.

fellowship of the brethren. It can be understood that men of this kind would not accept the apostle Paul either. For in the Epistle addressed to the Corinthians he speaks carefully about prophetic gifts, and knows of men and women who prophesied in the Church. Sinning in all these ways against the Spirit of God, they fall into the unforgivable sin.[80] But the followers of Valentinus, putting away all fear, bring forward their own compositions and boast that they have more Gospels than really exist. Indeed their audacity has gone so far that they entitle their recent composition the Gospel of Truth, though it agrees in nothing with the Gospels of the apostles, and so no Gospel of theirs is free of blasphemy. For if what they produce is the Gospel of Truth, and is different from those which the apostles handed down to us, those who care to can learn how it can be shown from the Scriptures themselves that [then] what is handed down from the apostles is not the Gospel of Truth.[81] That those alone are true and firm, and that there can be no more Gospels than have been mentioned before, nor any fewer, I have shown by these many great arguments. For since God made all things in due order and harmony, it was proper that the outer form of the gospel should be well ordered and well fitted together. So having examined the view of those who handed the gospel down to us, from their very first principles, let us proceed to the other apostles, and look into their view about God; and after that let us hear the very words of the Lord.

[80] Irenaeus' view of the Montanists; he objects to their exclusive Puritanism, and not so much to their claim to prophetic gifts as to their denial that these gifts already existed in the Church, which shows them to be false prophets who thus sin against the Holy Spirit by denying his working in others (Matt. 12:31; Mark 3:28; Luke 12:10).

[81] Which is preposterous.

THE TEXT: (BOOK V) REDEMPTION AND THE WORLD TO COME

DOCTRINE OF REDEMPTION IN REPLY TO THE GNOSTICS

We could in no other way have learned the things of God [1] unless our Teacher, being the Word, had been made man. For none could declare to us the things of the Father, except his own Word. For who else has known the mind of the Lord, or who has become his counselor? [82] Nor again could we have learned in any other way than by seeing our Teacher, that we might become imitators of his works and doers of his words, and so have communion with him, receiving our increase from him who is perfect and before all creation. We were but recently made by him who is the highest and best, by him who is able to bestow the gift of incorruptibility, made according to the image which is with him and predestined according to the foreknowledge of the Father to be what we were not yet. Made the beginning of [his new] creation, we have received [this gift] in times foreknown by the dispensation of the Word, who is perfect in all things, for he is the mighty Word, and true man. Redeeming us by his blood in accordance with his reasonable [83] nature, he gave himself a ransom for those who had been led into captivity. Since the apostasy tyrannized over us unjustly, and when we belonged by nature to God Almighty had unnaturally alienated us, God's Word, mighty in all things, [reclaimed us], making us his own disciples. Not failing in his quality of justice, he acted justly against the apostasy itself, not redeeming his own from it by force, although it at the beginning had merely tyrannized over us, greedily seizing the things that were not its own, but by persuasion, as it is

---

82 Rom. 11:34.
83 The Logos acted *logikos*, a play on words which cannot be rendered exactly in either Latin or English.

fitting for God to receive what he wishes by gentleness and not by force. [84] So neither was the standard of what is just infringed nor did the ancient creation of God perish.

So, then, since the Lord redeemed us by his own blood, and gave his soul for our souls, and his flesh for our bodies, and poured out the Spirit of the Father to bring about the union and communion of God and man—bringing God down to men by [the working of] the Spirit, and again raising man to God by his incarnation—and by his coming firmly and truly giving us incorruption, by our communion with God, all the 2 teachings of the heretics are destroyed. Vain are those who say that his appearance [on earth] was a mere fiction. These things did not take place fictitiously but in reality. If he had appeared as man when he was not really human, the Spirit of God could not have rested on him, as was the case, since the Spirit is invisible, [85] nor would there have been any truth in him, what was [then taking place] not being what it seemed to be. As I said before, Abraham and the other prophets saw him pro- phetically, prophesying by vision what was to be. If he then had appeared without really being what he appeared to be, this would have been just another prophetic vision for men, and they would have had to wait for another coming, in which he would be indeed what now was seen prophetically. I have shown too that to say that his appearance was only seeming is the same as to say that he took nothing from Mary. He would not have had real flesh and blood, by which he paid the price [of our salvation], unless he had indeed recapitulated in him- self the ancient making of Adam. Vain therefore are the Valen- tinians who teach this, and so reject the [new] life of the flesh and scorn what God has made.

3   Vain also are the Ebionites, who do not accept in their souls by faith the union of God and man, but remain in the old leaven of [merely] human birth—not wishing to understand that the Holy Spirit came upon Mary, and the power of the Most High overshadowed her, and so what was born [of her] is holy and the Son of God Most High, the Father of all who thus brought about his incarnation and displayed the new birth, so that as we by the former birth were heirs of death,. by this birth we should be heirs of life. They reject the mixture

[84] Cf. Diog. 7:4; Irenaeus here avoids referring to the prince of the apostasy, but in the process almost personifies the *apostasia* itself.
[85] And therefore presumably could "rest" only on a visible being, not on another invisible one.

of the heavenly wine, and wish to be only the water of the world, not receiving God into their mixture,[86] but remaining in that Adam who was conquered and driven out of paradise. They do not reflect that as at the beginning of our creation in Adam the breath of life from God, united with the created substance, animated man and made him a rational animal, so at the end the Word of the Father and the Spirit of God, united with the ancient substance of the creation of Adam, made a living and perfect man, receiving the perfect Father, so that as in the animal we were all dead, in the spiritual we are all made alive. For Adam never escaped those hands of God, to whom the Father said, "Let us make man after our image and likeness." And therefore at the last it was not by the will of the flesh, nor by the will of a man, but by the decree of the Father that his hands perfected a living man, so that there might be a [second] Adam after the image and likeness of God.[87]

Vain indeed are they who say that God [the Son] came to 2 things not his own, as if covetous of things belonging to another, in order to hand over the man who was made by another to the God who neither made nor created him, who indeed from the beginning had nothing to do with the true fashioning of man.[88] For a coming such as they allege, to what was another's, would not have been just. Nor would he have truly redeemed us by his blood if he had not been truly made man, restoring again to his own creation what was said [of it] in the beginning, that man was made according to the image and likeness of God—not snatching by deceit what was another's, but justly and graciously claiming what was his own—for with reference to the apostasy, he justly redeemed us from it by his own blood, but with reference to us, who have been redeemed, he acted graciously. For we gave nothing to him first, nor does he desire anything from us, as if needing it; but we are in need of communion with him. Therefore he graciously poured himself out that he might gather us together into the bosom of the Father.

Vain above all are they who despise the whole dispensation 2 of God, and deny the salvation of the flesh and reject its rebirth, saying that it is not capable of incorruption. For if this [mortal flesh] is not saved, then neither did the Lord redeem us by his

---

86 A reference to the Ebionite Eucharists, celebrated with water alone (cf. Epiphanius, *Haereses* 30:16).
87 I Cor. 15:45; John 1:13; the "hands of God" are presumably the Word and the Spirit.
88 I.e., the Marcionites.

blood, nor is the cup of the Eucharist the communion of his blood, and the bread which we break the communion of his body. For blood is only to be found in veins and flesh, and the rest of [physical] human nature, which the Word of God was indeed made [partaker of, and so] he redeemed us by his blood. So also his apostle says, "In whom we have redemption by his blood, and the remission of sins."[89] For since we are his members, and are nourished by [his] creation—and he himself gives us this creation, making the sun to rise, and sending the rain as he wills—he declares that the cup, [taken] from the creation, is his own blood, by which he strengthens our blood, and he has firmly assured us that the bread, [taken] from the

3 creation, is his own body, by which our bodies grow. For when the mixed cup and the bread that has been prepared receive the Word of God, and become the Eucharist, the body and blood of Christ,[90] and by these our flesh grows and is confirmed, how can they say that flesh cannot receive the free gift of God, which is eternal life, since it is nourished by the body and blood of the Lord, and made a member of him? As the blessed Paul says in the Epistle to the Ephesians, that we are members of his body, of his flesh and his bones.[91] He does not say this about a [merely] spiritual and invisible man, for the spirit has neither bones nor flesh, but about [God's] dispensation for the real man, [a dispensation] consisting of flesh and nerves and bones, which is nourished by his cup, which is his blood, and grows by the bread which is his body.

And just as the wooden branch of the vine, placed in the earth, bears fruit in its own time—and as the grain of wheat, falling into the ground and there dissolved, rises with great increase by the Spirit of God, who sustains all things, and then by the wisdom of God serves for the use of men, and when it receives the Word of God becomes the Eucharist, which is the body and blood of Christ—so also our bodies which are nourished by it, and then fall into the earth and are dissolved therein, shall rise at the proper time, the Word of God bestowing on them this rising again, to the glory of God the Father. It is he who indeed grants to this mortal immortality, and gives

[89] Col. 1:14.
[90] " And blood" lacking in Greek (quoted here by John of Damascus), but doubtless correctly present in Latin; Irenaeus thinks of consecration of the Eucharist by the power of the Word (as in the Eucharistic prayer of Sarapion), or perhaps by the divinely ordered pattern of prayer (cf. Justin, Apol. I, ch. 66).
[91] Eph. 5:30.

to the corruptible the gracious gift of incorruption, for God's power is made perfect in weakness, [92] so that we should not be puffed up as if we had life from ourselves, and be exalted against God, developing ungrateful minds. But we learn by experience that our survival forever comes from his greatness, not from our nature, so that we may neither ignore the glory that surrounds God as he is nor be ignorant of our own nature, but may see what it is that God can do, and what man receives as a gift [from him], and so may not wander from the true conception of the reality of things, with reference to both God and man. May it not be, as I have said, that God allows our dissolution into the earth for this very purpose, that being instructed in every way we should for the future be quite definite about all [these] things, being ignorant neither of God nor of ourselves?

THE NEW CREATION IN CHRIST "RECAPITULATES" THE OLD

So the Lord now manifestly came to his own, and, born by **19** his own created order which he himself bears, he by his obedience on the tree renewed [and reversed] what was done by disobedience in [connection with] a tree; and [the power of] that seduction by which the virgin Eve, already betrothed to a man, had been wickedly seduced was broken when the angel in truth brought good tidings to the Virgin Mary, who already [by her betrothal] belonged to a man. [93] For as Eve was seduced by the word of an angel to flee from God, having rebelled against his Word, so Mary by the word of an angel received the glad tidings that she would bear God by obeying his Word. [94] The former was seduced to disobey

---

[92] I Cor. 15:53; II Cor. 12:9.

[93] The rhetorical balance of this sentence is clear, but in detail it evidently baffled the Latin translator, whose version is all but unintelligible, so that a literal English rendering is scarcely possible; the key word *recapitulare* doubtless represents Greek *anakephalaioō* (cf. Eph. 1:10)—it is clearly used with a variety of associations, and I have ventured to translate "renew." The idea has a considerable history in both theology and devotion; cf. the liturgical preface for Passiontide, "Who on the Tree of the Cross didst give salvation unto mankind; that whence death arose, thence life also might rise again: and that he who by a tree once overcame, might likewise by a Tree be overcome, through Christ our Lord" (translation from *Common Service Book of the Lutheran Church*, p. 59. Philadelphia, 1917).

[94] Luke 1:38; in this sentence I have rendered *verbum* by "Word" and *sermo* by "word," as probably representing *logos* and *rhēma*, respectively, although the difference here may not be significant.

God[95] [and so fell], but the latter was persuaded to obey God, so that the Virgin Mary might become the advocate of the virgin Eve.[96] As the human race was subjected to death through [the act of] a virgin, so was it saved by a virgin, and thus the disobedience of one virgin was precisely balanced by the obedience of another. Then indeed the sin of the first-formed man was amended by the chastisement of the First-begotten, the wisdom of the serpent was conquered by the simplicity of the dove,[97] and the chains were broken by which we were in bondage to death.

20, 2   Therefore he renews these things in himself, uniting man to the Spirit; and placing the Spirit in man, he himself is made the head of the Spirit, and gives the Spirit to be the head of man, for by him we see and hear and speak.[98]

21   He therefore completely renewed all things, both taking up the battle against our enemy, and crushing him who at the beginning had led us captive in Adam, trampling on his head, as you find in Genesis that God said to the serpent, "And I will put enmity between you and the woman, and between your seed and her seed; he will be on the watch for your head, and you will be on the watch for his heel."[99] From then on it was proclaimed that he who was to be born of a virgin, after the likeness of Adam, would be on the watch for

[95] Latin MSS. offer two unsatisfactory readings for this phrase: "*Si eum obaudiret* [emended by Massuet to *ea inobedierat*] *deo*," and "*Sicut illa seducta est ut effugeret deum*" (see discussion in Harvey, Vol. II, p. 376); the balance of the sentence demands something like "*Sicut illa seducta est ut inobedierat deo*," which seems to be supported by the Armenian (for notes on which I am indebted to Mr. Garabed Poutoukhian of the Berkeley Divinity School); probably one Latin scribe tried to correct the partial repetition of the previous sentence, while another carried the repetition still further.

[96] Nothing more recondite is implied by this phrase than that the ultimate salvation of Eve came through the incarnation, which began with the obedience of Mary, the angelic message of Luke, ch. 1, thus reversing the diabolical temptation of Gen., ch. 3. The Armenian here has one of the diffuse renderings to which it often resorts in difficult passages—"That the Virgin Mary may become to the virgin Eve consolation and exhortation and intercessor."

[97] A curious use of Matt. 10:16.

[98] As in the old creation the breath of life was the highest thing in man (Gen. 2:7), making him what he is, so in the new creation the gift of the Spirit is the highest thing in the new man; the word "head," *kephalē*, is used with reference to various aspects of "recapitulation," suggesting mainly perhaps the highest or organizing principle of the new creation.

[99] Gen. 3:15; the LXX here reads "watch" for "bruise," a slight difference in Greek.

the serpent's head—this is the seed of which the apostle says in the Letter to the Galatians, "The law of works was established until the seed should come to whom the promise was made." He shows this still more clearly in the same Epistle when he says, "But when the fullness of time was come, God sent his Son, made of a woman."[1] The enemy would not have been justly conquered unless it had been a man [made] of woman who conquered him. For it was by a woman that he had power over man from the beginning, setting himself up in opposition to man. Because of this the Lord also declares himself to be the Son of Man, so renewing in himself that primal man from whom the formation [of man] by woman began, that as our race went down to death by a man who was conquered we might ascend again to life by a man who overcame; and as death won the palm of victory over us by a man, so we might by a man receive the palm of victory over death.

SOME GLIMPSES OF IRENAEUS' TEACHING ON THE LAST THINGS [2]

Since the opinions of some have been affected by the dis-**32** courses of the heretics, and they are ignorant of the dispensations of God, and the mystery of the resurrection of the just and the Kingdom which is the beginning of incorruption, by which Kingdom those who are worthy will gradually be accustomed to receive [the fullness of] God, it is necessary to speak about these things. For the righteous must first rise again at the appearance of God to receive in this created order, then made new, the promise of the inheritance which God promised to the Fathers, and will reign in this order. After this will come the judgment. It is just that in the same order in which they labored and were afflicted, and tried by all kinds of suffering, they should receive the fruits of [their suffering]—that in the same order in which they were put to death for the love of God they should again be made alive—and that in the same order in which they suffered bondage they should reign. For God is rich in all things, and all things are his.[3] It is right, therefore, for this created order to be restored to its pristine

---

1 Gal. 3:19 (with a reminiscence of Rom. 3:27); 4:4.
2 The five final chapters are missing in most MSS. and were published first by Feuardent; but their genuineness is indicated by Greek and Syriac quotations and the Armenian version, and they were doubtless omitted in most copies after the Church had come generally to repudiate the millenarianism supported by Irenaeus.
3 Rom. 10:12.

state, and to serve the just without restraint. The apostle made this clear in the Epistle to the Romans, saying: "For the expectation of the creature awaits the revelation of the sons of God. For the creature was subject to vanity, not willingly, but because of him who subjected it in hope; for the creature itself shall be freed from the servitude of corruption into the freedom of the glory of the sons of God."[4]

2   So, then, God's promise which he promised to Abraham remains firm. For he said, "Lift up your eyes, and look from the place where you now are, to the north and south and east and west; for all this land which you see I will give to you and to your seed forever." And again he says, "Arise and go through the land in its length and its breadth, for I will give it to you.[5] Yet he received no inheritance in it, not even a footprint, but was always a pilgrim and a stranger in it. And when Sarah his wife was dead, and the Hittites wanted to give him freely a place for her burial, he would not accept it, but bought a tomb, for which he gave four hundred didrachmas of silver, from Ephron the son of Zohar the Hittite.[6] He awaited the promise of God, and did not wish to seem to accept from men what God had promised to give him, saying to him again, "To your seed will I give this land, from the river of Egypt to the great river Euphrates."[7] If, then, God promised him the inheritance of the [promised] land, but in all his sojourning there he did not receive it, it must be that he will receive it with his seed, that is, with those who fear God and believe in him, at the resurrection of the just. For his seed is the Church, which receives through the Lord adoption to God, as John the Baptist said, "That God is able from these stones to raise up sons of Abraham."[8] The apostle also says in the Epistle to the Galatians, "But you, brothers, are like Isaac the sons of the promise." Again in the same he says clearly that those who have believed in Christ will receive Christ, the promise of Abraham, saying, "To Abraham were the promises uttered, and to his seed; and it does not say, And to seeds, as of many; but as of one, And to your seed, which is Christ." And again he says, confirming what has been said: "Even as Abraham believed God, and it was counted to him for righteousness. You know therefore, that those who are of faith, they are the sons of Abraham. Now the Scripture, foreseeing that God would justify the Gentiles by faith, foretold to Abraham, In you will

---

[4] Rom. 8:19–21.   [5] Gen. 13:14, 15, 17.   [6] Gen., ch. 23
[7] Gen. 15:18.   [8] Luke 3:8; Matt. 3:9.

all nations be blessed. Therefore those who are of faith are blessed with faithful Abraham." [9] So, then, those who are of faith are blessed with faithful Abraham, and they are sons of Abraham. Now God promised the inheritance of the land to Abraham and his seed, and neither Abraham nor his seed, that is, those who are justified by faith, have any inheritance in it now, but they will receive it at the resurrection of the just. For God is true and faithful, and therefore he says, "Blessed are the meek, for they shall inherit the earth." [10]

Because of this, when he came to his Passion, that he might [33] declare to Abraham and those with him the glad tidings of the opening of the inheritance, after he had given thanks as he held the cup, and had drunk of it, and given to the disciples, he said to them: "Drink of this, all of you. For this is my blood of the new covenant, which is shed for many for the remission of sins. For I say to you, that I will not drink of the produce of this vine, until that day when I shall drink it with you new in the Kingdom of my Father." [11] Then he himself will renew the inheritance of the land, and will re-establish the mystery of the glory of the sons, as David said, "He who renewed the face of the earth." [12] He promised that he would drink of the produce of the vine with his disciples, thus showing both the inheritance of the earth, in which the new produce of the vine is drunk, and the physical resurrection of his disciples. For the new flesh that rises again is the same that has received the new cup. For he cannot be understood as drinking the produce of the vine when established on high with his own, somewhere above the heavens, nor again are they who drink it without flesh, for it belongs to flesh and not to spirit to receive the drink of the vine. Because of this the Lord said: "When you give a [2] dinner, or a supper, do not invite the rich, nor your friends and neighbors and relations, lest they should invite you in return, and you receive a reward from them; but invite the lame, the blind, the beggars, who have nothing with which to reward you; for you will be rewarded at the resurrection of the just." [13] And again he says, "Whoever has left fields, or houses, or parents, or brothers, or sons for my sake, shall receive a

[9] Gal. 4:28; 3:16, 6-9.
[10] Matt. 5:5; Ps. 37(36):11. For "God" one should perhaps read "the Lord," in accordance with what follows, since the abbreviations DS and DNS could easily be confused.
[11] Matt. 26:27-29.
[12] Ps. 104(103):30, somewhat misquoted.
[13] Luke 14:12-14.

hundredfold in this world, and in the one to come will inherit eternal life." [14] Where are the hundredfold rewards in this age, the dinners offered to the poor, and the suppers for which a reward is received? These things are [to be] in the times of the Kingdom, that is, on the seventh day, which is sanctified, in which God rested from all his works which he made; this is the true Sabbath of the just, in which they will have no earthly work to do, but will have a table prepared before them by God, who will feed them with dainties of all kinds.

3   This is also the sense of the blessing of Isaac, with which he blessed Jacob, his younger son, saying, "Behold the smell of my son is as the smell of a rich field, which God has blessed." The field [here referred to] is the world—and therefore he added: "God give you of the dew of heaven, and of the fertility of the earth, abundance of grain and of wine. And the nations will serve you, and princes will worship you, and you will be Lord over your brother, and the sons of your father will worship you. He who curses you will be accursed, and he who blesses you will be blessed." [15] If one does not take this as referring to the destined [times] of the Kingdom, he finds himself in great contradiction and confusion, as the Jews have found themselves completely puzzled [in interpreting this passage]. For not only did the nations not serve Jacob in this life, but he, when he set forth after this blessing, served his uncle Laban the Syrian for twenty years. Not only was he not made lord of his brother, but he himself worshiped Esau his brother, when he came back from Mesopotamia to his father, and offered many gifts to him. How did he inherit an abundance of grain and wine who, because of the famine that took place in the land in which he dwelt, migrated to Egypt [and became] subject to Pharaoh, who then reigned in Egypt? So the aforesaid benediction undoubtedly refers to the times of the Kingdom, when the just, rising from the dead, will reign, when the created order will be made new and set free, and will produce an abundance of all kinds of food, from the dew of heaven and of the fertility of the earth. So the elders remembered, who had seen John the disciple of the Lord, that they had heard from him how the Lord taught about those days and said: "The days will come, in which vines will be produced, each one having a

[14] Matt. 19:29; Luke 18:29, 30; Jerome, commenting on Matt., ch. 19, notes and rejects the literal interpretation, pointing out that the reference to wives (which Irenaeus quietly omits) makes it ridiculous.
[15] Gen. 27:27–29.

thousand branches, and in each branch ten thousand twigs, and on each twig ten thousand shoots, and on each shoot ten thousand clusters, and in each cluster ten thousand grapes, and each grape when pressed will give twenty-five metretes of wine. And when one of the saints takes hold of a cluster, another will cry, 'I am a better cluster, take me, bless the Lord through me.' Similarly a grain of wheat will produce ten thousand ears, and each ear will have ten thousand grains, and each grain [will yield] ten pounds of clear pure flour; and the other fruits and seeds and grass will produce in the same proportion, and all the animals, using the foods which come from the earth, will be peaceful and harmonious with each other, and perfectly subject to man." [16]

Papias, who was a hearer of John and an associate of Poly- 4 carp, a fine old man, bore witness to these things in writing, in his fourth book, for there were five books that he compiled. And he went on and said, "These things are credible to believers, and when Judas, the traitor, did not believe, and asked, 'How can such kinds of production be accomplished [even] by the Lord?,' the Lord answered, 'Those who come to these things will see them.' " Isaiah, prophesying about these times, said: "And the wolf will feed with the lamb and the leopard will lie down with the kid, and the calf and bull and lion will feed together, and a little boy will lead them. The ox and the bear will feed together, and their young ones will be together, and the lion will eat straw like the ox. A little child will put his hand in the den of the asps, and into the nest of the young of the asps, and they shall do no harm, nor will they be able to injure anyone in my holy mountain." And again, summarizing, he says, "The wolves and sheep will feed together, and the lion will eat straw like the ox, and the serpent earth like bread; and they will not injure nor disturb in my holy mountain, says the Lord." [17] I am not unaware that some try to refer these [prophecies] to fierce men of diverse nations, and of different kinds of behavior, who have believed, and when they have believed have come to agree with the righteous. But although this be now true of various kinds of men who have come from different nations to the one conviction of the faith, nevertheless [it will also be true] in the resurrection of the just with reference to these animals, as it is said, "God is rich over all." [18] And when the created order is renewed, then the animals

16 Cf. Eusebius, *Hist. eccl.* III. 39:12, 13.   17 Isa. 11:6–9; 65:25.
18 Rom. 10:12.

ought to be subject to man, and return to the food which God gave them at the first, the fruit of the earth, as they were subject and obedient to Adam. Some other time, not now, [will be the occasion] to show how the lion will eat straw. But this is enough to show the size and richness of the fruits [then to be produced]. For if such an animal as the lion feeds on straw, what kind of grain must it be whose very straw is suitable food for lions?

36   Since men are real, they must have a real existence, not passing away into things which are not, but advancing [to a new stage] among things that are. Neither the substance nor the essence of the created order vanishes away, for he is true and faithful who established it, but the pattern of this world passes away,[19] that is, the things in which the transgression took place, since in them man has grown old. Therefore God, foreknowing all things, made this pattern of things temporary, as I showed in the book before this, pointing out as far as I could the reason for the creation of the temporal universe. But when this pattern has passed away, and man is made new, and flourishes in incorruption, so that he can no longer grow old, then there will be new heavens and a new earth. In this new order man will always remain new, in converse with God. That this state of things will remain without end, Isaiah says, as follows: "As the new heavens and the new earth, which I make, remain before me, says the Lord, so your seed and your name will stand."[20] As the elders say, "Then those who are thought worthy of abode in heaven will go there, others will enjoy the delights of paradise, others will possess the splendor of the city; for everywhere the Saviour will be seen, according as those who

2 see him will be worthy."[21] This is the distinction of the dwelling place of those who bring forth fruit a hundredfold, sixtyfold, and thirty[22] respectively; for some will be taken up into the heavens, others will dwell in paradise, and others will inhabit the city. This is why the Lord said, "In my Father's house are many mansions."[23] For all things are of God, who provides for all a suitable dwelling place. As his Word says, "The Father divides to all according to what each is or will be worthy of; and this is the couch on which those who are invited to the marriage will feast."[24] This is the ordering and arrangement of those who are saved, say the elders, the disciples of the

---

[19] I Cor. 7:31.   [20] Isa. 66:22.
[21] Irenaeus' "elders" seems to represent a collection of traditions from the churches of Asia Minor.
[22] Matt. 13:8; Mark 4:8.   [23] John 14:2.   [24] Matt. 22:2–10.

apostles, and they advance by such degrees, and by the Spirit they ascend to the Son and by the Son to the Father. Finally the Son will yield his work to the Father, as is said by the apostle: "For he must reign, until he shall put all enemies under his feet; death will be destroyed as the last enemy." For in the times of the Kingdom the just man then upon earth will already have forgotten how to die. "For when he says, All things will be subject, he clearly excepts him who subjected all things. But when all things are subject to him, then will the Son himself be subject to him who subjected all things to him, that God may be all in all." 25

John therefore predicted precisely the first resurrection of 3 the just, and [their] inheritance of the earth in the Kingdom,26 and the prophets prophesied about this in agreement with each other. The Lord also taught thus, promising that he would enjoy the new mixture of the chalice with [his] disciples in the Kingdom. The apostle also confessed that the creature would be free from the bondage of corruption into the freedom of the glory of the sons of God. In all and through all these things the same God the Father is manifest, who formed man, and promised to the Fathers the inheritance of the earth, who brings this [promise] forth at the resurrection of the just, and fulfills the promises in the Kingdom of his Son, afterwards bestowing with paternal love those things which eye has not seen, nor ear heard, nor have they entered into the heart of man.27 Then there is one Son, who accomplished the Father's will, and one human race, in which the mysteries of God are accomplished, which angels long to behold.28 For they cannot search out the wisdom of God, by which what he had fashioned is perfected by being conformed and incorporated with the Son—or how that his offspring, the first-begotten Word, could descend into his creature, that is, into what he had fashioned, and be contained within it—and that the creature again should lay hold on the Word and should ascend to him, passing beyond the angels, and be made [anew] according to the image and likeness of God.29

25 I Cor. 15:27, 28. 26 Rev., ch. 20. 27 I Cor. 2:9. 28 I Peter 1:12.
29 This final paragraph is a fine example of the vigorous and epigrammatic style of Irenaeus' writing at its best, with barely a trace of the ponderous sentences in which he sometimes loses himself elsewhere in the effort to be impressive or to squeeze all aspects of a topic into one period.

INDEXES

GENERAL INDEX

Strataeus, 122
Suetonius, 256n
Sunday, 23, 96, 108n, 178, 185, 287, 348
Swearing, 252
Syria, 33, 40, 75n, 93, 97, 101, 104, 106, 111 and n, 115, 120, 136, 163, 166, 242, 285n

Tartarus, 317 f., 320, 323 and n
Tatian, 15, 17, 25, 226, 237, 295
Tavia, 116
Teachers, Christian, 176, 177, 178
Teaching of the Twelve Apostles. See Didache
Telesphorus, 373
Temple, Jewish, 89n, 262
Tertullian, 17, 25, 125n, 224n, 226, 227, 243n, 258n, 296
Testament of Our Lord, 165
Tethys, 316, 325
Thales, 324
Theophilus of Antioch, 15, 17, 18, 209 and n, 226, 228, 350 and n
Theophorus, 76 f., 87n, 94n, 110n
Thyestean Feasts, 258 and n, 292 f., 303 and n, 335, 338 f.
Thyestes, 303n, 336
Titans, 317 and n, 318, 320
Tradition. See Apostolic tradition
Trajan, 75, 83, 122, 124
Travelers, Christian, 177
Trinity. See God

"Two Ways," 161–165, 167, 171–174
Typhon, 323, 331

Uneducated, many Christians, 281, 310, 374 f.

Valens, presbyter, 122, 123, 135
Valentinus and Valentinians, 24 f., 78, 123, 187, 345, 349, 354, 359, 362 f., 369, 371, 374 f., 379, 382, 384, 386
Valerius Bito, 73
Victor, Pope, 123, 348
Virgin birth, 92, 255 f., 261, 263, 285, 360, 375, 376
Virginity. See Celibacy
Virgins, order of, 116 and n
Visions, 295, 330

Widows, order of, 116 and n, 119, 133
Word. See Logos

Xystus, Pope, 373

Zacharias, 382
Zeus, sons of, 235, 255 f., 276–279; impurities of, 244, 256, 263, 336; Euripides on, 304 and n; Empedocles on, 322 and n; Stoics on, 306, 322; birth and death of, 334; illimitable, 319
Zosimus, 135
Zotion, 95

MODERN AUTHORS

Altaner, B., 27, 30, 170, 191, 212
Amann, E., 129
Andrews, H. T., 129
Andriessen, P., 206, 207 and n, 209, 219n
Archambault, G., 240
Arnould, L., 298
Aulén, G., 344n, 357
Ayer, J. C., 29

Bardenhewer, O., 27, 30, 129, 170, 191, 357
Bardy, G., 42, 298
Bareille, G., 298
Bartlet, J. V., 169, 186, 191
Bartsch, H. W., 85
Batiffol, P., 129
Bauer, K. F., 298
Bauer, W., 28, 84, 128
Bell, H. I., 126

Bethune-Baker, J. F., 28
Beurer, J. J., 206
Beuzart, P., 356
Bigg, C., 168, 169
Bihlmeyer, K., 40, 84, 127, 128, 145, 146, 168, 190, 206
Blunt, A. W. F., 240
Bonner, C., 209 and n
Bonwetsch, N., 129, 356
Bosio, G., 41, 84, 127, 128, 145, 146, 169
Bruston, E., 85
Buchanan, N., 29
Bunsen, C. C. J., 206, 209n
Burghardt, W. J., 85
Burkitt, F. C., 162n, 169, 239, 357
Byrennios, P., 40, 161, 163n, 167, 168, 190

Cadoux, C. J., 28, 121, 129, 130, 147
Calder, W. M., 142

BIBLICAL REFERENCES

Printed in the United States
51296LVS00002B/142-204